W9-ARI-324

Evolution and Ecology

EVOLUTION AND ECOLOGY

Essays on Social Transformation
by JULIAN H. STEWARD

Edited by Jane C. Steward and Robert F. Murphy

UNIVERSITY OF ILLINOIS PRESS

Urbana   Chicago   London

Library of Congress Cataloging in Publication Data

Steward, Julian Haynes, 1902-1972.
  Evolution and ecology.

  Includes bibliographies.
  1. Social evolution—Addresses, essays, lectures.
2. Social change—Addresses, essays, lectures.
3. Steward, Julian Haynes, 1902-1972. 4. Indians—
Addresses, essays, lectures. I. Title.
GN360.4.S73 1976   301.24   76-46341
ISBN 0-252-00612-7

for Garriott and Michael Steward

Contents

Preface

This volume is a retrospective of the professional interests, theories, and ideas of Julian Steward. The essays presented here cover the full range of his interests—cultural ecology, multilinear evolution, social and economic development, the study of regions and complex societies, and archeological methodology. A shortened version of his doctoral thesis is included.

It had been Julian Steward's hope to write a book much like *Theory of Culture Change*, using as the substantive material various papers written and published during the 1960s. Illness and his death in 1972 prevented his completing this book. In 1974 I suggested to the University of Illinois Press that I put together a small commemorative volume of some ten or twelve essays which I hoped would be a convenience for students and others. The press and its readers, however, strongly recommended that I compile a much larger book representative of Julian Steward's many interests during his long professional life.

At this point I asked Robert F. Murphy (Columbia University), my husband's student and colleague, and our long-time friend, to write an introduction and advise me on the selection of material to be included. This he most kindly agreed to do. Eric Wolf (Lehman College of the City University of New York) and Morton Fried (Columbia University) reviewed Murphy's introduction and also suggested material to be used.

My most sincere gratitude and thanks to all three.

JANE C. STEWARD

Introduction: The Anthropological Theories of Julian H. Steward

by Robert F. Murphy

American anthropology has since its beginnings been characterized by an expansiveness of mood and a sweeping diversity of interests and vision. It has harbored many "schools," but it has never constituted a school in and of itself, except perhaps for the ascendancy of Franz Boas and his students in the early part of this century. Growing at a geometric rate, spilling over into every intellectual niche open to it, optimistic and occasionally incautious, American anthropology was much like the country that spawned it, which should hardly surprise any anthropologist. It would be impossible to define a center of the discipline in this country, but there have been a number of consistent strains and directions that are not always evident in the welter of its endeavors. These are a persistent historicism coexisting in an uneasy and often dissonant relationship to an equally tenacious evolutionism, a concern for ecology that must be seen in part as an outgrowth of our remarkable variety of landscape, and a rather loose-jointed functionalism that sought to bring the various strands together. Most American scholars followed one or another of these lines of inquiry, but few attempted to bring them together in a unified and internally self-consistent theory. Julian Steward was one of these very few, and many of his contemporaries and successors will agree with the present assessment that he was the greatest of the synthesizers. He was indeed the complete American anthropologist.

AN ACADEMICIAN'S LIFE

Julian Steward was born on January 31, 1902, in Washington, D.C. Reared in the city until the age of 16, he took pleasure in his uniqueness as a native Washingtonian, though he never expressed any particular fondness for the capital. Steward loved to indulge in reminiscence, but he rarely spoke of his earliest years, and if he received any impetus at all toward a vocation in science from his family, it was as a reaction to the Christian Science of the household. At the age of 16, he went west to the Deep Springs Preparatory School, near Owens Valley, California. This was a most important episode in Steward's life, for it was during this time that he formed what was to be a lifelong attachment for the West, and it was then also that he first met the Shoshoni and Northern Paiute Indians he was later to study.

After preparatory school Steward spent a freshman year at Berkeley, where he was first exposed to the teachings of Alfred Kroeber, Robert Lowie, and Edward Gifford. He then transferred to Cornell University, which had no anthropologist on its faculty at the time, though its president, Livingston Farrand, had taken his degree in the subject under Boas at Columbia. Steward was forced by this circumstance to major in zoology and geology, which undoubtedly did much to mold his naturalistic model of culture. After graduation in 1925, he went back to Berkeley to pursue graduate work, a choice dictated largely by finances, according to Robert Manners.[1]

The 1920s were Berkeley's vintage years, a period of growth and intellectual excitement, unmarred by later depression, war, and the ultimate emergence of what Clark Kerr has referred to as the "multiversity." Anthropology was a young discipline, but it prospered under the sometimes censurious patronage of Phoebe Hearst, the wife of the publisher. One of the more amiable aspects of life in Berkeley at the time was a thriving, western-style bohemianism, which in anthropology was pursued under the spiritual leadership of Jaime d'Angulo, erstwhile anthropologist, bon vivant, Modoc shaman, and certainly one of the greatest characters produced by anthropology. Steward was a willing participant in the activities of the Berkeley group, which provided him at the very least with a rich fund of anecdotes for the future. Whether owing to the intellectual atmosphere or to d'Angulo's parties, Steward developed a strong tie to Berkeley and, however rich his later experiences at Columbia and the University of Illinois may have been, he regarded it as a sort of home.

At the time of Steward's residence, the Department of Anthropology at Berkeley effectively consisted of its founder, Alfred L. Kroeber, and Robert H. Lowie, who joined the department in 1921 after a long period as a curator at the American Museum of Natural History. Both Kroeber and Lowie were trained at Columbia by Boas, and both were almost by default students of the North American Indian, Kroeber specializing in California and the Great Basin and Lowie in the Plains. Anthropology at that time had neither the resources nor the personnel to expand its purview much beyond North America, and the discipline was still beset by the need to salvage as much data as possible on the native life of the Indian tribes. Today it is customary for new graduate students to cast about for the area in which they are going to specialize,

[1] Manners, 1973: 889. Further biographical information on Steward, as well as his full bibliography, may be found in this source, the *American Anthropologist* obituary.

but when Steward was a student the choice was predetermined, one simply chose which Indian group, and it is understandable that he gravitated toward the people he knew as a teenager in Deep Springs.

Part of the Kroeber stamp upon the Berkeley department was a broad orientation to the holistic aspects of anthropology, a concern for seeing mankind from the biological, cultural, historical, and linguistic viewpoints. This is a continuing aspiration of the discipline, honored more in word than in practice, and those who seek such unification today usually work at the boundaries between cultural anthropology on the one hand and linguistics or physical anthropology on the other. Lowie saw himself as an "ethnologist" only, though he did publish linguistic notes on the Crow Indians, but Kroeber worked actively in linguistics and archeology as well as in cultural anthropology. It was common for Berkeley students in the latter field to develop competence in archeology also, an overlapping of interests that was to continue until the mid-1950s, when the department grew in size, and specialization was correspondingly intensified. Steward was part of the earlier tradition, and throughout his earlier years as a professional he was just as much an archeologist as a cultural anthropologist. Most of his writings in the late 1920s and early 1930s were in archeology, and fully one-third of his publications in the period 1927 through 1939 were in that field. This had an impact upon his later thinking which will be explored further in this essay.

Steward was one of the most creative minds in anthropology, and his theoretical writings were striking in their transcendence of the work of his teachers. Kroeber carved out a domain of culture that stressed symbol and style, whereas Steward became deeply involved in the study of interaction and the work of ordinary life. Lowie was a cautious scholar who shied away from generalizations, or hedged them as soon as he made them, but Steward squeezed every last bit of conceptual inference out of his data. Both Kroeber and Lowie were steeped in the historicism, and sometimes nominalism, of the Boas group, while Steward reacted to this relativism by a search for cross-culturally valid social laws. Though much of Steward's work may be profitably regarded as in part a counterformation to what he was taught at Berkeley, many of his directions were set there. However different his historical theories may have been from those of Kroeber and Lowie, he nonetheless was concerned with history as an integral part of anthropological study. And if his own preoccupation with the natural environment differed sharply from Kroeber's bent, both he and Kroeber made major contributions to an understanding of the relations between cultures and their natural settings. Finally, Steward's writings showed an abiding focus upon social organization as a fundamental subject of study of equal conceptual importance to culture; this is more certainly a product of his work with Lowie, who, after all, guided his thinking as much as did Kroeber. This should become more evident in ensuing pages.

Steward received his Ph.D. degree in anthropology in 1929 on the basis of a thesis entitled "The Ceremonial Buffoon of the American Indian," a study of ritualized clowning and role reversals.[2] The thesis explored the distribution of various culture elements associated with formalized buffoonery, as it would have to if it were to meet the approval of Kroeber and Lowie, but it was also an inquiry into the psychology of humor. Most of those acquainted with Steward's work express puzzlement at his choice of thesis topic, for his later writings were not at all on psychological subjects, and he was known as a trenchant critic of the "personality and culture school" when he was at Columbia. Even Steward found it amusing that he should have been one of the first practitioners of psychological anthropology, a deviation that he himself saw to have been influenced by Lowie.

Modern students of anthropology may also find it curious that he had written a "library dissertation," for the discipline has been characterized by a tradition of first-hand ethnographic field research that has made it almost unseemly to write one's thesis on the basis of literary sources. The library thesis was not at all uncommon in Steward's day, however, and the usual procedure was to collect data in the field for descriptive purposes but to do comparative ethnology for the dissertation. The kind of problem-oriented field research in which one goes out armed with a set of hypotheses or theoretical premises to be tested, the very stuff of the dissertation format, had not yet come into vogue; one did fieldwork to collect data which would be published in the standard descriptive monograph. Theoretical formulations, to the contrary, were derived inductively from a broad set of data from a number of societies, a device that was seen to yield historical controls over general inference. It should be said that Steward's later research among the Great Basin Shoshoni pioneered future ethnography, for it was done as part of a larger theoretical venture founded in good part on a set of deductive premises. Steward was, as will be seen, a complete believer in the comparative method, but his Shoshoni research exemplified Emile Durkheim's dictum that one case, exhaustively studied, is sufficient to establish a social law.

Steward's early professional years saw him groping his way toward the program that was to occupy his life. It was also a period of shifting between jobs. In 1928 he went to the University of Michigan at Ann

---

[2] A shortened version of this work is reprinted in the present volume, pp. 347-365.

Arbor, where he originated instruction in anthropology. He stayed there for two years and then moved to the University of Utah to found a program of teaching and research. Steward had done archeological research in the Dalles area of the Columbia River during the 1920s in collaboration with Egbert Schenck and William Duncan Strong, and, as Utah's only archeologist, it was logical for him to continue work in that state. He did some cave archeology in northern Utah, but most of his efforts were directed toward the southwestern part of the state, an area into which the classical Anasazi variety of Puebloan culture had extended. His archeology was supplemented by extensive reading in both historical and ethnographic sources, and Steward became a leading authority on the Southwest. Four years after his work in Utah had ended, he published a truly path-breaking synthesis of archeological, historical, and ethnological data entitled "Ecological Aspects of Southwestern Society" (1937), which is universally regarded as a landmark in the study of Pueblo society and a model of methodology. The southwestern United States is a complex region, both historically and culturally, but Steward somehow managed to pull it all together into a coherent whole. It was this ability which was his greatest gift.

Steward's contributions to the study of the Southwest have been all but overshadowed by his later work in the Great Basin. His Shoshoni and Northern Paiute fieldwork had its beginnings when he was still a graduate student, taking him back to Deep Springs Valley for a short archeological sojourn and to Owens Valley, where he discovered the first known instance of irrigation of wild food plants (Steward, 1930). His work began in earnest when he left Utah in 1933 to return to Berkeley as a lecturer during the 1933-34 academic year. In 1934 and 1935 he was able to devote full time to a study of the Shoshoni, traveling with his bride, Jane (Cannon), from California northward through Nevada to Oregon and Idaho. More will be said about this most important research later, but it was notable for its extensiveness as well as its intensity. Not only did Steward do a complete analysis of Shoshoni economy, social organization, and ecology, but he also carried out a culture element survey (Steward, 1941a) as part of Kroeber's well-known effort to statistically plot the distribution of culture traits in Nevada and California. The major result of the Shoshoni research was, however, his *Basin-Plateau Aboriginal Sociopolitical Groups* (Steward, 1938), which is one of the great classics of descriptive analysis in anthropology and is required reading for anybody who pretends to having a serious thought about ecology.

Twenty years later my wife and I retraced the Stewards' path in the Duck Valley Reservation of northern Nevada. It soon became apparent that we could add nothing to his earlier work, for the older informants were mostly dead. Our final discouragement came when we visited the house of an elderly couple whom the agent said could be helpful. A lady responded to our knock and asked us our business. We carefully explained to her that we were interested in Shoshoni history, especially how the people had gotten their subsistence, where they camped, and so forth, all delivered in the simplest words possible. She listened politely, then said, "Why, you're anthropologists. Why didn't you say so?" To add to our embarrassment, she asked whether by chance we knew Julian and Jane Steward. I mumbled "Yes, ma'am," and she explained that her husband had been Julian's interpreter in 1934. "A very serious man, but a fine fieldworker," she continued. We chatted for a while and then left. The next day we were on our way back to the Wind River Reservation in Wyoming, determined never to talk down to an informant again.

A curious interaction goes on between a scholar and his work, through which the facts are rearranged and transformed by his mind, but in which the data themselves also have the same effect upon the thought of the scholar. An anthropologist's theories, then, are to a very considerable degree written by the circumstances and times in which he works, and by the people whom he studies. In just this sense the Great Basin Shoshoneans were the catalysts of Steward's theories. Characterized as these were by emphasis upon the material conditions of life and the struggle of man against his environment, the Shoshoni became the model of man at the threshold of survival. Living in a forbidding country of high desert and harsh landscape, the single dominant fact of their lives was the necessity to eke out subsistence through the seasons of the year. Given the simple technology at their disposal, the environment offered few alternatives to the ways in which they lived, and their very patterns of social life had to be understood as an adjustment to bleak physical reality. Steward grasped and developed this essential truth of Shoshoni society and made it into a general theory. That he was able to find analogues even in modern life is perhaps a function of the depression period during which he worked. Even the Shoshoni were better off than millions of Americans in the 1930s.

In 1935 Julian Steward joined the Bureau of American Ethnology of the Smithsonian Institution, leaving teaching for the next 11 years. His years at the Smithsonian were most productive in terms both of publications and organizational activities. It was also a period during which his active participation in field research slackened off, for, except for ethnographic research among the Carrier Indians of British Columbia in 1940, he became largely an organizer and manager of research projects. One of the most ambitious and successful of Steward's research enterprises was the six-volume *Handbook of South American*

Indians (1946-50). Little systematic anthropological research had been done among South American Indians up to the time of World War II, and most of our information on the Indian tribes of the continent was scattered through explorers' chronicles, missionary accounts, government reports, and the like. A limited number of intensive studies had been made, but most ethnography was of the survey type, for data were lacking even on locations and identities of tribes. Under the urging of the noted Swedish anthropologist, Baron Erland von Nordenskiold, a committee of the National Research Council was named in 1932 to promote an encyclopedic compendium of all that was known of the ethnography, prehistory, languages, and physical types of the South American Indians. The project was turned over to the Bureau of American Ethnology, and work began in 1940 under the editorship of Julian Steward.

Steward amassed a group of contributing scholars which included almost every anthropologist who had an interest in South America, a list that was limited by the fact that war made correspondence with European scholars difficult or impossible. He established a typology of South American cultures as a basis for ordering the volumes and managed to persuade all the many writers to keep to the same format. And, despite the many obstacles thrown up by the war, he somehow produced the first two volumes in 1946, only six years after the inception of the project. Two more followed in 1948, a comparative volume appeared in 1949, and the section on languages, physical anthropology, and cultural geography was published in 1950. It was a truly monumental achievement, for, in addition to editing all six volumes, Steward authored several substantive and theoretical sections. The *Handbook* did more than simply summarize our knowledge of South America. It set the background for three decades of subsequent empirical research and defined most of the major theoretical problems of the area.

While engaged in the editing of the *Handbook,* Steward also published a series of important papers on South America which did much to encourage postwar interest in the continent (1943a, 1943b, 1943c, 1947). More significant for his future work, he had become deeply interested in problems of acculturation and modernization in the area, a concern that stemmed from a belief that the science of anthropology could have predictive powers that would be of incalculable applied value, an optimistic creed that he later abandoned (Steward, 1969). In 1943 he founded the Institute of Social Anthropology of the Smithsonian Institution and served as its first director. The institute sponsored an extensive program of field research in Mexico, Brazil, and highland South America in both anthropology and cultural geography. Its aim was not so much the promotion of applied anthropology in the narrow sense as the conduct and publication of basic research that could be of practical value in understanding and dealing with culture change. The work of the institute did much to encourage the study of complex societies and to foster interdisciplinary effort. It also set the stage for the entire study of development and modernization.

Steward returned to academic life in 1946, when he accepted a professorship at Columbia University. Prior to this time he had exerted an enormous influence on the profession through his publications and the work of the institute, but he had had little experience in the training of graduate students. Columbia provided this for him and with a vengeance. At that time the Columbia department was almost entirely devoted to graduate teaching, and until the 1950s the only Columbia College courses were a one-year introduction to general anthropology and a senior seminar, both taught by Charles Wagley. There were also a few general studies courses taught mostly by Gene Weltfish. Steward's only contacts with undergraduates were with Columbia College students who took his graduate courses.

There were, however, more than enough graduate students to keep busy the small Columbia faculty of that time. Steward arrived in the immediate post–World War II period amid the great influx of students supported by the so-called "GI Bill of Rights." Since many of the returned veterans were only beginning their undergraduate work at the end of the war, the mid-1950s still saw many of them working on doctorates. There were well over 100 graduate students in the Columbia department during Steward's residence (the exact number was never really known and could have been as many as 150), and his classes were heavily attended. Steward was a splendid teacher; his courses were crammed with empirical detail, beautifully organized, and held together by theoretical purpose and consistency. Most people who have taken anthropology courses are familiar with two basic types of lecturers. There are the ones who engage in windy generalities that never engage the facts of social life, and there are the others who assail and stultify the students with undigested tidbits of data that issue interminably from bell to bell. Either type can make 50 minutes seem like a full day. Steward's lectures were different. They were indeed replete with mountains of fact, but all the data had their place within the overall framework of his thought. The facts became transformed, meaningful, and retainable, while each lecture had the fascination of a complex construction project as each piece was carefully fitted into an overall design. His favorite aphorism was that "there are no theories unless based upon fact, but facts exist only within the context of a theory." Whatever course he taught, whether on South American Indians or the American Southwest, each was an excursion into his synthetic view of culture.

Students were attracted to Steward for other reasons than his style of lecturing. Most of the Columbia graduate students were products of the Great Depression, enured to a hardscrabble, uncertain existence, cognizant of the economic realities of life, and attuned to a critical view of their social milieu. And as a finishing school, most had gone to war, which at least had provided the means for their further education. The kind of relativism that had prevailed at Columbia had little meaning for them, for they had lived in a world in which some facts were clearly more important than others, and they had experienced the inexorable forces of history as its victims. Above all, they sought some kind of consistent interpretation of culture which would help them understand their own lives. Steward's courses provided the intellectual format for these concerns, and they also conveyed a sense of surety and conviction that few of us can muster today.

I dwell on this period in Steward's life for the obvious reason that it was then that I first knew him. But it was also the time when his career reached a crest, for he had behind him a history of major productivity, he was embarking on new projects, and he was training a large number of graduate students who were to preserve and spread his view of anthropology more surely than did his writings. The final claim to fame of any scholar is his students, and Steward supervised some 35 doctoral dissertations during his six years at Columbia. He served on many more committees, and during one year alone read almost 20 dissertations. Steward always seemed to become overinvolved and overcommitted against his own best interests and judgment. While at the Smithsonian, he undertook the *Handbook,* the Institute of Social Anthropology, and the River Valley Archeology project. He escaped to the "quiet" of academia only to be buried under a mountain of dissertations and advisees—the hallway outside his office resembled a busy internist's waiting room.

However beset he was as a teacher, he filled the part; indeed, Steward was one of the few professors I have known who looked like a professor should look. A tall man, he had a brush of graying mustache that matched his graying hair and his gray tweeds. He was serious, intense, reserved, and wholly committed to his work. The commitment was so strong, and his synthesis so broad and inclusive, that he appeared dogmatic to some persons. In actuality, he was not authoritarian as a teacher. He listened carefully to the views of his students, and was very often moved by them to modify or refine his positions. His students came to feel that they were partners in a venture, and the venture was nothing less than the founding of a true science of society.

Steward was pushing toward a general theory, and general theorists, as a category, have a difficult time accommodating themselves to radically different frameworks of thought. They develop a set of concepts and a language for viewing their domain that tend to exclude other metaphors. In this sense, there were certain people with whom Steward could communicate, yet there were others whose view of anthropology was couched in a language apart from his own. He did not insist upon rigid conformity with his own ideas as the price of discourse, but he minimally hoped that anthropologists would accept the position that culture is an orderly domain in which causality operates, and the operation of which is accessible through scientific method. Given the complexity of our subject matter, this may have been a naive expectation, but to Steward these were the unstated premises which underlay the rest of his theories.

The Columbia department to which Steward came in 1946 was not exactly fertile ground for his ideas, however receptive the students may have been. Columbia was the home of Franz Boas and, though he had retired in 1936 and died in 1942, the general tradition of Boasian historicism and relativism was continued by his successors. Boas's student Ruth Benedict had never realized her full potential in the Columbia department because of the fact that she was a woman, but her long association with the faculty had attracted many students and had helped turn the department's interest to the personality and culture field.[3] Ralph Linton, though hardly a Boas student or appointee, had been chairman of the department since 1937; he, too, worked in the personality and culture field, though a long and famous feud between him and Benedict precluded their cooperation. Linton left Columbia for Yale in 1946, and Steward was appointed as his replacement, a move that owed much to Columbia's new chairman and Steward's old fellow graduate student, William Duncan Strong. Steward's relationship with Benedict was always cordial, and he strongly backed her promotion to full professor, but he made no secret of his generally low opinion of personality studies in anthropology. After Benedict's death in 1948, Steward moved into an even more central position in the department, and the psychological interests of Columbia anthropology went into a long decline from which it has not yet turned.

Steward's most important research activity at Columbia was a collaborative effort with the University of Puerto Rico in 1948-49 that attempted nothing less than a study of the major institutions of Puerto Rican culture. The actual fieldwork was carried out by five Columbia graduate students: Robert Manners, Sidney Mintz, Elena Padilla, Raymond Scheele, and Eric Wolf. Ambitious in design and scope, the project was important for a number of reasons. It represented Stew-

---

[3] In all fairness to Columbia, however, it should be remembered that Benedict was the first woman in anthropology to hold a tenure appointment in a major university department; things were bad everywhere for women in academia.

ard's first major research in an area in which he had sponsored much work through the Institute of Social Anthropology, and was thus a logical culmination to the development of his scholarship in both the Indian and Hispanic cultures of Latin America. The fieldwork was also significant as the first attempt in anthropology to study the cultures of an entire area; as such, it was a precursor of the great area institutes that began to burgeon in American universities during the later 1950s. Finally, the Puerto Rico project was one of anthropology's first attempts to understand the institutions of a complex culture in their historical dimension, as a function of ecological relationships, and within the context of a larger political and economic community.[4] A parallel effort in Brazil was launched by Charles Wagley a few years later, making Columbia a center of some of the major directions taken by anthropology in the next two decades.

During the latter part of his Columbia tenure, Steward suffered from a series of health problems, some of which stemmed from an earlier period of field research in the South American highlands. Health and the pressures of teaching at Columbia made the offer of a research professorship at the University of Illinois an attractive prospect, and Steward left in 1952. When one considers the composition and orientation of the Columbia department today, it seems difficult to believe that he left over two decades ago, and after only six years in residence. Steward's young World War II veterans of the late 1940s are now senior professors in universities throughout the country; they are mostly in the same fiftyish age bracket that Steward was in at Columbia, and at the top of their productive careers. Some of them either stayed at Columbia as faculty members or were invited back after some years away, and they embody in various ways and forms the ecological and evolutionary interests of their teacher. The persistence of the Steward tradition at Columbia is a striking testimonial to his influence as a teacher and to the personal devotion that he gave to us all, and which we returned.

The Department of Anthropology at the University of Illinois included in 1975 some 35 full-time faculty members and 144 graduate students. When Steward arrived in Urbana in 1952, the Department of Sociology and Anthropology, headed by the late sociologist William Albig, had two other full-time anthropologists and no anthropology graduate students at all. John McGregor, a specialist in the prehistory of Illinois and the Southwest, handled archeology, and cultural anthropology was the province of Oscar Lewis; both were mainly involved in undergraduate instruction. Steward had gone from too

---

[4] Steward's introduction to the Puerto Rican report (Steward *et al.*, 1956a) outlined the methods and results of the project; it is reprinted below, pp. 240-296.

many graduate students to none at all. Under the terms of his appoint-ment Steward could engage in full-time research if he pleased or teach whatever he wanted, whenever he felt so inclined. It was in every respect an ideal position, but he felt lonely outside the classroom and without students. One of the conditions of his research professorship, however, was the provision that he could appoint two full-time, paid research associates in anthropology, who would work on projects under his direction. He solved the personnel search, and his own feel-ing of isolation, by appointing two Columbia graduate students, Ben Zimmerman and Frederic K. Lehman, who is now a professor in the Illinois department.

The Illinois position made possible a research plan that Steward had given some thought to while at Columbia. This was a large-scale investi-gation of the processes of change that occur in peasant agricultural systems that have been exposed to outside markets and wage labor. In a sense, several of the Institute of Social Anthropology researchers had worked on this subject, and it was also a direction of the Puerto Rico Project. Steward believed that empirical data available at the time indi-cated that the same processes of change could be found in a number of areas and that the cross-cultural validation of the conditions under which they arise would yield regular laws of development. The pro-gram was to design a field research project that would recruit anthro-pologists to the venture, convene them in preliminary sessions to determine a common framework and methodology of research, send them out to do their respective ethnographies, and then reconvene them to sift through the results. He started work under the rubric "Studies in Cultural Regularities."

The first few years of the project were spent in researching background, refining theory, writing supporting research papers, and drawing up proposals. One of Steward's problems in getting the work off the ground was a fairly rapid turnover of research associates. Leh-man spent the 1952-53 academic year in Urbana and then returned to Columbia to finish his doctorate. He was replaced by me, but Zimmer-man left in 1954. Fortunately, Eric Wolf had been teaching at Illinois on a temporary basis and was available to fill that vacancy, but at the end of the 1954-55 academic year both Wolf and I left. We, in turn, were replaced by Charles Erasmus and Louis Faron, who stayed with the project through its research phase. The major problem of all the earlier appointees was their desire to go into regular teaching positions having some prospect for advancement and tenure. Steward under-stood our anxieties as Depression-bred—and he was right.

Steward's life was far more relaxed at Urbana than in New York.

The family settled in a house on Champaign's University Avenue, but after two years in town they opted for a rural setting and moved to the little village of Fithian, some 17 miles east of Urbana. Life in Fithian suited Steward's style, as did residence in semirural Alpine, New Jersey, during his Columbia stay. One of the finest tributes that can be given him, perhaps, is recognition of the fact that he despised university social life and avoided it as a loathsome disease. Steward liked people, but he was not a gregarious man. He enjoyed seeing people on his own terms and in his own time, and the usual patterns of academic sociability did not meet these criteria. He did most of his work at home rather than in the office, and the more secluded the home, the better.

Social science departments always seem to be the last to get new space, and the University of Illinois did not depart from this rule. The anthropologists were lodged in Davenport Hall in a small suite of offices made vacant by the fact that the School of Agriculture had just moved into new quarters. Most of the building, however, was still occupied by agricultural departments, and our closest neighbor was the Department of Meat, chaired by an amiable gentleman named Sleeter Bull. One of the duties of the meat department was evidently to test the produce of the university farms, and each morning Eric Wolf and I were tortured by the scent of thick rashers of prime bacon frying in their labs. At noon, as we ate dry sandwiches, a sirloin would often be sizzling down the hall; we were grateful that they at least went home to dinner. Steward was especially bitter when the best secretary he had had in three years quit to work in the meat department, after having been invited on several occasions to lunch with them. Wolf and I tried to tell Julian that her desertion was a reaffirmation of his theories—there is indeed a Shoshoni in all of us—but he uncharacteristically argued that we all need values that transcend our stomachs.

In 1956 the Ford Foundation granted the project in cultural regularities the then princely sum of $225,000 to carry out the field research phase of the program. In terms of what was accomplished, however, the grant was not at all large or lavish. A total of eleven fieldworkers were sent to four continents: one to Mexico, two to Peru, one each to Nigeria and Kenya, two to Tanzania, one to Burma, another to Malaya, and two to Japan. Most of the fieldwork was carried out during 1957 and 1958, and the results were published·in three volumes in 1967. The work, consisting of Steward's introduction and ten monograph-length studies and published as *Contemporary Change in Traditional Societies* (1967), was an important study that somehow did not receive proper recognition by reviewers. As Manners tells us (1973:895), Steward was very disappointed at the reception and

planned to write a paper in defense and clarification of the work which
was to have appeared in this volume; he never finished it.[5] This was
one of the very few Steward products to have been so treated, at least in
the period since the 1940s, and the reason must lie more in changes in
academia and the discipline than in the work itself. The volumes, like
all of Steward's work, were based upon anthropology construed as a
positive science and appeared at exactly the point when positivism in
the social sciences began to fall under attack. And it reached the re-
viewers in the spring of 1968, which is as convenient a marker as any of
the end of the age of optimism and innocence in the American university. It was a time of collapse of a vision of indefinite progress and
failure of faith in the ultimate rationality of society, if not of man. We
still have not fathomed the dramatic change that occurred in the Western world through the decade of the 1960s, but the work of Steward
and his associates may well have been one of its casualties.

Steward's Illinois years were productive ones. In 1955 he published
his widely read collection of essays *Theory of Culture Change,* to which
this volume is a sequel; *Native Peoples of South America,* co-authored with
Louis Faron, appeared in 1959. The latter work largely represents a
summarization of the *Handbook,* but it remains the only general text on
South American Indians. Toward the end of his life he published a
short biography of Alfred L. Kroeber, his old teacher, with a selection
of Kroeber's essays (1973). He remained active until his last days and,
despite failing sight, published several important papers. At the time
of his death in 1972 he was working on a general synthesis of the
cultures of the Great Basin for the projected "Handbook of North
American Indians." During the time since he had joined the Illinois
faculty, anthropology grew steadily on the campus, and in 1960
Steward was given the charge of forming a new department independent from sociology. He expanded the staff and recruited the able
administrative talents of Joseph Casagrande for the regular chairman-
ship. He then went back to occasional teaching, guiding graduate
students, and writing.

Steward received almost every honor that can come to an anthropologist. In 1952 he was named the Viking Medalist by the Wenner-
Gren Foundation, and only two years later he became one of the few
scholars outside the hard sciences to be named to the National
Academy of Sciences. In the academic year 1956-57 Steward went to
Japan as director of the Kyoto American Studies Seminar, a trip which
helped extend his interests to Japan and the Orient. Twenty-six of

[5] An unpublished essay on the theoretical scope of the project, reprinted in this
volume on pp. 297-330, will provide some of the explication that Steward had intended
for the unfinished paper.

Steward's colleagues and former students honored him in 1964 with a *Festschrift* edited by Robert Manners (1964), and the graduate students at the University of Illinois have founded a journal in his name. It should be mentioned that Steward never sought the honors that came to him. Like everybody else, it was important to him that his abilities and the quality of his work be recognized, but he never engaged in self-promotion. Steward never held a position within the American Anthropological Association, despite having been offered the editorship of the *American Anthropologist* once and the presidency of the association twice. He turned down all these offers on the grounds of overcommitment, but I doubt if that was truly the reason. Rather, he really hated the annual conventions and rarely went to them. This should be taken not as a sign of lack of professional devotion but, rather, as an indication of good taste.

Before moving on to a presentation of Steward's theories, we should pause a moment to consider the man. The characteristic I remember most strongly was the impression of enormous inner tension and conflict, full of countervailing tendencies that were less a disability than a source of his creativity. He could shift from sociability to isolation swiftly, but the periods of seclusion were commonly germinal ones. He liked people, and he enjoyed the company of friends, but he shied away from large groups even though he was frequently their center—but this, perhaps, is exactly why he shunned crowds. Steward had a good sense of humor, and he especially enjoyed bawdy limericks, but his younger colleagues could make him wince with a really nastily vulgar ditty. Jaime d'Angulo's parties had not erased all the rigidity of the childhood household, and there was even a touch of ambivalence when he took a drink. He would usually find some rationale of health or work, such as fighting off incipient flu or relaxing in order to think better, before he would allow himself to unwind a bit. Steward lived for his work and operated on the premise that enjoyment for enjoyment's sake was somehow frivolous and unseemly. That he did, nonetheless, enjoy himself was part of his inner struggle, and a constant goad to his sense of total committedness.

Steward was a kindly man and a very vulnerable one. Just as he was always considerate of the feelings of others, so also was he hurt by affront. He had no stomach whatsoever for the occasional rough and tumble of academic or disciplinary politics, but his research goals were such that he did have to become involved. This is one of the reasons for the paradox of Steward as a research manager, the director of large projects, and the essentially introverted man who sought only the quiet of his farm and his study. He had a passionate dedication to a research program that took up his entire life and to which he devoted his career, yet he was repelled by the kinds of things that had to be done in order to carry out the program. He was one of the first and greatest of the "grantsmen," yet he never could bring himself to practice "grantsmanship."

There was a kind of old-fashioned honesty about Steward that was part of a conservative cast of character and style. His clothes were always as sober as his demeanor could become, and his manners stemmed from a more genteel time. Yet he was openly and avowedly liberal and left-of-center in politics at a time when such professions were dangerous. Steward was at Columbia during the McCarthy years, but the direction of his theories was undampened by the intellectual squalor of the times, nor was he hesitant to speak his mind on controversial issues. Nonetheless, he later distinguished between the forms of advocacy of the social scientist as private citizen and as social scientist. He kept the two separated, said what he believed or had determined, and let the chips fall where they may.

Finally, Steward was a family man in both the specific sense and in a general way. He was devoted to his wife and their two sons and never let professional involvements interfere with the rites and duties of the home. He extended this kind of warmth and loyalty to his close younger associates and students. Many of us drifted off into various lines of research and into theoretical interests that were divergent from his own, just as he had decades earlier asserted his own independence from Kroeber. But just as family ties are diffuse and enduring, involving unquestioned loyalties, the student-teacher bond endured through all the vicissitudes of our thoughts and through our own aging. And what he really had given us all was not a theory or a method but a faith that somewhere underlying things there is an order, and the curiosity to search for it.

PREMISES AND CONCEPTS

Steward's model for social science research was derived from the natural sciences. He dealt with a mechanical world in which there was cause and effect and in which the nature and locus of reality were never much of a question. Like most of the anthropologists of his time, Steward paid little attention to epistemological problems, adopting the positivism that was current in both sociology and anthropology. In this kind of cosmos the facts of society were seen as having an autonomous existence and could be apprehended in their essences by the human mind, just as could the objects of the natural world. Social institutions, customary practices, and the like were treated as part of an objective universe, as positive entities that could be counted and measured, as part of an irreducible reality. More important, these components of the social and cultural universe had a natural order; the parts were related one to another, and the work of science was to discover these relations as they existed in both space and time. One of Steward's fundamental premises was drawn directly from the natural sciences: in a natural order anything that happens can happen again, and, given the same conditions, it probably will. This was the rationale for his study of causality and his use of the comparative method, and it was an unstated part of his entire approach in anthropology. The natural sciences have, of course, changed greatly since Steward studied them, and the faith that there is an objective order of reality has been couched in many doubts, but most of anthropology still adheres to positive science and its assumptions.

Within this ordered universe of social things, there are relationships. Steward looked upon these relations both in space at a moment of time, or synchronically, and in a temporal-historical dimension, or diachronically. Actually, synchronic and diachronic relationships were exactly the same to him, and the distinction lay only in how the investigator looks at the data. Thus two cultural items can be regarded as related in some mutually supporting way, such that the operation of each one is to some degree necessary to the operation of the other; this is a synchronous view of the relation, a statement of *function* couched in terms of the operation of interrelated variables. The same two cultural items, however, can be studied in their interaction with each other over time and then, to the extent that we can determine that one is essential to the existence of the other or at least is partly determinative of the form of the other, we have stated a relationship of *causality*. Steward, we will see, was a student of *process*, but process to him referred largely to any social or cultural change that was directional and determined. For example, there were processes of state formation related to irrigation agriculture in early times, and there are processes today by which peasant agriculturalists are becoming subject to outside markets, with a series of concomitant changes in the family, landholding, and so forth. Process, then, is a causal sequence that underlies the unfolding and emergence of institutions.

To continue our review of the basic assumptions and working concepts, both implicit and explicit, in Steward's theories, he considered the search for causal connections to be, in effect, the search for general laws. Steward operated in what Robert Merton calls "the middle range" of theory. He was not a general theorist in the sense that he looked for some underlying, austerely economical formula that would unify a universe of phenomena, but rather he attempted to develop a series of cause-and-effect relations that would be applicable to a delimited range of phenomena. These could be stated in the order: Given conditions A, B . . . , then C will probably result. The operation of these laws was demonstrable through history, and their validity was verifiable through comparison, according to a methodology that will be detailed presently. The basis of his use of the comparative method was essentially the same as in the rest of anthropology. Assuming the kind of naturalistic view of culture and society I have outlined, the demonstration of the relatedness of two elements in society or culture depends upon a test of co-variance. This can be effected in the hard sciences by experimentation, the setting up of an artificially bounded and isolated situation in which one or more of the variables under study may be manipulated. In human societies it is impossible to isolate the variables, just as it is often politically or ethically undesirable or impossible to change them. The only way that we can study co-variation in natural setting situations is to find a variety of such situations in our inventory of cultures. Thus, if we are interested in demonstrating a relationship between A and B on one hand and C on the other, then we can review all the societies that have A and B to see whether C is always present; or we may look at all the societies where C is found in order to determine whether A and B are present. The actual situation in comparison is always more complex than this, of course, but this is the essential method in anthropology, and the one followed by Steward. It was his means of posing the significance of recurrent institutions in the cross-cultural study of society and of deriving from these regularities empirical laws.

Contemporary students are often puzzled by the frequent discussions in Steward's writings of the controversy between "diffusion" and "independent invention" and find it hard to appreciate the dimensions of this practically moribund issue. Steward was trained in a historicist tradition that dealt less with history as we usually understand it than with the geographical distribution of culture elements. Where Steward would see a striking similarity of institutions in different cultures to be possibly due to the operation in each of the same causes, his teachers tended to see the similarity to be a result of the spread of the institution from one of the societies to the others. Of course, diffusion is a cause of a sort, but Steward shied away from such "historical" explanations because they introduced a capricious element in the development of culture. Diffused items, according to many of the students of Boas, were accepted or rejected for reasons of psychology, and the availability of a diffusable culture trait was, in any event, dependent upon geographical conditions and thus adventitious. Steward unequivocally rejected diffusion as a sufficient cause: "The use of diffusion to avoid coming to grips with problems of cause and effect not only fails to provide a consistent approach to culture history, but it gives an explanation of cultural origins that really explains nothing. Diffusion becomes a mechancial and unintelligible, though universal, cause, and it is employed, as if in contrast to other kinds of causes, to account for about 90 percent of the world's culture" (1955:182).

This did not mean that Steward rejected diffusion's existence or importance. Rather, he saw diffusion as providing an explanation of similarities of detail and style, parallels of external form, and he also saw it as a means by which the development of institutions is hastened. The major operating institutions of society did not spread through diffusion, in Steward's view, unless there was a pre-existent basis for them. Thus the state did not diffuse either as idea or as organization unless the recipient society already had at least the makings of a class structure, a certain level of population density, and a reasonably complex division of labor. In short, the state can diffuse in a situation in which it would have soon developed anyhow, with or without diffusion. Both diffusion and independent development were part of the same underlying process. In this way Steward resolved the question by dissolving the antinomy. The issue is indeed a dated one that today's students do not much worry about, but this is only because Steward argued the matter to a resolution.

One source of Steward's rejection of mechanical and superficial explanations such as that of diffusion lay in his view of society. Although he would acknowledge the pre-eminence of the diffusion explanation for isolated elements such as tobacco smoking, myths, ritual forms, and the like, he rejected it when it concerned entire institutional complexes. The latter he saw as possessing a functional unity and a possible centrality for the culture that made their simple spread through imitation most implausible, let alone defeating for the goals of science. Steward, like most American anthropologists, was a functionalist, but, also in keeping with the American tradition, his was a specific kind of functionalism, operating within the context of a rather loose-jointed notion of structure. His idea of "function" was of the mathematical type; that is, it concerned the operation of a variable in relation to a limited set of other variables rather than to a social system seen as the entirety of the institutional life of a society. Steward's comparative method differed, however, from that of G. P. Murdock (1949) in that it was nonstatistical, drew upon a limited universe of societies of the same type, and involved the comparison of a larger number of variables, seen as structures. Moreover, given the simultaneously causal nature of these relationships, the notion of function was just as productive of a theory of change as of a theory of structure.

Steward did not use the term "function" to refer specifically to the maintenance of a system in a state of equilibrium, as was the usage of the British anthropologists of his day. This stemmed just as much from a difference in concepts of structure as of function. The tendency in most of structural-functionalism has been to look upon structure as the groupings, roles, and institutions of a society in their totality and as a bounded system, indeed as a closed and balanced system. One can start a functional analysis at any point in the system and follow it through the whole structure to the beginning point. The referent of function is the structure as an organic whole, and no logical priority can be attributed to any part of the system as opposed to the others. This position was not taken by all the British anthropologists, of course, and Raymond Firth is one very prominent exception, but it was true of the genre. Steward, on the contrary, did not operate with ideas of total social system, system boundaries, equilibrium maintenance, and so forth. He generally used system or structure to refer only to what he saw as the principal institutions within a society, and the relations between them were generally interpreted as far looser than in most functional analysis. Moreover, even within the limited purview of what he saw as systems, some parts were more important than others; this, of course, is at the heart of his theory of cultural ecology, which will be reviewed below. This sense of priorities and the very open-endedness of his concept of structure allowed him to operate in a temporal-causal dimension at almost the same time that he was handling the material in a synchronic-functional fashion. Even when he was operating as a functionalist, then, causality was implied.

Along the lintel above the entrance to Columbia's Schermerhorn Hall, where Boas presided, where Lowie and Kroeber went to school, and where Steward taught, is the inscription: "Speak to the earth and it shall teach thee." So went the great faith of the inductivist age of science, and Lowie and his classmates rejected Lewis Henry Morgan while hoping for a new evolutionism that would emerge directly from the facts. The belief that somehow the information, if only enough were collected, would fall into place by itself, that general laws were immanent within the data, died in the natural sciences while Schermerhorn Hall was still new, but it lasted much longer in anthropology. Steward did not eschew the world of evidence and the senses, of course, but he was among the first anthropologists to introduce a strong element of deductive process in his scientific reasoning. He formulated hypotheses on the basis of scattered evidence combined with logic and then went to the field, or to the library, for fuller corroboration. He was one of the first anthropologists to undertake fieldwork with a firm sense of problem, formulated in advance, rather than to simply obtain a general description of a culture. This affinity for educated conjecture was paralleled by an equally strong propensity toward generalization. He was criticized for not keeping an open mind when embarking on research and he was criticized also for pushing his data too far and generalizing too broadly when he presented his results. Lowie and Kroeber were rather ambivalent about their student. Both felt that he always went a bit too far, but both admired him completely. Caution, care, and restraint were a matter of style and character to them, but they understood its relative lack in others. And they knew also that the age of induction, of the German science they had learned from Boas, was dead—but they did think it was a pity.

CULTURAL ECOLOGY

Julian Steward's greatest contribution to anthropology was his earliest: the theory of cultural ecology.[6] The reawakening of interest in man's impact upon the environment in the 1960s and the growing public alarm at ecological degradation and the exhaustion of the earth's resources also make this the most timely of his ideas today. When Steward first wrote on the subject in the mid 1930s, he was one of the very first anthropologists to have given serious attention to the problem. There were a scattering of environmental determinists of various stripes throughout the nineteenth and early part of the twentieth centuries, but most of their work was characterized by a simplistic mechanism that tended to look for direct connections between weather and topography and the character or ethos of a people. Thus the progress of the peoples of Europe and North America might be attributed to the invigorating and varied climate, while heat and humidity accounted for the presumed slothful and backward ways of tropical peoples. It did not take much research, of course, to show that civilization was flourishing in many tropical areas during centuries when the "vigorous" Europeans were looked down upon as howling barbarians by their southern neighbors. Nor did one need to know much history to see that the great cities of North America stood on top of the poor remains of very simple Indian societies. If there were indeed a causal relationship between culture and the environment, it clearly had to account for the complexities of history.

Alfred Kroeber's *Cultural and Natural Areas of Native North America* (1939), which had been sitting in manuscript form long before its publication, was the nearest precursor to Steward's theories. It was, however, more a compendium of useful plants and animals and their distribution relative to the culture areas of North America than a systematic

---

[6] Steward did not write a great deal on ecology, per se, and most of the theory was emergent from empirical studies. One of his few general statements on cultural ecology is reprinted in this volume, pp. 43-57.

exploration of a relationship. In this sense Kroeber was following the path of Clark Wissler and others, who found a correlation between culture areas and the dominant economy or food pursuit of these regions. The way of life of mounted bison hunters of the Plains contrasted sharply with that of the sedentary agriculturalists of the southwestern pueblos, which in turn differed radically from the cultures of the impoverished hunters and collectors of the Great Basin. But the contrasts given within the culture area classifications tended to be obvious and analytically gross. It remained for Steward to develop a theory that could be stated in abstract and universalized terms.

The theory of cultural ecology has less to say about the environment than about culture, and this is its strength. Steward wrote that the concept involves both a problem and a method: "The problem is to ascertain whether the adjustments of human societies to their environments require particular modes of behavior or whether they permit latitude for a certain range of possible behavior patterns" (1955:36). The method for investigating the problem contains three steps. The first is to analyze "the interrelationship of exploitative or productive technology and environment" (*ibid.:* 41). In short, the theory and method of culture ecology posit a relationship between the resources of the environment, the tools and knowledge available to exploit them, and the patterns of work necessary to bring the technology to bear upon the resources. The organization of work, in turn, is hypothesized as having a determinant effect upon other social institutions and practices. The key element in the equation is not the environment, nor is it the culture. Rather, it is the process of work in the fullest sense: the division of labor and the organization, timing, cycling, and management of human work in pursuit of subsistence. Steward's theory may not have been the first in anthropology to treat the environment, but it was indeed the first to examine the creative and determinant effects of the organization of production.

Despite the clear emphasis upon the material base of society, Steward did not consider the theory to be a form of economic determinism. He regarded it instead as a strategy and a method which did not prejudge a relationship but simply set it as a problem for inquiry. It was not the only subject to be investigated, but merely the first to be considered in any analysis. The reasons for the priority are clear. First, in all societies the quest for subsistence has an immediacy and urgency that set it apart from other human activities. Second, the relationship is peculiarly accessible to a causal analysis because there are strict limits to the patterns of work that can be used with a particular technology on particular resources. The relationship is not invariant and absolutely determined in a one-to-one way, but it is circumscribed. There may indeed be more than one way to skin a cat, but if your only tool is a bamboo sliver, there are not many. There is thus an element of necessity in the ways a group gains its subsistence that any analysis must account for.

Nowhere is the cultural-ecological equation more evident than among the Western Shoshoni, where there was little latitude of range of possible behavior patterns, following Steward's phrasing of the problem.[7] Steward systematically interviewed informants for information on hunting and collecting patterns in every district of the Shoshoni habitat, getting from them data on actual behavior and aggregations, a far more difficult chore than collecting normative, cultural material. Shoshoni technology was of the simplest sort known, and the food-getting equipment was limited to the bow and arrow, digging stick, winnowing flail and pan, stone-flake knives, and the like. The men hunted deer, antelope, rabbits, an occasional mountain sheep, and rodents, and the women gathered various grass seeds, roots, and berries. Steward demonstrated for almost every activity that the lone worker was the most effective unit and that the environment was so poor in resources that people had to scatter thinly over the landscape to gather enough to eat. The only large-scale cooperative economic activities were the antelope surround and the rabbit drive. These endeavors drew people together for only limited periods and infrequently, and they yielded only temporary aggregations and leadership.

The critical part of the year in Nevada was the winter, when the Shoshoni depended upon stored foods for survival. The principal winter provender was the pine nut, which was gathered each fall on the mountainsides, brought to a sheltered spot nearby in the valleys, and cached; the people made their winter camps nearby. The winter villages were the largest gatherings of the year, except for occasional game drives and dances, but their populations were unstable and shifting, their existences often ephemeral. Under ordinary circumstances one might expect groups of Shoshoni to return to the same pine-nut grove and village every year, thus producing a stable social unit, but the vagaries of pine-nut harvests prevented this. Each grove would fail to yield fruits about every third year or so, and the occupants of a winter village of one year might have to scatter in different directions in the following year to find a grove that was producing. The result was a great fluidity of population, of movement of families from one valley to another, of changing patterns of association. The

[7] Steward gave an excellent summary of Western Shoshoni society and ecology in one of his last essays (Steward, 1970), a contribution to the festschrift for the Swedish linguist-ethnologist, Sven Liljeblad. The paper is reprinted below in this volume, pp. 366-406.

cultural-ecological equation produced social fragmentation and amorphousness.

The basic camp group involved in hunting and foraging was a cluster of some four or five nuclear families. These, however, were of shifting composition and had no distinct identities or patterns of leadership. There were loosely recognized neighborhoods in Shoshoni country, but no populations having stable memberships were linked to these areas. In effect, there were no bands in either a territorial or a political sense. The truly stable and durable unit was the nuclear family. There was thus maximum impact of the adjustment to the environment upon other patterns of behavior. The Shoshoni case, however, did not make for a theoretic mold that all societies fitted into, and Steward hypothesized that the immediate impact of environment upon culture would decrease with the increase of social complexity and the growth of man's domination of the environment through technology: "In proportion that societies have adequately solved subsistence problems, the effect of ecology becomes more difficult to ascertain. In complex societies certain components of the social superstructure rather than ecology seem to be determinants of further development" (Steward, 1938:262).

Steward's first important article on the ecology of hunters and collectors was not on the Shoshoni but was based on research in secondary sources and dealt with what he termed the "patrilineal band" (Steward, 1936). Surveying the Bushmen, Pygmies, Semang, Australian aborigines, the Ona, and other groups, he found the basic social aggregation to be a patrilocal, patrilineal, exogamous, and territory-owning band. The ecological conditions for these parallelisms were low population density, foot transportation, and the hunting of scattered and nonmigratory animals, making it of strategic value for a man to remain in the territory of his birth. In the same article he distinguished the patrilineal band from the "composite band." The latter had eclectic memberships, were generally larger than the patrilineal groups, and found their principal subsistence in the hunting of large, gregarious, and migratory animals. Later research has shown some of these patrilineal band societies to be bilateral in descent, with a strong tendency to patrilocality, but, in another direction, Elman Service has argued the patrilocal band as an early and general form in social evolution (Service, 1962). In either case Steward's work on hunters and gatherers during the 1930s posed a good many of the major problems for later research, as the results of the conference on "Man the Hunter" (Lee and deVore, 1968) amply demonstrated.

Cultural ecology placed emphasis on the study of behavior patterns, of movement and sensate activity, of the performance of work. It was in this respect, little noted by historians of anthropology, that Steward made one of his sharpest breaks with the past. American anthropology had been notable for its emphasis on the culture trait, as a basic symbolic unit, and on jural rules and matters of form and style. One might indeed choose to define culture as being the realm of the normative, as does much of American anthropology, but this hardly means that this is the only domain of anthropology, however much it might be termed "the study of culture." Norms are articulated and expressed in terms of action, and the interplay between rules, values, and style on the one hand and activity on the other is at the very heart of anthropological research. Steward's third step in ecological analysis, the investigation of the ways that work patterns affect other aspects of culture, calls at once for meticulous analysis of interaction patterns and for a theory that sees social activity as underlying culture. This underlying dimension of ecological theory may well prove to have been its most important message.

Ecological studies have flourished in anthropology during the past ten years, simultaneously expanding their theoretical scope and interests. One direction of research has seen the introduction of biological models that reduce human behavior and institutions to items within ecosystems. The general methodology in the newer ecologies has been functionalist, but the referent of function is either to the biosphere seen as a system or to the population as an aggregate of human organisms. Mindful of the old Darwinian premise that population maximization is the end product of the struggle for survival and thus the measure of adaptation, attention has been directed to the calories obtained from subsistence (which is good) at the expense of emphasis on the ways in which the subsistence is obtained (which is bad). Steward, to the contrary, never forgot that the goal of anthropology is the study of human behavior, and that human behavior is intelligible only in a cultural context.

The theory and method of cultural ecology is not concerned with the environment per se as much as with an interaction, even an opposition, between man and his surroundings. Its treatment of technology takes full account of the fact that technology is a cultural realm, dealing with historically derived tools and knowledge, whether diffused or independently invented. Moreover, Steward emphasized that his interest was less in the gross environment than in the resources it offered, and resources to him were a matter of culture. They were subjects of the knowledge of the people, and they were of value only to the extent that the available technology made them both accessible and usable. Steward's ecology was always a *cultural* ecology, for he was ever suspicious of biological reductionism, an inheritance, no doubt, of his studentship under Kroeber.

HISTORY AND EVOLUTION

His early experience as an archeologist no doubt did much to predispose Steward toward historical explanation. He received no training
in archeology at all, and he termed his first research on the Columbia
River "improvised" and "unbelievably bad." That he was self-taught
may well have been one of his strengths in the field, for he at least did
not become indoctrinated with the passion for pottery sherds that
infected his contemporaries, and which still bedevils the field. While
other archeologists were mulling over the variations of Kayenta and
Anasazi ware, Steward was digging sites in southern Utah for data on
settlement pattern, an almost unheard-of preoccupation in those
times. From the locations, size, and numbers of dwellings and ceremonial kivas, he analyzed the development of Puebloan society from its
origins in seed-gathering economies through agriculture. As part of
the same process, increases in population and settlement size were seen
to take the social organization from simple bands to localized lineages
to multilineal communities and clanship. The result, published as the
aforementioned "Ecological Aspects of Southwestern Society" (1937),
is one of the most original and creative works ever published in archeology, and it was undoubtedly for this reason that the American
journals turned it down. That it was not too daring for a German
journal in the year 1937 is perhaps a commentary on the openness of
American academia, in which we have taken such pride.

Steward's role in pioneering settlement-pattern archeology did
much to make archeology a social science and to redirect its efforts
toward the writing of social history rather than the study of style. It was
through settlement pattern and associated material culture having
economic inference that he was able to extrapolate back in time and
retrodict the shape and size of social units in the past. In essence, he was
doing cultural ecology with archeological data, and he founded environmental archeology 30 years before it became a recognized sub-
field. But the same profession that turned down his article on the
Southwest was not about to embrace anything so new. Robert Braidwood began to do settlement-pattern work in Mesopotamia, but little
else was done on the subject until the joint Viru Valley, Peru, project in
1946, which was inspired and planned by Steward and the late Wendell
Bennett of Yale. Gordon Willey of Harvard University writes that he
was assigned the settlement-pattern phase of the research, while his
seniors took the pottery and similar prizes (Willey, 1974:154). He was
quite annoyed with Steward, a cultural anthropologist, for having
given him so odd and unpromising an assignment, and felt that he had
been given a rather raw deal. As it turned out, the settlement-pattern

research was the most notable part of the project and formed the cornerstone of Willey's reputation. Interest in a broad-based and sociologically oriented archeology lapsed again until its re-emergence in the 1960s, but by then Steward had drifted almost completely away from the field.

Steward's archeology was based upon both ecological and functional considerations, and he tried to integrate the field as an essential part of social anthropology. Where others were doing the most shallow kind of historicism, a perpetuation in archeology of diffusionism, Steward sought to extract from the evidence inferences on how the people lived. He argued for the necessity of wedding ethnology and archeology as a means by which we can extrapolate from known and documented ethnographic data to partial and fragmentary archeological material. Just as he sought a holistic approach in cultural anthropology and just as he was to argue for classification based upon functional relations, so also did he argue for configurational and functional perspectives in archeology.[8] In a way, he attempted to de-mystify archeology, which may be why his suggestions were not always welcome. He did not view the field as a highly specialized enterprise with its own arcane methods and knowledge—a field that was thought of as an earth science by the social scientists and as a social science by the earth scientists. Archeology was just plain history, albeit a history that worked rubbish heaps, not archives. In "The Direct Historical Approach to Archeology" (1942),[9] Steward pointed to ways that archeological and historical data could support each other and merge their findings. This, like many of his suggestions, was pursued by others some 20 years later. It is curious that Steward, one of the most important theorists and methodologists in the history of the archeological discipline, never thought of himself as an archeologist and only spent a few years in prehistoric research. Perhaps the reason for his success is that he regarded archeology as just one more means to the study of causality and the search for social laws.

Steward's historical interests were joined with a theory of evolution, an inevitable outcome of his belief that history, evolution, and structure had a unity as the study of social and cultural causality. Steward's aim was not at all to develop a substantive scheme for the evolutionary ordering of the world's cultures, nor was it even to develop a general theory of evolution. Rather, he looked upon evolutionism as one more avenue to the establishment of specific social laws. Most of evolutionary

---

[8] See Steward's "Function and Configuration in Archeology" (with Frank M. Setzler, 1938), reprinted in this volume, pp. 208-214.

[9] Reprinted below, pp. 201-207.

thought in anthropology was, at the time Steward was developing his own theories, of the so-called "unilinear" variety. Discussed in different ways by writers as diverse as Lewis Henry Morgan, Durkheim, and Herbert Spencer, evolutionary theory dealt with the emergence of more complex social forms out of simpler ones and of more inclusive social organisms out of less expansive polities. The growth of human society was painted in bold colors on a broad canvas, and the bewildering variety of cultures was seen by the early theorists as residues of the past, enabling them to order the living primitive societies into stages of universal development. It was this panoramic picture which fell before the attacks of Boas and his students in the United States, Radcliffe-Brown and Malinowski in England, and the *Kulturkreise* group in Germany. By the 1930s it was in shambles and without adherents; the efforts of Leslie White, Steward's successor at Michigan, to revive the work of Morgan must rate as one of the most courageous intellectual stands ever taken by an anthropologist.

White had managed to at least make evolutionism thinkable again by the time Steward advanced his own theory in the early 1950s, but it was still considered a bold step, especially in light of the regnant McCarthyism. Steward's evolutionism had its immediate antecedents in the work of the Viru Valley group and the historical theories of Karl Wittfogel, a long-time friend and a colleague at Columbia. Wittfogel had formulated his theory of the emergence of the Oriental despotic state from his work in Chinese history. Starting from Karl Marx's well-known writings on the British rule in India, Wittfogel wrote on the role of irrigation agriculture in promoting the emergence of a state based on absolutist controls over the construction of hydraulic works and the distribution of water and, thence, over populations and agricultural lands.[10] The results of the Viru project similarly showed the development of state institutions in an arid valley of coastal Peru, an area where irrigation was necessary to cultivation. In an important paper entitled "Cultural Causality and Law" (1949), Steward surveyed the literature on the growth of the earliest and primary state civilizations—primary in the sense that in each case the state could not be looked upon as a secondary response to other states—and found that all rested on an economy based upon irrigation agriculture. The functional relationship between an arid environment, irrigation, and the growth of state institutions should have been enough to demonstrate causality in Steward's view, but he also had the corroboration of

---

[10] Steward's most extensive discussion of Wittfogel's work appeared in an unpublished paper, "Wittfogel's Irrigation Hypothesis," which is presented for the first time in this volume, pp. 87-99.

history. This allowed him to see causal process working out over a period of time, to see cause and effect in a temporal sequence.

The five type cases chosen were Mesopotamia, Egypt, North China (where irrigation was used for flood control more than to overcome an arid environment), northern Peru, and Meso-America. Steward found in the histories of each a remarkable parallelism that saw a development from a preagricultural period, a short era of "incipient agriculture" in which the use of cultigens originated in a dry farming regime, and a following "formative" period which saw the beginning of irrigation and the emergence of small states. The Formative period laid the bases for the subsequent eras of "regional florescence," which saw the full-scale development of irrigation, the growth of largely theocratic regional states, and the appearance of cities. In all five cases the Florescent period was followed by one typified by "cyclical conquests" with full urbanization, warfare, and militarism, a tendency toward state secularization, and the growth of dynastic empires. Behind the entire pressure toward stratification and the state was irrigation and, with it, the need for control over populations for the purpose of building public works and allocating the distribution of water.

Here indeed was evolutionary process as Steward understood it—the orderly and determined emergence of social forms. It was also a cross-culturally recurrent phenomenon, a regularity of social development. Steward thus had two controls over the formulation of generalizations, the temporal and the comparative. He found an association between a set of conditions: an arid environment, irrigation, and the state. The prehistory of the Viru Valley and the history of China showed a cause-and-effect sequence that could be further corroborated by comparative historical research. He next sought other areas where the state developed to determine whether the same conditions were also found. He could have also begun his cross-cultural survey using the environment as the independent variable. This would lead, as he himself conjectured, to the valleys of the Salt and Gila rivers in Arizona, where something very close to state formation had occurred in the Mogollon period, but it could also have taken him to southern California, where the technology was too rudimentary to augur development. Actually, the best procedure was to play with the variables using each in turn as the independent one, searching back and forth through the data and refining hypotheses in the process.

Steward's evolutionism obviously aimed at something far less than a worldwide or universal scheme, for the kind of development he had traced in the irrigation states had transpired in only a limited number of areas. Evolution is a universal process, but it takes different forms in different areas at different times—it goes through many lines, of which that taken by the hydraulic civilizations is but one. Recognizing this, he chose to call his theory "multilinear evolution," a term he first used in 1953.[11] Steward himself was not sure where, or whether, the term had been previously used when he adopted it, and the only occurrence of the phrase that I have found is in Robert Lowie's *Social Organization,* in which he characterizes the *Kulturkreiselehre,* the German school of diffusionism, as a kind of "multilinear" evolutionism (Lowie, 1948:33-35). Steward was slightly dismayed when I told him this.

Steward was quite specific about multilinear evolution's salience as methodology: "Multilinear evolution is essentially a methodology based on the assumption that significant regularities in culture change occur, and it is concerned with the determination of cultural laws" (1955:18). Just as the irrigation civilizations constituted one line of evolution, so also could others, based upon limited sets of parallel developments, be found. There may be only two examples in a set, or there may even be only one; the major point of the search for parallelisms is the comparative control obtained, and not simply the generality of the phenomena. Moreover, multilinear evolution is not a universal scheme but an empirical one:

> What is lost in universality will be gained in concreteness and specificity. Multilinear evolution, therefore, has no a priori scheme or laws. It recognizes that the cultural traditions of different areas may be wholly or partially distinctive, and it simply poses the question of whether any genuine or meaningful similarities between certain cultures exist and whether these lend themselves to formulation. [1955:19]

The empiricism of the method was consistent with the kind of middle-range causal formulations that Steward considered exemplary of general process. But it also had the purpose of keeping the theory tied to the ethnographic data and to the cultural-ecological considerations that underlaid his entire approach.

An article entitled "Tappers and Trappers,"[12] which I coauthored with Steward in 1956, is illustrative of the ecological underpinnings of multilinear evolution (Murphy and Steward, 1956). At the time I arrived in Urbana in 1953, I had recently done fieldwork among the Mundurucú Indians in South America, where I studied the effects of

---

[11] Steward published extensively on his evolutionary theory and method. Several of these essays were published in his *Theory of Culture Change* (1955), and three more are reprinted in this volume. These are "Cultural Evolution" (1956; see below, pp. 58-67), "Evolutionary Principles and Social Types" (1960; see below, pp. 68-86), and "The Evolution of Pre-Farming Societies" (1968; see below, pp. 103-127).

[12] Reprinted in this volume, pp. 151-179. Steward, a connoisseur of limericks and a lover of euphony, made up the title.

involvement in extraction of wild rubber for trade upon the native social system. One of the results of this commerce with Brazilian patrons was a tendency toward community fragmentation, dispersal of families through the rubber areas, and a recentering of interaction upon the trading posts. Steward noted that much the same thing happened among the Northern Athapascans. There, however, the aboriginal communities were hunting bands, as opposed to horti-cultural villages, and the commodity traded was fur from wild animals, as contrasted to wild rubber. And the locales were as different as could be, tropical jungle and subarctic forests. In effect, we had demon-strated a case, however limited in occurrence and time, of multilinear evolution, but we had also demonstrated that one can find the same cultural-ecological equation in radically dissimilar environments. Both populations were trading widely dispersed wild products within the structure of mercantile economies, and both were inexorably drawn more completely into this sytem by an escalation of their demands for Western goods. And the key parallelism between the two was in the organization of work, the central variable in cultural ecology.

Whatever its theoretical implications, our paper was empirical. Stew-ard was an admirer of Leslie White's trenchant, even pugnacious, defense of Morgan, and he felt that his attempt to relate evolutionary progress to man's control of energy was a positive contribution. He was, however, troubled by the "universalism" of White's evolutionary scheme, by the fact that it did not deal with organically linked historical sequences, and that it paid little attention to ecology—a lapse that he found curious in an avowedly materialistic theory. "The whole thing could just as easily take place on Mars," he sometimes commented. Steward was indeed a generalist, but he was also wholly committed to empiricism.

METHODS AND STRATEGIES

Steward disavowed universal schemes of evolution, but he curiously enough authored what was to become one without really intending to do so at the time. On the basis of the experience of the Puerto Rico project, Steward wrote a monograph entitled *Area Research: Theory and Practice,* which was published by the Social Science Research Council in 1950 (Steward, 1950).[13] The book was one of the early charters for the area study approach, but it also was Steward's attempt to overcome the difficulties that anthropologists, whose experience had been in small

---

[13] Chapter three of this book, which outlines his view of "levels of sociocultural integration," is reprinted in the present volume, pp. 217-239.

tribal societies, were encountering in conceptualizing complex cultures. One of the suggestions made in the volume was that complex, national societies be looked upon as being composed of a number of modes of integration, of various degrees of complexity. Just as there are a plethora of institutions, groupings, occupations, etc., in the modern nation, and just as there are local institutions and others that are nationwide in scope, so also are there small-scale kinds of integration within the overall national system, as well as broader integrating mechanisms. These modes of "sociocultural integration" differed in scope of social unit systematized and also in complexity. Thus, within the modern nation-state, one can see the family or kinship network as one mode of integration, the community as another, and finally the nation itself, held together as it may be by a national bureaucracy, an overall ruling class, a state religion, and so forth. Each represents a different "level" of organization and thus could be referred to as a "level of sociocultural integration."

The idea of levels represented an effort to come to grips with the relationship between the whole and the parts of any system and was, in a sense, the nearest Steward came to a structural-functional kind of analysis. Following the notions of integrative levels in biology, and the writings of Whitehead among others, he stipulated that the whole was more than the simple sum of its parts, and, equally important, the parts were conditioned by the whole:

> According to the principle of sociocultural sublevels, each higher sublevel is more complex than the lower ones not only in the qualitative[14] sense that it has more parts but, as in biological sublevels, that it has qualitatively novel characteristics or unique properties which are not evident in or foreshadowed by the lower ones. That is, the new whole at each higher sublevel induces change in the very nature of the parts and creates new relationships between the parts and to the whole. [Steward, 1950:110]

According to this reasoning, the family system within an industrial state, for example, must be understood to have quite different functions from formally similar units in a primitive society. It would follow from this, then, that the American family cannot be subjected to a scientific comparison with the Eskimo family, since Steward's comparative method looked for regularities of function more than of form. This is an important point, for Steward never tried to find analogues, let alone regularities, between the rather isolated American family and the similarly autonomous Western Shoshoni family. And it was for this

[14] Steward undoubtedly meant to use the term "quantitative" rather than "qualitative."

reason that he was critical of the treatment of the Eskimo and "Yankee" families as representative of a single type in G. P. Murdock's book *Social Structure* (1949).

Steward published a separate paper on the levels concept entitled "Levels of Sociocultural Integration: An Operational Concept" (1951), which further developed the utility of the idea in the study of social change and acculturation. He noted that acculturation among the Western Shoshoni was not as traumatic, either individually or culturally, as among other tribes because there were no tribal integrative mechanisms to be disrupted by American society. Given the family level of integration of the Shoshoni, "The individual families were quite free to adjust to changed circumstances in the most expedient way without facing conflict" (Steward, 1951:386). In contrast, the Spanish conquest of Peru brought about the total and sudden disruption of the Inca state, the state religion, and other national institutions, although family cults and the structure of local communities persisted even into the present. Steward wrote that "it is clear that social and cultural interaction takes place on different levels" (*ibid.:*389), a salutary reminder to those who viewed acculturation as the confrontation of alien cultures, in their totality.

Any concept so broad as to provide a framework for the conceptualization of complex societies and for studies of social change could clearly have evolutionary significance as well. The concept of integrative levels in biology was part of a theory of emergent evolution, and Steward's theory was quickly received in this way. In fact, many contemporary students are unaware that levels of sociocultural integration has anything other than an evolutionary referent. The concept deals, after all, with scope and complexity of systems, the very essence of evolutionism. Steward was aware of this and wrote "The concepts of level of organization and developmental continuum indicate the need of recognizing that in each world area the sequences of sociocultural units consist of successions of new kinds of wholes qualitatively different from previous ones but genetically related to them" (1950:114). The problem he thought, was to develop a taxonomy that had true evolutionary significance, and this would not prove easy.

Steward believed that taxonomy and classification were necessary to the work of making comparative generalizations. By the time he had finished his Southwest and Shoshoni research, he found dissatisfaction with the culture area classifications that were then popular in anthropology. Culture area divisions were too often based upon items of style and discrete traits that had diffused within a certain geographical area. The Southwest culture area was a glaring example of this. Included within it were the quite complex Puebloan societies, some of which used irrigation agriculture, the pastoral Navajo, and the hunting and gathering Apache groups. From the point of view of social structure and ecology, each was radically different from the others, however much they may have shared certain traits, such as sand painting and the like. In the light of his overall program, which remained the search for developmental laws, he urged instead a classification that would be based upon central economic, political, and social features, a typology of function and structure rather than of secondary traits.

His first attempt at such a taxonomy was in his formulation of *culture types* in the *Handbook of South American Indians*. He divided the continent into four types, which yielded a certain geographical continuity owing to common ecological factors. These were: the Andean civilizations, a type characterized by class stratification, the state, urbanization, and irrigation agriculture; the Circum-Caribbean, whose salient features were intensive agriculture, marine fishing, large communities, small multicommunity states and chiefdoms, and stratification; the Tropical Forest, which was typified by lack of classes and the state, large sedentary villages, slash-and-burn horticulture, and limited or no development of multicommunity forms of integration; and the Marginal tribes, which were largely hunting and collecting populations living in bands as well as some marginal horticulturalists. The actual dividing lines between the types were somewhat fuzzy, as is true in any taxonomy, and the division between Marginal and Tropical Forest was sometimes based on culture area characteristics such as presence or absence of the dugout canoe and the woven hammock. Despite the rough edges, the purpose was clear: the typological division related to differences in ecology and to what he would later call levels of integration. Within the typology was an evolutionary theory (cf. Steward, 1947).[15]

At the basis of Steward's later formulation of types was the concept of "culture core," which he defines in one source as "functional interdependency of features in a structural relationship" (Steward, 1955:94). He also used the term "core" to mean ". . . the constellation of features which are most closely related to subsistence activities and economic arrangements. The core includes such social, political and religious patterns as are empirically determined to be closely connected with these arrangements" (*ibid.:*37). In short, the core represented the cultural-ecological nexus of a society. A culture type, then, would include all societies having a fundamental similarity of core features, such that parallel causal processes may be hypothesized. The

---

[15] Steward's interpretation of South American cultural evolution is summarized in an article reprinted in this volume, pp. 128-150.

delineation of a type, therefore, was not simply a taxonomic exercise, but the definition of a problem. And it would follow from our previous discussion that the component groups of any type must be at the same level of sociocultural integration.

The concepts of core, type, and level of integration were not products of terminological virtuosity, though they did become bewildering at times, but part of an overall framework for the discovery of general laws through functional and historical analysis of cross-culturally recurrent phenomena, bringing our discussion back to where it started. Developed and elaborated at different times and in different contexts, the parts of the theory fitted together into an overall edifice of concept and method that had a remarkable internal consistency. This unity was the expression of a single-minded and central purpose that enveloped Steward's life and career. But in all this unswerving quest he remained a scientist, for he sought not truth but understanding.

ENDNOTE

Anthropological interests and directions have grown exponentially within the past decade, as much a consequence of the loss of confidence that climaxed the period as of the internal growth of the discipline. Steward's theories are probably holding their own as well or better than most. One reason for this is that his never became the predominant ideology in anthropology. If any school of thought was paramount during the period from 1950 to 1965, it was structural-functionalism, a movement to which Steward's work related but did not belong. Structural-functionalism, whether in the anthropological writings of Radcliffe-Brown or in the sociology of Talcott Parsons, was fatally flawed, however, and had reached an intellectual dead end by 1955. It became one of the casualties of 1968, itself an epiphenomenon of the end of an era and a denouement from which Steward's work emerged relatively unscathed.

The recent period has seen, among other currents of thought, a reawakening of interest in academic Marxism and the blossoming of French structuralism. Steward's work took a fuller and franker account of the material conditions of life than any of the other persuasions in professional anthropology, and Marvin Harris, in his grouchy but brilliant book *The Rise of Anthropological Theory* (1968), has argued that it is above all a form of "cultural materialism." This, to Harris, is the highest praise, and he devotes most of his final chapter to a laudatory treatment of Steward's contribution, with some complaints at his failure to have taken a doctrinaire position. It is doubtful whether Steward would have accepted the materialist label, however, for he always stressed the fundamentally methodological and empirical nature of his work, avoiding any ideological commitment to one or another kind of determinism.[16]

It is worth stressing that, although Steward's work had an undeniable affinity to materialist theory, he was repelled by ideology and never found Marxian thought to be personally congenial. Nonetheless, he did sounder and more sophisticated work on what could be called the means and mode of production than the Marxists of his time. He took more meticulous and detailed account of technology than did orthodox Marxists, and he incorporated a dynamic theory of environment, whereas theirs was primitive or wanting. The deepest difference between Steward's work and that represented by the Marxian tradition, however, lies in the total absence of dialectical process in Steward's view of history. In this sense Steward's theories were consistent with almost the entire corpus of anthropological literature, for, aside from the often crude dialectics of the Russian theorists, the discipline was innocent of the philosophy until the writings of Claude Lévi-Strauss.

The current vogue of Lévi-Strauss's structuralism inevitably begets the question: what has this to do with cultural ecology? Perhaps Lévi-Strauss answered the query himself when, in 1972, he delivered the Gildersleeve Lecture at Barnard College on the subject "Structuralism and Ecology." A large audience gathered in tribute to the noted French scholar and also to listen to what they hoped would be one of the great syntheses of our time. They were quickly disabused of this expectation when Lévi-Strauss launched into a discussion of the ways in which the environment was conceptualized and ordered in Northwest Coast mythology. It was clear that structuralism had nothing to do with ecology as most of his audience understood the term. Structuralism and cultural ecology are not in competition with each other in a situation where one is right, or righter, and the other is wrong, or wronger, for this would assume that they are asking the same questions and addressing the same problems. Quite to the contrary, like most academic arguments, they go past one another, and the student torn between the two, or between these and other directions for that matter, should only ask which one interests him more and seems most worthy of using up his time. He could do far worse than to choose cultural ecology, for it addresses itself to the very basic question

---

[16] Steward specifically eschewed unilateral theories of determinism in an article entitled "Determinism in Primitive Society?" (1941b), an essay on Carrier culture change. This paper and another on Carrier acculturation (1961) are reprinted in the present volume, pp. 180-187 and 188-200.

of work and survival. This is becoming less and less an academic issue today.

Steward's work will have a lasting impact upon the anthropological profession for another reason. This is that he posed a series of problems around which one can organize substantive field research—and fieldwork is the defining characteristic of anthropology more than any of its theories. More than this, he left to us some of the finest documents on native American society ever published, his work on the Great Basin Shoshoneans. Steward's theories will be transcended, something that he himself would have wished, for it is the measure of progress of a profession. His fieldwork, however, can never again be duplicated, and it remains a model for future research, as well as his testimonial to the American Indian.

BIBLIOGRAPHY

HARRIS, MARVIN
    1968. *The Rise of Anthropological Theory.* New York: Crowell.

KROEBER, ALFRED L.
    1939. *Cultural and Natural Areas of Native North America.* University of California Publications in American Archaeology and Ethnology, vol. 38. Berkeley: University of California Press.

LEE, RICHARD B., and IRVEN DE VORE, eds.
    1968. *Man the Hunter.* Chicago: Aldine.

LOWIE, ROBERT H.
    1948. *Social Organization.* New York: Rinehart.

MANNERS, ROBERT, ed.
    1964. *Process and Pattern in Culture: Essays in Honor of Julian H. Steward.* Chicago: Aldine.

MURDOCK, GEORGE P.
    1949. *Social Structure.* New York: Macmillan.

MURPHY, ROBERT F., and JULIAN H. STEWARD
    1956. Tappers and Trappers: Parallel Processes in Acculturation. *Economic Development and Culture Change* 4:335-355.

SERVICE, ELMAN
    1962. *Primitive Social Organization.* New York: Random House.

STEWARD, JULIAN H.
    1930. Irrigation without Agriculture. *Papers of the Michigan Society of Science, Arts and Letters* 12 (1929):149-156.

    1936. The economic and Social Basis of Primitive Bands. In *Essays on Anthropology in Honor of Alfred Louis Kroeber*, ed. Robert H. Lowie. Berkeley: University of California Press. Pp. 311-350.

1937. Ecological Aspects of Southwestern Society. *Anthropos* 32:87-104.

1938. *Basin-Plateau Aboriginal Sociopolitical Groups.* Smithsonian Institution, Bureau of American Ethnology, Bulletin 120, Washington, D.C.

1941a. *Culture Element Distributions: XIII. Nevada Shoshoni.* University of California Publications in Anthropological Records 4:208-259. Berkeley: University of California Press.

1941b. Determinism in Primitive Society? *Scientific Monthly* 53:491-501.

1942. The Direct Historical Approach to Archaeology. *American Antiquity* 7:337-343.

1943a. Acculturation and the Indian Problem. *América Indígena* 3:323-328.

1943b. Acculturation Studies in Latin America: Some Needs and Problems. *American Anthropologist* 45:198-204.

1943c. Anthropological Research Needs and Opportunities in South America. *Acta Americana* 1:20-37.

1946-50 (ed.). *Handbook of South American Indians.* 6 vols. Smithsonian Institution, Bureau of American Ethnology, Bulletin 143, Washington, D.C.

1947. American Culture History in the Light of South America. *Southwestern Journal of Anthropology* 3:85-107.

1949. Cultural Causality and Law: A Trial Formulation of the Development of Early Civilizations. *American Anthropologist* 51:1-27.

1950. *Area Research: Theory and Practice.* Social Science Research Council Bulletin 63:1-164.

1951. Levels of Sociocultural Integration: An Operational Concept. *Southwestern Journal of Anthropology* 7:374-390.

1954. Types of Types. *American Anthropologist* 56:54-57.

1955. *Theory of Culture Change.* Urbana: University of Illinois Press.

1956a. *The People of Puerto Rico.* With Robert A. Manners, Eric R. Wolf, Elena Padilla, Sidney W. Mintz, and R. L. Scheele. Urbana: University of Illinois Press.

1956b. Cultural Evolution. *Scientific American* 194:69-80.

1960. Evolutionary Principles and Social Types. In *Evolution After Darwin,* vol. 2, ed. Sol Tax. Chicago: University of Chicago Press. Pp. 169-186.

1961. Carrier Acculturation: The Direct Historical Approach. In *Culture in History: Essays in Honor of Paul Radin*, ed. Stanley Diamond. New York: Columbia University Press. Pp. 732-744.

1967 (ed.). *Contemporary Change in Traditional Societies*. 3 vols. Urbana: University of Illinois Press.

1968. Causal Factors and Processes in the Evolution of Pre-Farming Societies. In *Man the Hunter*, ed. Richard B. Lee and Irven de Vore. Chicago: Aldine. Pp. 321-334.

1969. Limitations of Applied Anthropology: The Case of the American Indian New Deal. *Journal of the Steward Anthropological Society* (Urbana) 1:1-17.

1970. The Foundations of Basin-Plateau Shoshonean Society. In *Languages and Cultures of Western North America: Essays in Honor of Sven S. Liljeblad*, ed. Earl H. Swanson, Jr. Pocatello: Idaho State University Press. Pp. 113-151.

1973. *Alfred Kroeber*. New York: Columbia University Press.

STEWARD, JULIAN H., and LOUIS C. FARON
1959. *Native Peoples of South America*. New York: McGraw-Hill.

STEWARD, JULIAN H., and FRANK M. SETZLER
1938. Function and Configuration in Archaeology. *American Antiquity* 4:4-10.

WILLEY, GORDON R. (ed.)
1974. *Archaeological Researches in Retrospect*. Cambridge, Mass.: Winthrop.

PART I

Theory and Method

1
The Concept and Method of Cultural Ecology

It is appropriate that the first essay of this volume be on cultural ecology, for this body of method and theory has characterized Steward's work more than any of his other interests. "Cultural Ecology" was originally published in the *International Encyclopedia of the Social Sciences*, David L. Sills, ed. vol. 4, pp. 337-344 (New York: Macmillan, 1968), and is reprinted with permission of the Macmillan Company (© 1968 by Crowell Collier & Macmillan, Inc.). This is one of the very few summary statements written by Steward on cultural ecology, for he generally developed the theory in empirical interpretations. Another article on the subject formed Chapter 2 of his *Theory of Culture Change* (Urbana: University of Illinois Press, 1955).

Cultural ecology is the study of the processes by which a society adapts to its environment. Its principal problem is to determine whether these adaptations initiate internal social transformations of evolutionary change. It analyzes these adaptations, however, in conjunction with other processes of change. Its method requires examination of the interaction of societies and social institutions with one another and with the natural environment.

Cultural ecology is distinguishable from but does not necessarily exclude other approaches to the ecological study of social phenomena. These approaches have viewed their special problems—for example, settlement patterns, the development of agriculture, and land use—in the broad context of the complexly interacting phenomena within a defined geographical area. Explanatory formulations have even included the incidence of disease, which is related to social phenomena and in turn affects societies in their adaptations. This modern concept of ecology has largely superseded other concepts, such as "urban," "social," and "human" ecology, which employed the biological analogy of viewing social institutions in terms of competition, climax areas, and zones.

Cultural ecology is broadly similar to biological ecology in its method of examining the interactions of all social and natural phenomena within an area, but it does not equate social features with biological species or assume that competition is the major process. It distinguishes different kinds of sociocultural systems and institutions, it recognizes both cooperation and competition as processes of interaction, and it postulates that environmental adaptations depend on the technology, needs, and structure of the society and on the nature of the environment. It includes analysis of adaptations to the social environment, because an independent tribe is influenced in its environmental adaptations by such interactions with its neighbors as peaceful trading, intermarriage, cooperation, and warfare and other kinds of competition, in the same way a specialized, dependent segment of a larger sociocultural system may be strongly influenced by external institutions in the way it utilizes its environment.

The cultural-ecological method of analyzing culture change or evolution differs from that based on the superorganic or culturological concept. The latter assumes that only phenomena of a cultural level are relevant and admissible, and it repudiates "reductionism," that is, consideration of processes induced by factors of a psychological, biological, or environmental level. The evolutionary hypotheses based upon this method deal with culture in a generic or global sense rather than with individual cultures in a substantive sense, and they postulate universal processes. Cultural ecology, on the other hand, recognizes the substantive dissimilarities of cultures that are caused by the particular adaptive processes by which any society interacts with its environment.

Cultural ecology does not assume that each case is unique. Its method, however, requires an empirical analysis of each society before broader generalizations of cross-cultural similarities in processes and substantive effects may be made. Cultural ecologists study highly diversified cultures and environments and can prescribe neither specific analytic formulas nor theoretical or ideal models of culture change; there can be no a priori conclusions or generalizations concerning evolution. The heuristic value of the ecological viewpoint is to conceptualize noncultural phenomena that are relevant to processes of cultural evolution.

Empirical studies disclose that among the simpler and earlier societies of mankind, to whom physical survival was the major concern, different social systems were fairly direct responses to the exploitation of particular environments by special techniques. As technological innovations improved man's ability to control and adjust to environments, and as historically derived patterns of behavior were introduced, the significance of both the environment and the culture was altered and the adaptive processes not only became more complex but also acquired new qualities.

The ecological concept of interacting phenomena draws attention to certain general categories of relevant data. The resources, flora, fauna, climate, local diseases and their vectors of occurrence, and many other features of the environment constitute potential factors in one part of the interacting system. The nature of the culture, especially its exploitative and adaptive technology but also features of the internal and external social environment, constitutes the other part. The interaction involves the social arrangements that are required in land exploitation; population density, distribution, and nucleation; permanence and composition of population aggregates; territoriality of societies; intersocietal relationships; and cultural values. In each case the empirical problem is whether the adaptation is so inflexible as to permit only a certain pattern or whether there is latitude for variation which may allow different patterns to be developed or borrowed.

Explanations in terms of cultural ecology require certain conceptual distinctions about the nature of culture. First, the various components of a culture, such as technology, language, society, and stylistic features, respond very differently to adaptive processes. Second, sociocultural systems of different levels of integration profoundly affect the interaction of biological, cultural, and environmental factors. Societies having supracommunity (state or national) institutions and the technological ability to expand the effective environment beyond that of the local or primary group can utilize resources within and outside the area controlled by the larger society. The adaptive responses of complex societies are thus very unlike those of a tribal society, which adapts predominantly to its own environment.

CULTURE HISTORY AND ECOLOGICAL ADAPTATIONS

The historical processes by which a society acquires many of its basic traits are complementary to studies of adaptive processes. The historical processes include the extensive borrowing of many cultural traits and trait complexes from diverse sources; the migrations of people; the transmission of cultural heritages to successive generations; and local innovations or inventions. Recognition of these historical processes, however, does not relegate environment to the circumscribed role of merely permitting or prohibiting certain cultural practices so that all origins must be explained by such history. It is obvious that fishing will have minor importance in desert areas and that agriculture is impossible in arctic regions. It is equally clear that abundant fishing resources cannot be exploited without appropriate techniques and that agricultural potentials cannot be utilized without domesticated plants. The presence of gold, oil, and uranium is unimportant until the society has demands for them and means of extracting them.

The Indians of the Southwest had at one time been predominantly food collectors, but the introduction of food crops, largely from Mesoamerica, provided the basis for the development of the more complex Pueblo village culture. Many details of this culture, such as ritual elements, were borrowed from the south, but the development of Pueblo sociocultural patterns are comprehensible only in terms of the processes of population growth, extension of biological families into lineages, eventual consolidation of lineages into larger settlements, and the appearance of many village institutions that cut across kinship groups.

Dissimilar ecological adaptations may also occur among societies that have been subjected to similar historical influences. The Indians of California and of the semiarid steppes and deserts of the Great Basin shared substantially the same devices for collecting wild foods and for hunting, but the vastly greater abundance of flora and fauna in California supported a population thirty times that of the Great Basin. The California Indians lived in fairly permanent villages which had developed some social elaborations, whereas the Great Basin Indians were divided into independent family units which foraged over large territories during most of the year and assembled only seasonally in encampments that did not always consist of the same families.

The investigation of cultural-ecological processes must consider the possibility that basic sociocultural patterns may have diffused or been carried by migrations from one kind of environment to another, but it also must examine whether these patterns have been modified. Assessment of modifications requires a distinction between the outer embellishments of the culture, such as ritual elements, art styles, and kinds of architecture, and those social patterns which are human arrangements for self-perpetuation.

BIOLOGICAL FACTORS

Man's adaptations to his natural environment cannot be comprehended in purely culturological terms because man not only shares basic biological needs with all animals but also has distinctively human characteristics. All activities are culturally conditioned, but ecological factors cannot be wholly distinguished from inherent biological and psychological factors which are the basis of behavior. Analyses that ascribe importance to inherent human qualities bear directly upon the validity of common hypotheses and raise new problems.

It has generally been assumed that the nuclear family consisting of parents and children has always been the irreducible social structure because the sexes serve complementary functions in meeting procreational and subsistence needs and in caring for and training the young during their long period of dependency. This assumption is generally valid for all ethnographically known societies, especially for primitive societies, among whom there is a clear sexual division of labor in subsistence, maintenance of the household, and child rearing. In contemporary industrial societies, however, the biological family has surrendered many of its functions, and cultural differences between sex roles have been diminished. Conceivably, the nuclear family might be reduced to little more than a procreational unit if its cultural functions are lost.

In primitive societies, larger suprafamilial bands or other groups that developed in response to cooperative needs, especially in subsistence activities, had a biological basis, especially through lineages. The patrilineages of hunting bands, for example, had the advantage that particular skills, knowledge of the the environment, and obedience to authority were transmitted from father to son in a male-dominated group. Biological relationships have so long been fundamentally important in culture history that they may be ascribed excessive importance, as when the position of head of a family or even kingship is transmitted through primogeniture. The biological basis survived because of the lack of patterned alternatives.

Another basic biological factor in cultural-ecological adaptations is the prolonged period of human growth. The factors of age and environment interact in many ways to affect behavior patterns. The Shoshoni child may help in rabbit drives but not in big game hunting; the east African boy may herd cattle but not go to war; modern American youths attend school for a required number of years; in areas of precarious subsistence the aged may be abandoned to die, while in other areas they may be accorded special consideration; and everywhere the marriage age group is determined by biological development, culture, and adaptations to the environment.

There are, however, many problems concerning the interaction of biological and cultural-ecological factors. One of these arises from the assumption that the nuclear or biological family is a basic part of every human society. This assumption might rest on the obvious biological nature of the family or upon the universal cultural functions the family is believed to serve. The higher primates usually live in fairly small bands that consist of females and their dependent offspring, a single powerful male, and subordinate adult males. In certain depressed segments of modern society, however, the matrifocal family or kin group, which consists of women and dependent children and some-what subordinate males who are loosely attached to the family, appears to be the irreducible social unit. This family represents an adaptive response to restricted territoriality, low income, and lack of opportunity for improvement.

Although the transition from a precultural primate society to the nuclear family has not been explained, the contemporary existence of the matrifocal kin group raises the question of origin. How did the nuclear family develop from an early kind of society which may have lacked the cultural-ecological processes that created and have subsequently supported it?

Speculation about the origin of the family must be based on what is known archeologically about the origins of technology and on ethnographic evidence. In all ethnographic cases of prefarming societies the nuclear family is based on clear complementarity of the sexes in subsistence activities. Women are food collectors because they must not leave their children, who are their inescapable responsibility, whereas men may spend long periods away from their families hunting large game or fishing, if the technology makes this possible. Prior to the invention of such distinctly male-associated hunting devices as spears, bows, nets, and traps, both sexes may have collected food in so similar a way that they were no more differentiated than were the higher primates. If so, there may have been a long transitional stage when some type of matrifocal kin group persisted. The hand ax, which was long the principal weapon, may attest to men's role in protecting the group but not specialization in hunting, for its use was in close combat.

SETTLEMENT PATTERNS AND THE ADAPTIVE PROCESS

A culture that is introduced into a wholly new environment must adapt in some ways to local conditions, but only empirical research can determine whether the adaptations are unalterably fixed or whether there is latitude for variations. In some instances, the case for narrow limits of variation seems clear. Simple societies that exploit only sparse and scattered resources obtained by food collecting must obviously fragment into small groups, for members of the society are in competition with one another. More abundant resources, such as rich areas of vegetable foods, large game herds, fisheries, or intensive farming, may permit variation in some features and thus allow latitude for borrowing or for local innovations.

There can, however, be no a priori conclusions: whether a society is dispersed over its land or clustered in large settlements may result from adaptive factors, from historical patterns, or from both. The

Indians of California and the Northwest Coast had very similar native population densities, but the dispersed acorns and game in California led to considerable dispersal of the villages, whereas the rich salmon fisheries of British Columbia and Alaska required the people to concentrate on the main streams in fairly large settlements. Similarly, agricultural areas dependent upon irrigation concentrated the population within the network of canals. On the rainless and barren deserts of coastal Peru, the people had to live in dense settlements along or near the rivers. The large communities on the coasts of British Columbia and Peru, however, were parts of unlike sociocultural systems. Each developed from a different historical background, and each had a distinctive local adaptation; there were fisheries on the Northwest Coast and intensive, irrigation farming together with ocean resources in Peru.

A dense population supported by a rich economy is not always concentrated in large centers. The native agricultural peoples of the northern Andes of Colombia and the Araucanian Indians of the central valley of Chile had very similar population densities, but the northern Andean peoples were organized in strong, class-structured chiefdoms with communities of five hundred persons or more, whereas the Araucanians were dispersed in many closely spaced villages, each a patrilineage of no more than one hundred persons. This contrast is not explained by farm productivity or other technological factors involved in maintaining large communities. The northern Andean chiefdoms were the result of a diffused cult-complex of temples, priests, warriors, and human sacrifice, which may have originated in Mesoamerica but was re-adapted to the diversified environment of high mountains and deep valleys. Presumably, the Araucanians could have supported chiefdoms, but the nucleating factors were absent. A limited pastoral nomadism based on llama herding may have been an ecological deterrent to community growth, although this factor did not inhibit the development of states and empires in Peru.

Nontechnological features of culture may also affect the adaptive arrangements through the external social environment of the society. Peaceful interaction of societies through marriage, trade, visiting, and participation in ceremonies, games, and other activities may take various patterns within the limits imposed by the environment. Intergroup hostilities, however, may have a decisive influence, because fear of warfare often causes peoples to cluster in compact settlements that are not required by subsistence patterns and sometimes do not give optimum access to resources. Thus, the palisaded villages of parts of the Amazon somewhat inhibited farming of the frequently shifting slash-and-burn farm plots. To judge by the prehistory of the Pueblo Indians, the nature of farming permitted considerable variation. Early settlements were small and widely scattered, but in later peiods the population declined as the settlements became large and tightly nucleated. This was the result of increased precariousness of farming in an area that had frequent droughts and was inhabited by marauders. In Tanganyika, people did not dare disperse along the fertile lands near the waterways until colonialism largely eliminated warfare. Throughout much of history, warfare has been a major factor in the interaction of culture and environment.

Exploitation of an environment by means of certain cultural devices may also drastically affect the environment, which again reacts upon the culture. In native California, as in many other areas, the Indians deliberately fired the grass in order to kill seedlings of brush and trees and thus increase the grazing land for game. Deforestation, overgrazing with concomitant soil erosion, the damming and rechanneling of rivers, drainage of swamps, and conversion of rural areas to urban or suburban land-use patterns also alter the environment. In such instances as the firing of grasslands, the development of irrigation works, or reclamation of swamps, the culture increases its basic resources. In others, such as overgrazing, lack of conservation, or the exhaustion of basic minerals, the culture destroys or impairs certain aspects of its local foundations.

CULTURAL VARIABLES VERSUS HOLISM

Although the culture of any society constitutes a holistic system in which technology, economics, social and political structure, religion, language, values, and other features are closely interrelated, the different components of a culture are not similarly affected by ecological adaptations. Technology, which exemplifies progress in man's control of nature, tends to be cumulative. A language, unless replaced by another one, slowly but continuously evolves into divergent groups of languages. Humanistic and stylistic cultural manifestations may retain their formal aspects during social transformations but acquire new functions. Societies change through a series of structural and functional transformations.

Social structures respond most clearly to environmental requirements. This basic structuring is related most immediately to cooperative productive activity, and it is manifest in community and band organization and in essential kinship systems. Among simple societies, any interpersonal or interfamilial arrangements necessary for survival in particular areas are virtually synonymous with social organization.

Because food collecting, such as in the case of seed gathering, is competitive, societies in unproductive environments tend to become fragmented into nuclear family units. Societies of hunters are more productive under cooperative arrangements and attain various patterns of cohesion. Societies that depend primarily upon farming tend to have permanent community organization, whether in dispersed or nucleated settlements, because cooperation in such activities as clearing plots and irrigation projects facilitates production. Increase in productivity is delimited by the environmental potentials, crops, and farm methods, but it may lead to larger communities and to internal specialization of role and status.

Productive increases achieved by social cooperation and improvements in exploitative technology became the bases of the transformation of small, homogeneous societies into large societies that were internally specialized by occupational role and social status. Structural aspects of cooperation are reasonably well known, but quantitative statements of productivity, potential and actual surpluses, manpower hours that might be available for pursuits other than production of basic necessities, numbers of persons engaged in special occupations, and other measurable activities are rarely available. These serious lacunae in our data leave open the question of the part that sheer quantities of people and things played in the transformations from simple to complex societies.

Even within the category of culture subsumed under social patterns, it cannot be assumed that all features are equally fixed by a given ecological pattern. Among simple societies, residence, kinship, and subsistence patterns are more fundamental and less alterable or variable than clans, moieties, religious and secular associations, and other elaborations which are secondary embroideries on the basic social fabric. Distributional evidence in many parts of the world clearly shows that such elaborations have diffused widely across different kinds of environments and to fundamentally different social structures adapted to use of the environments. In the Southwest, for example, matrilineal clans occurred among the western Pueblo farm villages and the seminomadic pastoral Navajo, and moieties were a secondary adjunct of the patrilineal hunting bands in southern California and some of the eastern Pueblo agriculturalists.

A final problem concerning the response of different aspects or components of culture to adaptive processes is whether old or traditional forms may acquire new functions. Among the Sonjo of Tanganyika, the man's age-group that served as warriors in precolonial times now spends several years performing wage labor in the new nonmilitaristic, cash-oriented context. Clan-owned or lineage-owned land and traditional types of ownership and inheritance of herds may persist under production for an outside market. Although traditional structures and trait-complexes tend to perpetuate themselves in all stages of cultural development, the evidence seems clearly to indicate that the new functions of the changing context eventually alter old forms beyond recognition, or that these forms wither and are replaced by new ones.

LEVELS OF SOCIOCULTURAL INTEGRATION

The adaptations of a complex or highly developed society differ in many ways from those of a simple society. The internal specialization that developed after the agricultural revolution and more so after the industrial revolution has affected the adaptive processes of the local segments of states and nations. Land use has increasingly reflected the importance of external economic institutions rather than local subsistence goals. Trade, improved transportation, mechanization, and other factors related to industrialization have made each local social group a more highly specialized and dependent part of the larger sociocultural system. There is a tendency toward monocropping in areas best suited to production of crops for external markets and toward specialization of local extractive industries, such as mining, oil, and timber, which have little intrinsic value to the local subsociety. Larger sociocultural systems have also created metropolitan and industrial centers and set aside special recreational areas.

Owing to technological achievements, the impact or conditioning effects of nature upon society are far less direct and compelling in a complex society than in a simple one. Culture increasingly creates its own environment. Foods and other necessities can be transported, water diverted, and electric power transmitted great distances. Reasonable comfort can be provided even for those who live for a time in Antarctica.

In a more fundamental sense, however, the distinction between primitive and developed societies is not merely one of social complexity or of technological knowledge. Among primitive peoples, the family, extended kin group, or fairly small village or band adapts directly to its own territory. Among more complex societies, there are suprafamilial and supracommunity institutions that are impersonal in that they do not involve the total cultural behavior of the people connected with them. State economic institutions—corporations, for example, that extract new materials and manufacture and distribute the products—serve the varied needs of the many subcultural groups within the state. They also extend the interaction of culture and environment far beyond state boundaries through the exploitation of distant resources and through extensive commerce. These vast economic extensions of the more developed societies penetrate local societies, and by creating new uses for land and other resources and imposing outside political and economic patterns, they fundamentally transform the local societies.

Within a modern, complex state, there is increasing specialization of land use within environmental potentials, but distinctiveness of local subcultures is partly leveled by the impact of national influences. The subcultures of ranchers in Nevada, sugarcane workers in Puerto Rico, tea-plantation workers in Kenya, and other subsocieties who live on the land are shaped by the outside economic institutions to which they are linked, as well as by the local environment. As technology develops and subsocieties become more dependent upon the larger society, direct adaptation to the local environment decreases. The way of life, or subculture, of business executives of New York City, for example, has become dichotomized: in part it is derived from their highly specialized occupational role in a city and in part from their residence in suburbia, where the family and neighborhood culture differs from that of their profession and neither is closely adapted to the local environment. Even more remote from direct environmental impact are certain urban institutions found in contemporary Nevada, where the divorce, gambling, and entertainment complexes are linked to special aspects of the total national culture rather than to the semideserts of the Great Basin.

SOME SUBSTANTIVE APPLICATIONS

The concept of cultural ecology may be clarified by a number of substantive applications. These cases range from simple to complex societies, from the most elementary level of sociocultural integration to higher levels.

The precursors of man lacked culturally derived devices for killing game and for gathering, storing, and preparing food. They were food scavengers, and any food they collected was preserved without culturally prescribed techniques. Because animals can best forage a known habitat, they may have lived in groups or bands that were somewhat territorially delimited. Any social structuring was probably biologically oriented around the male's dominance and protection of the group and the female's role of caring for the young.

When culture provided more efficient techniques for survival, the essential human biological facts of sex, age, and kinship continued to affect the nature of society but were patterned in various ways by cultural-ecological adaptations. Where the principal resource was seeds, roots, fruits, insects, small mammals, or shellfish, which occur sparsely, food gathering was necessarily competitive rather than cooperative because the yield decreases with the number of families that exploit the same site. If the local occurrence of principal resources varied each year, as it did among the Shoshoni Indians of Nevada, a multifamily society of permanent composition was not possible. Each Shoshoni family was linked with other families through intermarriage, through largely fortuitous association at a winter campsite, and through brief cooperation during antelope and rabbit hunts wherever there happened to be game. There were no bands of constant membership and no claims to territory or to resource areas. These families were not free wanderers, however, for any human society more effectively exploits a territory familiar to it.

The Chilean archipelago is completely unlike the Great Basin, but the erratic occurrence of shellfish, which was the principal food of the Alacaluf Indians, was functionally similar to Great Basin resources in preventing the formation of permanent social units larger than the nuclear family. That the nomadic, food-collecting family was the irreducible social unit in both cases is a function of the biological factors underlying marriage, division of labor, and child rearing. The independent nuclear family, however, is rarely reported ethnographically, and its occurrence in history is an empirical question rather than a matter of deduction from evolutionary principles.

Many societies fragment seasonally into family units of food collectors, but if the resources are sufficiently abundant and their whereabouts is predictable, the same families maintain contact with one another in loose groups that associate for suprafamilial activities. Examples are the Indians of California, who subsisted on acorns, and the Indians of Lake Superior and the upper Paraguay River, who gathered wild rice. It appears that such groups tended to consist of extended families or lineages, although the evidence is not clear on this point.

Hunting generally requires cooperation, but there are various kinds of hunting societies, each reflecting special ecological adaptations. The Central Eskimo, whose population density was one person to 250 square miles or more, lived in small, somewhat isolated family clusters. Since some cooperation was necessary in arctic hunting, nuclear families could not well have survived alone.

In societies that hunted large herds of bison, the concentrated resources supported bands of several hundred persons that exceeded the size of traceable lineages and consisted of many unrelated kin groups. The clans among certain Plains Indians were fictitious kinship extensions and an embellishment of the basic subsistence group. The Plains bands were more tightly integrated than the hunting bands of Canada, because game herds were larger, cooperative hunts were more highly developed, and warfare, especially after horses were acquired, became a major factor. By contrast, hunters of small and less migratory game herds cooperated in bands of thirty to sixty persons who constituted a patrilineal lineage that controlled territorial resources, married outside the band, and brought wives to the husband's band.

The basic social structure of these types of bands is essentially an interfamilial arrangement that is a necessary—or an optimum —organization for survival depending on the conditions. A historical explanation that they originated elsewhere and were introduced to the areas through diffusion or migration is not credible, especially in the case of the patrilineal hunting bands that occurred in South Africa, Australia, Tasmania, southern California, and Tierra del Fuego. Each is a special kind of evolutionary development.

Societies of early farmers seem also to have been small, except where intercommunity warfare forced the people to concentrate in protected villages, and each probably consisted of lineages that tended to bud off as long as land was available. Although few analyses of the ecological adaptations of such farmers have been made, several types are suggested. In tropical rain forests such as the Amazon basin, where root crops were staples, slash-and-burn cultivation together with rapid soil exhaustion required the frequent shift of plots and sometimes villages. In addition, dietary needs made riverine protein foods of major importance, and canoe transportation facilitated the concentration of the population along rivers. In temperate areas, such as the United States, there was a marked contrast between the small villages of woodland farmers, who contended with prairie sods or forests, and the riverbottom farmers, as in the Mississippi system, whose fertile soils, once cleared of vegetation, supported large communities that were able to adopt the temple-mound complex from Mesoamerica.

In several temperate, arid areas, early farming was restricted to flood plains or to the rainy highlands. Increased population density in the valleys—made possible by irrigation in such cases as Peru—led to theocratic and militaristic states, whose power extended over wide areas, and to urban centers, which were the containers of civilization. It is not now clear to what extent trade, based upon increasingly specialized local production in adjoining areas, religious cults, and militaristic controls regimented the people to achieve maximum production and fill special statuses and roles.

Animal domestication entailed other kinds of ecological adaptations. Herds require more land for subsistence purposes than farming, have to be tended and moved about, and may be subject to theft. Claims to exclusive grazing areas were difficult to enforce until barbed wire was mass-produced in the last century. Cattle stealing and consequent intergroup hostility could therefore develop, as they did among many cattle breeders of east Africa. Free-roaming livestock, moreover, is a threat to crops, and until recently, farmers had to fence out the animals.

When societies became mounted, for example, the horse or camel nomads, other special adaptations occurred. They became more efficient hunters or herders and could transport foods a greater distance, thus extending their areas of exploitation and permitting larger social aggregates to remain together. They could also engage in predatory activities against one another and their settled neighbors. Mounted predators even created several ruling dynasties in the empires of the Middle East, China, and India.

After the agricultural revolution, the development of supra-community state- or imperial-level institutions extended the areas of resource exploitation beyond those occupied by any of the subsocieties that were welded into the larger sociopolitical unit. Each local subsociety, although adapted in some measure to its terrain, became a specialized part of a new kind of whole to which it contributed different foods, raw materials, products, and even people—all for state purposes.

The industrial revolution enormously expanded the areas of exploitation through its improved transportation, mass manufacturing, communications, and economic and political controls. Its technology also gave importance to many latent resources. Modern nations and empires embrace highly diversified environments and draw upon areas beyond their political boundaries. Their technology may modify environments to meet their cultural needs, and, above all, any localized subsociety reacts to a complex set of state institutions, to a diversified social environment, and to a large number of goals other than survival. Although people necessarily live in particular places, members of highly industrialized nations must be viewed as increasingly non-localized to the extent that their behavior is determined by a great overlay or elaboration of cultural patterns that are only remotely connected with particular environments and are even minimizing some of the child-rearing and economically complementary functions of members of the nuclear family. It can be imagined that nuclear power, hydroponic and synthetic food production, and other technological developments might create wholly artificial environments, as in a permanent space station.

BIBLIOGRAPHY

BARTH, FREDERIK
    1956. Ecologic Relationships of Ethnic Groups in Swat, North Pakistan. *American Anthropologist* New Series 58:1079-1089.
HELM, JUNE
    1962. Ecological Approach in Anthropology. *American Journal of Sociology* 67:630-639. Includes a review of the literature of cultural ecology.
LATTIMORE, OWEN
    (1940) 1951. *Inner Asian Frontiers of China*. 2d ed. Irvington-on-Hudson, N.Y.: Capital.
SAHLINS, MARSHALL D., and SERVICE, ELMAN R. (editors)
    1960. *Evolution and Culture*. Ann Arbor: University of Michigan Press.
STEWARD, JULIAN H.
    1955. *Theory of Culture Change: The Methodology of Multilinear Evolution*. Urbana: University of Illinois Press.
WASHBURN, SHERWOOD L. (editor)
    1961. *Social Life of Early Man*. Viking Fund Publications in Anthropology, No. 31. Chicago: Aldine.

2

Cultural Evolution

As Steward's professional note grew, expanding beyond the confines of anthropology, he was increasingly called upon to present his theories to a broader public. This essay (*Scientific American*, vol. 194, pp. 69-80, 1956), is of such a gender; the original illustrations have been omitted in this edition. Reprinted with permission. Copyright © 1956 by Scientific American, Inc. All rights reserved.

It is almost 100 years since evolution became a powerful word in science. The concept of evolution, which Charles Darwin set forth so clearly and convincingly in his *Origin of Species* in 1859, came like a burst of light that seemed to illuminate all of nature—not only the development of the myriad forms of life but also the history of the planet earth, of the universe, and of man and his civilization. It offered a scheme which made it possible to explain, rather than merely describe, man's world.

In biology the theory of evolution today is more powerfully established than ever. In cosmology it has become the primary generator of men's thinking about the universe. But the idea of evolution in the cultural history of mankind itself has had a frustrating career of ups and downs. It was warmly embraced in Darwin's time, left for dead at the turn of our century, and is just now coming back to life and vigor. Today a completely new approach to the question has once more given us hope of achieving an understanding of the development of human cultures in evolutionary terms.

Before considering these new attempts to explain the evolutionary processes operating in human affairs, we need to review the attempts that failed. By the latter part of the nineteenth century Darwin's theory of biological evolution had profoundly changed scientists' views of human history. Once it was conceded that all forms of life, including man, had evolved from lower forms, it necessarily followed that at some point in evolution man's ancestors had been completely without culture. Human culture must therefore have started from simple beginnings and grown more complex. The nineteenth-century school of cultural evolutionists—mainly British—reasoned that man had progressed from a condition of simple, amoral savagery to a civilized state whose ultimate achievement was the Victorian Englishman, living in an industrial society and political democracy, believing in the Empire and belonging to the Church of England. The evolutionists assumed that the universe was designed to produce man and civilization, that cultural evolution everywhere must be governed by the same principles and follow the same line, and that all mankind would progress toward a civilization like that of Europe.

Among the leading proponents of this theory were Edward B. Tylor, the Englishman who has been called the father of anthropology; Lewis H. Morgan, an American banker and lawyer who devoted many years to studying the Iroquois Indians; Edward Westermarck, a Finnish philosopher famed for his studies of the family; John Ferguson McLennan, a Scottish lawyer who concerned himself with the development of social organization; and James Frazer, the Scottish anthropologist, historian of religion, and author of *The Golden Bough*. Their general point of view was developed by Morgan in his book *Ancient Society*, in which he declared: "It can now be asserted upon convincing evidence that savagery preceded barbarism in all the tribes of mankind, as barbarism is known to have preceded civilization." Morgan divided man's cultural development into stages of "savagery," "barbarism," and "civilization"—each of which was ushered in by a single invention.

These nineteenth century scholars were highly competent men, and some of their insights were extraordinarily acute. But their scheme was erected on such flimsy theoretical foundations and such faulty observation that the entire structure collapsed as soon as it was seriously tested. Their principal undoing was, of course, the notion that progress (i.e., toward the goal of European civilization) was the guiding principle in human development. In this they were following the thought of the biological evolutionists, who traced a progression from the simplest forms of life to *Homo sapiens*. Few students of evolution today, however, would argue that the universe has any design making progress inevitable, either in the biological or the cultural realm. Certainly there is nothing in the evolutionary process which preordained the particular developments that have occurred on our planet. From the principles operating in biological evolution—heredity, mutation, natural selection, and so on—an observer who visted the earth some half a billion years ago, when the algae represented the highest existing form of life, could not possibly have predicted the evolution of fishes, let alone man. Likewise, no known principle of cultural development could even have predicted specific inventions such as the bow, iron smelting, writing, tribal clans, states, or cities.

THE FACTS

When, at the turn of the century, anthropologists began to study primitive cultures in detail, they found that the cultural evolutionists' information had been as wrong as their theoretical assumptions. Morgan had lumped together in the stage of middle barbarism the Pueblo Indians, who were simple farmers, and the people of Mexico, who had cities, empires, monumental architecture, metallurgy, astronomy, mathematics, phonetic writing, and other accomplishments unknown to the Pueblo. Field research rapidly disclosed that one tribe after another had quite the wrong cultural characteristics to fit the evolutionary niche assigned it by Morgan. Eventually the general scheme of evolution postulated by the nineteenth century theorists fell apart completely. They had believed, for example, that society first developed around the maternal line, the father being transient, and that marriage and the family as we know it did not evolve until men began to practice herding and agriculture. But field research showed that some of the most primitive hunting and gathering societies, such as the Bushmen of South Africa and the aboriginal Australians, were organized into patrilineal descent groups, while much more advanced horticultural peoples, including some of the groups in the Inca Empire of South America, had matrilineal kin groups. The Western Shoshoni of the Great Basin, who by every criterion had one of the simplest cultures, were organized in families which were not based on matrilineality. Still another blow to the evolutionists' theory was the discovery that customs had spread or diffused from one group to another over the world: that is to say, each society owed much of its culture to borrowing from its neighbors, so it could not be said that societies had evolved independently along a single inevitable line.

The collapse of the theory that cultural evolution had followed the same line everywhere (what we may call the "unilinear" scheme) began with the researches of the late Franz Boas, and the *coup de grâce* was dealt by Robert H. Lowie in his comprehensive and convincing analysis, *Primitive Society*, published in 1920. When the evolutionary hypothesis was demolished, however, no alternative hypothesis appeared. The twentieth-century anthropologists threw out the evolutionists' insights along with their schemes. Studies of culture lost a unifying theory and lapsed into a methodology of "shreds and patches." Anthropology became fervently devoted to collecting facts. But it had to give some order to its data, and it fell back on classification—a phase in science which F. S. C. Northrop has called the "natural history stage."

The "culture elements" used as the classification criteria included such items as the bow and arrow, the domesticated dog, techniques and forms of basketry, the spear and spear thrower, head-hunting, polyandrous marriage, feather headgear, the penis sheath, initiation ceremonies for boys, tie-dyeing techniques for coloring textiles, the blowgun, use of a stick to scratch the head during periods of religious taboo, irrigation agriculture, shamanistic use of a sweat bath, transportation of the head of state on a litter, proving one's fortitude by submitting to ant bites, speaking to one's mother-in-law through a third party, making an arrowhead with side notches, marrying one's mother's brother's daughter. Students of the development of culture sought to learn the origin of such customs, their distribution, and how they were combined in the "culture content" of each society.

Eventually this approach led to an attempt to find an overall pattern in each society's way of life—a view which is well expressed in Ruth Benedict's *Patterns of Culture*. She contrasted, for example, the placid, smoothly functioning, nonaggressive behavior of the Pueblo Indians with the somewhat frenzied, warlike behavior of certain Plains Indians, aptly drawing on Greek mythology to designate the first as an Apollonian pattern and the second as Dionysian. The implication is that the pattern is formed by the ethos, value system, or world view. During the past decade and a half it has become popular to translate pattern into more psychological terms. But description of a culture in terms either of elements, ethos, or personality type does not explain how it originated. Those who seek to understand how cultures evolved must look for longer-range causes and explanations.

MULTILINEAR EVOLUTION

One must keep in mind Herbert Spencer's distinction between man as a biological organism and his functioning on the superorganic or cultural level, which also has distinctive qualities. We must distinguish man's needs and capacity for culture—his superior brain and ability to speak and use tools—from the particular cultures he has evolved. A specific invention is not explained by saying that man is creative. Cultural activities meet various biological needs, but the existence of the latter does not explain the character of the former. While all men must eat, the choice of particular foods and of how they are obtained and prepared can be explained only on a superorganic level. Thanks to his jaw and tongue structure and to the speech and auditory centers of his brain, man is capable of speech, but these facts do not explain the origin of a single one of the thousands of languages that have developed in the world. The family is a basic human institution, but families in different cultures differ profoundly in the nature of their food-getting activities, in the division of labor between the sexes, and in the socialization of the children.

The failure to distinguish the biological basis of all cultural development from the explanation of particular forms of culture accounts for a good deal of the controversy and confusion about "free will" and "determinism" in human behavior. The biological evolutionist George Gaylord Simpson considers that, because man has purposes and makes plans, he may exercise conscious control over cultural evolution. On the other hand, the cultural evolutionist Leslie A. White takes the deterministic position that culture develops according to its own laws. Simpson is correct in making a biological statement, that is, in describing man's capacity. White is correct in making a cultural statement, that is, in describing the origin of any particular culture.

All men, it is true, have the biological basis for making rational solutions, and specific features of culture may develop from the application of reason. But since circumstances differ (e.g., in the conditions for hunting), solutions take many forms. Moreover, much culture develops gradually and imperceptibly without deliberate thought. The growth of settlements, kinship groups, beliefs in shamanism and magic, types of warfare, and the like are not planned.

This does not mean that there is no rhyme or reason in the development of culture, or that history is random and haphazard. It is possible to trace causes and order in the seeming chaos. In the early irrigation civilizations of the Middle East, Asia, and America the inventions were remarkably similar and ran extraordinarily parallel courses through several thousand years. There was clearly a close connection between large-scale irrigation agriculture, population increase, the growth of permanent communities and cities, the rise of specialists supported by agricultural workers, the appearance of unprecedented skills in technology, the need for a managerial class or bureaucracy, and the rise of states.

There have been other patterns in the development of man's institutions, each adapted at different times and places to the specific circumstances of a specific society. The facts now accumulated indicate that human culture evolved along a number of different lines; we must think of cultural evolution not as unilinear but as multilinear. This is the new basis upon which evolutionists today are seeking to build an understanding of the development of human cultures. It is an ecological approach—an attempt to learn how the factors in each given type of situation shaped the development of a particular type of society.

Multilinear evolution is not merely a way of explaining the past. It is applicable to changes occurring today as well. In the department of sociology and anthropology of the University of Illinois my colleagues and I are studying current changes in the ways of rural populations in underdeveloped areas of the world; it is called "The Project to Study Cross-Cultural Regularities." During the past three years my colleagues—Eric Wolf, Robert F. Murphy, F. K. Lehman, Ben Zimmerman, Charles Erasmus, Louis Faron—and I have constructed research models to be tested by investigations in the field. These models consist of several types of populations—peasants, small farmers, wage workers on plantations and in mines and factories, primitive tribes. The objective is to learn how the several types of societies evolved and how their customs are being changed by economic or political factors introduced from the modern industrial world. Such studies should obviously have practical value in guiding programs of technical aid for these peoples.

HUNTERS, TRAPPERS, FARMERS

To illustrate the ecological approach, let us consider very briefly several different types of societies, using the ways in which they made their living as the frame of reference. The first example is the form of society consisting of a partilineal band of hunters. This type of organization was found among many primitive tribes all over the world, including the Bushmen of the deserts in South Africa, the Negritos of the tropical rain forest in the Congo, the aborigines of the steppes and deserts in Australia, the now extinct aboriginal islanders in Tasmania, the Indians of the cold pampas on the islands of Tierra del Fuego, and Shoshoni Indians of the mountains in Southern California. Although their climates and environments differed greatly, all of these tribes had one important thing in common; they hunted cooperatively for sparsely scattered, nonmigratory game. In each case the cooperating band usually consisted of about 50 or 60 persons who occupied an area of some 400 square miles and claimed exclusive hunting rights to it. Since men could hunt more efficiently in familiar terrain, they remained throughout life in the territory of their birth. The band consequently consisted of persons related through the male line of descent, and it was required that wives be taken from other bands. In sum, the cultural effects of this line of evolution were band localization, descent in the male line, marriage outside the group, residence of the wife with the husband's band, and control by the band of the food resources within its territory.

Another line of evolution is exemplified by rubber-farming

Mundurucú Indians in the Amazon Valley and fur-trapping Algonquian Indians in eastern Canada, of whom Murphy and I recently
made a comparative study. The common feature in these two groups is
that both were transformed by contact with an outside economy from
simple farmers or hunters to barterers for manufactured goods. Although the aboriginal Mundurucu villagers and the Algonquian
bands had had very different forms of social organization, both converged to the same form after they began to pursue similar ways of
making a living. As the Indians came to depend on manufactured
goods, such as steel axes and metal utensils, obtained from traders,
they gradually gave up their independent means of subsistence and
spent all their time tapping rubber trees and trapping beaver, respectively, eventually depending upon the trader for clothing and food as
well as for hardware. Since tapping and trapping are occupations best
carried out by small groups on separate territories, the Indians' villages
and bands broke down into individual families which lived in isolation
on fairly small, delimited areas. The family became part of the larger
Canadian or Brazilian national society, to which it was linked through
the trader. Its only relations with other families were the loose social
contacts created by dealing with the same trader.

IRRIGATION CIVILIZATIONS

Irrigation farming is the major organizing factor of another line of
evolution, which covered a considerable span of the early prehistory
and history of China, Mesopotamia, Egypt, the north coast of Peru,
probably the Indus Valley, and possibly the Valley of Mexico. This line
had three stages. In the first period primitive groups apparently began
to cultivate food plants along the moist banks of the rivers or in the
higher terrain where rainfall was sufficient for crops. They occupied
small but permanent villages. The second stage started when the people learned to divert the river waters by means of canals to irrigate large
tracts of land. Irrigation farming made possible a larger population
and freed the farmers from the need to spend all their time on basic
food production. Part of the new-found time was put into enlarging
the system of canals and ditches and part into developing crafts. This
period brought the invention of loom weaving, metallurgy, the wheel,
mathematics, the calendar, writing, monumental and religious architecture, and extremely fine art products.

When the irrigation works expanded so that the canals served many
communities, a coordinating and managerial control became necessary. This need was met by a ruling class or a bureaucracy whose

authority had mainly religious sanctions, for men looked to the gods for the rainfall on which their agriculture depended. Centralization of authority over a large territory marked the emergence of a state.

That a state developed in these irrigation centers by no means signifies that all states originated in this way. Many different lines of cultural evolution could have led from kinship groups up to multi-community states. For example, feudal Europe and Japan developed small states very different from the theocratic irrigation states.

The irrigation state reached its florescence in Mesopotamia between 3000 and 400 B.C., in Egypt a little later, in China about 1500 or 2000 B.C., in northern Peru between 500 B.C. and 500 A.D., in the Valley of Mexico a little later than in Peru. Then, in each case, a third stage of expansion followed. When the theocratic states had reached the limits of available water and production had leveled off, they began to raid and conquer their neighbors to exact tribute. The states grew into empires. The empire was not only larger than the state but differed qualitatively in the ways it regimented and controlled its large and diversified population. Laws were codified; a bureaucracy was developed; a powerful military establishment, rather than the priest-hood, was made the basis of authority. The militaristic empires began with the Sumerian Dynasty in Mesopotamia, the pyramid-building Early Dynasty in Egypt, the Chou periods in China, the Toltec and Aztec periods in Mexico, and the Tiahuanacan period in the Andes.

Since the wealth of these empires was based on forced tribute rather than on increased production, they contained the seeds of their own undoing. Excessive taxation, regimentation of civil life, and imposition of the imperial religious cult over the local ones led the subject peoples eventually to rebel. The great empires were destroyed; the irrigation works were neglected; production declined; the population decreased. A "dark age" ensued. But in each center the process of empire building later began anew, and the cycle was repeated. Cyclical conquests succeeded one another in Mesopotamia, Egypt, and China for nearly 2,000 years. Peru had gone through at least two cycles and was at the peak of the Inca Empire when the Spaniards came. Mexico also probably had experienced two cycles prior to the Spanish Conquest.

Our final example of a specific line of evolution is taken from more recent times. When the colonists in America pre-empted the Indians' lands, some of the Indian clans formed a new type of organization. The Ute, Western Shoshoni, and Northern Paiute Indians, who had lived by hunting and gathering in small groups of wandering families, united in aggressive bands. With horses stolen from the white settlers, they raided the colonists' livestock and occasionally their settlements.

Similar predatory bands developed among some of the mounted

Apaches, who had formerly lived in semipermanent encampments consisting of extended kinship groups. Many of these bands were the scourge of the Southwest for years. Some of the Apaches, on the other hand, yielded to the blandishments of the U.S. government and settled peacefully on reservations; as a result there were Apache peace factions who rallied around chiefs such as Cochise, and predatory factions that followed belligerent leaders such as Geronimo.

The predatory bands of North America were broken up by the U.S. Army within a few years. But this type of evolution, although transitory, was not unique. In the pampas of South America similar raiding bands arose after the Indians obtained horses. On an infinitely larger scale and making a far greater impression on history were the Mongol hordes of Asia. The armies of Genghis Khan and his successors were essentially huge mounted bands that raided entire continents.

BIOLOGY AND CULTURE

Human evolution, then, is not merely a matter of biology but of the interaction of man's physical and cultural characteristics, each influencing the other. Man is capable of devising rational solutions to life, especially in the realm of technical problems, and also of transmitting learned solutions to his offspring and other members of his society. His capacity for speech gives him the ability to package vastly complicated ideas into sound symbols and to pass on most of what he has learned. This human potential resulted in the accumulation and social transmission of an incalculable number of learned modes of behavior. It meant the perpetuation of established patterns, often when they were inappropriate in a changed situation.

The biological requirements for cultural evolution were an erect posture, specialized hands, a mouth structure permitting speech, stereoscopic vision, and areas in the brain for the functions of speech and association. Since culture speeded the development of these requirements, it would be difficult to say which came first.

The first step toward human culture may have come when manlike animals began to substitute tools for body parts. It has been suggested, for example, that there may have been an intimate relation between the development of a flint weapon held in the hand and the receding of the apelike jaw and protruding canine teeth. An ape, somewhat like a dog, deals with objects by means of its mouth. When the hands, assisted by tools, took over this task, the prognathous jaw began to recede. There were other consequences of this development. The brain centers that register the experiences of the hands grew larger, and this in turn gave the hands greater sensitivity and skill. The reduction of the jaw, especially the elimination of the "simian shelf," gave the tongue freer movement and thus helped create the potentiality for speech.

Darwin called attention to the fact that man is in effect a domesticated animal; as such he depends upon culture and cannot well survive in a state of nature. Man's self-domestication furthered his biological evolution in those characteristics that make culture possible. Until perhaps 25,000 years ago he steadily developed a progressively larger brain, a more erect posture, a more vertical face, and better developed speech, auditory, and associational centers in the brain. His physical evolution is unquestionably still going on, but there is no clear evidence that recent changes have increased his inherent potential for cultural activities. However, the rate of his cultural development became independent of his biological evolution. In addition to devising tools as substitutes for body parts in the struggle for survival, he evolved wholly new kinds of tools which served other purposes: stone scrapers for preparing skin clothing, baskets for gathering wild foods, axes for building houses and canoes. As cultural experience accumulated, the innovations multiplied, and old inventions were used in new ways. During the last 25,000 years the rate of culture change has accelerated.

The many kinds of human culture today are understandable only as particular lines of evolution. Even if men of the future develop an I.Q. that is incredibly high by modern standards, their specific behavior will nonetheless be determined not by their reason or psychological characteristics but by their special line of cultural evolution, that is, by the fundamental processes that shape cultures in particular ways.

3

Evolutionary Principles and Social Types

"Evolutionary Principles and Social Types" (in *Evolution after Darwin*, vol. 2, ed. Sol Tax, Chicago: University of Chicago Press, 1960, pp. 169-186) was first presented as a paper in the symposium honoring the centennial of Charles Darwin. It is reprinted with permission of the editor and publisher. © 1960 by the University of Chicago.

THE MEANING OF CHANGE

One can add little to the kudos so abundantly bestowed on Darwin for his role in establishing the idea that change or historicity is inherent in all phenomena. For the biological sciences, Darwin not only convinced the world of change but provided evolutionary principles which describe the essential orderliness of biological transformations. The physical scientists, too, have formulated change in the inorganic realm, both microscopically and macroscopically, in such a way as to reveal orderly process. It is, in fact, inconceivable that change in biological and physical phenomena should be random, quixotic, chaotic, and without regularities which are described as "causes." Moreover, hypotheses, descriptions, or formulations of recognized order are presumed to apply to all places and times within the universe.

That cultures have changed is also unquestioned, but the social sciences and humanities have achieved little agreement regarding what constitutes orderly principles in cultural change. It is sometimes held that cultural change is not amenable to formulations; or that a series of special histories must constitute our only categories; or, again, that there are principles underlying all cultural change. If no principles whatever are recognizable in cultural change, it is probably inappropriate to insist that there has been cultural evolution. On the other hand, contention that there has been cultural evolution certainly imposes the obligation to identify the orderly alterations of structures or systems, the principles that have operated at all times and places. This poses extremely difficult problems of cultural taxonomy and of determination of process.

SOME VIEWS OF CULTURAL EVOLUTION

There have probably been more papers written on cultural evolution during [the Darwin] centenary than during the last half-century, but they exhibit a very wide variety of individual interests. While some are more or less directed to the problem of orderliness in culture change, they constitute little more than a barely discernible trend. The essential meaning of cultural evolution has by no means been clarified, and some of the views expressed in the present symposium [on evolution] are so disparate that they are hardly even in conflict.

One view, which is expressed by Huxley (in "Evolution of Life") if I understand him correctly, and by others, is that cultural evolution expresses the distinctive creativity of the human mind. A somewhat different emphasis is Kroeber's interest in the major streams of world cultural history. A deliberate effort to cut across these streams and, in fact, to disregard them as major categories, is found in the hypotheses of worldwide developmental stages postulated by Leslie A. White (1959a) and to a certain extent by the nineteenth-century unilinear evolutionists. A rather different means of seeking order is the more recent tendency to begin with the particulars of change in culture areas or special streams of history and then formulate tentative and limited cross-cultural hypotheses of what seems significant in structure and process.

These views are not necessarily in direct conflict. The creativity of the human mind is beyond doubt. If culture is conceived as the continuity of a social pattern or value system, it unquestionably has flowed in major channels. At the same time, it is perfectly clear that the agricultural revolution of several millennia ago and the later industrial revolution profoundly altered structures within all the cultural historical traditions. There is also no question that transformations have occurred repeatedly, on a smaller scale, within each of the many streams of history. The obvious need at the moment is to reconcile these diverse interests in a common search for orderliness in culture change.

Emphasis upon the capacity for reason, creativity, and communication naturally highlights the distinctively human qualities resulting from the biological evolution of the human brain, hands, and bipedal locomotion. This evolution created the preconditions of cultural evolution and thus suggests that cultural evolution is an extension of biological evolution. But this does not imply that cultural evolution follows the principles of biological evolution. Cultural behavior is really phenotypical behavior, as contrasted with the rigid patterns of genotypical or instinctual behavior, but it is infinitely more adaptive in man than in any other animal. More specifically, the abilities to use speech and other symbols, to reason, and to manipulate tools underlie the development of the vast variety of known human behavior patterns.

Acknowledgment that man is a rational and creative thinker—or at least can be rational upon occasion—in no way tells us what he will think, and it can easily involve us in sterile discussion of free will. We have to assume that the application of reason is reasonable in the sense of following some orderly pattern, and that creativity, as manifest in ethos, value systems, styles, religions, and philosophy, has some comprehensible relationship to other activities and is not wanton, random, causeless, or without relevant antecedents and cultural correlates.

The more fundamental difficulty in discussing cultural evolution is the absence of any generally accepted system of classification. Kroeber stresses repeatedly that anthropology's cultural taxonomy is pre-Linnean; it lacks systematization and classificatory criteria for cultural categories, except those which are evident in distinctive areas, histories, or traditions. It is as if culture had no order other than the accident of each history. Kroeber's own classification reflects his lifelong interest in history, which gives primary emphasis to the many streams of history that develop through time, criss-cross, diffuse, and interact. The main streams are more often characterized by their intellectual achievements, specific inventions, philosophies, and value systems than by structural components. Their identification and characterization result more from deep insights, sometimes from what is more nearly intuitive feelings, as in the recognition of styles, than from emphasis upon formal criteria. Structural transformations during time are made secondary to the stylistic continuities.

The nineteenth-century unilinear evolutionists have been attacked for their philosophical presuppositions, especially for their use of the idea of progress as a basic principle, and for the inadequacy of their facts. I believe, however, that their more serious limitation was that they never came to grips with the question of structures and types of structures. Preoccupied with cultural origins, as many of them were, and inclined to deal topically with religion, the family, technology, law, and other special subjects, primitive culture was treated as a very generalized but not well-characterized category. It is germane to this point that anthropologists left the great cultural transformations or growth of civilizations in Egypt, Mesopotamia, the Indus Valley, and China to the orientalists and sinologists, and that, although they accepted Middle America and the Andes as a legitimate part of their subject matter, they have understood the structural changes in these areas only recently.

The question of the developmental typology of whole cultures never became a major issue in nineteenth-century anthropology except that a small number of scholars offered world schemes of cultural evolution. For example, L. H. Morgan (1877) postulated classificatory diagnostics for each of seven stages from savagery to civilization and thereby became vulnerable on many scores. Most of the nineteenth-century anthropologists treated the whole primitive world as a single category from which facts were drawn at random to illustrate their points, while the question of social change was left to Engels, Marx, and their followers. The great impact that V. Gordon Childe (1951) has had upon understandings of culture change arises less from theoretical claims than from the fact that he bridged the gap from the primitive to the civilized in the Middle East and was directly concerned with the profound structural changes involved. But Childe knew little about other areas.

Certainly the clearest taxonomy has come from Leslie A. White (1949; 1959a, b), who proclaims complete allegiance in principle to the nineteenth-century writers. White, however, deals not only with the origins of primitive culture but with the great transformation— "revolution," he calls it—that occurred among all societies which were fundamentally affected by plant and animal domestication. He has no place in his scheme for Kroeber's streams of history or for culture areas or local traditions. White's two main structures are: kin-based tribal societies, which controlled little energy; and the internally differentiated, class-structured, territorial states, which controlled high energy. If we understand him correctly, he postulates that a third major structural change occurred after the industrial revolution and believes that a fourth is being initiated by the use of nuclear energy.

It can hardly be argued that White's stages or categories do not represent major structural transformations, although it may be noted parenthetically that they do not constitute a tree of culture comparable to the tree of life. Presumably, each culture was transformed independently whenever the impact of domestication was sufficiently great; or rather, primitive culture as a single entity was transformed.

There is question, however, concerning certain implications of White's categories and evolutionary principles. Since anthropologists have traditionally dealt with preliterate, primitive societies, few accept White's contention that variations within the primitive world that resulted from local cultural-ecological adaptations, area traditions, diffusion, and other factors are unimportant. Moreover, White's characterization of primitive society as essentially based on classificatory kinship systems, i.e., extended kinship, disregards the principles of sexual and age divisions. Again, his discussion of agrarian states or civilized societies after the agricultural revolution draws freely from such diversified societies as those of the Andes, Middle America, Egypt, Mesopotamia, Islam, the ancient Hebrews, and the Roman Empire, as if all these were essentially similar (cf. Steward, 1960, review of White, 1959a). What is similar taxonomically among these societies represents a high degree of generalization. The role of such factors as religion, irrigation, warfare, and commerce in their development can only be understood through much fuller archeological information and detailed comparisons.

Much of the discussion of evolution has hinged upon the question of what order of generalization is required to justify using the term. White seems to argue that evolutionary changes must be universal. I have maintained that processes may operate cross-culturally only a few times to produce similar structures and suggested that the many lines of development could be described as "multilinear evolution." But, if evolution requires universal principles, I willingly forego the term and continue, along with many others, to interest myself in limited generalizations before undertaking to make the grand scheme.

Limited and detailed comparison, I believe, characterizes the present trend. It grows out of the influence of Franz Boas, who introduced unrelenting empiricism and field research into cultural studies. In its extreme of "cultural relativism," Boas' influence led to the denial of evolutionary categories and causal relationships. It also led to re-examination of earlier evolutionary claims. Perhaps today, proceeding from the particular to the general, we can arrive at evolutionary principles that fill the bill better than those offered in the past.

THE IMPLICATIONS OF CULTURAL RELATIVISM AND THE CULTURE AREA

In American research, following Boas' influence several decades ago, the culture area became the basic taxonomic category. Defined in terms of distinctive element-content and unique integration, the so-called "pattern" of each area was sometimes conceived more stylistically than structurally, as in Ruth Benedict's *Patterns of Culture* (1934). While no one, of course, claimed that these area patterns were god-given, they were treated as if they were part of an original creation. Little interest was taken in their origins, except to trace the diffusion of their elements. When the concept of cultural personality entered social science, the normative aspects of patterns became emphasized, and interest centered on how the distinctive cultural content and the psychological patterning of individual behavior constituted mutually reinforcing factors that tended to resist change of culture patterns. Explanations of origins and transformations were avoided.

Some scholars became definitely antihistorical. However, others who retained an interest in history and prehistory operated with area-bound cultural taxonomy, which ascribed developmental periods secondary importance. Style, as manifest in ceramics, weaving, architecture, and other material remains rather than structure, became diagnostic of culture areas, spheres, traditions, and co-traditions. The very use of such terms as "developmental" and "florescent," even for the long and complicated sequences of the Central Andes and Meso-America (for example, by Strong, Bennett, and Willey in Bennett, 1948), implied change that was more like the germination, growth, and flowering of a plant than the transformation of one species into another.

In part, this emphasis upon aesthetic florescence is an Americanist characteristic, derived from the primacy of the culture area and from the exclusion, until recently, of Old World civilizations from anthropological classifications and formulations. Yet we find that historians, with their strong humanistic orientation, still ascribe major importance to style; for example, Coulborn (1959) sees aesthetic style as the enduring characteristic of each of the early civilizations in his discussion of the concepts of water-gods.

THE PRESENT TREND

To judge by many recent writings which bear "evolution" in their titles, and by many more which do not, there is increasing interest in finding causes of culture change other than diffusion. It should not be necessary to state that no one denies the massive diffusion of cultural elements and element complexes. The point is that acceptance of diffused traits generates internal changes, which have become the focus of interest. More specifically, attention is increasingly paid to changes in social structure.

In prehistoric archeology, this trend has brought a shift from a predominating concern with implement typology to settlement pattern in relationship to environment, for example, Braidwood, Beardsley *et al.* (1955), Willey (1953), and Steward (1937). The universality of stages postulated by Braidwood and by Beardsley *et al.* is certainly not confirmed, and I question on ethnographic grounds whether there has ever been a "free wandering" stage. Whether this approach will fill the requirements of evolution is less important than the new problems which orient it. While diffusion is amply evident in the distribution of types and stylizations of early implements, the nature of human organizations which use these implements in the food quest is now commanding attention.

Intensive analyses, with attention to structural change and process within the Old World, have been carried out especially by V. Gordon Childe (1934, 1946, 1951) and by Braidwood (1952, 1958, 1959), and within the New World by Willey and Phillips (1953, 1955) and others. These understandings have been generalized in cross-cultural hypotheses concerning the development of irrigation civilizations in a symposium by Donald Collier, Angel Palerm, Robert Adams, Karl Wittfogel, Ralph Beals, and the present writer (Steward, 1955, ed.), and by Adams (1956). Wittfogel (1957) has written far more broadly upon the subject.

Social organization is also the center of interest in Murdock's typological and developmental studies, which are treated essentially statistically (1959). Kinship, marriage, residence, and descent are primary taxonomic criteria, but universal principles as such are not suggested. Goldman, in an excellent review of the theory of cultural evolution (1959) and in two studies of Polynesia (1955, 1957), deals with the critical change in structure from kinship to class. Among Polynesian variations, he sees status rivalry as "basic in all evolutionary sequences leading to civilization" (1959, p. 74). He has not demonstrated, however, that status rivalry is a univeral principle. Moreover, the very fact of status differences in kinship societies generally implies some control of surplus or other perquisites which themselves have to be explained if any causality is to be found.

Goldman in 1941 and the present author in his contribution to the Radin Festschrift—"Carrier Acculturation"—studied change of simple bands or lineages into a strong status system among the Carrier Indians; the fur trade was the key factor in introducing the required surplus. The relationship of the status system to the wealth of the fur trade has also been the subject of many other analyses of Northwest Coast Indians. Along somewhat similar lines, studies of the conflict of the principles of kinship and state institutions in West Africa have received much attention since the writings of Maine in the last century.

Other studies directed at the problem of cultural typology with reference to causality are Oberg's (1957) discussion of South American lowland types and Steward and Faron's (1959) on five South American types. These studies are less concerned with the universality of their findings than with significant structural diagnostics and the relationship of these to land use, environment, and socially integrating factors.

THE PROBLEM OF PRINCIPLES

It is noteworthy that most attempts to take a large view of cultural evolution focus upon change in structure, principles, and processes at that crucial point when internal specialization and social classes begin to supersede kinship groups, that is, when productive surplus and means of controlling it become central considerations. This is as true of Goldman's limited evolutionary sequence in Polynesia as of Willey's (Centennial Paper) shift of evolutionary criteria from technological to social features in the High civilizations of America and White's world stages.

White seems most keenly aware of any writer that evolutionary principles should be universal. He points to some principles that are common not only to the cultural realm but to the universe, such as a tendency to segmentation, and to others common to biological organisms and societies, such as utilization of external energy. So far as culturological phenomena are concerned, however, the general principle that improved technology increases command of energy and thus transforms societies and, in turn, their ethos is presumed to apply at all times and places. It might be contended, however, that the utilization of energy really involved many mechanisms that differ greatly according to the specificity of local histories. White does not solve the difficulty that after the agricultural revolution, new processes appeared, resulting in structures based upon the nonkinship principles of internal specialization, class structure, and state institutions. The required universality of evolutionary principles seems to break down.

There is a possible way of viewing these phenomena, however, which may enable us better to hew to the line of principle. Primitive societies are, with few exceptions, structured basically not only upon lines of kinship but also of age and sex. Kinship takes many forms; age entails assignments of roles according to maturity and often is formally graded; and sex is manifest not only in reciprocity within the family but in organizations that follow sex lines. These might all be considered variations upon the universal, biological fact that human beings have chronic sexual interest, that the human infant has a prolonged period of helplessness, that the human learning potential and language capacity make complicated socialization possible, and that the nuclear family is universal because of sexual, procreational, and socializational needs. Modified and often elaborated as these principles are, they are rarely superseded or eliminated in the primitive world. Purely culturological principles had not taken complete command. It is, perhaps, as if we were studying the primordial, chemical-laden swamp where self-replicating atoms were taking form but the principles of biological evolution as known today had not yet come clearly into being.

My point is not to minimize culture. But Hallowell's observation (1959) has cogency—that, since primate society has fairly definite form in precultural times, we cannot look upon the emergence of culturally determined societies without reference to their biological basis. In the primitive world the cultural arrangements have not suppressed the biological themes. It is only in societies which have specialists and hereditary classes that wholly nonbiological structural principles begin to emerge.

The primitive variations upon sex, age, and kinship principles are determined largely by two additional factors: tools and environment. Everywhere the nuclear family, whether polygynous, polyandrous, or monogamous, is the basic expression of the biological facts of life, but whether such families constitute independent societies, or are grouped in patrilineages, matrilineages, or other larger structures, depends largely upon how their technology is used in a particular environment, that is, upon the process of cultural ecology. Important as this process is in determining the organization of independent primitive societies, where it is somewhat analogous to biological ecology, it becomes a minor factor in complex states.

Ecological adaptations are highly inferential where we have only a scant archeological record. Evidence as to the nature of society consists of settlement pattern and environment as much as tool inventory. Howell and Washburn conclude from cave middens that the australopithecines changed from scavengers to hunters, even though archeology discloses only stone hand tools. Hunting, however, normally either requires spears or bows to kill medium and large mammals at a distance, fairly elaborate traps and snares, or else such cooperation as surrounds and drives. Unless the culture utilized stone- or bone-pointed spears or arrows, or, as Leakey suggests, bolas, we would have no archeological record of the techniques involved in very early periods.

The causal implications of technology, cultural ecology, and other purposes for which human beings organize are much clearer in ethnographic cases. The Great Basin Shoshoni (Steward, 1938) and the southern Chilean Alacaluf and Chono (Steward and Faron, 1959) were split into independent families because their subsistence was based upon sparse and scattered foods that were collected—seeds and small mammals in the Great Basin, shellfish in Chile—and because such food collection is competitive rather than cooperative. Although both groups had bows and in other environments could well have been large game hunters and although the Shoshoni held occasional cooperative rabbit and antelope hunts, the family was the basic social unit in each case. Technology per se and environment in its totality had very secondary importance. The adaptation to a collecting subsistence caused the family to assume virtually all cultural functions: sexual cooperation in the provision of subsistence and shelter, socialization of children in the mode of life, and care in sickness. Additional cultural functions, such as Chono initiation ceremonies, brought clusters of families together briefly at intervals of several years.

The similarity or typological category of these independent family units represents a certain order of abstraction, though not nearly so great an abstraction as that which places all societies prior to the agricultural revolution in a single category. Structurally, these societies are more similar to one another than they are to patrilineal hunting bands or sedentary farm communities. The similarities are still greater when the functional rather than formal aspects of the culture content are emphasized. Houses, despite formal differences, were temporary and improvised, clothing was made of locally available materials, supernaturalism, except for the Chilean deities connected with initiation ceremonies, concerned individual and family welfare, and so on. These provide the synchronic basis for the type. Diachronically, also, identity of process is implied. Whatever the cultural antecedents of the Shoshoni, Alacaluf, and Chono, the cultural-ecological adaptation was the same in each case.

With reference to the streams of culture history, these people would be classified differently. The Chilean societies might be viewed as part of an archaic American cultural stratum, or, with reference to their stone tools, as of an "early lithic" type, or again in view of their relationship to higher cultures of South America they would be "marginal." The Shoshoni would also be "marginal" with reference to the Southwestern climax of the Anasazi area from which they probably drew much of their basketry, rabbit skin blankets, rabbit nets, and other technological features. But in each case, the population density and distribution and the organization of the people for the meager repertory of cultural activities, which were principally concerned with survival, developed internally from evolutionary processes rather than externally from diffused patterns.

This family-type society is not a universal stage or survival of such a stage, but those who claim that all human societies consist of territorial grouping of clusters of families are in error. Such independent family units must have existed in the past under suitable conditions. A very different type, the patrilineal hunting band, is found in Tierra del Fuego, southern California, Australia, Tasmania, and among the Bushmen, and Congo Negritoes. This type consists of an extended patrilineal family, that is, a half-dozen or so nuclear families, which are related in the male line and which own territory and bring wives from outside the band. This essential structural similarity is related to hunting of fairly sparse but non-migratory game; it represents maximum efficiency in terms of cooperative hunting in a terrain which hunters can know and traverse, and it involves an optimum number of cooperating families.

Other types of hunters and gatherers are the matrilineal bands of the Sirionó and Guayakí forest nomads of Bolivia and Paraguay (Steward and Faron, 1959), the Eskimo family clusters of arctic hunters, which is seemingly a unique type, the multifamily bands of Canadian caribou hunters, and various more settled communities of acorn gatherers of California and fishermen of the Northwest Coast.

These types are not definable in terms of culture-element content nor mere technology. They are not, as White (1959) implies, all based upon extended and classificatory kinship systems. The Shoshoni have a descriptive system, and the other societies have many kinds of systems. They can be categorized only partly by Murdock's (1959) criteria of kinship, descent, marriage, and residence.

Viewed in its particulars, any primitive society is an organization of human beings which is necessarily adapted to the requirements of survival in its habitat. But the organization involves sexual unions and child rearing, which are biological constants. Upon this biological basis develop reciprocal sexual divisions of labor and sometimes formal structures which follow sexual lines, as in men's tribal societies. Cooperation beyond the nuclear family tends usually, although not always, to involve relatives in one line or the other and hence provide a basis for extended, formal kinship-structuring. The long human span of life tends to assign the individual different roles as a child, adult, and elder, and often it underlies formal age-grading.

In the absence of internal specialization and social classes, primitive societies are organized upon the basis of these three principles. In the varied streams of cultural development, especially where more abundant resources permit denser populations and more complex societies, these principles frequently find elaboration and emphasis that amount to structural transformation, but rarely a break through to new principles. Thus, certain East African cattle breeders are distinguished by their age-grade societies and clan development; the Hopi Indians, by a complex system of matrilineal clans, kiva groups, a kachina society, and associational groups; certain Ge tribes of eastern Brazil, by several pairs of moieties and in some instances age-grades; and many Amazon tropical forest farm villages, by patrilineal clans and a men's house or men's society.

THE EVOLUTION OF AGRARIAN STATES

The transformation from primitive to civilized communities entails some conflict between the egalitarian principles of the former and the differentiation of status and role of the latter. This conflict has long been noted, more in sociological than in anthropological literature, and it is reflected in the dichotomy expressed by such pairs as *Gemeinschaft* and *Gesellschaft, societas* and *civitas,* and folk and urban. The conflict does not mean that societies cease to be structured along lines of sex, kinship, age, and associations. Instead, the earlier structures are modified and adapted to the functions of the newer and larger structure. The family and household surrender certain functions to the community, the community becomes integrated within the state, and so on, as a series of internal sublevels within higher levels of cultural integration. Such levels are merely constructs for analyzing particular societies and histories. They do not represent cross-cultural abstractions or evolutionary stages, although they may be employed for this purpose.

The most profound transformation was that which followed the agricultural revolution. Some of the very general effects of this revolution are clear. There was an agricultural surplus which supported non-food-producers, dense and stable populations, class stratification, and political, religious, or military institutions that controlled the state. Beyond these simple generalizations, the problem of cultural classification is greatly complicated by the complexity of structures and apparent multiplicity of processes. At the same time, it is facilitated because of primitive societies. It becomes possible to define change partly in terms of culminations of one or more major processes.

The process of cultural-ecological adaptation becomes increasingly subsidiary to other processes which underlie state formation, for local societies cease to be independent structures that are organized primarily for survival in situations of very direct man-to-nature relationships and become subsocieties, or part-societies, whose interaction with the environment is increasingly modified by a special relationship to the larger society and culture. Adaptation to environment continues to be a factor in culture change, but the higher civilizations provide a greater spectrum of adaptive possibilities, such as purely agrarian, commercial, militaristic, or theocratic communities whose place in the total cultural structure is maintained by the larger society. Meanwhile, the larger society evolves in response to new kinds of processes which really do not have homologues among primitive societies. Thus, multi-community structures may attain cohesion as states because of cooperation in irrigation works, militarism, theocratic controls, or other factors. Merely to list these processes so succinctly, let alone to ascribe primary importance to one or another, however, is to make much too high a level of generalization.

It is a highly generalized statement to say that in the Andes, Egypt, Mesopotamia, the Indus Valley, and Yangtze Valley irrigation was obviously a key factor in increased farm productivity, and at some point the water systems were so great as to require a state managerial control. We need to know, in each case, what this point was and whether some pre-existing institution, such as a priesthood, took over this function, or whether a new institution evolved. We need to know better how the growth of population related to expansion of farming and waterworks. We are by no means certain when and under what circumstances militarism became an institution of state aggression, which enforced amalgamation of local groups into a single political unit. The nature and role of commerce in state growth needs clarification. The same is true of other institutions, such as property, slavery, or peonage of different kinds, and urbanization.

The processes just mentioned seem to have operated cross-culturally and produced rather similar structures, but this is so highly generalized a statement that it adds little to knowledge. The processes themselves can be broken down into smaller connecting links. For example, instead of proposing the broad theory that military conquest created states, we would have to examine the emergence of militarism in the apparent theocratic, nonmilitaristic state of Teotihuacan in Mexico and compare it with militarism in early Andean states. One hypothesis might suggest that militarism came to Mexico as conquest from the outside, whereas it began in Peru with the capture of sacrificial victims, then became an instrument of state control, and only later a means of territorial conquest.

With reference to processes, cultural structures may then be viewed as culminations of predominant processes rather than as static, formal structures. This does not obviate the necessity of some kind of classification, however, for processes can only be recognized through their concrete manifestations at particular moments. Prior to the industrial revolution, there were many kinds of states in which agriculture, commerce, militarism, religion, and other factors played different roles. None was static, but all tended strongly to consist of hereditary classes and thus to have structures which were fairly enduring until conquest or revolution overthrew them or until they were affected by the industrial revolution.

We return at this point to the role of man's creative capacity in culture development. The food revolution that was the basis of these agrarian states resulted from the application of certain scientific knowledge, while state administration, conquest, and religious and aesthetic developments were all creative expressions of sorts. But it is doubtful whether anyone in the course of the rise of agrarian states was aware of their outcome, let alone consciously directed their growth beyond the pattern in which he was involved.

The age of exploration, science, invention, and the industrial revolution applied reason on a more massive scale. The technological effect of this is an incredible acceleration of change in means of production. The social effect is the continued and accelerating individual mobility, which increasingly destroys the possibility of hereditary status and classes. There is no need to discuss the mechanisms of education, mass communications, and the like involved. The central fact is that new skills are demanded almost every year for all statuses and roles throughout society. This was no more foreseen by political philosophers of the West than by Marxian philosophers who envisaged a dictatorship of the working class. Russian communism has changed radically during its brief forty years owing to an increase of individual mobility which has probably accelerated faster than in the Western democracies.

While this acceleration of internal rearrangements has, of course, been recognized, its magnitude could not have been foreseen, and it is difficult even now to project its consequences so as to alter them through intelligent planning. And, of course, planning involves social or moral standards that are not susceptible to scientific validation. The most we can say perhaps is that with new sources of energy and automation foreseeable, society will face the problem of leisure and what to do with it.

SOME CONCLUSIONS

This paper is largely an admission of the general uncertainty now surrounding the concept of cultural evolution. Excellent critical analyses of the concept can be found in White's writings, in Lesser (1952), in the papers by Kluckhohn, Murdock, Hallowell, Haag, Braidwood, and Greenberg in the Centennial Symposium of the Anthropological Society of Washington (1959), and in Goldman (1959), but the methodological difficulties of cultural evolution still lack clarification.

In the physical and biological universes, evolution implies change which can be formulated in principles that operate at all times and places, although the particular principles of biological evolution differ from those of the physical realm. Expectably, or at least by analogy, then, cultural evolution should contain its own distinctive principles, which also underlie all cultural change.

By this criterion, no one has yet demonstrated cultural evolution. Some of White's principles are common to physical, biological, and cultural phenomena. Others differ when primitive, kinship-based societies are transformed into civilized societies. The "principle" of energy levels per se has little meaning; the question is how energy is used. The individual mobility that followed the industrial revolution was the process or connecting link between energy and society; it destroyed the earlier hereditary classes of agrarian states. If an age of nuclear energy brings further transformations, it will be through the agency of automation and other arrangements contingent upon quantities of energy rather than the nature of the source.

At the other extreme are the interests in histories, culture areas, or traditions, which become "evolutionary" only by being so designated.

In between is an increasing large number of papers, some that deal with the particulars of what is called "evolution" within single culture areas, and others that compare change between areas. The latter necessarily generalize in some degree in order to recognize structures that are similar formally or functionally and to ascertain relevant processes or causes of change.

What can we say, then, of cultural evolution? Are transformations within a single area or tradition evolutionary? Can we say that limited cross-cultural generalizations that formulate different but recurring lines of change are evolutionary? Or must we conclude that cultural evolution, unlike physical and biological evolution, generates new principles as it evolves? This last proposition is implied in the emphasis upon the creativity of the human mind, except that reference to principles surely requires recognition of ascertainable order in culture change. It challenges us to show what new principles of order emerge at successive stages.

Perhaps the wholesale proclamation of allegiance to cultural evolution in 1959 is principally to do honor to Darwin. Nevertheless it has constituted an important theoretical stocktaking, even though the new evolutionists will undoubtedly continue to do what they have been doing during the last two or three decades. This recent research, however, constitutes an important trend, consisting of interest in transformation, however large or small, and a search for causes. Emphasis is now upon society, which is conceived more narrowly as kinship systems in the case of primitive peoples and more holistically in the case of civilized peoples. As hypotheses are constructed and modified, there is reason to hope that some sort of solid taxonomic basis will be found. As hypotheses are validated and broaden, perhaps universal principles will emerge. These may not differ greatly from those of the nineteenth-century writers, but they will have a more solid empirical basis.

BIBLIOGRAPHY

ADAMS, ROBERT M.
1956. "Some Hypotheses on the Development of Early Civilizations," *Amer. Antiquity*, XXI, No. 3.

BEARDSLEY, RICHARD K. *et al.*
1956. "Functional and Evolutionary Implications of Community Patterning" in *Seminars in Archaeology: 1955*. (Memoir No. 11, Society for American Archaeology.)

BENEDICT, RUTH
1934. *Patterns of Culture*. Boston: Houghton Mifflin.

BENNETT, WENDELL C.
1948. "The Peruvian Co-tradition," pp. 1-7 in *A Reappraisal of Peruvian Archaeology*, Wendell C. Bennett, ed. (Memoir No. 4, Society for American Archaeology.)

BRAIDWOOD, ROBERT J.
1952. *The Near East and Its Foundations for Civilization*. (Chicago Natural History Museum Popular Series in Anthropology, No. 37.)

1958. "Near Eastern Prehistory," *Science*, CXXVII, 1419–30.

1959. "Archaeology and Evolutionary Theory," pp. 76–89, in *Evolution and Anthropology: A Centennial Appraisal*. Anthropological Society of Washington.

CALDWELL, JOSEPH R.
1958. "Trend and Tradition in the Prehistory of the Eastern United States," *Amer. Anthropologist*, LX, No. 6, Part 2. (Memoir No. 88, Scientific Papers of the Illinois State Museum, Vol. X.)

CHILDE, V. GORDON
1934. *New Light on the Most Ancient East*. London: Routledge and Kegan Paul.

1946. *What Happened in History*. London: Penguin Books.

1951. *Social Evolution*. London and New York: H. Schuman.

COOPER, JOHN M.
1942. "Areal and Temporal Aspects of Aboriginal South American Culture," *Primitive Man*, XV, 1–38.

COULBORN, RUSHTON
1959. *The Origin of Civilized Societies*. Princeton: Princeton University Press.

GERARD, R. W., CLYDE KLUCKHOHN, and ANATOL RAPAPORT
1956. "Biological and Cultural Evolution," *Behavioral Science*, I, 6–34.

GOLDMAN, IRVING
1955. "Status Rivalry and Cultural Evolution in Polynesia," *Amer. Anthropologist*, LVII, 680–97.

1941. "The Alkatcho Carrier: Historical Background of Crest Prerogatives," *Amer. Anthropologist*, XLIII, 396–418.

1957. "Cultural Evolution in Polynesia," *Journ. Polynesian Soc.*, LXVI, 156–64.

1959. "Evolution and Anthropology," *Victorian Studies* (September, pp. 55–75.)

GOODENOUGH, W. H.
1957. "Oceania and the Problem of Controls in the Study of Cultural and Human Evolution," *Journ. Polynesian Soc.*, LXVI, 146–53.

HAAG, WILLIAM A.
1959. "The Status of Evolutionary Theory in American Archeology," pp. 90–105 in *Evolution and Anthropology: A Centennial Appraisal.* Anthropological Society of Washington.

HALLOWELL, A. IRVING
1959. "Behavioral Evolution and the Emergence of the Self," pp. 36–60 in *Evolution and Anthropology: A Centennial Appraisal*, Anthropological Society of Washington.

HARRIS, MARVIN
1959. "The Economy Has No Surplus?" *Amer. Anthropologist*, LXVII, 185–99.

HUXLEY, JULIAN S.
1958. "Cultural Process and Evolution" in *Behavior and Evolution*, Anne Roe and George Gaylord Simpson, eds. New Haven: Yale University Press.

KLUCKHOHN, CLYDE
1959. "The Role of Evolutionary Thought in Anthropology," pp. 144–57 in *Evolution and Anthropology: A Centennial Appraisal.* Anthropological Society of Washington.

KROEBER, A. L.
1939. "Cultural and Natural Areas of North America." *University of California Publications in American Archaeology and Ethnology*, Vol. 38, 242 pp.

1945. "The Ancient Oikoumene as an Historic Cultural Aggregate." (Huxley Memorial Lecture for 1945.) London: Royal Anthropological Institute of Great Britain and Ireland. Reprinted in 1952 in his *The Nature of Culture*, Chicago: The University of Chicago Press.

1946. "History and Evolution," *Southwest. Jour. Anthrop.,* II, 1–15.

LESSER, ALEXANDER
1952. "Evolution in Social Anthropology," *Southwest Journ. Anthrop.,* VIII, 134–46.

MORGAN, LEWIS H.
1877. *Ancient Society, or Researches in the Lines of Human Progress from Savagery, through Barbarism to Civilization.* New York: Henry Holt & Co.

MURDOCK, GEORGE P.
1959. "Evolution in Social Organization," pp. 126–43 in *Evolution and Anthropology: A Centennial Appraisal.* Anthropological Society of Washington.

MURPHY, ROBERT F., and JULIAN H. STEWARD
1956. "Tappers and Trappers: Parallel Process in Acculturation," *Econ. Develop. and Culture Change,* IV, 335–55.

OBERG, KALERVO
1955. "Types of Social Structure among the Lowland Tribes of Central and South America," *Amer. Anthropologist,* LVII, 472–88.

PHILLIPS, PHILIP, and GORDON R. WILLEY
1953. "Method and Theory in American Archaeology: An Operational Basis for Culture-Historical Integration," *Amer. Anthropologist,* LV, 615–34.

SINHA, S.
1955. "Evolutionism Reconsidered," *Man in India,* XXXV, 1–18.

SOUTH, STANLEY
1955. "Evolutionary Theory in Archeology," *Southern Indian Studies,* VII, 10–32.

STEWARD, JULIAN H.
1937. "Ecological Aspects of Southwestern Society," *Anthrop.,* XXXII, 87–104.

1938. *Basin-Plateau Sociopolitical Groups.* (Bureau of American Ethnology, Bulletin 120.)

1956a. *Anthropological View of Contemporary Culture Change,* "Kyoto American Studies Seminar Publications," No. 2: "Anthropology." Kyoto, Japan.

1956b. "Cultural Evolution," *Scien. Amer.,* CXCIV, 69–80.

1958. "Problems of Cultural Evolution," *Evolution,* XII, 206–10.

1960. Review of Leslie White's *The Evolution of Culture* in *Amer. Anthropologist,* LXII, 144-148.

STEWARD, JULIAN H., ed.
 1955. *Irrigation Civilizations: A Comparative Study.* Pan American Union, Social Sci. Monographs, No. 1, Washington, D.C.

STEWARD, JULIAN H. (with ROBERT F. MURPHY)
 See Murphy and Steward, 1956.

STEWARD, JULIAN H., and LOUIS C. FARON
 1959. *Native Peoples of South America.* New York: McGraw-Hill Book Co.

WHITE, LESLIE A
 1949. *The Science of Culture.* New York: Farrar, Strauss.

 1959a. *The Evolution of Culture.* New York: McGraw-Hill Book Co.

 1959b. "The Concept of Evolution in Cultural Anthropology," pp. 106-25 in *Evolution and Anthropology: A Centennial Appraisal.* Anthropological Society of Washington.

WILLEY, GORDON R.
 1953. *Settlement Patterns in the Virú Valley.* (Bureau of American Ethnology, Bulletin 155.)

WILLEY, GORDON R., and PHILIP PHILLIPS
 1955. "Method and Theory in American Archaeology II: Historical-Developmental Interpretation," *Amer. Anthropologist,* LVII, 723–819.

WISSLER, CLARK
 1922. *The American Indian.* New York and London: Oxford University Press.

 1923. *Man and Culture.* New York: Thomas Y. Crowell.

WITTFOGEL, KARL
 1957. *Oriental Despotism: A Comparative Study of Total Power.* New Haven: Yale University Press.

4

Wittfogel's Irrigation Hypothesis

During Steward's years at Columbia University, he became deeply interested in the work of the noted historian of China, Karl Wittfogel. The relevance of Wittfogel's theories on the relation between irrigation agriculture and the development of "Oriental despotism" to the growth of the state in other regions formed the basis of Steward's original formulation of the theory of multilinear evolution. This essay was written late in Steward's life, and his death came before he could revise it for publication. It was intended as a reflection upon the idea of the "hydraulic society" and as a tribute to an old friend.

1. A MATTER OF PROBLEMS AND INTERESTS

A scholar's contributions to science should be judged more by the stimulus he gives to research—by the nature of the problems he raises and the interests he creates—than by the enduring qualities of his provisional hypotheses. Karl Wittfogel's hypothesis concerning the role of irrigation in the development of early civilizations was first formulated during the 1930s (Wittfogel, 1935, 1938, 1939-40, 1946), when most students of the development of culture were still basically oriented toward descriptive and historical rather than explanatory analyses. Anthropology and history were mainly concerned with cultural differences. Any formulations of cultural development which recognized cross-cultural similarities, and especially any which postulated causal processes which might account for these similarities, were thought to be impossible and almost certainly erroneous.

There was, however, an undercurrent of interest in identifying cross-cultural regularities or developmental similarities, but in America this was largely a tenuous heritage of earlier theories of cultural evolution (White, 1959). Even after the stimulus of the centennial of Darwin's *Origin of the Species* in 1959, evolutionists were still largely concerned with the question of general stages of cultural evolution (e.g. Sahlins and Service, 1960) rather than with the determination of the specific causes of different kinds of cultural development or evolution (Steward, 1960; Steward and Shimkin, 1961). Interest in cultural causality, however, has continued to grow even though comparatively little research is guided by interest in the still nebulous theory of cultural "evolution."

Wittfogel's contribution to recent trends originated in his extensive research on China, which had created vast hydraulic works including irrigation systems, drainage canals, and internal routes of water transportation. He developed the hypothesis that the early civilized states of both the eastern and western hemispheres were integrated by the managerial controls required to construct and maintain the irrigation—and more broadly hydraulic—systems. As water was brought to arid lands, food production and population increased and became the basis for class-structured states and the achievements of civilization. While historians of culture were emphasizing differences between civilizations, Wittfogel was postulating a single basic factor that brought all of the civilizations into being.

The thirty years since Wittfogel's first publications, especially the two decades since World War II, have produced a vast amount of field research which has thrown doubt upon the universal applicability of the irrigation hypothesis. It is clear that in many instances irrigation had been ascribed excessive importance and that in others, its development seems to have been the result rather than the cause of the growth of states. Much of this research has obviously been directly stimulated by Wittfogel's theory, and it is safe to say that even Wittfogel's most vigorous critics have advanced our understanding of the role of irrigation precisely because their interest had been directed to the subject and they had a theory which could be tested. Inadequacies of the irrigation hypothesis leave us with the challenge of finding alternative hypotheses to explain the growth of early states.

The basic problem is broader than irrigation and states. It is one of seeking explanatory formulations for the development of any culture. My own interest in this was first published in 1936 (Steward, 1936) and dealt with primitive bands. Later (Steward, 1949), Wittfogel's irrigation hypothesis stimulated me to ascertain whether apparent cross-cultural regularities in the development sequence of early civilizations could not be extended farther back in time and made to include features of culture other than those concerned with the emergence of states. This "trial formulation" included Meso-America, Peru, Egypt, Mesopotamia, and China, and provisionally postulated similar developmental eras which were designated Hunting and Gathering, Incipient Agriculture, Formative (of States), Regional Florescent States, and Empires and Conquests. Research since 1949 has required many revisions of these sequences and many modifications of the assumed role of irrigation (see Steward, 1955).

In the criticisms of Wittfogel's and my formulations, three trends are discernible. First, there are some who have delved so deeply into the details of single areas that they not only repudiate any cross-cultural formulation but apparently hold an a priori conviction that general causes do not exist. Some even seem to assume on philosophical grounds that the creative operations of the human mind are not reducible to causal understandings. Second, an opposite extreme is represented by the more systematic evolutionists who are content to place all these early civilizations in a stage called the "agricultural" or "urban revolution." There is a third, or intermediate, position which is empirical in its attention to the details of individual cases and which applies the insights of each case to other cases to be tested and revised. That factors and processes of culture change must be abstracted from the hundreds of minutiae in each instance in no way invalidates the methodology.

This third view, unfortunately, is often obscured by confusion in its application. In a recent symposium on the prehistory of Latin America (Meggers and Evans, 1963), experts on special areas from Mexico to Argentina described their areas in some detail, but the period diagnostics ranged from presence or absence of agriculture or pottery to presumed development of states and cities. Cross-cultural comparability was badly obscured in most of the articles. The increasing knowledge of early history and cultural developments in the Near East lacks systematic presentation owing to the diversity of interests, as illustrated by the essays in *City Invincible* (Kraeling and Adams, 1960). The classical orientalists tend to pay so much attention to humanistic achievements that no two subareas seem comparable. Even general concepts, such as "urban revolution" and "civilization," lose validity in the assumption that a civilization had to have writing and, since cities were the "containers of civilization," Jericho is in doubt while the Inca Empire, despite certain huge urban centers, is completely disqualified.

The sociologists and anthropologists, especially the dirt archeologists, have generally given us more insight into what is significant cross-culturally in the Near East. The sociologists who contributed to *City Invincible* rightly pointed out that the apparent absence of cities in Dynastic Egypt did not necessarily disqualify it from the stage of "urban revolution," since no one had defined a city. The diagnostics of a city plague students of the New World for the same reason. Whether Classical Mayan ceremonial centers should be called "cities" has not yet been decided. The concept of urbanization will remain vague until it is recognized that there are many kinds of cities, each with one or more special functions. This requires an empirical comparative study, which must have a starting point and some provisional hypotheses.

We are really on more solid ground in comparisons of societies during the initial phases of agriculture, probably because irrigation was of minor importance, communities were small, writing was absent, and there were no state institutions to confuse the issues. Many studies of the New World have traced the origins of plant cultivation and reported on the earliest farm communities. Braidwood (1964) has raised interesting questions about the degree of incipiency of agriculture and possible differences in the natural environments where farming first sustained permanent villages. In each case the sequence started at some point when dependency upon domesticated crops began to supersede reliance upon wild foods. There have been no genuine civilizations which lacked agriculture, or agriculture and a partially symbiotic animal husbandry dependency.

My first essay (1949) attempted to trace the sequence of sociopolitical types and of cultural achievements from what we must now consider a vague and ill-defined era of primary village-farm communities (Braidwood, 1964), through later eras, and to define each era in terms of its achievements and culminations. In all early civilizations the sequence of these cultural features was extraordinarily similar. Virtually all basic plants were domesticated before the higher civilizations developed. The increased populations and stability of communities based on better food supply entailed amalgamation of formerly independent villages into larger sociopolitical units. The trend also entailed social differentiation into classes and specialized occupations as well as roles.

Whereas the era of incipient or early agriculturalists had pottery, permanent houses, and other simple technologies, ensuing developmental eras witnessed remarkable parallels in other achievements. Metallurgy began quite early with gold and culminated in the age of empire in the New World with bronze and in the Old World with bronze and later iron. Specialization of role freed certain groups of individuals or classes, perhaps priests, so that they developed astronomy, mathematics, and writing. Writing was not common to all civilizations, and systems of writing differed, but it appeared, if at all, in about the same developmental era in both hemispheres. Similarly, the wheel was invented at about the same stage, although it was only a toy in America and was later abandoned.

The development of monumental architecture, elaborate priesthoods, state religions, and humanistic expressions of state political and religious concepts in art, literature, architectural style, music, and other media were understandably manifestations of state development and of classes of specialists. The sequence of cultural achievements of all kinds was surprisingly similar in each early civilization, and there was little disjunction. The Inca had no writing, the New World abandoned the wheel, and the stylistic and symbolic expressions of state development were largely unique in each case. In a functional sense, however, the particular styles of art and architecture, the various religious ideologies, and other humanistic extensions of state development were similar in sanctioning the basic institutions.

This brief recapitulation of similarities in the development of early civilizations oversimplifies the picture. It will be unacceptable to the cultural relativists who, in the name of empiricism, must push examination of minutiae to the point that each case seems unique and any valid cross-cultural understandings are ruled out. As a broad, cross-cultural hypothesis, however, it is concerned with basic factors and processes that underlie cultural growth. The value of such a generalization is that it provides a foil or a target for criticism which, devastating as it may be, will hopefully advance understandings a step further.

II. THE IRRIGATION FACTOR

The importance of water to any civilization is becoming painfully evident today. If the value of irrigation to pre-industrial civilizations has been overemphasized as the all-important factor in creating the state—or Wittfogel's "oriental absolute state"—the hypothesis, like many others, is first presented in bold strokes and later requires modification. The crucial issue of whether large-scale irrigation created the state or was created by a developed state is an academic issue to the extent that neither could exist without the other in extremely arid lands. More concretely, however, the issue must be broken down into special considerations of soils, terrain, topography, climate, and other factors. The principal criticism of Wittfogel's hypothesis, like that of so many pioneering hypotheses, is that "irrigation" is far too broad a rubric to have precise heuristic value. One must ask in each case such questions as "how arid is arid?" The rainless Peruvian coast will support no vegetation without irrigation except along the stream borders. How adequate is rainfall? In some areas it barely supports plant life. In many areas, even the eastern United States, there are drought years when irrigation would be a tremendous asset. What is the nature of stream flow? In some areas rivers deposit alluvium, overflow and change their channels to the extent that they can be readily tapped by short ditches or canals. In others streams are deeply entrenched and require major construction of dams and complicated systems of canals. What features of social structure may affect maximum use of land, whether irrigated or not? Warfare may expose dispersed settlements—and their irrigation works—to disastrous raids. The nature of the state may involve specialized production for trade with its attending hazards. What capital, advanced technology, and control of manpower can a state put into maximum development of irrigation? There is incredible expansion of irrigation today, based upon water storage in huge dams and construction of long canals. How much land is available for cultivation? This may be related on the one hand to topography and water flow and on the other to terracing of hills where flat land is scarce, as in the Philippines, Peru, Japan, and elsewhere. How much water is needed by the crops? Rice requires far more water than some of the grains.

Empirically, revisions of Wittfogel's hypothesis are clearly required by much recent research. It has been shown by Adams (1964) that in the Diyala Plains of lower Mesopotamia significant enlargement of irrigation systems was a sequel to, not a precondition or antecedent of, state development and planning and of urban growth. Meso-America, despite much recent search, has not yielded convincing evidence of large irrigation systems prior to the Spanish Conquest. The prehistory of Peru, however, reveals a fairly concomitant growth of population, states, and almost certainly irrigation, except that population seems to have dropped off just prior to the Inca Empire. China's early well-and-ditch irrigation probably did not require much supracommunity coordination, but its great irrigation and navigational canals of later periods were clearly state-controlled. The cycles of population rise and fall which were closely associated with China's dynasties may or may not imply periodic neglect and reconstruction of irrigation.

The obvious difficulty of correlating irrigation works, land use, population, and community and urban development is in dating irrigation systems and determining their extent at any given period. Any irrigation system would require an enormous amount of excavation and, since canals were undoubtedly used over long periods—often re-excavated—they are difficult to date (Woodbury, 1955). Undoubtedly, the most comprehensive study of this problem is Adams's reconstruction of some 6,000 years of the Diyala Plains of Iraq (1964).

In all the world areas classified as arid and semiarid, crop production is increased through irrigation. In all cases, moreover, irrigation requires some kind of supervision. The problem, then, is whether a society has centralized authority which developed apart from needs of food production and which took over the managerial functions of irrigation or whether irrigation itself created a managerial class. Suggestions are provided by some of the simpler cases.

The most elementary irrigation known was that of the Paiute of eastern California, who lacked domesticated plants (Steward, 1930).

These Indians, who lived along the eastern escarpment of the Sierra Nevada mountains of California, diverted streams by means of small dams and ditches which were carried a mile or so in order to further the growth of wild seeds. This practice was evidently the logical sequitur of their observation of the great natural growth of these plants along the stream margins and marshy terrain as compared with the extremely arid areas between streams. The small, localized bands of these Paiute had no chiefs or headmen, and "irrigation bosses" therefore had to be accorded power to get the job done.

In the arid Southwest, the Indians irrigated in varying degrees and for different crops. The Hopi, who were among the most developed and culturally complex, had adapted maize, beans, and squash to the meager rainfall of the high Colorado Plateau. Some of their maize was exceptionally deep-rooted. Occasionally, the Hopi built dams in the arroyos to catch the periodic rainfall, but these were local enterprises and they involved no changes in the sociopolitical organization of the Indians. It is interesting that the Hopi developed a new kind of irrigation in post-Spanish times. Onions and a few other garden crops adopted from Europeans were planted near small springs which irrigated a few hundred square feet of land.

The prehistoric Hohokam peoples of the Salt-Gila River valleys of hot, arid southern Arizona, however, had constructed irrigation systems wherein the canals and ditches totaled several hundred miles and served many communities. These canals brought large areas of desert under cultivation. This magnitude of planning and labor seems to imply some centralized authority, and recent archeological research suggests that a state-like sociopolitical system somewhat resembling that of Meso-America, but diminished in scale, was involved. Whether the state developed first and created the large irrigation system or resulted from it cannot be known. If the Hohokam were migrants from much farther south, the state may have preceded the irrigation.

There are other examples of very impressive irrigation works, such as the mountain terracing in the Philippine Islands, which resembled that of the Central Andes in land use but not in size. In the Philippines, however, fairly small "tribes," communities, or clusters of peoples who were not at all organized into states seem to have managed their hydraulic problems by informal understandings. The Andean irrigation systems, on the other hand, were vastly more extensive, and they must have resulted from large-scale planning over a long period. The canals extend far back into the mountains, collect water from a vast highland area of considerable rainfall, and distribute it within valleys. In some cases they even combine the waters of several valleys.

A contrast of two irrigation areas in Japan is illustrated by the findings of Toshinao Yoneyama, who worked on my recent study of native communities. In the Nara Basin, a fairly small stream irrigates the land of 24 hamlets which occupy only two or three square miles and have a total population of about 3,000 persons. Maintenance of ditches and distribution of water are entirely a matter of local concern. Interestingly, however, Kaminosho, the last hamlet downstream, has first rights to the water and enforces the cooperation of other communities through certain ditch-cleaning ceremonies each year. Possibly Kaminosho was the first settlement in the area and later hamlets remained subordinate to it. The other community is Kurikoma in the mountainous area of the northern Tohoku district. It had no access to irrigation water until several centuries ago when an overlord put his people to work building a dam and ditches. The regions differ in that streams in the Nara Basin flow sluggishly from the mountains over alluvial fans, and irrigation requires minimal dams and ditches, whereas in the Kurikoma area the river is deeply entrenched in gravels as it comes out of the mountains and requires extensive work on dams and ditches.

The importance of topography in Peru is unparalleled. In the great highlands or puna, potatoes and quinoa were grown with rainfall up to an altitude of 15,000 feet, but the population seems always to have been dispersed with few cities prior to the growth of Tiahuanaco and later of the Inca capital at Cuzco. Rainfall decreases with altitude, and the coast is virtually without rain. Except for limited flood-plain farming along the immediate margins of the rivers, the farm productivity in the lower altitudes could not have compared with that of later periods. Unlike aggrading rivers, such as those in the Nara Basin, the Hohokam area, and the lower Tigris-Euphrates system, Andean streams are deeply entrenched in mountain valleys and gorges. The earliest irrigation seemingly expanded until whole valleys were included in single systems. Later, several adjoining valleys might be integrated. Construction of these irrigation systems in Peru clearly required central managerial controls, whether by priests, warriors, civil rulers, or special engineers.

The applicability of the irrigation hypothesis in its extreme form to lower Mesopotamia has clearly been discredited by the work of Robert Adams. The larger area has many microvariations in landscape and climate. The earliest known farming was on the "hilly flanks," where rainfall was adequate for plant cultivation and where the first permanent farm villages are found. In the lower valley, however, as in the Diyala Plains of Iraq, the rivers aggrade to the extent that they overflow their banks, change courses, and create swamps. Under these conditions cultivation could be carried on through construction of fairly short lateral canals and drainage ditches which did not require highly centralized state management. Between 4,000 B.C. and the beginning of the Christian era, there were some fluctuations in population which evidently represented sociocultural factors, such as militarism, but there were no urban centers and the population never exceeded 100,000, in contrast to several later periods when cities of several hundred thousands and a total population of more than 800,000 were reached. The many factors other than use of water and land indicated by Adams's research (1965) will be discussed subsequently.

3. ADDITIONAL FACTORS

While it is clear that managerial controls of irrigation or hydraulic works alone were not everywhere the principal factor underlying the growth of early civilizations, it is equally certain that irrigation of some form increased food productivity in all these areas. No matter how small the irrigation system, cooperative effort in its construction and maintenance and in distribution of water had to be coordinated. Many local factors of physical geography caused variations, ranging from the need for small amounts of water to supplement rainfall to complete dependence upon irrigation, and they presented engineering problems ranging from drainage of swamps caused by river overflow to damming of deeply entrenched streams.

In every case some forms of managerial controls were needed. In each culture, however, there were apparently early developments of theocratic and perhaps other controls and later of militaristic authority. The question, then, is how these ruling classes came into being, whether they assumed control of irrigation, and whether the expansion of irrigation systems, increase of population, appearance of cities, and development of civilization were enhanced by the irrigation factor. To the extent that a society depended upon irrigation water and/or lands to which water could be diverted, the role of sociocultural institutions and hydraulic controls must have been intricately interrelated. The identification of the critical factors, however, requires far more research into the nature and antiquity of irrigation on the one hand and far better understanding of the early social and political structures on the other. Several basic propositions, however, seem tenable.

First, the agricultural revolution in different parts of the world—the domestication of what were to become the plant staples—occurred in areas where rainfall farming, flood-plain cultivation, or small-scale irrigation sufficed. At some later time large-scale irrigation (and/or drainage) increased production.

Second, a precondition of early states—that is, of regionally integrated sociopolitical units consisting of many villages—was sufficient farm yield to support permanent communities and to relieve a portion of the population from work in the fields. As the nonfarming population increased, a variety of specialists in construction, crafts, and religious and political functions developed.

Third, amalgamation of formerly independent communities into states required integrating factors. Assessment of possible factors must take into account state functions and enterprises other than managerial controls of irrigation.

Initial state integration around theocratic controls has been postulated for several areas. In the western hemisphere warfare for conquest, slavery, tribute, or territories seems to have been absent during the culmination of pre-imperial states. The early Maya and highland Mexican cultural culmination prior to about the eighth century A.D. (the so-called Classical Periods) probably was based in part on a religion in which victims were captured for religious sacrifice, but they seemed to have lacked true nationalistic warfare. A similar culmination apparently occurred in the Central Andes, and perhaps also in the Mississippi Valley Temple Mound cultures.

Just why thousands of people submitted to theocratic controls is not clear. It has been suggested that the early Chavinoid cultures of Peru had qualities of a messianic cult. Eric Wolf has speculated that Teotihuacan, like historic Mecca, combined the functions of trade and religion. In Mesopotamia state integration seems to have been peaceful, while warfare was beginning in the hilly flanks. The case for nonmilitaristic, theocratic integration in pre-Dynastic Egypt and China is strong but not wholly convincing.

In all these instances it is obvious that eventually a populous state that was internally specialized and socially stratified required centralized controls. Allocation of labor, distribution of goods, adjudication of disputes, and performance of religious rites could no longer be carried out by the kin group or the isolated village. A civilian, or civil-religious, government had to develop.

Control of hydraulic works passed from the implicit authority within a small cluster of villages to the explicit authority of the state. In some cases this transfer was necessarily early; in others it came late. Little farming could have been carried out on the coastal deserts and the steep mountain slopes of intermediate altitudes of Peru unless a central authority mobilized the people of many localities to construct the necessary dams and ditches. Whether state organization had already existed in Peru is probably unimportant. The growth of the state and of agricultural production are aspects of a single process. The Peruvians, however, increased their public works after the Andes were unified under one huge empire. At the same time, population possibly declined, which might be interpreted to mean that farm production had previously reached the limits of environmental potentials and productive technology. By contrast, the low flat valley of the Tigris-Euphrates was easily watered by short ditches from the river. Indeed, its swampy nature had made drainage as much a problem as irrigation. The irrigation maximum in this area came much later, when authoritarian and militaristic governments built enormous canals and created cities in areas previously uninhabited.

Other world centers probably represent intermediate situations. Where farming had to expand into arid areas, centralized control over the waterworks were required as local conditions imposed various difficulties. Expanded farming concomitantly increased the population, strengthened state controls, and permitted further state expansion.

With the fairly primitive technology and engineering skills of these early civilizations, however, a limit had to be reached. In some cases strong authoritarian states realized maximum productivity. In others, state expansion was accomplished by military conquest rather than by peaceful, internal development. Thus all early civilizations sooner or later reached an era of conquests or successions of dynasties.

As comparative studies are pursued, and an empirical, case-by-case approach is utilized, each study illuminates others. It now begins to appear that the factors and processes in any cultural development are fairly limited in number and are rather similar cross-culturally. The differences lie more in their combinations and relative importances than in any total uniqueness of given cases.

Irrigation is not a single factor, but the varieties of irrigation and the effects of each variety differ in ways which have scarcely been touched by research. The other factors in the context of state and urban development, especially in prehistoric periods, are just beginning to enter the realm of speculation. A strong religious factor is evident everywhere, but its varieties and influence have not been clearly assessed. Militarism is widely evidenced by capture of sacrificial victims, but the time when wars of conquest became a factor that integrated independent states is speculative. The nature of land ownership, production, and control and trade of commodities is virtually unknown except in eras of written history.

In short, instead of "throwing out the baby with the irrigation water," the need is to recognize the particular combinations of factors, *including the kind of irrigation,* which operated in each case. Wittfogel's hypothesis challenges the disbelievers to produce alternative explanations which are more than accounts of the uniqueness of individual cases.

BIBLIOGRAPHY

ADAMS, ROBERT McC.
1962. Agriculture and Urban Life in Early Southwestern Iran. *Science,* vol. 136, pp. 109-122.

1965. *Land Behind Baghdad: A History of Settlement of the Diyala Plains.* University of Chicago Press, Chicago.

BRAIDWOOD, ROBERT J.
1964. More Complex Regularities? In *Process and Pattern in Culture,* pp. 411-417 (Robert A. Manners, ed.). Aldine Publishing Co., Chicago.

KRAELING, CARL H., and ADAMS, ROBERT McC. (eds.)
1960. *City Invincible.* University of Chicago Press, Chicago.

KROEBER, ALFRED L.
1948. *Anthropology* (Revised edition). Harcourt, Brace, New York.

MEGGERS, BETTY J., and EVANS, CLIFFORD (eds.).
1963. *Aboriginal Cultural Development in Latin America: An Interpretative Review.* Smithsonian Misc. Coll., vol. 146, No. 1.

SAHLINS, MARSHALL D., and SERVICE, ELMAN R. (eds.)
1960. *Evolution and Culture.* University of Michigan Press, Ann Arbor.

STEWARD, JULIAN H.
1930. Irrigation without Agriculture. *Papers,* Michigan Acad. Sci., vol. XII, pp. 149-156.

1936. The Economic and Social Basis of Primitive Bands. In *Essays in Honor of Alfred Louis Kroeber,* pp. 311-350. University of Calif. Press, Berkeley.

1949. Culture Causality and Law: A Trial Formulation of Early Civilizations. *American Anthropologist,* vol. 51, pp. 1–27.

1955 (ed.). *Irrigation Civilizations: A Comparative Study.* Pan American Union, Washington, D.C.

1960. Evolutionary Principles and Social Types. In *Evolution after Darwin,* pp. 169–186 (Sol Tax and Charles Callender, eds.). University of Chicago Press, Chicago.

1961, with Demitri B. Shimkin. Some Mechanisms of Sociocultural Evolution. In Evolution and Man's Progress. *Daedalus,* vol. 90, no. 3; *Proc. Amer. Acad. Arts and Sciences,* pp. 477-497.

WHITE, LESLIE B.
1959. *The Evolution of Culture.* McGraw-Hill Book Co., New York.

WILLEY, GORDON R.
1953. *Prehistoric Settlement Patterns in the Viru Valley, Peru.* Bur. Amer. Ethnol. Bull. 155.

WITTFOGEL, KARL A.
1935. The Foundations and Stages of Chinese Economic History. *Zeitschrift für Socialforschung*, vol. 4, pp. 26-60. Paris.

1938. Die Theorie der Orientalischen Gesellschaft. *Zeitschrift für Socialforschung*, vol. 7, nos. 1–2. Paris.

1939-40. The Society of Prehistoric China. In *Studies in Philosophy and Social Science.* Institute of Social Research, vol. 8 (1939), pp. 138–186. New York, 1940.

1946. General Introduction (to History of Chinese Society, Liao, by Karl A. Wittfogel and Feng Chia-Sheng). Amer. Philos. Soc., *Trans.*, vol. 36, pp. 1–35.

1957. *Oriental Despotism: A Comparative Study of Total Power.* Yale University Press, New Haven.

WOLF, ERIC R.
1959. *Sons of the Shaking Earth.* University of Chicago Press, Chicago.

WOODBURY, RICHARD B.
1960. The Hohokam Canals at Pueblo Grande, Arizona. *American Antiquity*, vol. 26, pp. 267–270.

PART II

Culture Change and History

5

The Evolution of Prefarming Societies

Under the longer title "Causal Factors and Processes in the Evolution of Pre-farming Societies," this essay was presented to a symposium on hunting and collecting societies (*Man the Hunter*, ch. 34, ed. Richard Lee and Irven DeVore, Chicago: Aldine, 1968, pp. 321-334). It is reprinted here with the consent of the editors and the publisher.

METHODOLOGICAL TRENDS

The papers of this conference as well as of the recent conferences on the Great Basin and on bands seem to me notable for the interest in causality that runs through the comparisons of prefarming societies. This interest has led to the scrutiny of concepts and to the reporting of kinds of data that were accorded little attention two or three decades ago. But, as these papers clearly demonstrate, we have not yet perfected a methodology for determining cause-and-effect relationships in the evolution of different kinds of cultures. I wish, therefore, to examine some of the methodological implications of these conferences, especially in the conceptualization of the nature of causes and effects. Specifically, I stress that a distinction needs to be made between causal factors and processes. If any of my comments appear to contradict my earlier statements, it is because I endeavor to sharpen and, if necessary, redesign old tools rather than discard them.

Because cross-cultural comparisons are the essence of the present papers and discussions—although they are not the only means of examining causality—the nature of cultural taxonomies and their use in determining causal factors is of major concern. The ethnographic cases reported in these papers, however, are not holistic descriptions, and such descriptions do not lend themselves to explanatory analyses. This raises the question of which aspects of culture shall constitute diagnostic characteristics of cross-cultural types. The present papers accord major attention to social structures, and they generally start with small aggregates of nuclear families and extend analysis outward through kinship and marriage systems. This emphasis reflects the empirical importance of kinship ties, which are very responsive to the inescapable requirements of subsistence activities within these difficult environments, rather than any theoretical presuppositions according to which certain characteristics are ascribed greater importance than others. Even though structural characteristics have a continuity with past tradition, and in some cases may have been influenced by culture contacts, all must have sufficient adaptability to remain viable.

Cross-cultural comparisons have shown many cases of near similarity of social structure. There is danger, however, of committing a methodological fallacy in assuming that similar structural manifestations or effects are always caused by identical factors. The validity of the reverse hypothesis, that similar causes will have similar effects, does not prove that causes can be deduced unfailingly from effects. The data of these conferences have repeatedly demonstrated that similar effects may be traced back to various combinations of dissimilar causes. One must, of course, start with analysis of structures having similar characteristics. A preliminary taxonomy is inescapable. But thorough empiricism demands that causality be traced in each case.

In this methodology, it is necessary to distinguish causes, processes, and effects or manifestations. Although processes may be considered causes in one sense, I conceptualize them for present purposes as changes set in motion when more ultimate cultural and environmental factors are utilized by human societies. I define these ultimate factors as sets of cultural devices and practices and environmental features, which are no more than inert potentials and which may be classified in separable categories until they are activated and interrelated by human behavior. Thus, fire, carrying baskets, and weapons are merely part of the cultural inventory and fishing resources or edible seeds are features of the natural landscape. These have effects on society only when put to use, whereupon they initiate processes that affect the nature of society. Processes such as demographic trends and seasonal aggregation and dispersal of the population may bring about very similar structures of the social groups even though initiated by use of very dissimilar cultural practices in quite unlike environments. In large measure, these processes among simpler societies consist of cultural-ecological adaptations.

At the present stage of investigations, there may be some question of whether we have any cross-cultural types that are truly identical structurally. Detailed analysis discloses tendencies rather than fixed structures. For this reason, the term "model" may be preferable, provided it is understood to indicate a fairly high degree of abstraction, as in the case of Birdsell's models. "Type" perhaps denotes too great a degree of substantive similarity.

A striking illustration of two cases in which very different combinations of causal factors have produced generally similar social structures is provided by a comparison of Lee's !Kung Bushmen and Helm's Dogrib Athapaskans. In each case the minimum social aggregate consists of a core of consanguinal kin together with affinals from other aggregates. My concept that the nuclear family is structurally the irreducible social unit does not imply that it is the isolated independent social unit. To the contrary, among the Shoshoni, Bushmen, Athapaskans, and certain other prefarming societies, several nuclear families that are consanguinally and affinally related generally comprise the irreducible aggregate, for isolated families would ordinarily not be viable. These basic aggregates vary with circumstances and may range from ten to fifty persons, but usually average between twenty and thirty persons. Such small groups necessarily intermarry with one another.

Owing to their fluctuating composition and size, these minimum groups have been designated local bands, microbands, task groups, and camps. Since they have great cohesion, owing to their strong kinship bonds and joint subsistence activities, the term "primary subsistence band" seems to me a useful term for distinguishing them from larger groups or maximum bands.

Because members of primary bands become closely interrelated, kinship ties extend to other such bands. It seems probable, although I am unaware of supporting genealogical evidence, that a network of kinship ties as well as of visiting and cooperation extends to a maximum band—the "regional band" of the Dogrib—of 300 to 400 persons, where they become more diffuse. The equivalent among the Bushmen may be the 350 residents of the Dobe area. These maximum limitations appear to be determined partly by the accessibility of primary bands to one another, partly by distribution of food and water, and partly by bounding deserts or other barriers beyond which contacts are difficult.

Owing to seasonal and often annual changes in the processes that induce nucleation and dispersal, primary bands may associate in varying numbers for varying periods of time, so that intermediate groupings of different sizes and compositions form and dissolve. These processes and their social consequences are similar in an abstract sense among both Bushmen and Athapaskans, although very detailed comparison of marriage patterns and other interband ties, discloses special factors and processes that affect particular features. In certain other areas primary subsistence bands may have strong lineage tendencies.

My basic point is to show that the specific cultural and environmental factors that initiate these processes are very dissimilar. The Bushmen are 80 per cent vegetarians and occupy an environment where plant foods are perennially available, whereas the Dogrib are largely fish and game eaters. Dogrib territories are ten to forty times greater than those of the Bushmen, yet about the same number of primary bands interact in each case. The factors that make this possible are, first, the population density of the Bushmen, which is ten to forty times greater than that of the Dogrib and permits small bands that use only human carriers to maintain contacts with one another over short distances, and, second, the use of canoes and toboggans by the Dogrib, which enables the local bands to traverse enormous distances. In addition, survival in Canada requires clothing, shelters, and devices for taking fish which the Bushmen lack.

In my early efforts to classify and explain band types (1936, 1938), a distinction between causal factors and processes was implied in my stress on the great differences in environmental factors where similar social types, such as the patrilineal band, occurred. As late as 1949, however, the necessary conceptualizations remained unclarified in my paper on the development of early state civilizations, wherein I ventured to call attention to the strikingly similar sequences of social structures and cultural achievements of these states. Because basic research on the development of these civilizations really produced relevant data only after World War II, I inferred that similar cultural manifestations resulted from similar causes, and I took Wittfogel's sweeping generalization about irrigation to be the basic cause in each case. Subsequent research, which Adams (1966) has summarized and interpreted for Mesoamerica and Mesopotamia, has shown that irrigation was definitely an unimportant factor in these two areas, although its role may have been greater elsewhere. In all of these early states, however, similar processes such as those creating interdependencies of local population segments, specialization, stratification, centralization of authority, and others were initiated by a number of factors that have not yet been clearly identified.

In the case of the prefarming societies reported in these conferences, my effort to identify causes has revealed an astonishingly small number of factors. Viewed in terms of their formal and stylistic characteristics, thousands of cultural elements might be listed as causal factors. The provisional list given later is based on function—on whether a society has the means of getting certain kinds of jobs done. It involves such basic categories of activity as food collecting, fishing, hunting, transportation, food preservation and preparation, and, in some areas, clothing and shelter. Some of the categories have been accorded detailed attention in these conferences, but others have been largely ignored. The importance of transportation to interband contacts and activities, which I have suggested in comparing the Bushmen and Dogrib, has been almost wholly neglected, perhaps because it is so obvious. One wonders, however, by what means men got about over the deep snows of glacial-age Europe.

The present conference clearly demonstrates that hunting is not a primary diagnostic characteristic of social types. Hunting is not even a single causal factor. Comparison of societies that do some hunting— and only inhabitants of oceanic islands are nonhunters —indicates that there are many kinds of hunting, each involving different cultural means, distinctive kinds of game, and varied social processes that cause different kinds of societies. Hunting cannot be isolated from other factors, but a comparative study of hunting would have enormous value in indicating the subcategories into which it may be divided.

An empirical approach that extends inquiry from cultural manifestations through processes to ultimate causes may theoretically have great value for reconstructing lines of past evolution. If cultural and environmental factors can be reduced to a limited number of basic functional categories, we should be able within the limitations of prehistoric identification of these factors to infer the nature of the society. Thus the inherent difficulty of using ethnographic models, especially holistic models, to interpret prehistoric materials will be avoided. This matter has properly concerned many persons, such as Freeman, L. R. Binford, S. R. Binford, Sackett, Deetz, and others. Although analysis starts with cultural manifestations, it does not infer causality by correlating such manifestations, as in "factor analysis" (for example, Sawyer and Levine, 1966), and it does not project ethnographic types backward as hypothetical evolutionary stages. So far as my method is distinctive, it might be designated "causal factor identification" or "causal factor determination."

FACTOR DETERMINATION

The effects of the cultural factors listed below are vividly suggested if we can imagine what human societies would be like if any were absent. The comparison of men and apes made subsequently discloses sharp contrasts between cultural and noncultural beings, but what would human societies be like if they lacked human carrying devices, means of processing or storing food, or devices for obtaining animals that may run, fly, or swim away?

All recent societies have means of collecting vegetable foods, hunting, fishing, transporting and preparing food. So far as these factors are concerned, local differences must be ascribed to environmental variables. But certain environments have entailed additional factors. Imagine, then, the Eskimo without dog sleds, skin boats, and special apparatus for marine hunting and fishing, the Northwest Coast without sea-going canoes and elaborate techniques for fishing and hunting sea mammals, the northern Athapaskans without canoes and toboggans, any peoples of the extreme north without adequate shelter and clothing, or desert dwellers without means of transporting water. (One case of the last has been reported in Mexico.) Food preservation and storage is necessary when there are seasons with no vegetable growth, when game migrates away or fish runs cease. In tropical and subtropical latitudes, preservation and storage may not be necessary if, as Lee has shown for the Bushmen and Woodburn for the Hadza, foraging is possible perennially. This crucial matter, however, has been largely ignored.

A related problem is how much processing is necessary to utilize all possible resources. This involves not only the role of cooking and other processing of vegetable foods, but the very important matter of meat eating. Did man's physiology undergo evolutionary changes as he became a carnivore? Did fire, which apparently appeared after meat eating, help make spoiled meats digestible?

In my list, large game hunting is a single factor because it includes ways of taking large, mobile animals. Closer scrutiny of hunting might warrant several major subcategories based especially on the nature of the game. In the Great Basin, deer were ambushed or pursued by relays of hunters, mountain sheep were taken with the help of dogs in the high peaks, and antelope were driven by men, women, and children into enclosures. Although any of these animals might be taken by a single hunter, each of the more productive hunts involved a different kind of cooperation. An individual lucky enough to wound a deer might have to trail it for hours or days before it died.

Without making a detailed comparative study of hunting, I treat this category with considerable misgivings. Quantification of the yield of hunting in comparison with food collecting has shown that it is astonishingly small—perhaps 30 per cent of the food—except in higher latitudes. Intimate knowledge of the habits and habitats of game of different kinds—the size, migratory patterns, extent of herding, and reactions to human beings—as well as of the cultural devices available for hunting are also necessary. The lone Hadza hunter armed only with a bow and arrow must have been at some disadvantage in confronting an African buffalo or rhino. What of lower Paleolithic hunters whose artifacts include only hand axes and perhaps bolas? Did they construct pitfalls large enough for elephants, confront rhinos with bolas or throwing sticks, or bring down fleet antelope with untipped wooden spears? Did they hunt mainly the young of these animals or seek smaller species? Did they scavenge?

The cultural-ecological factors with which we are concerned obviously cannot be divorced from environmental, historical, and biological factors, which may constitute preconditions for their operation. These other factors are also reducible to a few basic categories, and they require only brief mention.

BIOLOGICAL FACTORS

Contrary to the culturological assumption that evolution must not be reduced to biological factors, the latter cannot be ignored, first, because certain fundamental characteristics of human beings changed during cultural evolution and, second, because they are preconditions of all modern cultures.

In the course of biological evolution, the early hominids acquired bipedalism, which enormously extended their range as compared with that of their quadrupedal ancestors. At a very early time, they also became meat eaters, which vastly increased their subsistence potentials and may have been a precondition of living in northern climates. The period of dependency of the immature hominid became greatly lengthened, thus strengthening mother-child bonds but also restricting women's activities. In ethnographic cases, where males have the complementary function of hunting, women's roles in the nuclear family became more specialized and restrictive.

Enlargement of the brain and all that this implies have become distinctive human characteristics, but they do not explain any particular features of culture. It might be said that, to the contrary, the vast human adaptability they permit is basic to the increasing range of cultural variations.

CULTURAL FACTORS

The subsequent list of cultural factors is drawn from ethnographic cases, and it is intended to explore the possibilities of a functional classification of causal factors. It is remarkable that so many of these factors are present where they are useful. All societies have some means of collecting, hunting, preparing, and transporting foods, and all that occupy regions of seasonal shortages have some means of storing foods. All that live in winter climates have adequate clothing and shelter. Those which occupy areas where water craft expedite fishing and transportation have canoes, skin vessels, or simple balsa rafts. This is not to say that all hunting and gathering societies have achieved maximum efficiency in the exploitation of their environments, but their knowledge of resources and cultural devices is extraordinarily extensive. Absence of certain factors in marginal areas—Australia and the extreme south of Africa and of South America—is expectable, since some late inventions did not diffuse to all societies. Some absences, therefore, may have made a greater difference than has been noted. But, unless the effect of each factor is carefully analyzed, we could be misled.

Could the Australians have hunted marsupials more effectively with bows and arrows? Even if true, was their hunting success primarily limited by the quantity of game? Are there major fisheries that remained unexploited for lack of canoes and fishing gear? Perhaps, but the Chilean archipelago, which has been cited as backward for want of diffused culture traits, simply had very minor marine resources. Could populations have increased in certain areas had the people stored a maximum amount of food when it was available? This is a complicated question, for it involves factors other than subsistence, but it seems likely that what Birdsell calls the "equilibrium system" rather than nutrition alone controlled the population density.

Another aspect of the question of maximum use of the environment is whether these societies might, without any changes in environment or improved cultural devices, have augmented their subsistence, sustained larger populations, and nucleated in greater aggregates, if they had been more industrious. If food getting required only one-third to one-half the total time, an increase of food would seem possible. I think, however, that Sahlins's picture of "affluent" hunters and gatherers is very unrealistic. Any abundance during brief periods dwindled until, as in the case of the Shoshoni, it ended in near starvation before new supplies became available. When the necessary food trek began, travel in temperatures over 100° away from water sources while carrying children, gear, and water was a thoroughly unpleasant necessity. Again, one must conclude with Birdsell that the equilibrium of factors maintained a population at fairly constant levels over periods of time. Any local or temporary abundance of foods could not be laid up to ensure more abundant nutrition throughout the whole year or a succession of years to increase the population.

Distinctions made in the following list are handicapped by the absence of unambiguous subsistence terms. *Foraging* denotes eating foods as they are gathered, and it is an activity that man shares with many other animals. *Food extraction* has been employed to designate utilization of natural resources and *food production* for use of plant and animal domesticates. *Food gathering* or *food collecting* are traditional terms for extraction of vegetable foods, larvae, and other small items, but they do not imply what is done with the food collected. An additional term such as *food storing* could be used to indicate that the foods are transported to another locality, sometimes to a central encampment, where they are stored to provide sustenance for varying lengths of time. *Food scavenging* is a useful concept if delimited to the consumption of animals that have been killed by predators, crippled, accidentally entrapped, or stranded, as in the case of whales. Scavenging does not involve the question of whether hominids, like vultures, ate putrescent meat. There are many ethnographic reports of scavenging, although *hunting* implies the killing of live animals.

1. *Foraging.* If the only foods eaten are those foraged, but not hunted or stored, occupation of areas of cold winters must have been rare or impossible. Subsistence, moreover, would not differ greatly from that of the apes, except in the larger area covered by bipedal animals.

2. *Collecting.* Many foods, such as fruits, nuts, shellfish, eggs, insects, and larvae were eaten as they were gathered, that is, foraged, although they were obtained in greater quantity by means of various cultural devices, for example, containers, digging sticks, climbing rings, poles, and others. All societies carried on this activity by one means or another.

Assembling food at a central point requires transportation, which can be considered a separate factor. If storage involves accumulation of more than enough for immediate needs, and especially enough for long periods, it requires special preparation. Storage is not a universal factor and it is therefore listed separately.

3. *Small game hunting.* This category is distinguished from large game hunting because it does not always require men to absent themselves from their band for arduous and extensive cooperative efforts. Small game such as rodents, rabbits, hares, small species of ungulates, marsupials and mammals, monkeys, various reptiles, and birds are taken by an extraordinary variety of traps, nets, snares, pitfalls, deadfalls, throwing sticks, spears, arrows, blowguns, bird lime, and other devices more often than by methods used for large, far-ranging mammals. To the extent that hunters did not have to leave their bands for long periods, this factor supplemented food collecting.

Because most societies had reasonably effective means of hunting small game, variation in the effects of this factor depended more upon the nature and abundance of game than on culture. It was probably of major importance in northern latitudes where small game could be a major source of food during the winters. Traplines exploited for a commercial market, however, may have very different effects than native trapping and do not fall under "small game hunting."

4. *Large game hunting.* This category is distinguished from the last in its reference to hunting large, herbivorous, fairly mobile, terrestrial animals, whose means of self-protection present serious problems.

These animals are either fleet, have tough hides, or make formidable foes. Hunting them by digging pitfalls or preparing ambushes, surrounds, and pursuits required great effort and entailed cooperation as well as endurance. Confrontation of such animals as rhinos and elephants also required caution.

The Upper Paleolithic seems to have marked a climax in hunting. Many animals, including now-extinct giant species, were taken with stone-tipped spears and atlatls and probably by other means. How large animals were killed in lower Paleolithic times is perplexing, for use of wooden spears or any other means is inferential. Yet Isaac describes an Acheulian site in East Africa containing bones of elephants, rhinos, and hippos. Early Paleolithic stone industries include choppers or fist hatchets, and later traditions include flake tools that suggest skin working, but nothing indicates weapons for killing or wounding from a distance. The use of bolas by men on foot to entangle large, tough-skinned mammals until they were killed with wooden spears or stones would seem to be a difficult feat. To excavate a pitfall large enough for any of these animals would be a prodigious task. It will be interesting to learn how often a Hadza hunter armed only with a bow could seriously wound a rhino or elephant.

Other possible methods were, as Isaac suggests, poisoning water holes, or, to use ethnographic analogies, drives with fire over cliffs or into bogs. Possibly, like some of the Congo Negritoes, elephants could be induced to impale themselves on spears, although this hardly seems to commend itself as a routine procedure.

A simple method of taking these large species would be to hunt only the young or crippled stragglers. Still simpler would be scavenging.

5. *Aquatic hunting.* In many areas water mammals such as whales, seals, walrus, otter, dugongs, and others were a fairly important subsistence resource, and the local societies seem always to have possessed some effective means of taking them, such as spears, harpoons, arrows, and various accessories. Since these animals are riverine or marine, some kind of water craft were generally used to hunt and transport them. Their importance to social structures is similar to that of large game hunting in that they required much time, effort, and cooperation between males. Most areas of aquatic hunting, however, were also major fishing areas.

6. *Fishing.* This category is enormously variable, for it includes cases in which fishing was so unimportant as to be a type of food collecting and other cases in which its effect was comparable to aquatic mammal hunting. Except for certain coastal and island areas, most major fisheries were riverine and required traps, weirs, baskets, and nets as well as canoes. Where fishing was of major importance, a high degree of

social cooperation was required. Even where fishing was only an important supplement to other subsistence, as in the Amazon, there was considerable cooperation in use of poisons, canoes, and other methods.

There may be areas of rich fisheries that were unexploited for want of canoes, nets, hooks, or other devices, but simple societies seem to have made excellent use of their resources by one means or another. Fish drugs, for example, are very widely distributed, and in South America alone several hundred different plants are used for this purpose.

7. *Transportational devices.* The importance of transportation has been mentioned in connection with accumulating and storing foods at some central point. It is also essential for transporting children and basic gear as a society moves about. Ethnographically, there are four subcategories of transportation.

a. Human carriers. All societies have some means of carrying foods, children, and various impedimenta. These devices, though highly varied, are generally limited in efficiency by human strength.

b. Sleds and toboggans. Where snow provides suitable surfaces, human beings can pull greater loads than they can carry. Dog traction adds further to the transportational potentials. It seems certain that the great territorial range of societies in the far north were a function of such transportation, complemented by water craft in the summer. It should also offset the need for infanticide, in which case Eskimo infanticide was practiced for reasons other than women's limitations on carrying children (see Balikci, 1964).

c. Water craft. Umiaks, kayaks, bark or dugout canoes, and balsa rafts give an enormous advantage in such subsistence activities as fishing, aquatic hunting, and even gathering wild rice, and they also increase transportational potentials. Except for certain marginal areas, such as Tierra del Fuego and parts of Australia, where better use might have been made of water craft, few societies lacked some kind of water transportation adequate to their needs.

The relatively high population density of coastal areas is obviously correlated with the combined land, sea, and littoral resources, but these areas usually have canoes which facilitate subsistence activities and permit concentration in large, permanent communities. In the Amazon, communities increased in size after steel axes enabled the people to range farther from the villages for foods.

d. Dog traction and packing. Use of dogs is probably comparatively recent, and it has limited distribution. The dog sled is certainly a major factor in the enormous range of some of the arctic societies and therefore also a factor in permitting large periodic aggregations. The dog-drawn travois and dog packing of the Plains were also of considerable value. Lowie (1963, p. 42) cites Coronado that dogs could draw 35 to 50 pounds on travois.

8. *Food preparation.* Many methods of treating vegetable and perhaps animal products extend the number of foods beyond that of precultural animals.

a. Mechanical processing. Certain hard-shell seeds and nuts must be opened before eating, but this can be accomplished with crude stones nearly as well as with metates and mortars. Greater efficiency may have increased leisure time rather than the amount of food. Other processing, such as winnowing seeds or cutting raw meat presents no problem, and stone-cutting tools have great antiquity.

b. Poison extraction. Some foods, such as acorns in California and elsewhere and the cycad of Australia, are made edible by extracting harmful ingredients. Domesticated manioc (*Manihot utillisima*) is elaborately treated with the tipití to remove the prussic acid, but Goldman states (1948, p. 772) that the acid readily boils off or disappears with drying or soaking in water. The Great Basin staple, pine nuts (*Pinus edulis* and *P. monophyla*), may be eaten raw, but roasting seems to change if not remove much of the resin.

c. Cooking. Although many fruits, greens, buds, and nuts require no treatment, probably the majority of foods, including roots, seeds, fish, and game, were cooked when necessary, and sometimes when not necessary. In addition to tenderizing foods, cooking may change deleterious chemicals and perhaps kills bacteria in overripe meat. If, however, the use of fire was not general until the second interstadial period (Clark and Piggott, 1965, p. 49), perhaps at about the first appearance of *Homo sapiens,* the earlier species of *H. erectus,* avoided poisonous plants and consumed meats raw. In this case the conversion to a meat diet was accomplished without the aid of cooking.

All ethnographic cases have some means of cooking foods of all kinds—roasting on coals or in earth ovens, boiling in pots or with hot stones in containers of hide, basketry, bark, wood, etc., broiling over coals or on babracots, and others. Cooking, therefore, is another universal or constant factor.

9. *Food preservation and storage.* It has been noted that certain tribes in low latitudes do not preserve or store foods—for example, the Bushmen and Hadza—because vegetable resources can be obtained at any time. Storage is difficult in tropical areas because of heat and humidity, but farming societies were able to preserve certain foods. In higher latitudes, however, where preservation and storage of foods are essential during certain seasons, all societies have appropriate techniques.

This factor has many subcategories: protection of seeds against moisture and marauding animals, drying and smoking flesh, and preservative mixtures such as pemmican in which the meat is protected by adding fat.

10. *Shelter and clothing.* Special factors are necessary to survive in certain environments. These include for cold climates adequate clothing and footgear, which the Clactonian stone flake industry shows were probably made by the second interstadial period of Europe, perhaps fire which appeared about the same time, and possibly means of travel on deep snow of which we have evidence only from ethnographic sources. Clothing and shelters were less imperative in warm climates, although all known societies improvised temporary lean-tos and in some of the tropics protected the body against insects with capes or with grease.

ENVIRONMENTAL FACTORS

Environmental features are significant in terms of their functional importance to ecological adaptations rather than their intrinsic properties such as climate, topography, or biota; for dissimilar environments may support somewhat similar societies if exploited in certain ways.

First, there are environmental potentials which, if exploited by appropriate cultural devices, determine the overall population density.

Second, there are factors which affect the nucleation of social segments. Natural barriers may separate major population groups and sometimes fairly small groups. Distribution of foods, as along shorelines, rivers, or lakes, and localization of water may entail special kinds of nucleation. Transportational devices other than human carriers will profoundly affect nucleation in areas where these can be used.

Third, the nature of the flora and fauna requires various kinds of subsistence activities, including certain patterns of cooperation and sharing.

Fourth, subsistence in some zones necessitates no food storing, whereas in others, especially in hard winter climates, it is impossible without considerable storage and methods of preservation. Accessories, such as clothing, shelters, and possibly fire, are also required by winter climates.

CULTURAL-HISTORICAL FACTORS

Perhaps 90 per cent of any tribal cultural inventory including subsistence devices is borrowed. Whether borrowed or locally innovated, the important consideration is the function of cultural features of different kinds to varying kinds of social aggregates. Exploitative devices are readily borrowed if they are useful. Restrictive marriage institutions, such as clans and moieties, will ordinarily be impossible among small, widely separate primary groups or bands whose choice of marriage partners is already limited. Clans, although highly developed in the Southwest and part of the Plains, did not spread to the sparsely populated Great Basin or the Mackenzie River drainage. Among societies of sparse population, the only institutions pertaining to aggregates larger than the subsistence bands were ceremonialism, including initiation rites in some areas, and games, contests, and dances that became functional only when the larger group was assembled.

On the other hand, large permanent communites or strongly integrated bands or tribes permitted complex social and ritual elaboration, as on the Northwest Coast or the Plains. It is of historical interest but minor importance functionally whether the clans, moieties, social stratification, and potlatches of the Northwest Coast and the strong chieftanship, sun dance, war patterns, and proliferation of associations of the Plains were borrowed from elsewhere or developed locally. These supra-kin-level institutions were possible only if ecological preconditions existed, although they became functionally intertwined with subsistence activities.

EVOLUTIONARY FACTORS AND PROCESSES

Noncultural Adaptations

The effects of cultural-ecological factors becomes most readily apparent when projected against the noncultural adaptations of certain of the primates. The most instructive primates are the chimpanzees, gorillas, and baboons, for they have received greatest attention and are most similar to hominids in several respects. These primates have greatest body size, dimorphism, perennial sexuality, some degree of terrestriality, a varied subsistence basis mainly within the range of plant foods, and high adaptability. Their behavior discloses patterns within the limits of these biological potentials, and it is not therefore a genetically determined archetype from which hominid behavior was necessarily derived. It represents patterns of the ancestors of hominids only to the extent that ecological adaptations may be assumed to have been similar.

1. *Subsistence.* These primates are herbivorous, except that some consume small insects and mammals (DeVore, 1963, p.32) and the chacma baboons eat shellfish, crabs, birds' eggs, and young birds (Hall, 1963, pp. 6-18). Goodall reported only three occasions during eighteen months when chimpanzees scavenged meat (1963, p. 46). Food is

found predominantly in trees—90 per cent among the chimpanzees (Goodall, 1963, p. 40)—which limits subsistence areas to stands of appropriate trees. Lacking transportation and storage devices, these foragers do not accumulate surpluses to establish even temporary encampments. There is no food sharing, even between mothers and offspring—which is true of herbivores generally in contrast to carnivores—and consequently no cooperation or dependencies based on subsistence activities.

2. *Territoriality.* Evidence on territorality is conflicting, partly, I suspect, because of the meaning attached to the term. Habitual use of a delimited territory and familiarity with the members of one's own troop apparently inhibit free association with strangers within the same species. In addition, as Schaller (1963, p. 27) clearly states of gorillas, the territory of each troop is separated from that of other troops by uninhabitable areas. Unequal concentrations of resources, therefore, would predispose any species to a degree of troop isolation. Owing to natural vicissitudes of troop expansion and contraction, however, there would be budding off in some cases and amalgamation in others.

The tendency toward territoriality is explainable by the ecological adaptations of various types of animals rather than by some genetically determined possessiveness which Ardrey in sensational articles in *Life* (1966a, 1966b) represents as the basis of conflict in man. Grazing herbivores of many species intermingled freely, and their herds are limited only by the extent of fodder. They defend themselves against predators rather than other herbivores. Male competition for estrous females is irrelevant to territoriality. Carnivorous predators, on the other hand, defend their kill and, unlike herbivores, share it. If game is locally scarce, they may come into competition with other groups of their species.

3. *Group and territory size.* Ape troops vary in size with population density, for the home range of these quadrupeds is only a fraction of that of human beings. To travel the length and breadth of a troop's territory would require a minimum trip of about three miles and rarely as much as nine miles.

Baboon troops are reported to occupy two to fifteen square miles (DeVore and Hall, 1965); gorillas, ten to fifteen (Schaller, 1965); and chimpanzees six to twenty (Goodall, 1965).

Gorilla troop size has been reported at two to thirty individuals (Schaller, 1965); chimpanzees at twenty to thirty (Reynolds, 1963); and baboons, thirteen to 185 at Amboseli (DeVore and Washburn, 1963); and twelve to 750 in Ethiopia (Kummer and Kurt, 1963).

4. *Group composition.* Conflicting data on group composition probably reflect differences among troops observed rather than errors of re-

porting; although distinction between troops may be difficult in densely populated areas and identification of individual members requires
familiarity with the group. In addition, troops on game reserves such as
that adjoining Nairobi, which is visited by hundreds of tourists daily,
are not truly in a state of nature.

There is unanimity that mature males and females do not form
permanent attachment, orangs possibly excepted. Male dominance
and dimorphism are strong among the more terrestrial primates,
which may be a function of sexual competition for the females and of
the need to protect the troop against predators rather than against
other troops. Whether a troop consists of a single dominant male and
several females and immature animals, whether it includes several
"harems," or whether there is a hierarchy of dominance, or pecking
order, seems to vary with the troops observed. Comparable male
dominance cannot be assumed for all hominid societies, because sexual
roles are determined more by cultural functions than by physical
strength, and the female reproductive functions preclude some activities women might otherwise carry out.

EFFECTS OF CULTURAL FACTORS

The general effects of cultural factors added to biological potentials
bring cultural-ecological adaptations into sharp focus. Human bipeds
may range at least twenty to thirty miles, and with certain transportation devices they may cover several hundred miles. Means of
collecting, hunting, transporting, and preparing foods vastly augment
man's subsistence basis. Primary human subsistence groups are little
larger than those of the apes, but specialized functions in subsistence
and child rearing have set lower limits on social groups, while exploitation of a wider environment and the kind of transportation have
set upper limits. In all ethnographic cases, cultural complementarity is
the basis of the nuclear family, and, because this involves marriage
prosciptions and preferences, kinship relations extend from one minimal or primary group to another, their nature being determined by
ecological adaptations and their limits by the size of the maximum
group.

Cultural devices have also permitted occupation of higher latitudes,
which nonhominids and early hominids probably could occupy only
during warm interstadial periods (see Carpenter, 1942, pp. 303-311).

In analyzing the various social responses to ecological factors, it is
convenient to start with the irreducible social unit, the family, although
social evolution almost certainly began with such larger aggregates as a
prehominid troop. Since the nuclear family is the focal point of all
kinship analysis, it is important to ascertain the factors that underlie it.

1. *The nuclear family.* Although a nuclear family—a minimal unit of father, mother, and children—is basic to all ethnographic cases, it may not have existed in early periods. The family among hunters and gatherers is based on strong sexual complementarity, men being primarily hunters and women carriers of wood and water, seed collectors, camp keepers, and child tenders. Unproductive as hunting may be in certain areas, it nonetheless gives men a distinctive and important subsistence role and was presumably the principal factor that created the nuclear family. If the early hominids were not hunters, their family may have been matrifocal in that it consisted of females and immature offspring. Food collecting, as far as we know, does not create a sexual division of labor, for it is carried out by both sexes in the same way.

Hunting of large game is clearly implied by Upper Paleolithic sites in Europe, and it was undoubtedly the special task of men, wherein masculine strength was probably less important than hunting devices and the considerable time spent away from the family. Fishing and aquatic hunting would have similar effects. Whether comparable specialization by the male was required to obtain large game during the Lower Paleolithic is wholly conjectural, for hunting methods are unknown. Scavenging, if practiced, probably did not require special masculine activities, while hunting small animals cannot have imposed activities on men similar to those of large game hunting. Net hunting of rabbits among the Great Basin people, for example, involved women and children along with men.

Although it is now impossible to date the appearance of the nuclear family, the assumption that it is based on cultural complementarity rather than on some inherent or "natural" tendency means that it may be weakened. This is happening today, especially in certain economically depressed segments of society where males form such loose and transient unions with females that the stable social unit is the women and children, which has been designated the "matrifocal family." Sexual complementarity has also been decreasing for many reasons in nuclear families of all segments of Western society.

2. *The minimum or primary band.* Completely isolated nuclear families are very exceptional, for clusters of several families provide greater security. This symposium has made it strikingly clear, however, that many of the larger aggregates, which were formerly designated bands, are composed of smaller groups and sometimes of intermediate but very fluid groups. Since relations that begin with the nuclear family are of major importance to the minimum group, even though they extend beyond it, it is convenient to consider these first. Variations are clearly related to the major factors previously discussed, although space prevents adequate analysis of some of the problems raised by comparisons of marriage and kinship systems.

Except for those areas of abundant subsistence, special transportation, and permanent villages, the minimum group as exemplified by Australians, Athapaskans, Bushmen, Hadza, Western Shoshoni, and probably many others is very close to Birdsell's model of 25 persons, although there is great seasonal variation and change over periods of years. (The patrilineal band discussed below is, however, somewhat larger.) This approximate size is maintained, despite population densities that range from one person to one or two square miles to one per forty or fifty square miles, because of the effect of transportational devices other than human carriers in some areas and because groups may be restricted in their range in other areas, concentrating, for example, near water or special resources.

I have designated these "primary bands" because they are connected most closely with subsistence, but other terms such as "special task groups" have been used.

Although the kinship structure of primary bands depends upon several factors, all consist of closely related families. Food collecting can rarely be cooperative, but, as Rose points out in the case of Australia, child tending becomes a particularly important function. In the case of hunters, cooperation by a number of men is common, and the kill is ordinarily shared.

Multifamily primary bands. Owing to expectable fluctuations in the size of primary bands, a strongly patterned cultural ideal of band composition would be difficult to maintain, except where factors making for a unilineal tendency become reinforced by myths or other fictions of descent. Composition of the primary band therefore varies, although its core is a number of intermarried families.

Among the Western Shoshoni, the primary group consisted of several families related through multiple marriages—brother and sister to sister and brother or brothers to sisters—and reinforced by the levirate and sororate. Because members of such small clusters of families soon become consanguinally as well as affinally interrelated, these clusters were interlinked through a network of marriages that extended territorially to the limits of natural barriers. These local groups were not, as Service believes (1962), patrilocal bands, a fact supported by unpublished ethnohistorical data (Steward, 1953). In southern Nevada and the Death Valley area, the lower altitudes, great aridity, sparse resources, and widely spaced springs isolated Southern Paiute groups to the degree of restricting the marriage network (Steward, 1938), and the same pattern seems to have prevailed among the Southern Paiute of Utah (Kelly, 1964).

The primary unit or band is very similar in composition among the northern Athapaskans. There has been semantic confusion regarding my statement (1936) that these bands could marry endogamously because they consisted of unrelated families. These bands contrast to patrilineages in that each had some consanguinally unrelated families. This is obviously true of Morice's large bands, which seem to be the same as Helm's "regional bands," and it is also true of Helm's "local bands," according to her genealogies. In the two Dogrib bands described, many families were related consanguinally through parents and children and through siblings, but there were also members related only affinally. After marriage all band members became affinals but not all were consanguines. Presumably, many of the spouses were drawn from other local bands. Unlike the Shoshoni, however, there were few cases of multiple marriage ties between two families.

From Helm's data I gather that trapping and fishing are far more important to the local band than I had previously recognized. In modern times, at least, this apparently affected postmarital residence in unpredictable ways, for siblings of both sexes often remained with their parents' group, although consanguinal barriers would force many to marry elsewhere. Group composition among the Bushmen (Lee, 1965) seems also to be based on multiple marriage between families that extended throughout the maximum band of 430 persons. Further comparisons of group composition would require extended genealogical comparisons; but Australia has special interest.

If the primary Australian band is only some 25 to 40 persons and these bands are widely separated in arid areas, the imposition of exogamous clans and moieties might restrict the number of potential marriage partners to an impossible extent. Some of the marriage classes or sections may historically be a combination of patrilineal and matrilineal moieties. Viewed in terms of generations, this would place individuals of alternate generations in the same class. If, however, the tendency toward so-called gerontocracy is included and consanguinity is redefined, enough marriages are possible, especially between widely differing age groups. A possible means of clarifying this situation is the use of algebraic descriptions of marriage systems (for example, Reid, 1967).

Lineage-based bands. The primary band has undoubtedly been a lineage when stochastically predictable circumstances have produced only sons or daughters for two generations, but this implies no ideal pattern. In other cases specific factors may create tendencies toward a lineage, but this too does not become fixed. Woodburn describes the Hadza of Tanzania as matrilineal and matrilocal, with qualifications; the bands, which average eighteen persons and are attached to larger encampments up to a hundred persons, are highly unstable. A dominance of food collecting over hunting, wherein less than half the men hunt and these do so individually and ineffectively, may be a partial explanation.

Patrilineal bands. This is a more clear-cut type, and although my earlier formulation of the factors producing it (1936) have been doubted by some persons, others, including Birdsell, who takes his model from Australia, and Williams, on the basis of the Birhor, have made it the general model of all food hunters and collectors. There are several possible sources of confusion about the patrilineal band.

First, the factor of hunting may have lost importance with the reduction of game in the last four or five decades. Schapera (1926, 1930) and the sources on which he based his description of the Bushmen may have been correct for an earlier period, although, as Lee (1965) notes, the quantity of game in the area has decreased and Bantu have brought herds into a portion of the !Kung Bushman territory. The same is doubtless true of many areas, although assumptions about the game population must be made cautiously. It has recently been estimated that the total deer population of the United States today is greater than in aboriginal times, although its distribution is not the same, whereas bison now number but a fraction of that of pre-Columbian times.

Second, during early periods of ethnographic exploration many writers undoubtedly took structural types found in limited regions to be representative of large areas or continents. This does not necessarily invalidate what they observed, but it is expectable that in a continent as varied as Australia Radcliffe-Brown's "horde" would not occur everywhere.

Third, where the patrilineal band is reported it seems too large for a patrilineage based on known genealogy. If ancestry were not known beyond five generations, a group of twenty-five or thirty persons might continue to practice exogamy but their patrilineal consanguinity would become untraceable. These bands, however, are reported at thirty to 150 persons. In the absence of a strong genealogical sense, the fiction of relationship between all members could be perpetuated by myths of descent, which I believe were present among all the patrilineal bands previously described (Steward, 1936). In this case we can accept as descriptive of a strong tendency the accounts of Gusinde (1931-39; also Baer and Schitz, 1965) for the Ona, Radcliffe-Brown (1931) for at least some Australians, Schebesta (1929, 1931) for the Congo and Malayan Negritoes, Roth (1890) for the Tasmanians, and Strong (1929) for the southern California Shoshoneans.

The importance of the hunter's familiarity with his country is questioned by Williams on the basis of the Birhor of India, who have patrilineal bands. The Birhor, however, are very distinctive in that they mainly hunt hares by means of nets for trade to neighboring peoples for rice. The Shoshoni hunt rabbits in the same way and need only to know where the animals are abundant. Unlike the Birhor, who were not self-sufficient in subsistence, the Shoshoni had to be familiar with their terrain to obtain other foods.

The factors that explain the patrilineal band are more environmental than technological. Such bands occur where there are large, highly mobile animals that do not migrate long distances, where hunting exceeds collecting in effort and sometimes in quantity, where population is sparse, and where transportation is limited to human carriers. It may have other preconditions and causes. This structure is the result of a strong tendency but, for reasons previously particularized (Steward, 1936) not an unalterable pattern.

The Indians of the Plains exhibit the effects of contrasting factors. The vast bison herds made food collecting secondary, the nature of the animals was such that highly coordinated and even policed hunts were carried out by large numbers of men, and the dog travois and packing supplemented human carriers.

3. *The maximum band.* This is the group of maximum social interaction, which Birdsell (1953) designates the "dialectical tribe" and which rarely exceeds 500 persons. Although such groups may be somewhat integrated through subsistence activities, they are based principally on similar dialect, intermarriage, visiting, and other social interactions and, unlike permanent communities, are not strongly structured and rarely have leaders of any importance. The social, cultural, and dialectical frontiers of such bands may be delimited by distances within which people can associate or by such barriers as deserts, lakes, and mountain ranges. Devices for snow travel in northern latitudes and greater resource density in lower latitudes are factors that permit communications within the bands.

Not all maximum bands, however, conform to the model of the dialectical tribe. Owing to unpredictability of resources, the annual subsistence trek among the Western Shoshoni (Steward, 1938) and the Alacaluf of the Chilean archipelago (Bird, 1946) brings family clusters into association with different clusters from year to year. The larger network of social interaction, therefore, was a series of intermarriages that extended over hundreds of miles.

Territoriality and warfare. There have been many contentions that primitive bands own territories or resources and fight to protect them. Although I cannot assert that this is never the case, it is probably very uncommon. First, the primary groups that comprise the larger maximum bands intermarry, amalgamate if they are too small, or split off if too large. Second, in the cases reported here, there is no more than a tendency for primary groups to utilize special areas. Third, most so-called "warfare" among such societies is no more than revenge for alleged witchcraft or continued interfamily feuds. Fourth, collecting is the main resource in most areas, but I know of no reported defense of seed areas. Primary bands did not fight one another, and it is difficult to see how a maximum band could assemble its manpower to defend its territory against another band or why it should do so. It is true that durian trees, eagle nests, and a few other specific resources were sometimes individually claimed, but how they were defended by a person miles away has not been made clear.

Defense of the hunting territories of patrilineal bands has also been claimed, but this too is open to question. Slain animals are owned by the individual or group of hunters. Fishing weirs, dams, and other constructions are always owned by their builders, and the same is doubtless true of pitfalls, blinds, corrals, and the like. Whether a band defended live game within a territory against other bands with which it intermarried deserves re-examination.

Ethnographic and archeological models. An ethnographic model based on dialect, stylistic features, value systems, corporate limits, jural principles, and ritual patterns is quite useless and unnecessary for archeology. The starting point is to compare the special-purpose encampment of a primary band with a prehistoric site where the same factors can be inferred. Larger temporary encampments of ethnographic cases are more difficult to equate with archeological sites, for non-ecological factors may have operated. But where the ethnographic and archeological sites are reasonably permanent, factor determination of the pre-conditions of such sites is possible. Sackett has noted that Upper Paleolithic sites seem generally to represent more permanent, multipurpose habitations than Mousterian sites which lack evidence of the full hunting complex and has suggested that the functional nature of hunting and fishing in the Upper Paleolithic may have been comparable to that of the Northwest Coast. If the Upper Paleolithic people had some of the transportational devices known among modern Arctic societies, nucleation of populations would have been easier.

As for Sackett's question about the kind of future Paleolithic research needed, I suggest that in addition to information on the locations and on the depth and artifact content of sites, it is important to estimate the relative quantities of fish and game, to speculate about the kinds of social activities that were required in hunting both mature and immature animals of different species with the methods that may have been used, and to attempt to relate the purpose and permanence of the site to microenvironments of different resources.

BIBLIOGRAPHY

ADAMS, ROBERT MCC.
1966. *The Evolution of Urban Society: Early Mesopotamia and Prehispanic Mexico*. Chicago: Aldine Publishing Company.

ARDREY, ROBERT
1966a. "The Basic Drive—for Territory." *Life*, 61(9): 40-59.
1966b. "Man, the Territorial Animal." *Life*, 61(10): 50-59.

BAER, G., and C. A. SCHITZ
1965. "On the Social Organization of the Ona (Selk'nam)." *Journal de la Société des Américanistes* (Paris) (n.s.), 54: 23-29.

BALIKCI, ASEN
1964. *Development of Basic Socio-Economic Units in Two Eskimo Communities*. Bulletin of the National Museum of Canada, anthropological series, no. 202.

BIRD, JUNIUS
1946. "The Alacaluf." In J. H. Steward (Ed.), *Handbook of South American Indians*, vol. 1: *The Marginal Tribes*. Bureau of American Ethnology Bulletin, 143(1): 55-79.

BIRDSELL, J. B.
1953. "Some Environmental and Cultural Factors Influencing the Structure of Australian Aboriginal Populations." *American Naturalist*, 87(834): 171-207.

CARPENTER, CLARENCE R.
1942. "Characteristics of Social Behavior in Non-Human Primates." *Transactions of the New York Academy of Sciences*, series 2, 4: 248-58.

CLARK, J. GRAHAM D., and STUART PIGGOTT
1965. *Prehistoric Societies*. New York: Alfred A. Knopf.

DEVORE, IRVEN
1963. "A Comparison of the Ecology and Behavior of Monkeys and Apes." In S. L. Washburn (Ed.), *Classification of Human Evolution*. Chicago: Aldine Publishing Company.

DEVORE, IRVEN, and K. R. L. HALL
1965. "Baboon Ecology." In I. DeVore (Ed.), *Primate Behavior*. New York: Holt, Rinehart and Winston.

DEVORE, IRVEN, and SHERWOOD L. WASHBURN
1963. "Baboon Ecology and Human Evolution." In F. C. Howell and F. Bourlière (Eds.), *African Ecology and Human Evolution*. Chicago: Aldine Publishing Company.

GOLDMAN, IRVING
1948. "Tribes of the Uaupes-Caueta Region." In J. H. Steward (Ed.), *Handbook of South American Indians*, vol. 3: *The Tropical Forest Tribes*. Bureau of American Ethnology Bulletin 143(3): 763-98.

GOODALL, JANE
1963. "Feeding Behavior of Wild Chimpanzees: A Preliminary Report." In *The Primates: Proceedings of the Symposium Held on 12th-14th April 1962*. Zoological Society of London, *Symposia*, 10.

1965. "Chimpanzees on the Gombe Stream Reserve." In I. DeVore (Ed.), *Primate Behavior*. New York: Holt, Rinehart and Winston.

GUSINDE, MARTIN (Ed.)
1931-39. *Die Feuerland Indianer* (3 vols.). St. Gabriel-Mödling bei Wien: Verlag der internationalen Zeitschrift Anthropos.

HALL, K. R. L.
1963. "Variations in the Ecology of the Chacma Baboon, *Papio ursinus*." In *The Primates: Proceedings of the Symposium Held on 12th-14th April 1962*. Zoological Society of London, *Symposia*, 10.

KELLY, ISABEL T.
1964. *Southern Paiute Ethnography*. University of Utah Anthropological Papers, no. 69.

KUMMER, H., and F. KURT
1963. "Social Units of a Free-Living Population of Hamadryas Baboons." *Folia Primatologica* (Basel and New York), 1: 4-19.

LEE, RICHARD B.
1965. "Subsistence Ecology of !Kung Bushmen." Ph.D. dissertation, University of California, Berkeley.

LOWIE, ROBERT H.
1963. *Indians of the Plains*. New York: American Museum Science Books. (First published as *American Museum of Natural History Anthropological Handbook*, no. 1. New York: McGraw-Hill, 1954.)

RADCLIFFE-BROWN, A. R.
1931. *Social Organization of Australian Tribes*. Oceania Monographs, 1.

REID, RUSSELL M.
1967. "Marriage Systems and Algebraic Group Theory." *American Anthropologist* (n.s.), 69: 171-78.

REYNOLDS, VERNON
1963. "An Outline of the Behavior and Social Organization of Forest-Living Chimpanzees." *Folia Primatologica* (Basel and New York), 1(2): 95-102.

ROTH, H. LING
1890. *The Aborigines of Tasmania*. London: Kegan Paul, Trench, Trübner.

SAWYER, JACK, and ROBERT A. LEVINE
1966. "Cultural Dimension: A Factor Analysis of the World Ethnographic Sample." *American Anthropologist* (n.s.), 68: 708-731.

SCHALLER, GEORGE B.
1963. *The Mountain Gorilla: Ecology and Behavior*. Chicago: University of Chicago Press.

1965. "The Behavior of the Mountain Gorilla." In I. DeVore (Ed.), *Primate Behavior*, New York: Holt, Rinehart and Winston.

SCHAPERA, ISAAC
1926. "A Preliminary Consideration of the Relationship between the Hottentots and Bushmen." *South African Journal of Science*, 23: 833-36.

1930. *The Khoisan Peoples of South Africa: Bushmen and Hottentots*. London: Routledge and Kegan Paul.

SCHEBESTA, PAUL
1929. *Among the Forest Dwarfs of Malaya*. Trans. by A. Chambers. London: Hutchinson.

1931. "Erste Mitteilungen über die Ergebnisse meiner Forschungsreise bei den Pygmäen in Belgisch-Kongo." *Anthropos*, 26: 1-27.

SERVICE, ELMAN R.
1962. *Primitive Social Organization: An Evolutionary Perspective*. New York: Random House.

STEWARD, JULIAN H.
1936. "The Economic and Social Basis of Primitive Bands." In R. H. Lowie (Ed.), *Essays in Anthropology Presented to A. L. Kroeber*. Berkeley: University of California Press.

1938. *Basin-Plateau Aboriginal Socio-Political Groups*. Bureau of American Ethnology Bulletin no. 120.

1953. "Aboriginal and Historic Groups of the Ute Indians of Utah: An Analysis." Paper presented before the Indian Claims Commission for the U.S. Department of Justice. (Mimeo.)

STRONG, WILLIAM D.
1929. *Aboriginal Society in Southern California*. University of California Publications in American Archaeology and Ethnology (Berkeley) no. 26.

WOODBURN, J. C.
1964. "The Social Organization of the Hadza of North Tanganyika." Ph.D. dissertation, Cambridge University.

WOODBURN, J. C., and SEAN HUDSON
1966. *The Hadza: The Food Quest of a Hunting and Gathering Tribe of Tanzania*. (16mm film.) London: London School of Economics.

6

Cultural Evolution in South America

This essay was originally part of a volume presented to Ralph Beals (The Social Anthropology of Latin America: Essays in Honor of Ralph L. Beals, ed. W. Goldschmidt and H. Hoijer, Los Angeles: Latin American Center, University of California, 1970, pp. 199-223). Beals took his Ph.D. at Berkeley, though somewhat later than Steward, and went on to found the Department of Anthropology and Sociology (later split into two departments) at the University of California at Los Angeles. Beals and Steward enjoyed a long friendship, as well as a common interest in South American ethnology. In this article Steward goes back to interests developed during his editorship of the Handbook of South American Indians. It is reprinted with permission of the editors and publisher.

1. METHODOLOGICAL CONSIDERATIONS

The great amount of research done in South America since World War II, together with renewed interest in the meaning of cultural evolution, make a reassessment of South American cultural development timely. In addition, a common belief that *Native Peoples of South America* (Steward and Faron, 1959) was intended to present evolutionary stages prompts clarification. Although this paper deals substantively with South America, the methodological discussion has broader implications.

It is becoming evident that the value of most cultural studies that are designated evolutionary—and of many that are not—is essentially their objective of making explanatory analysis or determining particular causal factors and processes in substantive cases, rather than construction of evolutionary schemes (Steward, 1967a). Explanatory hypotheses may be broadened through cross-cultural comparisons, but none is so completely proven that it is beyond scrutiny and possible revision. Schematizations, whether "multilinear" or "unilinear" reconstructions, are likely to be understood as final and unalterable conclusions. By "multilinear" I intend merely to signify that cultural evolution follows an undetermined number of different lines, only a few of which have been postulated. It is not my intention to substitute a complicated scheme for a simple one. I am forced to recognize, however, two serious misconceptions that are inherent in any scheme: first, the rather sterile notion that an evolutionary taxonomy is an end in itself; second, the assumption that causes can be inferred directly from the cultural characteristics chosen as diagnostics of the taxonomic categories.

Comparative analysis understandably begins with consideration of sociocultural systems that have similar characteristics, although there is disagreement concerning what is diagnostic or fundamental and what is variable embellishment. Because like causes always produce like effects, it is then inferred that similar cultural manifestations were always caused by the same factors, but this reasoning is vulnerable on several points. First, the nature of causality in cultural phenomena remains obscure. Second, since factors operate in combination, the precise effect of a single factor is difficult to determine. In every case of causality, there are environmental as well as cultural factors. Third, causes are effective through generating processes of change, and not through a simple, direct cause-and-effect relationship between a cultural factor and its consequences.

My hypothesis concerning the evolution of early civilizations (Steward, 1955) illustrates this methodological hazard. From the striking similarity at each stage in the developmental sequence of these societies, I inferred that irrigation was the basic cause, therein accepting Wittfogel's hypothesis (1938, 1957). Wittfogel was not entirely wrong, although it became clear that in Mesopotamia irrigation was a major state enterprise only after the dynastic period had begun, and Adams's detailed comparison of state evolution in Mexico and Mesopotamia (1966) has disclosed that interdependency of local populations based on microterritorial specialization probably created a greater need for centralized state controls than irrigation. In Peru, however, the importance of the irrigation factor cannot be minimized, and elsewhere its role varied with climate, topography, whether rivers were deeply entrenched, and other factors that merit detailed comparative studies. The factor of microterritorial specialization has undoubtedly also operated in other areas of state evolution, although it had been accorded little attention previous to Adams's comparison.

There is an important distinction between microenvironmental and microterritorial specialization. The first signifies exploitation by a single society of the special resources peculiar to the different natural environments to which it has access—rivers, swamps, grasslands, various mountain elevations, and the like. A hunting, fishing, and gathering society may thus have several subsistence patterns, often requiring a seasonal trek. Microterritorial refers to local specialization by families or communities in some particular kind of production, whether they utilize different microenvironments or impose several types of special production upon a homogeneous environment.

There are other possible factors in the evolution of the state that will be discussed in section 4, just as there are many potential factors in the evolution of societies of food extractors and farm communities that will be discussed in sections 2 and 3. The present relevance of these factors is methodological. How shall a factor be identified?

Certain technological features have exerted an important influence on cultural evolution—for example, stone axes, spears, fire, domesticated plants. The specific effect of any of these, however, obviously depends also upon the particular environment in which they are used. As a cause of social features, the effect of a spear differs if it is used to hunt mastodons, guanacos, or rabbits. The influence of maize farming is very different in slash-and-burn areas and irrigation areas.

These technological features are causes because they enable the society to get certain jobs done, and they are therefore classifiable in functional or utilitarian categories. That is, several dissimilar formal and stylistic features may be more or less equally well adapted to serving the same purpose. In studies of prehistory, the varied functions of specific artifacts as well as the possibility that certain functions may be performed in several ways tend to be obscured by the archeologists' overwhelming preoccupation with forms and styles, especially of ceramics. It is in fact incredible that many major divisions of prehistory are only twofold: pre-ceramic and ceramic periods.

Some of the essential categories among food extractors are: hunting, fishing, food collection; transportation, preparation, and storage of food; making fire; in certain environments, warm housing and clothing; and transportation on water or snow (Steward, 1967b). It is entirely possible, of course, that a specific job requires a very specialized shape of tool or weapon, Multipronged spears or arrows have obvious advantages for fishing. Comparative ethnology, however, discloses that there are usually several ways of getting most jobs done and that particular implements are stylized in ways that have little relation to their utility.

Another functional category is containers for storage, cooking, serving foods, and related uses. This function, too, may be served by containers of many materials, and food may even be boiled in bark, skin, basketry, or pottery vessels. Pottery, despite its obvious advantages for certain purposes, is but one subdivision of this category. Its aesthetic attributes are nonfunctional and highly variable. Pottery has enormous value as a diagnostic of developmental periods and indicator of culture contacts, but it is trivial as a causal factor, and unless vessels are realistically shaped or painted, they afford little indication of other cultural features.

Hunting, although commonly presented under a single heading, really involves several very different kinds of activities that vary according to weapons, environment, game species, and hunting methods. A single society, in fact, usually has several different types of hunting. Individuals may trap some terrestrial species or use blowguns for arboreal game near the village or encampment. Surrounds of some animals may be used by men, women, and children hunting together, but surrounds or drives of large animals are more onerous and exacting masculine tasks. The bow may be used in the ambushing or stalking of mobile animals, which entails sustained effort as well as cooperation; it may be used by lone hunters to shoot various game; or it may be an adjunct of other methods. Bolas seem to have been extremely effective in hunting guanaco, and mounted stock breeders later used them instead of lariats. Their value for bison, rhinoceroses, or elephants, however, is difficult to imagine.

Since so much of the earth was inhabited in historic times by farming societies, the nature of earlier societies and of evolutionary factors in these areas must be inferred from archeological materials. There is serious danger, however, of ignoring factors not directly suggested by the artifacts and other remains, of attributing an identical function to all objects of the same style, and of assuming that objects of different styles and forms have dissimilar functions.

It has been postulated, for example, that the first migrants to South America were large-game hunters who possessed the Big-Game Tradition of North America. This tradition is characterized by large stone spear points and sites containing bones of large game, including now-extinct giant species. Wendorf and Hester conclude (1962) that spearing bison and mammoths at drinking places and "stampeding" in narrow canyons or over cliffs were basic methods. It should be noted, however, that even the smaller modern bison which occurred in enormous numbers supported a very sparse Plains Indian population. Unmounted hunters—of whom we know little, since even George Catlin, who travelled in the plains from 1832 to 1838, saw most hunting done on horseback—probably found direct assaults with spears or bows exceedingly dangerous unless done in deep snow. Despite the archeological remains, one must conclude that smaller fauna was also hunted and that vegetable foods were probably more important to the early Indians than to the recent mounted tribes. In other words, the picture must be modified by attention to the exploitation of other resources at different places and seasons.

The Desert Culture west of the Rocky Mountains has been reconstructed on the basis of basketry, stone implements for preparing vegetable foods, early stone spear points, and later arrow points. Because arid conditions have prevailed to the present, it is assumed that

Great Basin Shoshoneans exemplify the ancient type of society, which consisted of small groups that ranged throughout the year in search of vegetable foods. A major ethnographic error is the frequent statement that the social group was an extended family or patrilineal band, which was true only of southern California Shoshoneans (Steward, 1955) whereas the Great Basin had clusters of intermarried bilateral families (Steward, 1938). Another error is that all these societies were seasonally nomadic, which ignores the permanent communities in certain areas of abundant resources.

In disclosure of causes, comparison of the hunting and desert traditions also overlooks the fact that in areas of limited game, such as the Great Basin, hunting may require far more time than where game is abundant. The issue is not whether game or seeds supplied a greater percentage in the diet but what methods were employed, how much time was required, and what kind of social cooperation was involved in each kind of hunting or food gathering. The procedure requires functional analysis of each category of activity and avoidance of imposing holistic ethnographic models, especially oversimplified ones, on archeological data.

In the present stage of knowledge of South America, it is difficult to use insights gained from ethnology to interpret prehistoric materials, but it is obviously necessary to understand as fully as possible the total range of exploitative activities in each environment and microenvironment rather than to assume that the nature of the society can be inferred directly from distinctive styles or forms of implements or can be usefully classified in such catch-all categories as "hunting" or "food gathering."

Plant and animal domestication added new functional categories to survival activities, and each became a causal factor in evolution as particular crops or herds were tended in special ways in various environments. For example, methods of slash-and-burn farming, rainfall farming, and irrigation entailed very different social activities.

Analysis of the functional role of cultural features does not, of course, assume that all factors were independently invented. Many features of primary importance, such as spears, spear-throwers, bows, domesticated plants, and others, were obviously widely diffused. Whether basic social patterns were diffused is another matter. Diffusionist explanations provide facile answers, and theories of migration evade questions of causality almost completely. Diffusion, which has both preconditions and consequences, depending on the phenomena in question (Steward, 1967b), and migrations, which did not occur as simple transpositions of whole societies from one area to another without change, will be discussed subsequently in specific contexts.

2. EVOLUTION OF PREFARMING SOCIETIES

South American cultural evolution began more than 10,000 years ago with the first migrants, who were equipped with many technological devices of the palaeolithic and neolithic cultures that had been brought to North America. Many features that were specific to the colder northern latitudes, however, were probably filtered out in the tropical areas. Although generally simple, the cultures of the earliest periods did not constitute a uniform substratum, such as Monseignor John M. Cooper, Baron Erland Nordenskiöld, and others attempted to reconstruct on an age-area basis, or an archaic culture consisting of a certain artifact complex. We cannot assume that an early migration introduced a homogenous culture from which all subsequent cultures evolved. It is probable that there were many infiltrations of people and cultural features. As exploitative devices became employed in different areas, special social arrangements evolved in the use of local resources of fish, shellfish, game, and plant foods.

Early periods in coastal areas are best known, and certain of these indicate predominance of fishing and shellfishing. In Central America (Baudez, 1963) and Colombia (Valdés, 1963), the earliest remains include no projectile points, and the same seems to be true of north-western Argentina (González, 1963) and perhaps coastal Peru (Lanning, 1963). Whether there was a pre-spear stage or not, it would be incorrect to postulate that there was an original culture similar to the Big-Game Tradition of North America. South America had only a limited number of the now-extinct species of megafauna found in North America, and the size of their population is not known. There were no species of herbivores comparable to the bison and antelope of the North American plains or the caribou and elk farther north. The principal South American herding species is the guanaco, a member of the camel family, which occurs only in the southern area, especially the pampas, and in the Andes. This animal weighs only 250 to 350 pounds, as compared to the bison, which weighs up to 2,000 pounds, and it occurs in many small herds. Other modern game species are more tropical; monkeys, small deer, armadillos, innumerable rodents, peccaries, tapirs, and water mammals. Tapirs, which may weigh 500 pounds, and smaller peccaries form minor herds. Except for water mammals, other species are very small. Food collecting and fishing within the diverse environments, together with hunting guanaco and more tropical game, must have entailed very different cultural-ecological adaptations throughout the prefarming evolution of South American cultures.

In the Conference on Man the Hunter (see Steward, 1968), it was brought out that societies of food extractors depended primarily upon meats only at extremely high altitudes; subsistence elsewhere consisted of as much as 80 percent vegetable foods. Few South American Indians can have been primarily meat eaters. The perennial growth of tremendously rich and varied flora throughout most of South America afforded seeds, fruits, and roots of one kind or another throughout the year, and food storage was consequently less a problem than in areas of cold winters.

We know little of the early artifacts, except those made of stone, bone, and shell. Evidence of subsistence consists largely of projectile points, net sinkers, bolas, stones, skin scrapers, and stones for smashing and grinding seeds and nuts. Many recent types of subsistence devices, including traps, pits, blowguns, baskets, weirs, nets, harpoons, wooden arrows, canoes, rafts, and others, would leave evidence only in extremely arid regions, such as coastal Peru, while fish poisons, dams, and blowgun dart poison, and group activities such as surrounds, pursuit, stalking, and ambushes would leave no remains. In those portions of the tropical forests that lacked stone, there would be virtually no evidence of early subsistence.

The many survival activities known ethnographically must have been devised, or diffused, at various times during the ten millennia or more while man became familiar with his environment; and by historic times most societies seem to have possessed the principal methods appropriate to their environments. Any evolutionary sequences described in substantive terms would have to deal separately with each area or type of environment. For example, shellfish, which can be collected by individuals using digging sticks, may have been the principal subsistence on certain coasts before nets, hooks, and watercraft were acquired and before hunting became important, factors that led to increased population and greater social cooperation. Guanaco were hunted with spears and bolas before arrows were introduced, but all weapons were useful in both individual and cooperative hunting.

It is characteristic of most food collectors that they exploited the differing resources of several microenvironments and thus maintained considerable mobility. Certain resources, however, predominated, and social structure reflects the nature of the exploitative activities required for each.

The Chilean archipelago was occupied by small clusters of related families—small subsistence bands—which wandered along the shores, gathering shellfish and hunting sea birds and mammals from canoes. The meager fish and vegetable resources had minor importance. As among the Western Shoshoni of the Great Basin, these small bands were not permanently aligned in larger bands, and they could assemble together only on rare occasions of abundant food.

The inland guanaco and rhea hunters of Tierra del Fuego and very probably of pre-horse Patagonia were grouped in territorial patrilineal bands, which were the effect of the nature and quantity of game, the means of taking it, and the kinds of cooperative hunting involved. Such bands seem also to have occurred in southern California, among the Bushmen, in Tasmania, and in parts of Australia (Steward, 1955). These areas differed in particulars of the environment, hunting devices, and species of game, but the combination of these factors initiated similar cultural-ecological processes and produced similar effects.

A different kind of society occurred among the Guató of Paraguay, where seasonal abundance of wild rice, baskets for collecting it, and canoe transportation permitted families to disperse for the harvest and then assemble at permanent habitation sites for as long as the rice lasted.

There are other hunting, gathering, and fishing tribes scattered between major rivers and around the periphery of the Amazon basin, which Cooper designated "internal marginals." These are too little known to permit even sketchy characterization. Some, like the Sirionó of the Bolivian jungles, may have been dislocated farmers who all but abandoned cultivation. Others, such as the Warrau of the Orinoco Delta, who have a temple-idol cult characteristic of the state-structured societies, may have been forced into their swampy habitat, where they abandoned farming. It is highly implausible, however, that these areas were not inhabited in prefarming periods by societies which had developed various means of exploiting the rich varieties of natural resources.

3. COMMUNITIES OF FOOD PRODUCERS

Food production—farming and pastoralism—represented a new functional category of tremendous importance owing to its potential for causing demographic growth and population nucleation, which, under certain conditions, led to the factors and processes of state evolution. At first, however, food production was only a minor supplement to hunting, fishing, and gathering; in some areas, several millennia passed before it became the principal subsistence. Food production was a necessary antecedent of state evolution, but states did not evolve everywhere from communities of farmers and pastoralists. Only certain combinations of factors led to intercommunity integration, specialization of status and role, and overall political controls. Just as particular combinations of factors had prevented many societies of food extractors from adopting food production, other combinations apparently set limits to the evolution of food producers. There is an important distinction, therefore, between farming societies that went on to achieve states and those that did not.

Domesticated plants fall into three categories based on their adaptability, yields, propagation, and cultivation: (1) annuals, such as maize, beans, cucurbits, and many others, which were planted from seeds; (2) annual root crops, such as manioc, potatoes, and others, which were propagated by cuttings; and (3) perennials, usually trees, which include a considerable variety of fruits and nuts. The principal seed crops were highly adaptable, some of them having spread to hot tropical forests, the high cold Andes, arid areas, and temperate zones. The root crops were more specialized, one group being found principally in the tropical areas and another in the cool Andes and Chile. Fruits and nuts were most characteristic of the tropics and circum-Caribbean area. The annual plants could be grown in new plots or clearings each year, but the perennials would seem to presuppose a certain community stability, a point that has not been adequately investigated. In addition to foods, many fish poisons, dyes, drugs, and other miscellaneous crops were grown.

Farming entailed comparatively few basic innovations in the implements of production or the methods of food preparation or preservation. In the tropical forests, a stone axe was crucial for slash-and-burn operations, but everywhere soil preparation, planting, and root harvesting were accomplished by means of a digging stick—and in a few areas a hoe—while baskets or other simple containers served for harvesting and transportation. Methods of storage did not differ fundamentally from those of food collectors except in size of granaries. Hunting devices actually continued to be more numerous and complicated than those used in farming.

Food preservation merits special consideration because it is necessary to the storage of certain foods, which is required in regions of seasonal production to maintain permanent settlements and in states to guarantee a surplus that will support classes of non-food-producers. In the case of seeds, the principal need was to protect the harvest from rain and from rodents. In the case of tropical root crops, however, the problem was to prevent rotting in the hot, humid climate. I know of little information on crop storage in the tropics, except in the case of bitter manioc, which became the staple food of European travelers in the Amazon. Bitter manioc was grated and its poisonous juices squeezed out; it was then cooked in the form of cakes. The elaborate processing, however, seems to have been unnecessary, for heat alone will drive out the poison.

Farm production differed most importantly in the new methods that were related to environmental factors. Simple rainfall farming was carried on in various areas which had adequate precipitation, a warm growing season, and an absence of sodding grasses which would prevent digging-stick cultivation. Flood-plain cultivation was restricted to the margins of rivers in arid areas. Irrigation farming followed flood-plain cultivation when areas away from the rivers had to be watered. Tropical flood plains were cultivated between annual inundations. Slash-and-burn had to be practiced in the tropical forests. Llama pastoralism was carried on in the plains and pampas of the high Andes and Chile, in areas where crops could not be grown.

In addition to these methods of cultivation, continued exploitation of microenvironments and specializations within microterritories are potential factors in furthering or retarding both community and state evolution.

This section will deal principally with those areas which had independent farm communities at the time of the European conquest. These areas include most of the Amazon and Orinoco basins, the Brazilian coast, parts of Paraguay, Argentina, and Chile, and enclaves among the circum-Caribbean chiefdoms.

Maize, first domesticated in Mexico about 4000 or 5000 B.C., did not support permanent farm settlements until 1500 B.C. (Coe, 1967), and it spread to Colombia and Peru about this time. From archeological finds of graters, it is inferred that bitter manioc was domesticated on the northern coast of Colombia or Venezuela about 1200 B.C., whence it subsequently spread throughout much of the tropical forests. It is entirely possible, however, that these graters were used for other root crops. The attention accorded bitter manioc has probably given it undue importance; the historical tropical forest societies cultivated a variety of plants including maize, kidney and lima beans, cucurbits, peanuts, *Diascorea,* peppers, several palms and fruits, and other root crops such as sweet potatoes, *arracacha,* and sweet manioc.

What is more important about tropical forest subsistence methods is that the combination of farming with hunting in all regions, with riverine resources along the main rivers, and with marine resources along the Brazilian coast supported a dense population and large communities but also prevented integration of these communities in states. The communities varied in size from 150 to 3,000 persons, but there was no specialization in subsistence activities between communities or families. There was actually a triple subsistence pattern. Fish, turtle eggs, reptiles, and water mammals were taken in abundance from the rivers in an extractive economy, carried out in the same way by all men. Hunting was done in many ways in the forests away from the river, but it was also an activity of all men and not of particular groups. Farming utilized various zones bordering the rivers: sandy beaches and flood plains between inundations, and forests of large trees that were cleared by slash-and-burn. Farming could probably have been increased if men had devoted full time to it, but presumably the need for proteins caused by the starchy crops—a plausible but unverified hypothesis—motivated men to spend most of their time hunting and fishing. The existence of vast regions of unfarmed forest might indicate the recency of agriculturalists in the area, but as archeology has pushed back the probable date of farming this explanation becomes less plausible. It appears, therefore, that the present kinds of subsistence activities have lasted for many centuries with little change.

The hypothesis of the limiting effect of a triple subsistence pattern does not apply to tropical forests per se. Such forest cover combined with microenvironments within a sharp range of altitudes, as in the circum-Caribbean area, with absence of major rivers, as in Yucatán, and with possibilities for special flood irrigation, as in Bolivia, Ecuador, north Colombia, and Surinam (Parsons and Denevan, 1967), constituted methods of land use that may have been factors in state evolution.

There is no evidence elsewhere in the tropical forest that any peculiar methods of subsistence not known ethnographically were used in prehistoric periods. Some earlier settlements seem to have been large, although it has not been demonstrated that they surpassed 3,000 persons, and there were certain elaborations of ceramics, which led to adoption of the designations "formative" and "florescent." These stylistic manifestations, however, in no way disclose social elaborations or basic social transformations. The ethnographic social elaborations of these communities consisted of clans, moieties, age-grade societies, men's houses, men's and women's societies, and special priest-shamans, but they did not include the community and class specialization that is fundamental to states. The basic subsistence patterns probably prevented internal evolution of states, precluded diffusion of state institutions, caused migratory state societies to be precarious and impermanent, and made conquests transient.

The aboriginal population of Chile was much denser than that of the tropical forests and nearly equal to that of the areas of the chiefdoms, but it was grouped in many small independent lineages of about 150 persons each. On the assumption that a critical precondition of state development is sheer numbers of people, I previously postulated that Araucanian society was comparable to a supersaturated solution, containing the potentials of state organization and needing only the seed crystals, such as a diffused priest-temple complex or other institutions, to precipitate states. Community interdependence based upon microenvironmental and microterritorial specialization, however, did not exist in Chile, and, perhaps owing to the small number of crops and the considerable importance of llama pastoralism, could not have existed. The Inca conquest briefly enveloped part of Chile but left no state institutions.

Another factor in the evolution of different kinds of farm communities was so-called "warfare": more accurately, raids that were carried on against neighboring villages to take scalps, head trophies, and captives for torture and cannibalistic rites. True slaving was post-European, not aboriginal. Although raids to capture sacrificial victims were an important adjunct to religion in early Peruvian states and persisted as an extremely sanguinary characteristic of historic state practices in the northern Andes and Mexico, they failed to integrate tropical forest communities in a common purpose. To the contrary, their principal effect was to isolate many communities, which nucleated within palisaded villages; and this probably had two additional effects. First, owing to the hazards of venturing too far from the village, it may have restricted the subsistence areas. Second, if formerly small, independent communities amalgamated within large villages, it may have enriched the culture of each, as occurred during Pueblo III times and later in the Southwest.

Within this generalized type of independent farm villages, there were several variations for which causal explanations may be ventured. In the Amazon, villages tended to consist of patrilineal kin groups, perhaps owing to the economic importance of men. Some villages, as among the Cubeo and Witoto, consisted of a single patrilineage—so considered by myth if not by genealogy—which occupied a large house. Amalgamation of several such patrilineages in single communities would, if they retained the fiction of common ancestry and descent, produce multiclan societies, as among the Mundurucú. In such a case, evolution marks the emergence of multikin and community-level institutions which are superimposed on predominantly kin-based structures, such as those characteristic of many food collectors and hunters.

The strong matrilineal tendencies of the independent communities within the circum-Caribbean area have two provisional explanations, neither verified. First, these villages may be matrilineal because undisclosed factors produced a heritage shared by both the chiefdoms and the villages. Second, the independent villages may have borrowed this feature from the chiefdoms, among which it is very strong. Neither explanation, of course, postulates ultimate causal factors.

There is a gradation of political authority in the independent communities from the lineage head in certain small villages to a priest-

shaman in large ones. The role of such authorities was to direct ceremonialism rather than subsistence activities, which, in the absence of
economic specialization by kin groups, communities, or social classes,
were regulated by traditional kin-group heads.

4. THE EMERGENCE OF STATES

States constitute an extremely broad category of sociocultural systems,
which includes chiefdoms, statelets, sultanates, empires, and other
varieties. These are characterized by a constellation of interrelated
features: social classes based upon status and occupation, and supracommunity political, religious, economic, and sometimes military institutions which regulated certain activities of the component communities, classes, kin groups, and families. The communities may retain
certain traditional or prestate characteristics and thus constitute what
some persons would call subcultural segments of a plural society.

The true state must be distinguished from several protostates, such
as those of the Northwest Coast, the Natchez, parts of Africa and the
Pacific, and perhaps a few societies of South America such as the
Cocama, in which authority, status ranking, and certain privileges had
become assigned to special segments or lineages within kin groups
which also included commoners. Emergent characteristics of state
evolution, such as concentration of wealth or ritual authority, may be
recognized in such societies, but causes of a breakthrough to a structure of purely hereditary classes which control all state institutions
cannot be inferred from the characteristics alone.

At the Spanish Conquest several very different kinds of states had
evolved in South America: theocratic chiefdoms of somewhat distinctive characteristics in parts of the Venezuelan Andes and the Greater
Antilles, warring chiefdoms or statelets in the northern Andes and
Central America, and an empire in the central Andes.

Sequences of the principal characteristics of some of the New World
states, especially in parts of Meso-America and the Peruvian coast, are
fairly well known, although the incipient or formative phases are less
clear than later stages. On the basis of available knowledge several basic
factors and processes have been postulated: (1) demographic growth
induced by plant cultivation, which somehow directly causes state
institutions to emerge; (2) need for managerial control of expanding
irrigation systems; (3) specialized exploitation by and interdependency
of populations within microterritories; (4) a concomitant rise of
specialized groups of non-food producers; (5) extension of theocratic
controls beyond the independent villages; (6) spread through proselytization of a cultist religion; and (7) militarism. Explanations that

are historical rather than evolutionary include diffusion and migration.

Historical explanations cannot be assessed without reference to causal factors, for diffusion of state institutions must require certain preconditions, and if such preconditions exist, they may cause state evolution without diffusion. A migration theory must establish whether the local area will support a state-structured society and the extent to which the state must adapt to local conditions. Both diffusion and migration also involve the question of whether formal features derived from elsewhere may serve new functions.

Increase of populations and community size based on farming seems everywhere to characterize state evolution, but these are intelligible as causes of state institutions only if the processes through which they operate can be demonstrated. High concentration of individuals within a restricted area requires regulatory mechanisms, but it is possible that such controls can operate only within the independent community. The question is what kinds of intercommunity social relationships require regulation. Close spacing of large communities does not of itself necessitate supercommunity controls, as illustrated by the villages along the Amazon.

The irrigation factor, or need for centralized control of expanding systems of dams, canals, and ditches, has been mentioned previously. Its importance in Peru seems undeniable, for the coastal areas are so completely arid that, after an early period of flood-plain farming, extension of farm lands required diversion of rivers. Since these rivers are very deeply entrenched in the Andes, construction of irrigation systems required intercommunity cooperation under increasingly strong central authority until the limits of available water were reached. Irrigation was not the sole factor in Peru, nor was it negligible elsewhere. In the Hohokam area of Arizona, it seems to have reached a scale that supported states, and in the Tehuacán region of Mexico, Coe and Flannery state (1967, p.103) that "population density remained low until the introduction of complex irrigation works, about 600 B.C."

In assessing the factor of specialization of land use, a distinction has been made between microenvironments and microterritories. Pre-farming societies hunt, fish, and gather vegetable foods from the different natural micro-areas over which they are able to range, and, unless a particular resource, such as fish or shellfish, is exceptionally abundant in one locality, there must be considerable group mobility. Societies of farmers at first continue to utilize the resources of several microenvironments until food production becomes so efficient as to relegate other activities to a secondary role, but such farming does not necessarily create local specialization and interdependence.

Where major life zones are fairly small and contiguous, as in certain mountainous areas, a society may specialize in farming as well as in the extraction of natural resources from each zone, thereby encouraging exchange and interdependency of communities. Many South American states evolved in mountainous areas, especially in the northern and Venezuelan Andes and the Antilles, where a considerable range of altitude within a small territory afforded a great variety of natural resources and farming potentials. The Chibchan kingdom of Colombia drew on produce from the tropical lowlands up to altitudes of more than 10,000 feet. Microterritorial specialization, however, was not necessarily limited to such life zones. It might involve ocean and river valley, as on the coast of Peru. It is now impossible to infer microterritorial specialization from archeological materials, but the tendency of houses to cluster around a ceremonial center and of communities to be grouped around temples warrants the interpretation that, as needs arose for intercommunity secular controls, the community priest expanded his functions.

Macroenvironmental areas—that is, zones much larger than any society can directly exploit—have long engaged in trade, but a political interdependency is created only when the trade is regulated by a strong state authority. In Peru the very different macroenvironments represented by the arid coast and the highland massif yielded complementary products, the exchange of which was regulated by the Inca Empire. While these portions of the empire could probably have been self-sufficient in subsistence, greater security was afforded by specialization. This, like many other factors, may have been an effect of empire, but it also became a cause in strengthening imperial institutions and permitting imperial expansion.

Specialized production of nonsubsistence goods probably also became a contributory factor in state evolution after states had emerged, for this implied sufficient food surplus and control of surpluses to release classes of artisans from food production. A surplus does not necessarily accrue with improved farming, for it may merely increase leisure and remain a mere potential until central authorities enforce the necessary labor. Specialized craft production is usually associated with evolving urban centers, where administrative personnel, retainers, and craftsmen tend to be concentrated.

In examining the militaristic factor in state formation, it is necessary to recognize the many purposes and kinds of intergroup hostilities such as those in the tropical forests. Human sacrifice in early Peru may have been a pre-state heritage of a widespread practice that became incorporated into a state religion but was not a cause of state growth. The sanguinary character of state warfare and religion diminished in

Peru, but it became a major attribute of the historic states of the northern Andes and central Mexico. Once firmly established, the momentum of such warfare created increasing demands for sacrificial victims, while the victimized states fought perhaps at first for self-defense and later for religious reasons. National warfare could have spread by a chain reaction to peaceful states, and conceivably the need for defense might have amalgamated independent villages. There is surprisingly little evidence, however, that warfare was an integrating factor in the absence of other contributing factors. It seems to have been part of the religious complex until economic conquest gave it a function in its own right.

In both Peru and central Mexico, wars of conquest apparently began when local resources were reaching their limits. Imperial armies subjugated neighboring states to exact tribute and labor, and in Mexico they also took sacrificial victims.

Diffusion can account for the wide distribution of forms and styles that chacterize particular states, but it is difficult to see how it can explain the emergence of states. Elsewhere (1967b), I have discussed the sterility of an abstract concept of diffusion that is divorced from the nature of what is diffused, the preconditions of its acceptance,and its consequences. There is abundant evidence of the diffusion of religious features and institutions, such as the temple mound, the feline god, human sacrifice, and particular kinds of status burial. Any monumental architecture, however, requires regimentation of labor, while status burials presuppose a special privileged class. The feline god and human sacrifice acquire new meaning in the context of the society that borrows them. Human sacrifice was widely diffused, but it was fitted into many contexts.

It has been postulated that the wide distribution of certain religious motifs of the Chavín style, especially the temple at Chavín de Huantar, which seems to lack any supporting community, may represent a cult that was diffused by proselytization. Possibly religious fervor alone motivated a dispersed population to contribute their labor to the ceremonial center, but this cannot now be proved or disproved. There are many stylistic similarities between the Olmec center in Mexico and the Chavín culture (Coe, 1963; Meggers, 1963), some of which may have spread down the valleys of the northern Andes and others of which may have been carried by sea; but, like other such features, styles do not prove the diffusion of basic institutions.

The crux of the issue posed by the diffusion hypothesis is why, since state institutions had to evolve once, they could not have evolved whenever the same factors were present. Coe (1963, p. 36) states: "From the very beginnings of Olmec Culture [presumably the source of Meso-American states] in the Olmec area, monolithic states must have imposed a system of internal tribute and corvée labor which alone would have enabled peoples on a primitive, even slash-and-burn level of agricultural technology, to have built elite centers and produced the artifacts that are diagnostic of civilization"; and he says further that Classical Mayan culture and states elsewhere in Meso-America evolved without "any unusual changes in food production or technology." The irrigation factor was absent in Yucatán, and national warfare was very late. But the earliest states must have contained certain of the factors discussed here, for it is stretching the appeal of an ideology of statehood too far to suppose that other societies imitated an Olmec pattern of exaction of tribute and enforced labor. This kind of thing has never appealed to basic rural populations. If certain state institutions characterize a culture area, we must assume that comparable factors and processes operated throughout the area, or else that all the societies were subjugated by conquest, which no one seems to postulate.

Migration hypotheses have recently been offered, especially since Meggers, Evans, and Estrada (1965) have shown the striking similarity of Valdivia period pottery in Ecuador to that of Jomon, Japan. Ford (1966) has traced a similar style to Georgia and Florida, and many other features are now thought to have been transmitted between Meso-America and South America, even by sea travel. This first pottery is called "early formative," and it is presumed that additional features that constituted ingredients of state cultures originated and diffused between North and South America during the middle and late formative. Meggers, however, recognized that the Japanese influence in Ecuador consists mainly of stylistic embellishments (1963, pp. 134-45), and no one has yet demonstrated how traits of inter-American distribution proved the migration of state societies or led to evolution of states, let alone to different kinds of states. It seems to me that reinstatement of Spinden's theory of the "archaic" base of all civilizations of Nuclear America, followed by divisions of the formative, each represented by a trait complex, while not debatable factually, is mainly a methodology that describes trait history without explaining basic institutions. If one began with explanatory analysis, utilizing the insights afforded by the historic states, I am sure that many of the causal factors and processes previously discussed could be recognized in earlier periods, in which they may have had dissimilar evolutionary roles. Styles and forms of objects do not necessarily indicate function.

A persistent migration theory is that the highland Andean civilization had a tropical forest origin. One argument for this is that highland root crops, such as white potatoes, are, like lowland root crops, propagated by cuttings. If such propagation had not been developed independently, priority would have to be determined by dates. Lathrap (1965) argues that associated ceramics in the tropical forests are earlier than similar styles in the highlands, whereas Meggers, Evans, and Estrada (1965, pp. 175-76) take the opposite view. Even if ceramics of certain styles—and, therefore, propagation by cuttings—were proved earlier in one area than in the other, it would prove nothing whatever about diffusion of associated cultural features or migration of whole societies.

Various temple and habitation mounds, elaborate tombs, and irrigation works have been found outside the area of states of the historic period. These have been reported especially in tropical Bolivia, eastern Peru, eastern Colombia, northern coastal Colombia, various sites in Central America, and Venezuela. Most are near the area of states and may represent thrusts of states during an early pre-militaristic period. Only a few such remains have been reported in more remote, isolated areas, the ridged fields of Surinam and the large platform sites of the island of Marajó being among them. If these represent some kind of state society, whether introduced by migrations or based on diffused factors, their tenure was obviously very precarious. With the exception of the Marajó site (Meggers and Evans, 1957), brief accounts of the Mompós River, Titicaca region, Surinam, and the *llanos* of Bolivia, by Parsons and Denevan (1967), and of the latter, by Plafker (1963) and, many years ago, by Baron Nordenskiöld, these regions have been largely neglected by archeologists. Eastern Bolivia is of particular interest because historically it had centrally controlled societies integrated around the men's house and jaguar cult and, apparently, large-scale irrigation, which, however, did not necessarily involve the canals, causeways, and raised fields described recently.

5. SUMMARY

Cultural evolution has been presented as qualitative transformations in substantive social phenomena that occur through internal processes rather than incorporation of basic structures and institutions from external sources. Traditional patterns have a retarding effect, but, since cultures do evolve, however slowly, the cause must be sought outside traditional structures and value systems. In simple prefarming societies, these causes must inevitably be viewed in terms of basic survival technology, whether particular traits are diffused or locally invented. In more complex state-structured societies, causes must be related also to culturally derived needs, but they consisted largely of technological features.

If cultural evolution refers to internal transformations, it follows that borrowed features are of a distinctive order. Internal transformations are primary in that they are inevitable and unalterable. Borrowed features are secondary in that their adoption depends on the internal transformations and they may take various forms or be absent altogether. Although this distinction may at first appear arbitrary, I believe it is heuristically validated by empirical evidence.

The causal nature of a particular technological trait cannot be inferred from its specific qualities, especially from its stylization, for it may have dissimilar functions in different environments, while certain dissimilar traits may serve the same function. The size, composition, and movements of a society that subsists only on natural resources represent accommodations to the use of technological features in specific environments. Since an isolated nuclear family would not be viable, the minimum social unit everywhere tends to consist of a cluster of about a half-dozen intermarried families. Among the shellfishing and sea-hunting Alacaluf of Chile, such family clusters are also the maximum social units. In the pampas the predominance of hunting created patrilineages rather than bilateral kinship groups. There is little evidence outside the Northwest Coast that food extractors developed moieties or clans—it is misleading to consider a locally exogamous lineage a clan—or that they borrowed such features. Where population density is low and small societies are widely spaced, the imposition of nonlocalized exogamous social segments would seriously limit the number of potential marriage partners. A social elaboration such as the men's secret tribal society of Tierra del Feugo could be borrowed—or perpetuated from an old tradition—because its main ceremonialism occurred infrequently, when resources permitted multiband assemblies. A men's society was also part of the structure of certain large houses in the tropical forests. In both areas it was a secondary feature that lent specific character to the societies but was not essential to the basic structure and day-by-day functioning of the people.

Plant domestication was a general factor of fundamental importance in causing increased size and stability of communities. This in turn entailed settlements of multi-kin units and necessitated a degree of social regulation, a function performed by the priest-shaman. Farm communities permitted the borrowing or internal development of certain elaborations: clans, moieties, men's houses, age-grade societies, and men's and women's societies, all based on sex and age rather than on economic function.

Agriculture became a factor in state evolution not because it gave men access to a new source of energy external to man himself but because, when additional factors were present, it gave certain classes of men access to the energy of other men. These additional factors include: many varieties of crops, microterritorial specialization, exchange of produce, and irrigation. In various combinations these factors required a regulatory institution or class, which first consisted of priests who expanded their authority to include secular functions and extended their scope to include many communities. Many traditional features of earlier farm villages, such as human sacrifice, certain god concepts, ritual forms, and even a secret society, were perpetuated, though with new functions, in the emergent states. Other features, such as monumental architecture, ritual practices, and aesthetic stylization, could be borrowed from other states, but their adoption and particular functional roles presupposed that a state had evolved. It is my hypothesis, therefore, that the preconditions of borrowing state institutions were actually the causes of state evolution.

Superimposition of state institutions on local communities modifies but does not destroy the traditional character of the latter. Family and community structure, houses, dress, watercraft, and many other community features may persist. Certain community practices and patterns may even become woven into state institutions. In the northern Andean states the matrilineal tendencies of the circum-Caribbean area were combined with very bloody warfare and ritual, so that there were female as well as male warriors and rulers. Despite evidence of considerable diffusion from Meso-America, the state development was autochthonous.

The sequence of independent evolutionary transformations from simple farm villages at the mouths of rivers in coastal Peru to states and empires has been traced in more detail (Kidder, Lumbreras, and Smith, 1963), and it needs no theory of migration of state-structured societies. As agriculture became more varied and efficient, small settlements were made higher up the rivers and began to cluster around ceremonial centers. Between 300 B.C. and 200 A.D. regional states began to form on the basis of irrigation, and soon thereafter captive-taking for ritual purposes began. By 600 A.D. wars of conquest were initiated, and cities grew, signifying a strong bureaucracy of priests, warriors, and rulers and classes of servants and special craftsmen.

The structure of the Inca Empire had become pyramidal. More or less traditional-type farm communities persisted, although they were assigned production quotas, subject to sumptuary laws, and entailed in corvée labor. States that had first evolved at least 1,500 years earlier and had been imposed on local communities came under imperial control, first by the Chimu Kingdom on the northern coast and then by the Inca Empire.

BIBLIOGRAPHY

ADAMS, ROBERT McC.
1965. *Land behind Baghdad: A History of Settlement on the Diyala Plains.* Chicago: University of Chicago Press.
1966. *The Evolution of Urban Societies: Early Mesopotamia and Prehispanic Mexico.* Chicago: Aldine Press.

BAUDEZ, CLAUDE F.
1963. "Cultural Development in Lower Central America." In *Aboriginal Cultural Development in Latin America: An Interpretative Review,* edited by Betty J. Meggers and Clifford Evans, pp. 45-54. Smithsonian Miscellaneous Collections, vol. 146, no. 1. Washington: Smithsonian Institution.

BIRD, JUNIUS
1946. "Archaeology of Patagonia." In *The Marginal Tribes.* Vol 1. of *Handbook of South American Indians,* edited by Julian H. Steward, pp. 17-25. Washington: U.S. Government Printing Office.

COE, MICHAEL D.
1963. "Cultural Development in Southeastern Mesoamerica." In *Aboriginal Cultural Development in Latin America: An Interpretative Review,* edited by Betty J. Meggers and Clifford Evans, pp. 27-43. Smithsonian Miscellaneous Collections, vol. 146, no. 1. Washington: Smithsonian Institution.

COE, MICHAEL D., and FLANNERY, KENT V.
1967. *Early Cultures and Human Ecology in South Coastal Guatemala.* Washington: Smithsonian Press.

COE, MICHAEL D,; DIEHL, RICHARD A.; and STUIVER, MINZE
1967. "Olmec Civilization, Vera Cruz, Mexico: Dating of the San Lorenzo Phase." *Science,* 155:1401-1402.

FORD, JAMES A.
1966. "Early Formative Culture in Georgia and Florida." *American Antiquity,* 31:781-799.

GONZÁLEZ, ALBERTO REX
1963. "Cultural Development in Northwestern Argentina." In *Aboriginal Cultural Development in Latin America: An Interpretative Review,* edited by Betty J. Meggers and Clifford Evans, pp. 103-113. Smithsonian Miscellaneous Collections, vol. 146, no. 1. Washington: Smithsonian Institution.

KIDDER, ALFRED, II; LUMBRERAS, LUIS G.; and SMITH, DAVID B.
1963. "Cultural Development in the Central Andes—Peru and Bolivia." In *Aboriginal Cultural Development in Latin America: An Interpretative Review,* edited by Betty J. Meggers and Clifford Evans, pp. 89-102. Smith-

sonian Miscellaneous Collections, vol. 146, no. 1. Washington: Smithsonian Institution.

LANNING, EDWARD P.
1963. "A Pre-Agricultural Occupation of the Central Coast of Peru." *American Antiquity,* 28:363-371.

LATHRAP, DONALD W.
1965. "Origins of Central Andean Civilization: New Evidence." *Science,* 148:796-798.

MEGGERS, BETTY J.
1963. "Cultural Development in Latin America: An Interpretative Overview." In *Aboriginal Cultural Development in Latin America: An Interpretative Review,* edited by Betty J. Meggers and Clifford Evans, pp. 131-145. Smithsonian Miscellaneous Collections, vol. 146, no. 1. Washington: Smithsonian Institution.

MEGGERS, BETTY J., and EVANS, CLIFFORD, editors
1957. "Archaeological Investigations at the Mouth of the Amazon." *Bureau of American Ethnology Bulletin,* 167.

1963. *Aboriginal Cultural Development in Latin America: An Interpretative Review.* Smithsonian Miscellaneous Collections, vol. 146, no. 1. Washington: Smithsonian Institution.

MEGGERS, BETTY J.; EVANS, CLIFFORD; and ESTRADA, E.
1965. *Early Formative Period of Coastal Ecuador: The Valdivia and Machalilla Phases.* Smithsonian Contributions to Anthropology, vol. 1. Washington: Smithsonian Institution.

PARSONS, JAMES J., and DENEVAN, WILLIAM M.
1967. "Pre-Columbian Ridged Fields." *Scientific American,* 217:93-100.

PLAFKER, GEORGE
1963. "Observations on Archaeological Remains in Northeastern Bolivia (Beni Department)." *American Antiquity,* 28:372-378.

SANOJA, MARIO
1963. "Cultural Development in Venezuela." In *Aboriginal Cultural Development in Latin America: An Interpretative Review,* edited by Betty J. Meggers and Clifford Evans, pp. 67-76. Smithsonian Miscellaneous Collections, vol. 146, no. 1. Washington: Smithsonian Institution.

STEWARD, JULIAN H.
1938. "Basin-Plateau Aboriginal Sociopolitical Groups." *Bureau of American Ethnology Bulletin,* 120.

1955. *Theory of Culture Change.* Urbana, Ill.: University of Illinois Press.

1967a. "Cultural Evolution Today." *Christian Century,* 54(7): 203-207.

1967b. "Perspectives on Modernization." In *Contemporary Change in Traditional Societies,* edited by J. H. Steward, vol. 1, pp. 1-55. Urbana, Ill.: University of Illinois Press.

1968. "Cultural Factors and Processes in the Evolution of Pre-Farming Societies." In *Conference on Man the Hunter,* pp. 321-334. Chicago: Aldine Press.

1969. "Postscript to Bands: On Taxonomy, Processes and Causes." In *Contributions to Anthropology: Band Societies,* Proceedings of the Conference on Band Organization, edited by David Damas, pp. 288-295. National Museums of Canada, Bulletin no. 228, Anthropological Series no. 84. Ottawa: National Museums of Canada.

STEWARD, JULIAN H., editor
1946-1950. *Handbook of South American Indians.* 6 vols. Washington: U.S. Government Printing Office.

STEWARD, JULIAN H., and FARON, LOUIS
1959. *Native Peoples of South America.* New York: McGraw-Hill Book Co.

VALDÉS, CARLOS AUGULO
1963. "Cultural Development in Colombia." In *Aboriginal Cultural Development in Latin America: An Interpretative Review,* edited by Betty J. Meggers and Clifford Evans, pp. 55-66. Smithsonian Miscellaneous Collections, vol. 146, no. 1. Washington: Smithsonian Institution.

WENDORF, FRED, and HESTER, JAMES J.
1962. "Early Man's Utilization of the Great Plains Environment." *American Antiquity,* 28:159-171.

WILLEY, GORDON R.
1953. "Settlement Patterns of the Virú Valley." *Bureau of American Ethnology Bulletin,* 155.

1966. *North and Middle America.* Vol. 1 of *An Introduction to American Archaeology.* Englewood Cliffs, N.J.: Prentice-Hall.

WILLEY, GORDON R.; BULLARD, WILLIAM R., JR.; GLASS, JOHN B.; and GIFFORD, JAMES C.
1965. *Prehistoric Maya Settlements in the Belize Valley.* Papers of the Peabody Museum of Archaeology and Ethnology, Harvard University, vol. 54. Cambridge, Mass.: Peabody Museum.

WITTFOGEL, KARL A.
1938. "Die Theorie der Orientalischen Gesellschaft." *Zeitschrift für Sozial Forschung* (Paris), vol. 7 (1-2): 90-122.

1957. *Oriental Despotism: A Comparative Study of Total Power.* New Haven: Yale University Press. London: Oxford University Press.

7

Tappers and Trappers: Parallel Processes in Acculturation

This essay was first published in *Economic Development and Culture Change* (vol. 4, pp. 335-355, 1956) and is reprinted in this volume with the permission of that journal. The paper was written by Steward and Robert F. Murphy, the co-editor of the present work, when the latter was associated with the University of Illinois Project in Cultural Regularities. Based in the first instance on the field researches of the two authors, the article was intended as an exemplification of the methods of cultural ecology and multilinear evolution. © 1956 by The University of Chicago.

I. THE PROBLEM

The purpose of this paper is to show how two cases of acculturation exemplify parallel processes of culture change, that is, cross-cultural regularities of function and causality, even though differences in outward norm and substantive content are such that the acculturation might also be considered as convergent development.[1]

As subsequent sections will show in detail, the Mundurucú of the Tapajós River in Brazil and the Northeastern Algonkians in Canada differed during pre-contact times in social structure, in the general nature of their culture, and in their cultural-ecological adaptations. The first were tropical forest hunters and horticulturalists living in

[1] The acculturational phenomena described in this article were apparently found among many, although not all, Northeastern Algonkians, including native groups of New England as well as Canada. Speck, Steward, and others have considered this problem for many years. They were also found among certain Mackenzie Basin Athabaskans, as Jenness has shown. A very comparable case of acculturational process was studied by Steward among the British Columbia Carrier. These cases will be cited in the concluding comparative section. The Montagnais are taken as our principal example because Eleanor Leacock studied them in detail from this point of view.
The Mundurucú of Brazil are analyzed on the basis of a year of field research by Yolanda and Robert Murphy during 1952-53. The research was conducted under the sponsorship of the Department of Anthropology, Columbia University, and was made possible by a Research Training Fellowship granted by the Social Science Research Council and the William Bayard Cutting Traveling Fellowship, awarded through the Trustees of Columbia University.

semipermanent villages and given to warfare. The second were hunters of large migratory game and were loosely organized in nomadic bands. Despite these differences, however, both represented roughly the same level of sociocultural integration. That is, individual families were related to one another through certain suprafamilial patterns—village activities in the one case and band functions in the other—but the local unit in each instance was politically autonomous.

Since this paper is essentially an illustration of methodology, it is important to stress that the concept of level does not classify cultures according to concrete and substantive form and content. Different cultures may be wholly unlike in their particulars in that they are the products of distinctive area histories or traditions and of local adaptations to environments. At the same time, the largest integrated and autonomous social units may be of a similar order of inclusiveness. While, therefore, similarity of level must underlie formulations of cross-cultural regularities, such similarity alone does not at all imply typological identity. The aboriginal tropical forest Mundurucú and the subarctic Algonkian hunters were wholly unlike in most cultural particulars and in social structure, although both were integrated on comparable sociocultural levels.

They were alike, however, in the acculturative processes to which they were subjected and in the final cultural type which is now emerging in both populations. The processes were similar in the special manner in which outside commercial influence led to reduction of the local level of integration from the band or village to the individual family and in the way in which the family became reintegrated as a marginal part of the much larger nation. The resultant culture type was similar in each case in that the local culture core contained the all-important outside factor of almost complete economic dependence upon trade goods which were exchanged for certain local produce and because the functional nature of local production, the family, and other features were directly related to this new element. The common factor postulated to have causal importance is a kind of economic activity—the collection of wild produce—which entailed highly similar ecological adaptations. While rubber production differs as greatly in particulars from fur trapping as the tropical forests differ from the subarctic barren-lands of Labrador, the result of the acculturative processes in the two cases was the independent emergence of the same type of culture, as defined in terms of level of integration and culture core. We shall use the latter term to denote the structural interrelationships of the basic institutions of the culture.

This case study should also help clarify the heuristic concept of cultural ecology, and especially to illustrate how fundamentally it differs from environmental determinism. It will be shown that total environment is in no way the decisive factor in the culture-environment relationship. In analyzing the creative processes in the adaptation of culture to environment, it is necessary to determine the crucial features in the environment that are selectively important to a culture of a particular level and a particular area tradition. In this sense, it does not matter how different the subarctic and the tropical forests are in their totality. The primary fact is that each environment afforded a resource for trade purposes which could best be exploited by individual families controlling these products within delimited territories. These products did not achieve importance until the native populations became parts of larger sociocultural systems and began to produce for outside markets in a mercantilist pattern.

The process of gradual shift from a subsistence economy to dependence upon trade is evidently irreversible, provided access to trade goods is maintained. It can be said, therefore, that the aboriginal culture is destined to be replaced by a new type which reaches its culmination when the responsible processes have run their course. The culmination point may be said to have been reached when the amount of activity devoted to production for trade grows to such an extent that it interferes with the aboriginal subsistence cycle and associated social organization and makes their continuance impossible.

II. NORTHEASTERN ALGONKIANS

Our discussion of the acculturation of the Northeastern Algonkians assumes that the family-owned fur-trapping territories widely reported among these Indians were post-white in origin. The supposition of Speck (1915, 1939, 1942), Cooper (1939), and Eiseley (1939, 1942, 1947) that such territories were aboriginal lacks support in early historical documents. Moreover, indisputable cases of post-white formation of family territories have been reported by Leacock among the Eastern Montagnais (1954), Jenness among certain of the Mackenzie Basin Athabaskans (1932, p. 257), and Steward among the British Columbia Carrier (1941). Leacock's study (1954) deals with the processes of development of trapping territories in greatest detail and consequently provides the most illuminating material. We shall constantly refer to it in the following delineation of the aboriginal culture core and the subsequent changes in it.

According to Leacock, the Eastern Montagnais formerly possessed very loosely integrated bands. The basic aboriginal social unit was the "multifamily" winter hunting group consisting of two to five families. These groups were nominally patrilocal, but there was considerable deviation from this pattern, and individual families readily shifted from one group to another (*ibid.*, p. 34.) The continual splits and reamalgamations of these winter groups depended upon the vicissitudes of the subarctic Labrador winter. Game, never abundant or highly concentrated, became thinly scattered during severe winters. Families then had to break away from the winter multifamily group in order to exploit the country extensively. In better times they might reassemble with a different group of families. While each of these groups had a leader, his following was ill-defined and fluctuating in membership.

Despite the frequent necessity for the winter group to split into smaller units, the Eastern Montagnais preferred to live in larger social groups, for collective hunting was generally more efficient for taking large game. Leacock's more conservative informants, in fact, regarded solitary or semisolitary hunting as a white man's technique, and they expressly said that it was not appropriate for Indians. Moreover, in the absence of outside sources of food, which are available today, sharing of game was essential to survival since any family might be unlucky in hunting. The rigors of the environment necessitated a degree of social fluidity and amorphousness that was essential to physical survival. Owing to variations in environmental factors, especially in the quantity and distribution of game, crystallization of more rigid and permanent winter groups was impossible.

The Montagnais were, however, grouped into somewhat larger units during the summer season of fishing and caribou-hunting. Each summer, several multifamily winter groups gathered together on the shores of the lakes and rivers, where they could obtain fish in some quantity. These groups, according to Leacock, did not maintain ownership of well-defined territories in native times (*ibid.*, pp. 14-15). Each band had only a rough and generally recognized territorial locus of operations. But it would have been contrary to the interests of any one band to encroach upon the lands of other bands, for band areas represented an approximate division of resources in relation to population. But since local availability of game differed each year, it was customary that a temporarily favored band offer hospitality to one that was starving.

These "bands" had little or no formal organization. There were no band chiefs or definite mechanisms for integrating the band as a social entity. The bands existed principally upon the basis of economic reality. They had greatest functional significance during the season of hunting large, migratory animals. While both the Montagnais and the culturally indistinguishable Naskapi hunted caribou, the relatively greater reliance of the latter upon caribou probably accounts for the stronger development of band hunting territories in northern Labrador.

Leacock divides the development of the family trapping territory into three general phases (*ibid.*, p. 24). In the first stage, when the Indians were only slightly involved in the fur economy, the trapping of fur-bearing animals and trade for hardware and foodstuffs was secondary to native subsistence activities. In this stage the Indians were only partially dependent upon the trader and could still subsist on the native economy. Since the small, nongregarious, and nonmigratory fur-bearing animals were not killed in great numbers by the more primitive techniques of wooden traps and firearms and since they yielded inadequate meat, the primary winter dependence was upon deer and other larger game. The Indians could devote themselves to the luxury of securing trade articles only after assuring themselves of an ample food supply.

These marginal trappers, however, rapidly became so involved in the barter system that certain Western goods, such as pots, pans, knives, axes, steel traps, and firearms became necessities to them. Since these available manufactured articles were much more efficient than the corresponding native implements, the latter were rapidly displaced and knowledge of their manufacture was eventually lost. The basic process therefore was one of increasing dependency upon trade, which eventually brought the loss of many useful arts. During this early stage of dependency, the customary use of ill-defined territories by amorphous bands was still the only approximation of land ownership to be found, and bonds of intragroup dependency were still tight.

In the second period of Montagnais acculturation, the same fundamental process continued to the point where certain basic readjustments became necessary. Dependency upon the trader increased to such an extent that fur trapping became more important than hunting for subsistence. The Indian was now forced to buy the major part of his winter's provisions from the trader, the game formed only a supplemental food source. Owing to the difficulties of transporting a supply of food adequate for the entire family, the men began to leave their families at the trading post during the winter while they trapped in the company of other men. Debt obligations and credit facilities had already linked Indians with particular trading posts. The practice of leaving families at the posts throughout the winter tightened these bonds. The families depended upon the store for subsistence, and the post became the center of the trapper's social as well as economic world.

Leacock states that during this second stage, which is typified by the present-day Natashquan band of Eastern Montagnais, there is still considerable territorial shifting of fur trappers and that family trapline tenure is temporary and unfixed (*ibid*., pp. 30-32). Older informants expressed a preference for collective activity, which is exemplified today by trapping in groups, lack of definite proprietary rights in trapping territories, and the sharing among the men of the trapping groups of the fur from animals shot with guns. That animals trapped were claimed by the trap owner is probably also native.

The stages outlined by Leacock, however, are not presented by her as clearly distinguishable periods during which cultural stability was achieved. They are no more than transitory phases, and the Eastern Montagnais are now, in our terminology, moving toward the culmination of the processes of change. Certain men, says Leacock, show an increasing tendency to return to the same trapping territory year after year (*ibid*., p. 30). Within these more limited precincts, usually no more than two trappers can work together. To a certain extent, the example for this pattern has been set by the white trappers, but the Indians follow it primarily because it is the most efficient working arrangement. When a single Indian enjoys the yield and has a vested interest in the vital resource of his territory, he attempts to protect and perpetuate it by practices of fur conservation which were not native to the culture. The more conservative Montagnais trappers do not wholly approve of the new mode of work followed by their compatriots, but they respect their tenure of exclusive trapping rights to a limited region. What emerges is a system of ownership by usufruct, a system also found among the Western Montagnais and, in fact, in many other areas of the world in which controls of law and government are loose and population density is low.

As more and more Eastern Montagnais adopt this new exploitative pattern, the group as a whole increasingly acknowledges family rights to delimited fur territories. Such rights will extend over much if not most of this area, and it will undoubtedly encroach seriously upon the seminomadism of the more conservative Indians. Ultimately, these latter, too, will have to change. What finally emerges will be the classical family trapping territory system in which definitely limited tracts are held by the head of a family and inherited patrilineally.

In order not to confuse or oversimplify theories of the origin and development of property rights, it is important to recognize that rights to fur-trapping territories mean merely customary or usufruct rights to the furs of animals within a defined area. They by no means give exclusive rights to control of and profit from the land itself and everything thereon or even to all its wildlife. Anyone may pursue and kill deer or caribou on any fur area. In some instances, another may kill and take the meat of a beaver, provided only that he give the pelt to the man having exclusive rights to the furs within the territory in question.

Two basically different concepts of rights to resources within the same area coexist, each justifiable and explainable in its own way: the right to hunt large game for subsistence purposes practically anywhere and the right to monopolize fur-bearing animals within prescribed areas. In British Columbia the provincial government recognized these differences some years ago and registered family-owned trapping territories of the Carrier Indians and protected them by law while permitting moose-hunting anywhere.

This end product of acculturation is substantially Leacock's third stage. The nuclear family now becomes the primary economic and social unit, and the old bonds of interfamilial economic dependency become attenuated. The new individualism has even penetrated the nuclear family. Among the Western Montagnais, the son of a trapper owns the beaver lodges which he discovers, whereas among the most acculturated of the Eastern group, only the family head may own such a resource.

With the breakdown in interfamilial ties among the Northeastern Algonkians, the economic centers of gravity for the families are the trading posts. Leacock says: "The movement of trading posts has obviously been the most important factor determining recent shifts in the size and location of Montagnais bands. However, it would be wrong to infer from this that increasing dependence on trade has acted to destroy formerly stable social groups. The reverse seems to be closer to the truth—that the changes brought about by the fur trade have led to more stable bands with greater formal organization" (*ibid.*, p. 20).

Leacock gives the Seven Islands band as an example of this postcontact development. This new "band," however, is of a different order entirely than aboriginal hunting bands, for the principal bond between the members is that they all trade at the Seven Islands trading post. They claim no band territory; in fact, all present trends are towards familial tracts and not band lands. The modern band has a chief whose principal function is to act as intermediary with the Indian agent. Also, the Indians refer to themselves as the "Seven Islands" (derived from the name of the trading post) people, and are so called by other Indians. In the interest of taxonomic clarity it is best not to describe such an arrangement as a "band." Such a group is reminiscent of the post-white Shoshoneans of the Great Basin, who classify themselves principally by reservation, for example, Warm Springs Paiute, Burns Paiute, Owyhee Shoshoni, and so forth. Prior to the Reorganization Act, the only basis for these groupings was common residence on a reservation and representation by a spokesman, who generally attained his position partly through prestige but probably more important through recognition by the Indian agent. Since the agents preferred "cooperative" men, the chiefs often did not truly represent the Indians. These reservation people, like Leacock's Seven Islands band, had little formal structure and a very limited *raison d'être*. The stability of these groups is almost entirely a function of their linkage to the whites, an outside factor. Among the more acculturated Eastern Montagnais, the basic socioeconomic unit appears to be the nuclear family.

III. THE MUNDURUCÚ

We shall discuss the Mundurucú in somewhat greater detail than the Algonkians not only because they are less known ethnographically but because the special problem of acculturation toward individual families has not been adequately described for South America.

The Mundurucú have been in active contact with European civilization for the last 160 years, of which only 80 years have been spent in rubber exploitation. The following description of the pre-rubber-period Mundurucú does not purport to depict the *precontact*, or aboriginal, Mundurucú, but refers to the middle of the nineteenth century. Earlier changes in Mundurucú culture form the subject of another paper (Murphy, 1955).

The Mundurucú have inhabited the gallery forests and savannah lands east of the upper Tapajós River in the state of Pará, Brazil, for at least two centuries. The savannah in this region is quite limited, and the predominant flora are the high forest and thick vegetation typical of the Amazon basin. The Mundurucú chose the open country for their villages because remoteness from the larger streams afforded some protection from river-born enemy attack and relief from the swarms of insects which infest the river banks, while the absence of forests immediately adjoining the villages gave some security against the dawn surprise attacks favored by nearly all tribes of the region. These attacks were difficult to launch without cover. Since the Mundurucú used water transportation only slightly, isolation from the rivers was not a hardship.

It has been noted that the nineteenth-century Mundurucú and Northeastern Algonkians were on the same level of sociocultural integration. The simple, loosely structured nomadic hunting bands of the Algonkians were roughly equivalent to the semisedentary villages of the Mundurucú. In both instances the local group consisted of a multifamily, autonomous community. Under certain circumstances the various Mundurucú villages tended to integrate on a tribal level, but there were no permanent transvillage political controls. That no

Mundurucú village could function in isolation, since there was inter-village marriage and periodic cooperation in warfare and cere-monialism, does not necessarily imply a higher level of integration in economic or political activities. Similarly, it can be argued that North-eastern Algonkian bands were autonomous but by no means isolated from other such units.

The Mundurucú and Algonkians were integrated on the same level, but their cultures differed structurally or typologically and in content. Patrilineal clans and moieties in Mundurucú society made kinship ties more extensive and pervasive. Village subsistence was based on slash-and-burn horticulture. Although the heavy work of clearing the forest was done by work groups consisting of all the village males, garden care and manioc processing were carried out by the women of the matrilocal extended family. The chief occupations of the men were hunting and warfare.

Leacock's reconstruction of the aboriginal society of the Eastern Montagnais shows the nuclear family to have had greater functional importance than among the Mundurucú. The Montagnais family was a relatively stable unit within the shifting and amorphous hunting bands, whereas the Mundurucú pattern was the converse. Each Mundurucú household was a stable unit composed of women and their female offspring. The Mundurucú had the seeming paradox of matrilocal extended families in a society of patrilineal clans and moieties. The men married into these extended families from similar units in the same village or from other villages. However, there was no need to integrate a husband into the extended matrilocal family of the house-hold, because the focus of his activities was the men's house. All males upon reaching adolescence slept in the men's house, which was located on the western perimeter of the circle of houses composing the village. The females of each household prepared and sent food to the men's house to be eaten in a communal meal. The men's house was also the center of male work and relaxation. The most immediate economic tie of a man to his wife's house was that he brought his daily take of game there. Communal distribution of game, however, made this economi-cally unimportant. Otherwise, the husband visited his household for purposes of sex, to play with the children, or to take a between-meals snack.

Marital break-ups caused no great social maladjustment. The woman and her children simply lived on in the household and took another husband. If the ex-husband was originally from the same village, he did not even have to move his hammock from the men's house. The husband and wife performed no economic tasks together, and the sexual division of labor operated mainly within the context of the village as a whole rather than the nuclear family.

The yearly cycle of activity of the pre-rubber-period Mundurucú was not patterned by warm and cold seasons, as in Labrador, but by rainy and dry periods. At the end of each rainy season, April on the upper Tapajós River, the trees and vegetation in each projected garden were felled by a work party composed of all the men of the village and allowed to dry out. After clearing the forest, many families went in small groups to the larger streams where fishing was good during low waters and where they could hunt the many game animals which left the interior forests to feed and drink at the streams.

After two to three months it was necessary to return to the village to burn the felled vegetation in the garden clearings before the first rains wet the forests. After the early rains had sufficiently moistened the ground, individual gardens were planted to manioc by the cooperative efforts of all the men and women of the village. Other vegetables were planted by the women of the household of the man who initiated the gardens, and who was formally considered to own it.

Maize, squash, beans, and other vegetables were harvested by January or February and eaten immediately. The root crops, including bitter and sweet manioc, matured at the end of the rainy season in new gardens. A longer period of maturation was required for root crops in replanted gardens. Bitter and sweet manioc can be harvested as needed; this natural storage made these crops invaluable for year-around subsistence.

The bitter manioc, by far the most important garden product, required considerable labor to render it edible. The tubers were grated, the prussic acid was extracted by use of the *tipití*, or basketry press, and the pulp was then toasted either in the form of the native *beijú*, a flat manioc cake, or of *farinha*, the coarse Brazilian manioc flour. *Farinha* was sold to Brazilian traders. All phases of manioc processing were carried out by the women of the extended family household, who worked together under the direction of the oldest woman of the house. The labor was divided according to specialized tasks which, however, probably contributed as much toward making the operation pleasant as efficient.

Farinha was thus a collective product in that it involved the communal labor of the village in garden clearing and manioc planting, and the efforts of the women of the household in processing. Moreover, it was sold to the traders by the village as a whole and not by individuals. In this barter the hereditary village chief represented the village, and the proceeds from the sale were divided equally among the contributing households.

Bates, the British naturalist, describes the mode in which this trade was conducted in the mid-nineteenth century, when the first small quantities of rubber were traded by the Mundurucú along with larger amounts of other produce:

"They [the Mundurucú of the upper Tapajós River] make large plantations of mandioca, and sell the surplus produce, which amounts on the Tapajós to from 3,000 to 5,000 baskets (60 lbs. each) annually, to traders who ascend the river from Santarem between the months of August and January. They also gather large quantities of salsaparilla, india-rubber and Tonka beans, in the forests. The traders on their arrival at the Campinas (the scantily-wooded region inhabited by the main body of Mundurucús beyond the cataracts) have first to distribute their wares—cheap cotton cloths, iron hatchets, cutlery, small wares, and cashaça—amongst the minor chiefs, and then wait three or four months for repayment in produce. [1863, pp. 243-244]

When rubber became the major product of Amazonia, the same pattern of trade was perpetuated among the Mundurucú. All of the rubber collected was turned over to the chief, who alone negotiated directly with the trader. The merchandise given for the rubber was, insofar as could be ascertained through contemporary informants, equitably distributed to each man in proportion to the rubber he had produced. But since chiefs were commonly more prosperous than other men, it can be assumed that they did not suffer in their role of middleman. The share taken by the chief, however, was never so great as to result in truly significant wealth differences. In fact, the traders usually managed to keep the Indians in debt, and this debt was charged against the chief as the representative of the village. Tocantins, who visisted the Mundurucú in 1875, published a bill presented to one chief (Tocantins, p. 154). If this bill is typical, the Indians' indebtedness was frequently very heavy. These debts were used to force the chief to extract greater production from his followers.

As the Mundurucú depended increasingly upon trade, the chief became more subordinate economically to the trader, who manipulated him accordingly. The trader eventually was able to appoint "chiefs" to carry on the trade. An appointed chief was usually known as the *capitao*, or "captain," as distinguished from the hereditary village chief, who was called *anyococucat* or *ichöngöp*. By using the"captains"as local trade representatives, the traders were able to increase their control over the villages. At the same time, by robbing the hereditary chiefs of their trade function, they weakened the entire structure of leadership. In time, the *capitao* displaced the hereditary chief almost entirely. To increase the prestige of the trader-appointed chief, the trader often took his protégé on his annual trip to buy supplies in Belém, where the chief's position was confirmed by the governor or some other official.

The Mundurucú dependency upon trade at first evidently increased the peace-time authority of the hereditary chief, for the villagers relied upon him to promote and secure their best interests in trading activities. The appointment of *capitaoes* undermined the native chief and initially increased the trader's control over the village. The people became confused, however, as to whether the *capitao* or the *anyococucat* should be regarded as "chief." Ill-feeling toward and suspicion of the appointed chiefs began to develop, for the Indians were always aware of, although powerless to cope with, the sharp practices of the traders, and they usually assigned the *capitao* a share of the blame. Upon the latter fell the onerous task of goading the people to harder work in the rubber avenues. Since most Mundurucú do not even today consider rubber collecting a congenial occupation, the role of the *capitao* must have done little to increase his popularity. During the field research among the Mundurucú, the young, bilingual trader-appointed "chief" of the village of Cabitutú was in danger of losing his life. Distrust of the trader, whom the "chief" represented, was centered upon this young man and threatened his position so greatly that he was on the verge of flight.

In later years, as will be described subsequently, individual Mundurucú Indians have tended increasingly to deal with the trader directly rather than through the "chief." For this reason village political organization has been effectively shattered.

The white-appointed Mundurucú "chief," unlike his Northeastern Algonkian counterpart, mediated trade relations between a group of followers and the whites. After individual trading had become strongly established among one section of the Mundurucú, however, "chiefs" were chosen by the Indian agent and by missionaries in order to control the general behavior of the Indians, and not specifically for commercial purposes. This more nearly approximates the modern Montagnais situation, although it was reached through a different sequence of functional roles and from a different aboriginal base. In both cases the Indians themselves were very conscious that these men were not genuine chiefs in terms of aboriginal leadership patterns, and both groups apparently suspected that the white-recognized chief was promoting the interests of the white men rather than those of his own people. The new leadership patterns never became fully established. While these patterns were functional in terms of white-Indian relations, they were dysfunctional in terms of the native sociocultural structure.

Among the Mundurucú, therefore, the integrity of the local sociopolitical groups was, in part, temporarily maintained by a change in the functional role of the chieftain. That the changed pattern of leadership eventually became dysfunctional resulted in part from the ecological adaptations necessary to rubber collection. These adaptations, however, did far more than contribute to the disintegration of policial controls. They undercut the very economic basis of village life.

Hevea brasiliensis, the native and most common species of rubber tree, grows wild throughout the upper waters of the Amazon. It can be exploited only during the dry season, and, in the upper Tapajós River valley, the maximum length of the gathering season is from May to early December, approximately seven months. Since these trees are scattered throughout the lowlands near the watercourses, they are reached by circuitous paths cut through the undergrowth. The spacing of the trees and the work involved in rubber collection generally limit the number of trees tapped daily by one man to 150 or less. Some collectors improve their yield per tree by maintaining two or three separate avenues which they visit only ever second or third day. The distribution of rubber trees is such that each avenue gives access to trees within an area of about three to five square miles. The actual size of this territory depends, of course, upon the density of the rubber trees. In some sections of the Amazon drainage wild rubber is more abundant than in others. One may travel ten to twenty miles on reaches of river where rubber is sparse without passing a single habitation, but where rubber is more plentiful, one encounters houses at intervals of a mile or even a half-mile.

The rubber tapper must work in his avenue or avenues almost daily, and therefore must live near them. Since each tapper exploits a considerable tract of land, his physical remoteness from neighboring tappers is a matter of necessity. Thus, on the Tapajós River, which has a population of about 3,000 excluding the Mundurucú, there are only two Brazilian villages of any consequence. One of these has a population of about 700, and the other has only 150 people. The other settlements are merely hamlets consisting of a trading post and from two to seven houses. The majority of the population live in isolated houses on the river banks.

The exploitation of wild rubber is a solitary, individual occupation in that the tapping of the tree, the subsequent collection of the latex, and the final coagulation process are one-man jobs. The last phase, carried out at the end of the day, consists of solidifying the latex over a smoky fire. The simplicity and the daily time schedule of the entire rubber process in Amazonia are such that no one can profitably leave off collection to specialize only in tapping or collection or coagulation. For similar reasons, two men do not work in the same avenue. However companionable, it would not be a practicable means of increasing production.

This brief account of how wild rubber is exploited is necessary to an understanding of changes in Mundurucú society. In the earlier contact period the Mundurucú traded chiefly in manioc flour and wild products, and rubber was of secondary importance. Chandless's observation (1862, p. 277) that in 1860 the Mundurucú of the upper Tapajós "trade in salsa and sell provisions to the parties of India-rubber makers" indicates that important trade in articles other than rubber continued at least until 1860. Shortly after this date, however, the tempo of rubber extraction in the Amazon quickened, and in 1875, as Tocantins's account shows (1877, pp. 151-154), rubber was the most important Mundurucú product.

With the advent of the rubber trade, Mundurucú acculturation entered its second stage. During the first, when trade in manioc flour and certain wild products predominated, the hereditary chief mediated between the traders and his people, aboriginal social patterns were largely unchanged, and warfare was still vigorously prosecuted, frequently under the sponsorship of traders and colonial authorities. During the second stage, which lasted until 1914, warfare abated, the size of villages decreased owing to migration and European-introduced diseases, and the position of the hereditary chief was weakened by the imposition of appointed "chiefs." The period was characterized by a "loosening" of integration rather than by a change in mode of integration, or structure.

Work in the rubber avenues in the latter half of the nineteenth century did not upset the annual subsistence cycle as much as might be expected. Whereas many people had formerly left their villages during the dry season to hunt and fish along the streams, they now left to collect rubber. As in times past, they cleared their garden sites before leaving and returned to the village in time to burn them over and plant. The necessity to provide all their own subsistence limited the rubber-producing season to three months, mid-June to mid-September, out of a possible seven. This parallels closely the earlier phases of Northeastern Algonkian fur production, when the Indians' need to obtain their own meat supply by aboriginal cooperative techniques limited fur production and conflicted with their increasing desire for Western manufactures (Leacock, 1954, pp. 25-26).

During the nineteenth century (and to the present day) the Mundurucú, like the Algonkians and in fact most aborigines, had been acquiring a seemingly insatiable appetite for the utilitarian wares and trinkets of civilization. Firearms increased their efficiency in warfare and hunting, especially the individual hunting carried on during the rubber season when one or two families lived in isolation adjacent to their rubber trees. In communal hunts the game could be surrounded and the range and velocity of the weapons were not so crucial to success. Other items, too, became necessities to the Mundurucú. Contrary to popular belief that nudity is beneficial to tropical peoples, there are various reasons why clothing is desirable in the Amazon. Insect stings greatly annoy the Indians, and at night the temperature drops to from 55° to 65° F. Clothing, however, is expensive, and only in recent years has it been used consistently in some Mundurucú villages. The movement toward covering the body entailed the development within two generations of a sense of shame comparable to that of Europeans. The Mundurucú, especially the women, have also acquired a desire for finery for the sake of display. They have also developed a taste for many strictly nonutilitarian goods, such as the Brazilian raw cane rum and the beads and ornaments purveyed by the trader.

A full and adequate description of the growth of Mundurucú dependence upon trade would require a separate treatise, for reliance upon manufactured goods entailed further dependence upon many adjuncts of these goods. For example, firearms required powder and lead, while garments of factory-woven cloth had to be made and repaired with scissors, thread, and needles. The substitution of metal pots for native ones of clay and of manufactured hammocks for the native product has reached the point where many young women now do not know how to make these articles. The Mundurucú barely remember that their forebears used stone axes and bamboo knives, and they would be helpless without the copper toasting pan used to make manioc flour.

Despite the flourishing trade in gewgaws, the allure of most trade goods lay more in their sheer utility than in their exotic qualities. The increased efficiency of the Mundurucú economy made possible by steel tools must have been enormous.

The parallels in these basic processes of acculturation between the Mundurucú and the Montagnais are probably to be found also among most aborigines. In the case of the Mundurucú the displacement of aboriginal crafts by commercial goods better suited to meet local needs, both old and new, inexorably led to increased dependency of the people upon those who furnished these goods and therefore to a greater involvement in economic patterns external to their own culture.

The Mundurucú families, like those of the Algonkians, became dependents of the trading posts. More than a century ago Bates related that Brazilian traders made seasonal expeditions to trade with the Mundurucú. After rubber became important in the Amazon, permanent trading posts were established on the upper Tapajós River. These posts, whether owned by individuals or companies, exercised such control over tracts of rubber-producing forest that they compelled the rubber collector to trade exclusively with them. They accomplished this by their power of dispossession and by holding the collector in debt. The traders among the Mundurucú were never able to obtain title of ownership to the rubber regions within Mundurucú country proper,[2] but they made the Indians dependent upon them in a very real sense through their credit arrangements. In time, all of the Mundurucú villages came under the control of various traders, who were so influential by virtue of being necessary to the Indians that they were able to appoint the "chief," in violation of Indian tradition, and thereby intensified their control over the Indians.

The progressive weakening of the hereditary chief, whose authority was based upon aboriginal activities, was furthered by the decline in warfare. The post-white warfare, although frequently mercenary in character and auxiliary to Portuguese occupation and expansion, continued the native pattern of authority. The Indians were paid in trade goods. When, at the end of the nineteenth century, the central Amazon region had been pacified, the military help of the Mundurucú was no longer needed. Meanwhile, rubber collecting had become the principal means by which the Indians acquired foreign trade articles. Since the Indians were important to rubber production in labor-starved Amazonia, they were pushed to greater efforts by the traders. Increased devotion of the Mundurucú to rubber production correspondingly interfered with their warfare, for in earlier times the rubber season was the time for war. When in 1914 a Franciscan mission was established in their midst, the earlier political and economic basis of Mundurucú warfare was so undermined that the admonitions of the priests that they live in peace were quite effective.

At the end of the second stage of Mundurucú acculturation, only bonds of kinship and economic collectivity in producing food for the group held Mundurucú society together. Much of the old structure was gone. The chieftaincy had been undermined, warfare had ended, and reliance upon the outside economy was taking effect. During the nineteenth century increasing numbers of Mundurucú who had difficulties with their co-residents were able to leave their villages permanently. Many others left in order to participate more fully in the rubber economy.

Full dependency upon rubber collecting is not compatible with village life. Since the aboriginal Mundurucú villages were located several

---

[2] The tenuous and diverse legal rights of the traders to control of rubber areas have been discussed by Wagley (1953, pp. 91-92).

days' foot travel from the rubber areas fringing the rivers, a family participating both in collective village life and the rubber economy had to migrate seasonally between its village and its house in the rubber area. Families living in this manner could spend only three to four months in rubber production. The only way the Indians can devote their full efforts to rubber tapping is to leave the villages of the interior savannah and live permanently near the rubber trees along the river banks. A large portion of the Mundurucú, whose increased need of and desire for trade goods could no longer be satisfied by the yield of only three months' work in the rubber avenues, have made this choice.

These families represent the third stage of Mundurucú acculturation. Their resettlement in the rubber regions, however, has occurred in two ways. The first is a direct and complete adaptation to rubber collection, which can be studied in many contemporary inland villages. People desiring to increase their income from barter improve their rubber avenue house to make it more comfortable during the rains, plant gardens, and remain there. Although they maintain relationships with the inland villages, the loci of their social lives lie increasingly within the orbit of the communities of scattered families dependent upon the trading posts. The final step in their incorporation into the local Brazilian economy and the culmination of this acculturative process will come when they abandon horticulture to devote full time to work in the rubber avenues, and, like their Brazilian neighbors and the Western Montagnais, depend upon trade for the bulk of their food supply.

The second mode of readaptation to the rubber economy, while ending in the same type of settlement pattern and social organization as the first, involves passage through an intermediate stage. The previously mentioned mission on the Cururú River had indifferent success in attracting the Mundurucú until the 1920s, when a policy of trading with the Indians was adopted. The missionaries were honest and generous in their commercial relations, and rubber-tapping became more profitable to the Indians. Their intensified collecting activities resulted in a general movement to the banks of the Cururú River, and by the 1930s many interior villages had been abandoned.

The migrants settled so heavily on the river banks that they were able to nucleate in new villages. These villages, however, lacked the men's organization, division of labor, and collective patterns which structured the old type villages. Although the population shift from the old to new villages was heavy, it involved individual families rather than whole villages. The new villages grew as additional nuclear families arrived from the savannah communities. During this period of growth, since the new villages consisted of families, many of which had not previously been connected with one another, each family had to carry on the subsistence activities which were formerly the function of the extended family and village. Gardens were cleared and planted by husband and wife with whatever aid their children were capable of giving. Fish, taken by family members from the nearby rivers, rapidly replaced game formerly taken in collective hunts as the major source of protein. Meanwhile, increased rubber production enabled the Indians to buy the hooks, lines, and canoes with which fishing was made more effective. As the new villages grew larger, the atomistic division of labor was perpetuated, and the nuclear family became the basic unit of production.

Political authority on the Cururú River was almost nonexistent. The migrants began to trade as individuals, first with the missionaries and later with the newly established post. This economic trend stripped the "chiefs" of one of their last remaining functions, and their role was reduced to that of intermediary between the villagers and the priests and Indian agent.

The amorphously structured villages which arose on the banks of the Cururú River represent a transition to the family level and are not the culmination of adaptation to the ecology of rubber collection. Most of the residents of the Cururú River still have to reside away from their villages during the rubber season, but the easy communication made possible by canoe transportation allows the majority to return to rubber production after planting their gardens.

The new individualism and fragmented division of labor, combined with facets of the old culture which had become dysfunctional in the new situation, contributed to the disorganization of Cururú River society. The political authority of appointed "chiefs" was now a means of extending the influence of the whites. The continuing migration of young men from the remaining primitive villages of the savannahs caused an oversupply of men on the Cururú River, and conflicts over women became rife. Owing to the endless squabbles in villages which had lost their aboriginal basis of integration, dissidents moved off to live at their rubber avenues or formed new and smaller villages. This fission process is still going on. Concomitantly, the mission and the Indian post are becoming more important as focal points in a new mode of integration of the Mundurucú. Over one-third of the Cururú River population make their rainy season homes at these agencies, which serve as centers of trade and of social and religious gatherings. It is from the post and mission, also, that the lines of authority now radiate.

IV. COMPARATIVE SUMMARY

The accompanying table presents the major phases of acculturation in summary form, as abstracted from the historical continua. The basic acculturative factors in both cases exerted parallel influences, although the two societies were substantively different until the final culmination was reached. There were four causal factors common to each. First, both became involved in a mercantile, barter economy in which the collector of wild products was tied by bonds of debt and credit to particular merchants. Such involvement also occurred widely among native peoples who produced crops or livestock. This arrangement must be distinguished from cash transactions, in which, owing to the impersonality of money as a medium of exchange, the primary producer has greater freedom of choice as to with whom he will deal. In a pure credit-barter economy, all transactions are based on a personal relationship between the principals; the merchant must be able to rely upon the continued patronage of the primary producer whereby the latter liquidates past debts while assuming new ones. It seems to be a basic procedure that the pre-literate Indian is kept in debt by the trader. While the latter can manipulate accounts at will, and no doubt is frequently guilty of malfeasance, he usually allows the Indian to buy beyond his means. The debtor-producer is selling his future production, and the creditor will not extend payment unless assured of delivery. Where such an economy is found, it is common for merchants to refuse to deal with primary producers who are in debt to another merchant. This is a "gentleman's agreement" in the Amazon, although it is frequently violated by wandering traders. Second, the growing ties of dependency upon the traders are at the expense of collective bonds within the respective societies. Reliance upon individuals and institutions outside the native social system is intensified by a steady increase in demand and need for manufactured goods. This, as we have seen, goes beyond the mere initial allure of Western tools and ornaments. Luxuries soon became necessities—a process that can be found in our own culture. Third, while crude latex and animal furs are very unlike articles, they imply a common cultural-ecological adaptation. Both are natural products having a reliable occurrence in worthwhile quantity within an area which can be most efficiently exploited by one man. Both require conservation, for careless exploitation can seriously reduce the number of fur-bearing animals or render rubber trees worthless. The producer has an incentive to maintain the productivity of his resources. Finally, both rubber trees and fur animals are sufficiently dispersed to require that persons exploiting them live or work at some distance from one another.

These factors of change were essentially the same among both Mundurucú and Montagnais, and they were introduced through contact with the outside world. Their initial effects upon the aboriginal cultures were somewhat dissimilar, owing to aboriginal differences between the two groups. Whereas the Mundurucú chief served at first as intermediary with the trader, this seems not to have been true of the Montagnais chief. Montagnais family heads, however, traded on behalf of their sons. For a short time this pattern was followed by many Mundurucú during the period immediately after the Mundurucú chief had ceased to act as intermediary with the trader. After the breakdown of extended kinship bonds in both groups, individuals traded completely on their own.

TABULAR COMPARISON

Mundurucú	*Montagnais*
1. Pre-rubber	1. Pre-fur
Village consists of men's house, matrilocal extended family households; population divided into patrilineal clans and moieties.	Nomadic composite band hunts large migratory game animals.
Village males form collective hunting and garden-clearing group.	Frequent band breakup during winter scarcity.
Household females form the horticultural unit.	Amalgamation of several winter groups for summer hunting and fishing.
Intensive warfare for headhunting and as mercenaries allied to whites; partial dispersal of villagers in dry season for fishing and war.	Chieftainship weak and shifting—leader of winter group; no summer band chief.
Chief the war leader and representative of village in trade of manioc flour.	Residence bilocal, frequent shifts of winter group membership.
2. Marginal involvement	2. Marginal involvement
Chief continues as mediator with trader, but is now often trader-appointed—trader gains influence.	Trade by family heads—leaders do not trade for followers.
Dry-season population dispersal for rubber production rather than fishing and war—war continues, but lessened in importance.	Trapping secondary to subsistence hunting—subsistence still gotten traditionally, basic social patterns persist.
	No trapping territory.
	Linkage to trading posts.

Basic pre-rubber economy and settlement pattern unchanged.
Continuing displacement of aboriginal crafts.

3. Transitional

Further displacement of native crafts, increased need of trade goods, increased dependence on trader.

Chieftainship undermined owing to new type chiefs who now represent the trader.

Agricultural cycle and village life inhibit larger rubber production.

Trend toward individual trade.

4. Convergence and culmination

A. Intermediate

Move to new villages in rubber regions.

Chief now intermediary with Indian agent and missionaries.

Individual trade, individualized subsistence economy—end of men's house and traditional village—village held together only by weakening kin ties and sociability.

Centripetal factors (e.g., sorcery, sexual rivalry) cause fission of these villages and results in B, below.

B. Dispersal (follows upon 3 or 4A)

Leadership no longer integrative. Individual trade undercuts kin obligations.

Conflict with argicultural cycle resolved by moving to rubber avenue—family now in isolation except for trade bonds.

3. Transitional

Further displacement of native crafts, increased need of trade goods, increased dependence on trader.

Increased fur production interferes with subsistence hunting.

Individual trade conflicts with group solidarity.

4. Convergence and culmination

Fur trapping now predominant; winter provisions purchased.

Winter groups not necessary with end of collective hunt—family or individual hunting gives greater efficiency, allows conservation.

Shift of economic interdependencies from group to trader.

Emergence of a chief who serves as intermediary with Indian agents and missionaries.

Nuclear family basic unit at all times of year.

Trapper maintains and transmits right to a delimited hunting territory exploited only by his family.

The native kinship organization persisted longer among the Mundurucú than among the Montagnais, and this has been a factor in perpetuating village life today among the less acculturated Indians east of the Tapajós River. Aboriginal Mundurucú kinship structure was more extensive and socially integrative than that of the Montagnais. Moreover, the aboriginal production of subsistence crops survives even among Mundurucú families living in isolation in their rubber avenues. The Mundurucú still produce all their own subsistence, although there are some changes in emphasis, technique, and organization.

The Brazilian rubber tapper—the white man who has gone into the forest or the Indian of mixed blood who is completely acculturated and enmeshed in the mercantile economy—usually buys all his food from the trader and devotes the season when he could be growing his own food to tapping rubber or to working off his debt to the trader by performing personal services. At present, we know of only one case of a Mundurucú who bought most of his food, but we can confidently predict that as the population becomes more acculturated toward dependency in all ways upon the larger society, an ever-increasing number will buy food. When they are no longer able to feed themselves by their own efforts, they will have effectively become *caboclos*, or neo-Brazilian backwoodsmen.

The acculturative factors operated in two somewhat different ways among both the Mundurucú and Montagnais. First, they created a succession of modifications in the native societies, which gradually converged toward typological identity in the final family level. Second, during this evolution of the total groups they produced deviant families which broke away from their fellow tribesmen to devote themselves entirely to tapping or trapping. It was not until the processes had nearly reached their culmination that the surviving but greatly modified native society began to disintegrate.

Among the Mundurucú the bonds of leadership and kinship had undergone a steady and slow attrition during one hundred years. The end of warfare had robbed Mundurucú culture of a great deal of its vitality, and the chief was reduced to a mere figurehead, manipulated by the trader and the religious and governmental agencies. Work in the rubber avenues and dependence upon the trader had served to sever and weaken ties within the society. At the final point of transition to isolated residence, and total divorce from traditional communal life, the Mundurucú were not much more closely integrated than the Montagnais.

The culmination of the long acculturative processes shows a high degree of structural parallelism. Both Mundurucú and Montagnais populations are divided into loosely integrated and dispersed communities centering about particular trading posts with which the individual families have ties. The Indians still recreate, associate, and intermarry with one another, but the nuclear family is now the stable socioeconomic unit. It is the highest level of integration found among the native population itself, but it is linked to the nation through the intermediary of a regional economy. The integration of the family with the national level is highly specialized and limited. These families do not yet share a substantial part of the common denominator of the national culture or even of the regional subcultures of their non-Indian neighbors.

There is a final phase, which, though occurring at different dates in the different localities, is characterized by assimilation of the Indians as a local subculture of the national sociocultural system and virtual loss of identity as Indians. At this point the acculturational processes and results diverge, since the Indians participate to a much greater extent in the national culture. So long as the families maintain their marginal relation with the national society, they are quite unlike the basic populations of the nations in which they live and much more like one another. When, however, they learn the national language, intermarry extensively with non-Indians, and acquire many of the non-Indian values and behavior patterns, they have to be classed with the special regional subcultures that have developed in portions of these nations.

It can be predicted that the drastic shift in mode and level of integration will do much to hasten the loss of cultural distinctiveness. Fortes has cogently expressed the relationship between social structure and formal culture content in such a situation: "I would suggest that a culture is a unity insofar as it is tied to a bounded social structure. In this sense I would agree that the social structure is the foundation of the whole social life of any continuing *society*. . . . The social structure of a group does not exist without the customary norms and activities which work through it. We might safely conclude that where structure persists there must be some persistence of corresponding custom, and where custom survives there must be some structural basis for this" (Fortes, 1953, pp. 22-23).

V. FURTHER COMPARISONS

We can delimit and refine the Mundurucú-Algonkian parallel by the cross-cultural examination of structural changes caused by acculturation in other areas. We will not seek further parallels, however, but will discuss cultures in which divergence appears manifest. One instance of such apparent divergence is the Northwest Coast, where the fur trade at first strengthened or intensified rather than weakened the aboriginal social structure. The florescence of the potlatch and class system on the Northwest Coast as a result of new wealth in trade goods is a thesis which has been ably expounded by a number of students (cf. Barnett, 1938; Drucker, 1939; Collins, 1950; Codere, 1950). It would be very misleading, however, to consider *any* trade in furs as the crucial factor. What really matters is *individual trapping of fur-bearing animals*. The sea otter was the principal fur bartered by most Northwest Coast tribes, and collection involved neither individual effort nor delimited territories. The amount of land trapping was probably fairly limited and in any event did not offset the cultural effects of the great salmon wealth which created surpluses rarely if ever paralleled by hunting, gathering, and fishing people.

The trapping activities of the Skagit of Puget Sound more nearly paralleled those of the Northeastern Algonkians, according to Collins's description (1950, p. 335): "The [trading] posts played an important part in altering the economy of the Indians. First, they encouraged a shift in their hunting habits. The skins in which the traders were most interested were beaver and land otter. These animals had small value in the aboriginal economy, since they were less desirable for food than deer or elk, for example. At the traders' behest, however, hunters pursued these animals eagerly. Another economic shift took place when the hunters, instead of killing game for meat, began to exchange skins for food." The result of this trade was, however, quite different from its effects in Eastern Canada: "The effects of these changes upon Skagit social organization were pronounced. Distinctions in social rank began to be more marked—a shift made possible since, though social mobility had always been within the grasp of any person of good descent who could acquire the distinction of wealth, new sources of wealth were now available" (*ibid.*, pp. 337-338).

The new wealth acquired by the Skagit was funneled into the class structure and ultimately the potlatch. The difference, then, between the processes of change which occurred among Northwest Coast and Northeastern Canadian groups is that the former integrated the new wealth into a *pre-existent* class structure created and perpetuated by a fishing economy. Among the latter, since there were no cultural means or goals promoting the concentration of surplus wealth in the hands of a select few, the benefits rebounded to all persons. The same was true of Mundurucú society, which also was unstratified. The differences between the Skagit on the one hand as opposed to the Mundurucú and Montagnais on the other are attributable to the stratification of society among the former, which in turn is partially explainable by the greater aboriginal resources of the Skagit. In effect, this constitutes a difference of level of sociocultural integration.

The impact of trapping upon a pre-existing social structure can be even better appraised among the Carrier of the interior of British Columbia, where the wealth in salmon was far less than on the coast. The fur trade among the Blackwater River Carrier involved intimate interaction with Northwest Coast groups, especially the Bella Coola. Goldman summarizes the effects of this contact upon the simple, bilateral Carrier hunting bands (1941, pp. 416-417):

> Undoubtedly the Bella Coola, like all Northwest Coast tribes, became relatively wealthy as a result of this trade. And in Bella Coola where wealth was the decisive factor in building rank, the fur trade must have been particularly welcome. And the lowly interior Carrier who hunted for furs in order to trade with the Bella Coola, who traded them to the whites, became an important part of the scheme of elevating one's rank. Although a Bella Coola did not gain valuable prerogatives from a Carrier son-in-law, if he could get a monopoly upon his furs he could make enough wealth to purchase new prerogatives. And as the Bella Coola benefited by this trade, so did the Alkatcho Carrier. The latter took up products obtained on the coast and traded them to the Carrier villages eastward on the Blackwater River drainage. As they obtained guns and steel traps, economic productivity spurted so that they were able to build up the necessary property surpluses for potlatching. Potlatching obligations in turn stimulated economic activity, and the degree to which they were able to potlatch made possible the full integration of crests as honorific prerogatives.

Given our previous hypotheses, developments more or less parallel to those in Eastern Canada might be expected. But these Carrier did not trade with European traders; they dealt instead with stratified Northwest Coast tribes in the context of an economic system, the rationale of which was the validation of rank by potlatch. As the following example of the Stuart Lake Carrier suggests, direct trade with the whites and the end of potlatching result ultimately in the family trapping territory system.

The effect of the fur trade among the Carrier of Stuart Lake to the north of the Blackwater River ran a similar course but culminated in family trapping territories, according to Steward's research. In pre-white times the wealth of salmon fisheries, although far less than those of the coastal tribes, had provided some surplus, while contacts with the Tsimshian of the Skeena River had introduced a pattern for channeling this surplus to nobles who controlled the fishing rights of large territories in the name of matrilineal moieties. This wealth circulated through small-scale potlatches. The fur trade, carried on directly with the whites more than through coastal contacts, created a new source of wealth and intensified the native pattern. Although furs were trapped by individual moiety members, a noble had rights to a certain percentage of the furs taken in his moiety's territory.

In the course of about 50 years, however, several processes combined to bring about individual trapping territories as among the Indians of Eastern Canada. Most important, the new wealth in trade goods brought hardware that was of value to individuals. Pressures mounted to force the nobles to divide the trapping territories among their own children rather than to pass them on intact to their sister's sons, who had traditionally inherited their titles and rights. This process was aided by the activities of the Catholic missionary-ethnologist Father Morice, who effectively undermined the native religious sanctions of the class of nobles, and by the government, which banned potlatching. The older pattern survives only in isolated localities, where it is carried on clandestinely. At Fort St. James on Stuart Lake, where there is located a Hudsons' Bay Trading Post and some few hundred whites and Indians, the processes have reached a culmination almost identical to that of the Montagnais: "Present-day Carrier society at Stuart Lake consists of individual families that have exclusive rights to certain trap-lines that are registered with and protected by the Provincial Government. The family is the kinship and economic unit" (Steward, 1941, pp. 500-501).

It seems likely that the Blackwater River Carrier have not yet reached the final stage of acculturation. The same may be true of the Skagit. The critical consideration is whether wealth in salmon among these tribes was so great that it offset the importance of trapping. This was not the case at Stuart Lake. On the lower Skeena River salmon are so important that canneries have been built, and the Tsimshian and Tlingit have given up fur trapping to become commercial fishermen and cannery laborers.

Certain Plains Indians in North America also engaged in the fur trade but developed in distinctive ways. This is another illustration of the need to examine specific features in the taking of furs. There is a significant ecological difference between the collection of fur on the Great Plains and in the coniferous forests of Canada that lies essentially in the difference between hunting and trapping. It is incomplete and misleading therefore, to make comparisons simply on the basis of "fur trading." In the Great Plains, buffalo hides were the chief item traded, whereas in eastern Canada, small, nongregarious, and nonmigratory animals were trapped. The trade on the Plains resulted in an emphasis upon the buffalo hunt beyond the needs of subsistence and served to strengthen the collective and cooperative techniques traditionally used in the pursuit of migratory herds. Moreover, band cohesion in the Plains was enhanced by acquisition of the horse and gun and by intensification of warfare, the latter carried on in part to obtain horses.

It is possible that a nonstratified society which acquires surplus wealth may develop a class structure, but this involves special conditions not ordinarily found among collectors of wild products. Some of the North American Plains Indians showed an incipient development of a class society in the late eighteenth and early nineteenth centuries, but the tribes were decimated by epidemics and overwhelmed by the advancing frontier when intensified wealth and significant prestige differences had begun to emerge. A parallel between the Plains and the Mundurucú can be found in the increased authority of chiefs owing to their functions as intermediaries between the traders and the Indians. Jablow notes such a florescence of political controls among the Cheyenne (1951, p 86), and Lewis specifically states of Blackfoot trade (1942, p. 42): "In periods of monopoly (of the Indian trade by one company) the fur trade has a positive effect, that is, it increased the prestige and authority of the chiefs. In periods of competition it has a disruptive effect, that is, it weakened the power of the chiefs."

The Plains band chief traded a commodity which was obtained by collective effort. The Mundurucú chief served as middleman in the pre-rubber period when trade in manioc flour, which was also communally produced, was of primary importance. But he eventually lost his position when individually produced rubber became predominant. The Tenetehara Indians of northeastern Brazil have been in contact with civilization longer than the Mundurucú, but, according to Wagley and Galvao, the village chiefs and extended family heads still have a central role in the trading of collectively produced manioc flour and palm oils (1949, pp. 26-30). It seems apparent that, lacking some other basis for political authority, it is difficult for leaders to maintain control over trade in individually produced goods.

Our formulations, in effect, state that when certain acculturative factors, defined functionally rather than formally, are present, the core of a culture will change in expectable and predictable ways. These formulations assume the constancy of certain other preconditions, which, though well worth investigation of themselves, can be regarded as given factors for methodological purposes.

This can best be exemplified in our present cases by reference to the basic, though incompletely explained, acculturative factor common not only to the Mundurucú and Naskapi but to most primitive peoples throughout the world. This factor can be stated simply as follows: *When goods manufactured by the industrialized nations with modern techniques become available through trade to aboriginal populations, the native people increasingly give up their home crafts in order to devote their efforts to producing specialized cash crops or other trade items in order to obtain more of the industrially made articles.* The consequences of this simple though worldwide factor are enormous, even though they vary in local manifestation. The phenomenon is of such a high order of regularity that special explanations must be sought for the few departures from it. The main hypothesis arising from the present study is that: *When the people of an unstratified native society barter wild products found in extensive distribution and obtained through individual effort, the structure of the native culture will be destroyed, and the final culmination will be a culture type characterized by individual families having delimited rights to marketable resources and linked to the larger nation through trading centers.* Tappers, trappers, and no doubt other collectors come under this general statement.

BIBLIOGRAPHY

BARNETT, H. G.
1938. "The Coast Salish of Canada," *American Anthropoligist,* 40, pp. 118-141.

BATES, HENRY WALTER
1863. *The Naturalist on the River Amazons.* London.

CHANDLESS, W.
1862. "Notes on the Rivers Arinos, Juruena, and Tapajós," *Journal of the Royal Geographical Society*, 32, pp. 268-280.

CODERE, HELEN
1950. *Fighting with Property.* Monograph No. XVIII of the American Ethnological Society.

COLLINS, JUNE
1950. "Growth of Class Distinctions and Political Authority among the Skagit Indians during the Contact Period," *American Anthropologist,* 52, pp. 331-342.

COOPER, JOHN M.
1939. "Is the Algonquian Family Hunting Ground System Pre-Columbian?" *American Anthropologist,* 41, pp. 66-90.

DRUCKER, PHILLIP
1939. "Rank, Wealth, and Kinship in Northwest Coast Society," *American Anthropologist,* 41, pp. 55-56.

EISELEY, LOREN C.
1939. See Speck and Eiseley.

1942. See Speck and Eiseley.

1947. "Land Tenure in the Northeast: A Note on the History of a Concept," *American Anthropologist,* 49, pp. 680-681.

FORTES, MEYER
1953. "The Structure of Unilineal Descent Groups," *American Anthropologist,* 55, pp. 17-41.

GOLDMAN, IRVING
1941. "The Alkatcho Carrier: Historical Background of Crest Prerogatives," *American Anthropologist*, 43, pp. 396-418.

JABLOW, JOSEPH
1951. *The Cheyenne in Plains Indian Trade Relations, 1795-1840.* Monograph No. XIX of the American Ethnological Society, New York.

JENNESS, DIAMOND
1932. *The Indians of Canada.* 2d ed. National Museum of Canada Bulletin 65, Anthropological Series No. 15.

LEACOCK, ELEANOR BURKE
1954. *The Montagnais "Hunting Territory" and the Fur Trade.* American Anthropological Association Memoir 78.

LEWIS, OSCAR
1942. *The Effects of White Contact upon Blackfoot Culture.* Monograph No. VI of the American Ethnological Society, New York.

MURPHY, ROBERT F.
1955. "Matrilocality and Patrilineality in Mundurucú Society." Unpublished.

SPECK, FRANK G.
1915. "The Family Hunting Band as the Basis of Algonkian Social Organization," *American Anthropologist,* 17, pp. 289-305.

1939 (and Loren C. Eiseley). "The Significance of the Hunting Territory Systems of the Algonkian in Social Theory," *American Anthropologist*, 41, pp. 269-280.

1942 (and Loren C. Eiseley). "Montagnais—Naskapi Bands and Family Hunting Districts of the Central and Southern Labrador Peninsula," *Proceedings of the American Philosophical Society*, 85, pp. 215-242.

STEWARD, JULIAN H.
1941. "Determinism in Primitive Society?" *Scientific Monthly*, 53, pp. 491-501.

TOCANTINS, A. M. G.
1877. "Estudos sobre a tribu Mundurukú," *Revista do Instituto Historico e Geografico Brasileiro*, 40, Pt. 2, pp. 73-161.

WAGLEY, CHARLES
1949 (and Eduardo Galvao). *The Tenetehara Indians of Brazil.* New York.

1953. *Amazon Town.* New York.

8

Determinism in Primitive Society?

First published in the *Scientific Monthly* (vol. 53, pp. 491-501, 1941) and reprinted here with permission of that magazine, "Determinism in Primitive Society?" explores the question of economic causality in culture. Other articles by Steward address this theoretical issue more fully, but the essay is also important as one of his few publications on the Carrier Indians of the Bulkley River, British Columbia. The original illustrations have been omitted in this edition. Copyright 1941 by the American Association for the Advancement of Science.

There has recently been renewed interest in the general proposition, stated in many ways and with varying degrees of moderation, that technological and economic changes largely predetermine social and political trends. Politicians, businessmen, and laymen argue the power of some form of "economic determinism" as against ideologies. What has anthropology, centering its attention largely on the simpler peoples of the world where it should be easier to isolate the causes of social change, to say of this proposition?

Anthropologists have long recognized that the spread of customs from one group of people to another—"diffusion" in anthropological terminology—accounts for at least nine-tenths of the culture of any group. On its face, this would seem to assign any kind of economic determinism an insignificant role. An analysis of this problem, however, in the light of what is known of culture change among primitive peoples, both before and after they have experienced acculturation resulting from contact with European cultures, exposes its considerable complexity. Under certain conditions, subsistence patterns—that is, the activities concerned with acquiring food, clothing, shelter, and other things indispensable to existence—have imposed very narrow limits on possible variation of social and economic organization. Under other conditions, it is evident that considerable latitude is possible in the socioeconomic structure. Before attempting any generalizations, therefore, anthropology is compelled to ascertain in specific circumstances the manner and extent to which subsistence patterns have affected the total culture.

Subsistence patterns have been extraordinarily potent in shaping the social organization of a number of primitive hunting and gathering peoples in different parts of the world. Among the Bushmen, African and Malaysian Negritos, Australians, Tasmanians, Fuegians, southern California Indians, and several others, certain features of the relationship of man to his environment are very similar and have produced almost identical social patterns. All these peoples live in areas of slim food resources and low population density. To obtain adequate food, it is necessary that single families forage alone during most of the year. Larger population aggregates are possible only for brief periods of abundance when a few communal enterprises are carried on. Because hunting provides the most important food, it is customary for a man to remain in the territory in which he has been raised and has learned to know intimately. He hunts alone or with a few other men who do not venture beyond their territory and defend it from trespass by outsiders. As the local group rarely numbers more than 50 people, its members are usually related so that it is necessary that a man take his wife from another group. Each group consequently consists of people related through the male line. It is a patrilineal, patrilocal, exogamous, land-owning band. This pattern is repeated so consistently under identical economic and environmental conditions that a cause-and-effect relationship between the latter and the former is unmistakable (Steward, 1936).

Although the essential social patterns of the tribes just mentioned developed directly from factors that are mainly economic, diffusion was also at work in some cases. In northern Australia matrilineal moieties—dual divisions reckoning descent through the female line—had spread among many tribes and been superimposed on patrilineal bands to create a complicated system of marriage classes. In southern California patrilineal moieties had been adopted by several tribes with patrilineal bands. And among all these tribes, a number of minor details of society were clearly derived from neighboring areas.

Subsistence patterns imposed even narrower limits on the social structure of Shoshonean tribes in the Great Basin area of the western United States (Steward, 1939). In aboriginal days the Shoshoneans did little hunting, as game was too scarce. They relied predominantly on wild seeds that grow sparsely in the semideserts. Because these seeds occur somewhat erratically from year to year it was necessary that families, usually wandering alone in their food quest, gather seeds wherever they could be found. This brought overlapping subsistence areas and a complete lack of ownership of natural resources. The lone family, therefore, was usually the maximum economic unit, and, rarely enjoying the company of other families, it was the only stable social unit being linked to other families only through loose kinship bonds.

But the entire socioeconomic structure of certain Shoshoneans was altered by a single factor introduced by the white man. The horse was adopted at an early date by those groups occupying grasslands. The transportational advantages of the horse not only enhanced the importance of hunting among those near bison country, but enabled considerable numbers of people to live together in permanent association. It was no longer necessary that families remain near their stored foods in various parts of the country; food could be transported to a central point. These Shoshoneans quickly developed bands of considerable size.

The question of what limitation subsistence patterns imposed on the social structure of hunters and gatherers in a more fertile environment was investigated among the Carrier Indians of British Columbia. The Carrier Indians inhabit an area of comparatively abundant food resources. Like their Athapaskan-speaking relatives of the Mackenzie basin, they trapped fur-bearing animals and hunted large game characteristic of the north woods. But, like the tribes of the north Pacific coast, they also took considerable quantities of fish, especially salmon, from the headwaters of the Fraser and Skeena Rivers. Although less wealthy than the coast Indians, the Carrier found living not as precarious as among the tribes east of the Continental Divide beyond the habitat of the salmon.

The history of the Carrier Indians is known in considerable detail during the century and a quarter that has elapsed since the first European visited them in 1805. Certain events during the prehistoric period can be inferred with reasonable certainty.

The Carrier subsistence pattern that was known at the beginning of the historic period probably extends back several centuries. It rested on a balance of complementary activities carried on during the summer and winter respectively. In summer, people remained in permanent villages near their fisheries and caught great quantities of salmon. Communal enterprises, such as the construction of fish weirs, contributed to group solidarity. In late fall, when furs were prime, families, alone or in small groups, took to the streams and forests to trap beaver, muskrat, mink, fox, and other fur-bearing animals and to hunt deer, bear, and caribou. They remained, however, within easy distance of their villages because hunger compelled them to return home from time to time to their stores of smoked salmon.

Carrier socioeconomic organization must originally have been based on some kind of loose bands like those of the interior Athapaskans. If the Carrier were distinctive, it was probably because salmon gave them greater security and permitted permanent villages, whereas Athapaskans beyond the salmon habitat had to wander over their hunting lands throughout the year. There is no reason to believe that the Carrier had any kind of private ownership of food resources. As among other Athapaskans, all members of the village or band probably had the right of using the group's fishing stations and hunting area.

In the course of time, however, the Carrier were exposed to influence from the Pacific Coast, where the tribes had a strongly matrilineal society with an aristocracy based on wealth—a socioeconomic organization unique among American Indians. The Northwest Coast tribes are organized in totemic moieties and clans. A child belongs by birth to his mother's group. Each clan and moiety had certain hereditary titles of nobility which were held by individual men and passed on to their sisters' sons, thus remaining in the clan and family. With these titles went rights to the produce of certain fisheries and other natural resources and the privilege of requiring one's clansmen of the common class to help amass goods for great feasts at which presents were distributed to rival chiefs or nobles. These feasts, called potlatches, were essential to establish a title and the wealth it represented, for the Northwest Coast point of view held that proof of wealth lay in distributing rather than hoarding goods.

Completely foreign to Athapaskan society as this Northwest Coast pattern would seem, it spread up the Skeena River from the Tsimshian Indians to the Carrier of Babine Lake and finally to those of Stuart Lake. Its appearance among the Carrier, however, was in comparatively late prehistoric times, for it was still spreading when the white man arrived. Some Carrier adopted it only within the past hundred years. The Stuart Lake people, however, had the whole system when the Europeans first arrived, as several facts show. The succession of matrilineally inherited land and titles can be traced back to this time. Moreover, several historic incidents demonstrate the importance of wealth to the early Carrier. It is related that in 1823 James Douglas, who was in charge of Fort St. James, had two Indians put to death for the murder of two soldiers. The great chief Kwah entered the fort to avenge the matter. He objected not to the death sentence imposed on the Indians but to their bodies having been thrown to dogs. As Kwah threatened to kill Douglas, a quick-thinking woman began to potlatch him with tobacco, blankets, and other goods thrown from the loft. No Carrier nobleman could commit murder in the face of such gifts and Douglas's life was spared.

So far as can be ascertained, the transition from a simple band system to the Northwest Coast type of society occurred without a single important change in the methods of producing wealth. Hunting, fishing, and fur-trapping were still carried on with devices that are widespread and clearly old in the north—bows and arrows, traps, nets, and snares.

Innovations were not in methods of production but in ownership and distribution. Land that previously had belonged to the whole group was now divided among men holding potlatch titles. Other people continued to live on the produce of this land but might be obliged to supply the needs of their potlatching nobleman, who might also be a kinsman and a source of some pride to them. In short, wealth was now owned and much of it consumed by a hereditary aristocracy.

The only economic factor that must be considered in this new Carrier social order was salmon fishing. The wealth that salmon made possible was insufficient to create a new system, but without it the system could not have been introduced. This is shown by the distribution of clans and potlatching. Whereas they were finally adopted by practically all the tribes on the salmon streams west of the Continental Divide in northern British Columbia, they did not and almost certainly could not have spread to the poorer Athapaskans of the Mackenzie basin beyond the habitat of the salmon.

The first effect of contact with the white man was to intensify rather than alter the motivations and structure of Carrier society. Steel traps made it possible to take more furs, guns to shoot more game, and steel tools to construct weirs that would catch more salmon. The fur trade introduced a wealth of European goods. Potlatch guests enjoyed presents in greater variety and quantity than ever. But at best, Carrier potlatches were sorry affairs compared with those held by Indians on the coast, where natural resources are far greater. A wealthy coast noble might not only distribute quantities of food, hundreds of Hudson's Bay blankets, and other presents, but, to prove that his wealth was unlimited, kill a slave or burn a canoe in sheer bravado. A potlatching Carrier gave each guest a bit of food, perhaps a pair of moccasins or leggings, and a quarter or a sixth of a Hudson's Bay blanket. It was said that a man who had been potlatched often might receive enough pieces of blanket to sew them together into a whole blanket!

In the course of time, other influences emanating from the white man began to undermine the native Carrier system. But the transition to a new kind of society was effected gradually, through a series of cultural reintegrations. The Carrier experienced a minimum of the shock that has demoralized so many Indian tribes after the impact of European culture on their own. Some of the ease with which change was accomplished may be attributed to the powerful personality of Father Morice, a Catholic missionary among them during the crucial years of their transformation. A historian and ethnographer, Father Morice studied the native Carrier culture and succeeded not only in stamping out many features disapproved by the Church but in developing the Carrier along new lines.

One of the first blows at the native system was to disrupt the mechanism for inheriting wealth and titles by banning cross-cousin marriage. It had been the custom that a man marry his mother's brother's daughter, live for some years in his uncle's household, and finally inherit his uncle's land and title. With a prohibition on cousin marriage, this inheritance machinery was thrown out of gear. It was still possible, of course, for a man to give his wealth and titles to his sister's son but, without cross-cousin marriage, his own daughter received nothing, so that these were alienated from his immediate family. Moreover, the Carrier were continually exposed to the white man's system of patrilineal ownership and inheritance. In the course of time, therefore, certain men came to consider it better to divide their estates among their own sons and repudiate the ancient obligation to give them to their nephews. One of the first to follow this independent course was Chief Kwah, owner of the highest titles and largest territory at Fort St. James. He divided his land equally among all his sons. An increasing number of men followed Kwah's example so that today very few Carrier families lack trapping grounds. Descent from father to son is the rule.

The new system of land tenure and inheritance in turn destroyed the basis of the old titles and potlatching. For a few years men continued to pass their titles to their nephews even while giving their land to their own sons. But a title is worthless unless a potlatch feast can be held to establish it, and a potlatch can not be given without ample resources. Potlatching therefore was doomed and titles were empty. One of Kwah's sons attempted to usurp Kwah's title which, by the former rule, should have gone to the nephew. This not only violated native usage but, having little wealth, Kwah's son was unable to potlatch for his title. He was refused recognition. Today most Stuart Lake Carrier not only do not know who would be eligible for titles but have forgotten what most of the titles were.

Potlatching was also undermined when the Indians began to learn that it is better to husband goods than to give them away. The importance of this became very clear after the fur take had begun seriously to decline as a result of immoderate trapping with steel traps and after the salmon catch had all but vanished when the government prohibited the use of weirs and when the downstream canneries cut heavily into each salmon run. Under aboriginal conditions, depleted fortunes could have been restored in time with hard work. Now, with reduced resources, potlatching ate into capital that would take many years to replenish and tended to pauperize the common people who had to supply potlatch goods. In a few parts of British Columbia where secret potlatches are occasionally held today in defiance of Provincial law, public officials are no little annoyed that commoners who have impoverished themselves for potlatches should clamor for government relief!

Among the last features of the old Carrier social system to fade were the matrilineal, exogamous clans. These could, of course, have persisted after potlatching was abandoned. But they were weakened when the Indians accepted Catholicism. The clans had consisted of people who felt themselves related to one another because they had the common bond of an animal totem as well as economic functions. When the Catholic Church destroyed the system of myths and beliefs that had sanctioned the supernatural nature of these totems, the bond between clansmen was greatly weakened. The sense of kinship began to fade and marriages between clan members became more frequent.

Present-day Carrier society at Stuart Lake consists of individual families that have exclusive rights to certain trap-lines that are registered with and protected by the Provincial government. The family is the kinship and economic unit. Potlatching, status based on wealth, and exogamous clans have disappeared. The transition to the new socioeconomic system was caused mainly by noneconomic factors— absorption of the white man's ideology, especially Catholicism. Depletion of native resources was only an incidental, contributing factor. Its effect will probably be consummated in the future, when the native economy gradually gives place to a system of jobs and wages and the Carrier are absorbed in the broader economy of the white man.

From this review, it is evident that the influence of subsistence patterns on the general form of socioeconomic organization is great among the hunting and gathering peoples in areas of low productivity. Among the Carrier, at least, the framework of a given economy permitted several very unlike kinds of society, the choice between them depending on the influence of ideas from other peoples rather than upon economic necessity. Anthropology will not, however, be in a position to formulate any important generalizations about determinism in social change until this problem has been analyzed in many societies of different kinds. Each analysis must clarify the complex interaction of economic technology, environment, socioeconomic organization, and diffusion of ideas.

BIBLIOGRAPHY

STEWARD, JULIAN H.

1936. "The Social and Economic Basis of Primitive Bands." In *Essays in Anthropology in Honor of Alfred L. Kroeber*, pp. 331-350. Berkeley, Calif.

1939. "Changes in Shoshonean Indian Culture." *Scientific Monthly*, 49:524-537.

9

Carrier Acculturation: The Direct Historical Approach

"Carrier Acculturation: The Direct Historical Approach" (in *Culture in History: Essays in Honor of Paul Radin*, ed. Stanley Diamond, New York: Columbia University Press, 1961, pp. 732-744) was written almost twenty years after Steward's Carrier research and represents a historic focus that marked his work in both archeology and ethnology. It is reprinted here with the permission of Dr. Diamond and the Columbia University Press.

THE PROBLEM

In 1940 there were 1,666 Carrier Indians on 23 reserves scattered in the general area of Stuart Lake and Babine Lake, British Columbia. The population of the reserves ranged from 5 at Black Water to 257 at Fort St. James on Stuart Lake, where the present research was carried out. These Indians still spoke their own language as well as English, retained a few native crafts, and were fairly orthodox Catholics. They subsisted partly by hunting and fishing, but, more important, they depended upon the fur-trapping in the area. Carefully mapped trapping territories were registered in the names of individuals with the Provincial government of British Columbia (see map) and protected against exploitative trespass by the game warden.

A century ago these same people were divided into what Jenness and Morice call "phratries." "Phratry" is hardly the appropriate term, however, since the divisions were not strictly unilinear, exogamous, nonlocalized groups, and they were not subdivided into clans. Rather, they were localized groups which carried titles of nobility that theoretically were inherited matrilineally but in practice were acquired in various ways. The titles were validated by potlatches supported by the wealth in fur and fish taken from particular territories.

Two centuries ago the Carrier were hunters and fishers who lived in some kind of simple bands and lacked any nobility or potlatching.

The research problem was, first, to ascertain the process of change from the hunting bands to the nobility and potlatches and, second, to understand how the latter broke down into individual families, each with its trapping territory.

The nature of the earlier change from hunting bands to a society of nobles and commoners is inferential, since it took place before whites entered Carrier country. There are interesting similarities and differences between the northern Carrier, herein discussed, and the Alkatcho Carrier to the south, who were studied by Irving Goldman. The Stuart Lake Carrier derived their Northwest Coast patterns ultimately from the matrilineal Tsimshian of the Skeena River, who adjoined the Carrier of the Babine and Bulkley rivers, both tributaries of the Skeena, whereas the Alkatcho were influenced by their western neighbors, the patrilineal Bella Coola.

The breakdown of the "phratry" system during the last two or three generations and the division of territories of nobles into individual trapping territories are well documented. It was possible to begin with the Provincial British Columbian maps which showed registered trapping territories of 1939, and, by means of genealogies, to trace the inheritance of these back to the nobility holdings. These genealogies were especially well illustrated by the case of Kwah, the native chief of the Fort St. James village, whose grandson, the elderly and extraordinarily able "chief," Louis Billy Prince, was my main informant. The processes were also verified by tracing the genealogies and land tenure among holders of other trapping territories in the Stuart Lake region.

HUNTING BANDS

The nature of the early Carrier hunting bands can only be surmised. Throughout most of north-central Canada, Athabaskan bands were "composite," that is, multifamily societies which subsisted mainly by hunting large caribou herds. The Carrier live on the Pacific watershed and had access to salmon as well as caribou and, later, to moose. While their fisheries were not comparable to those of the downstream Indians—e.g. on the Lower Skeena and Fraser rivers—they yielded perhaps 50 percent of the foods. This densely forested, mountainous area with its thousands of lakes and streams was also rich in fur-bearing animals, which, however, were important to the aboriginal people more for their meat than their pelts.

There is nothing in recorded or recent Stuart Lake ethnography that clearly indicates the nature of early Carrier band organization. Goldman believes that the Alkatcho Carrier bands may have consisted of extended and predominantly patrilineal families which controlled trapping territories. Owing to the comparative scarcity of caribou, which later disappeared to be replaced by moose, and to the abundance of fish and nonmigratory small game, such localization may have characterized all the Carrier. These extended family units, however, should be distinguished from the nuclear families which held trapping territories in eastern Canada and which today hold such territories among the Carrier. While Cooper and Speck had argued that family territories were aboriginal, the evidence seems pretty conclusive that they represent the breakdown of hunting bands and the emergence of the family as the socioeconomic unit in response to the fur trade. The eastern Algonkian family territories, in other words, are the same as the registered Carrier territories of the present day, and they developed for the same reasons.

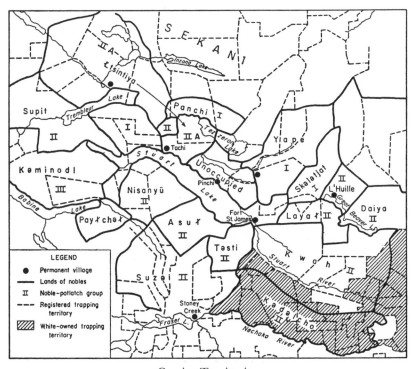

Carrier Territories

The map shows the principal permanent Carrier villages known in historic times. Probably the population was much more dispersed before the era of fur trade than it is today. Fort St. James, established in 1806 at an Indian village at the outlet of the lake, became a major trading post and religious center of central British Columbia by mid-century. In 1909 it had 198 persons, and in 1939 it had 257. That the function of village chief remained distinct from that of nobles and that it was inherited patrilineally, whereas the latter was in theory acquired matrilineally, accord with Goldman's data in indicating strong patrilineality among the hunting bands. Possibly the smaller communities were actual patrilineages.

FROM BAND TO NOBILITY AND POTLATCH

Since introduction of the Northwest Coast social and economic patterns to the Carrier probably took place two or three decades before the whites entered their country and without any change whatever in exploitative technology or local resources, this seemed to represent a case in which the cultural ecology or organization of society with respect to land use had considerable latitude for variation. If so, the change from bands to nobles and potlatching was caused by the fortuitous historic circumstance of contact with the coast.

As Goldman clearly implies, however, this interpretation is untenable. The fur trade reached important proportions on the Northwest Coast in the last two decades of the eighteenth century. The coastal Indians, acting as middlemen for the Indians living east of the Coast Ranges, created a new source of wealth in furs. Without any change in resources or productive technology (until steel goods began to filter in), the Carrier suddenly had a negotiable surplus.

In considering the processes by which the pattern of nobility spread inland to the Carrier, it is important to distinguish production of basic subsistence commodities—food, clothing, housing—from surplus goods, which were predominantly furs and secondarily fish. In a sense, two social arrangements for land use—two unlike cultural-ecological adaptations—coexisted.

At Stuart Lake, subsistence continued to follow the older pattern in that people could hunt food animals anywhere and, if in dire need, could kill fur-bearing animals for food provided they gave the pelt to the owner of potlatch rights. The village chief, *köyohodachum* ("village big tree"), had the duties of exhorting people to provide for their own needs, of arbitrating disputes over hunting boundaries (probably band boundaries regarding large game), and settling disagreements among villages. This position was strongly patrilineal, passing to the chief's brother or son or to someone chosen by the retiring chief for his ability. Later it tended to be elective, and in some cases the chief was appointed by government officials or Catholic missionaries.

A title of nobility might also be possessed by a village chief, but the two positions were separable. Thus Kwah at Fort St. James was *köyohodachum* and held the highest potlatch title, *agetas*. But the title of *agetas* was passed on to Yuwani, his nephew (probably his sister's son, which accords with the theory of descent), while the village chieftainship was taken over by Prince, his own son. In part, this latter succession reflected or at least accorded with white interests, for the government officials had designated Kwah as "king" and his son, of whom they approved, as "Prince."

There was less conflict between the hunting band pattern and the potlatching pattern among the Alkatcho Carrier than among the northern Carrier. The former retained their patrilineal pattern as the basic economic, social, and potlatching unit, although it is not clear whether these units were localized. Through intermarriage with the Bella Coola and establishment of titles of nobility supported by the new surplus, the old could be transformed into the new.

The mechanisms of diffusion from the matrilineal Tsimshian to the northern Carrier are more complicated and more hypothetical. The Bulkley River and Babine River Carrier unquestionably first acquired the coastal patterns through intermarriage or other direct contact with the Tsimshian and passed them eastward to Stuart Lake. In theory, a title of nobility is transferred to the sister's son, and marriage, especially of the eldest son, is with the mother's brother's daughter. My recorded genealogies go back to the parents of Kwah, who died in 1840, but they show no case of cross-cousin marriage, and Carrier kinship terminology in no way suggests such marriage. The wide distribution of cross-cousin marriage among the Athabaskan-speaking peoples east of the Coastal Range, however, makes the early occurrence of cross-cousin marriage among the Carrier plausible.

It is quite possible, then, that the introduction of a nobility inherited from a man by his sister's son was initially facilitated by the marriage of his own daughter to his sister's son. Cross-cousin marriage may, therefore, have provided the mechanism for the addition of matrilineal principles of a class of nobles into an otherwise patrilineal hunting and fishing people.

But among the Stuart Lake and Babine Lake Carrier the system of nobility and potlatching involved individuals rather than groups. Consequently, the term "phratry" is inappropriate. Individual men held titles which gave rights to the surplus from certain tracts of land which they used to potlatch. The common people who subsisted on this land were required to contribute furs and certain foods to the nobles. They were said to be of the same "company," that is, "phratry," as the nobles, but this probably did not imply genuinely exogamous matrilineal kin groups. The commoners may in fact have been related through either parent to their nobles, for it was the title to nobility rather than land use for subsistence purposes that was theoretically inherited by a man's sister's son.

While the earliest genealogical data are from the latter part of the nineteenth century, a time when the Hudson's Bay Company, Catholic missionaries, and other outside influences were beginning to undermine the pattern of nobility, it seems clear that matrilineal principles never became as firmly rooted as among the Tsimshian or coastal people. At Fort St. James there were only two so-called phratries, while a third was represented only at the western end of Stuart Lake. Of the first two, Ltsəməshyu (II), was predominant at Fort St. James, where at least six of its nobles resided. Each of these nobles controlled the surplus of a tract adjoining the lake. The other group, Lasilyu (I), had one noble residing at Fort St. James and several others to the north and east. Each controlled a tract.

Toward Fraser Lake to the south, the Ltsəməshyu titles seem to have been very recently introduced from Fort St. James. Just to the east of Stuart Lake live the Sekani, who, according to Jenness, attempted fairly recently to adopt the nobility-potlatch system but had to give it up for lack of resources. My own data show that the Carrier nobles were pressing eastward, incorporating Sekani tracts.

The determining factor in the spread of this pattern seems clearly to have been potential surplus. The Bulkley and Babine rivers were not far from the coast and received salmon runs. Since feasting as well as present-giving was part of the potlatch pattern, fisheries were extremely important. At Stuart Lake, which is virtually the source of the Fraser River and is far from the coast, the salmon were reduced in numbers and much decreased in weight by their long travel. While the country afforded beaver, fox, and other fur-bearing animals, it did not provide the quantity of trade pelts realized by the coastal Indians in sea otter. The quantitative basis of potlatching was meager at Stuart Lake but even poorer among the Sekani, who lacked salmon fisheries. In their failure to maintain a nobility-potlatch pattern, the Sekani are more like the many Canadian Indians who, under the fur trade, changed from hunting bands directly into individual families with trap lines.

These interpretative remarks are illustrated by the map and by specific data of the genealogies and land use. A comparison of this information with that of Morice and Jenness indicates the fading of the pattern toward the east. The table shows the "phratries" recorded from west to east.

The division of the Bulkley River people into five phratries, four of which were subdivided into three clans each, certainly represents a strong coastal pattern. My own informants recorded five divisions for Babine Lake, three of which clearly correspond with Bulkley River groups. The other two names, Kwanpahoten and Grand Trunk (named from the railroad), do not correspond to the phratries on Bulkley River, but Kwanpahoten means "fireside" and may have been derived from one of the Bulkley River Laksilyu clans. Morice's five Stuart Lake groups may actually include people farther afield, for my informants were very definite that Fort St. James had only two. Correspondences are in I (Lasilyu), II (Ltsəməshyu), and III (Tsayu). But the subdivision into clans breaks down, for Lasilyu was merely equated to frog, which Morice equated to Ltsəməshyu, and Tsayu was identified as owl. Moreover, the Stuart Lake people considered Lasilyu the same as Kwanpahoten, which was distinctive at Babine Lake; and they regarded Tsayu, which occurred between Stuart Lake and Trembleur Lake, as the equivalent of Ltsəməlshu, since it helped the latter potlatch.

While the significance of these divisions bears far more comparative study, it seems clear that as a status system spread eastward through intermarriage, control of surplus, and perhaps other factors, it became so simplified that Stuart Lake and Stoney Creek had only two main divisions and no subdivisions, and that nominal equivalents from one locality to another became confused. In fact they became so confused that such names as Grand Trunk and Japan were adopted in certain localities.

Within the framework of this somewhat erratic diffusion, most of the people of Fort St. James at Stuart Lake were brought into Ltsəməshyu, shown on the map as II. The group II nobles at Fort St. James holding land were Kwah, Asuł, Təsti, Kədəlcho, and Daiya, while Skələtjat of group I (Lasilyu) also lived in this village. While each of these five nobles of II controlled the surplus of the territory indicated on the map and potlatched after their own fashion, they were subservient to Kwah, who held the title of *agetas* and was thus supreme over all group II nobles. The equation of IIA, Tsayu to the northwest, to II is based upon the former's obligation to assist in potlatching.

In other words, group II diffused into the Stuart Lake area, especially to Fort St. James, and its several nobles held tiny feudal domains while being subservient to the principal lord or *agetas*, Kwah. But the existence of strong hereditary principles, marriage rules, or group organization beyond the obligation to supply surplus to the noble is very questionable.

Of ten marriages of Ltsəməshyu nobles at Fort St. James, four were with local Ltsəməshyu women, four with local Lasilyu women, and two with Stoney Creek women who apparently belonged to no nobility group. Marriages of nobles elsewhere near Stuart Lake show a similar lack of consistent exogamy either by noble group or locality.

There was, however, a strong feeling about keeping the title within the group. In the case of exogamous marriage, the title passed to the sister's son; in the case of endogamy, it often passed to a man's own son or to a son-in-law. However, the title required land to support it, and land was the object of some jockeying. New lands at Stoney Creek and among the Sekani were being brought under the control of Fort St. James nobles, while local land might be exchanged in return for assistance in potlatching or even acquired forcibly. Kwah, the village chief and supreme noble at Fort St. James arbitrated land disputes, but he also came out the richer himself.

FROM NOBILITY TO INDIVIDUAL FAMILY

The nature of the land rights of the nobility and of the factors which destroyed this pattern is best seen in the case histories of the nobles indicated on the map. The undoing of the nobles had already begun during the lifetime of the earliest men in the genealogies. The principal factors were the trading companies, the Catholic Church, and the social and political effects of the Provincial government and white settlers. The trading companies gave direct access to manufactured goods, the desire for which eventually overshadowed the importance of status. The interest in retention rather than ceremonial giving of material goods was enhanced as white trappers began to move into the country. In the course of time, new concepts of land rights came into conflict with and finally superseded the old; trap lines registered under Provincial law destroyed the domains of the nobles. (The territories indicated on the map by dotted lines were registered in 1926.) Meanwhile the Catholic Church, especially under the able missionizing efforts of the priest-ethnographer Father Morice, destroyed the religious sanction of the nobility and potlatch at Stuart Lake.

These processes had run their course more completely at Stuart Lake than elsewhere. In 1939, in certain isolated areas, the Carrier, though holding registered trap lines and nominally Catholic, had no resident priests and were still holding secret potlatches. This same year certain Skeena River Tsmishian, although largely deprived of their fisheries and other sources of wealth and still caught in the economic depression, were using relief money to potlatch. The long-run out-

NORTHERN CARRIER NOBLE-POTLATCH OR PHRATRY GROUPS

Bulkley River (Jenness)		Babine Lake (Steward)	Stuart Lake (Morice)	Stuart Lake (Steward)	Stoney Creek (Steward)
Phratry	*Clans*				
I. Laksilyu	Many eyes House On Flat Rock House Fireside House	I. Lasilyu	I. Yəsilyu	I. Lasilyu =Kwanpahoten Frog	I. Nułkwiten =Lasilyu
II. Laksamshu	Sun House Twisted House Owl House	II. Łtsəməshyu	II. Łtsəməshyu Frog	II. Łtsəməlshu Owl =IIA. Tsayu at Trembleur Lake	II. Ta'chekten =Łtsəməlshu
III. Tsayu	Beaver	III. Tsayu	III. Tsayu		
IV. Gitamtanyu	Grizzly House Middle of many Anskaski	IV. Grand Trunk	IV. Təm'tenyu		
V. Gilserhyu	Dark House Thin House Bark House	V. Kwanpahoten	V. Kwanpahotene		

come of individualization of sources of wealth, however, is clear. And at Fort St. James, the dependence upon certain European foods, hardware, clothing, and most material essentials had reached the point where each individual had to trade his wealth in furs in order to support his family.

The case history of Kwah is the most interesting. Kwah was the son of a Lasilyu nobleman from Fort St. James and a Łtsəməshyu woman from Stoney Creek. That he acquired control of several main tracts around Fort St. James—those mapped as Kwah, Təsti, and Asuł—suggests that his role as village chief was a main factor in gaining support for his title, *agetas,* which he inherited orthodoxly from his mother's brother. At some point Kwah shared the title with his brother, Howeapah. Later it passed to his nephew (his sister's son?) Yuwani, who seems to have acquired it by marrying Kwah's widow. Still later, Təsti, a possible relative of Kwah, who had trapped with him, acquired the title *agetas.* Meanwhile, Kwah's son, Prince, initiated the breakdown of nobility and their tracts. As village chief but not *agetas*, he forced Təsti back into the land shown on the map and in time divided the land mapped as Kwah's among his own sons and grandsons. During this time white trappers pressing in from the east had pre-empted the former territories of Kwah which are shaded on the map, and they now have legal rights to them.

Kwah's brother's (Howeapah's) son, Kədəlcho, belonged to group II but was a minor noble. He married a Stoney Creek woman who probably belonged to no group and claimed land just south of Stuart River. This was lost to the whites.

The case of Asuł and Skələtjat also shows failure to follow a fixed rule. Skələtjat's sister's son, Tylee, born of a marriage to Asuł, inherited his uncle's land but passed it on to his own son by a marriage to a Stoney Creek woman. Asuł, however, gave his land south of Stuart Lake to his own son, Song (Tylee's brother), who gave it to his son, Bacome Song. Asuł is thought to have acquired this land from his first wife's family.

Layał, who lived in the village on the western shore of Great Beaver Lake, obtained the land from his mother's brother, a member of the same village. In the absence of children he passed on a portion of it to the son of a part Cree, who in turn gave it to his stepson.

Daiya, of group II, married a woman of II and acquired from her father the territory east of Great Beaver Lake. Daiya took Asuł's pot-latch name and was then called "nephew" by Asuł, although they were not related. Part of Daiya's land was given to Sagalon, his friend, and part to his wife's sister's son, Louie Mattess.

SUMMARY

While the course of Carrier culture change is somewhat inferential in early times and confused in certain detail, its broad outlines can be seen in terms of two culminations which are closely paralleled elsewhere. Murphy and Steward have shown that the Mundurucú of the Amazon and the Montagnais of Labrador acquired a new source of wealth in rubber trapping and fur trapping respectively. At first, the village chief of the Mundurucú and the band chief of the Montagnais acquired great power through assuming the new role or function of entrepreneur in the trade. In time, however, individual tappers and trappers preferred to trade directly with the whites, whereupon band or village organization disintegrated and individual families acquired rights to their own delimited territories.

Among the Carrier, too, the fur trade created a new wealth, and local chiefs came into prominence. The specific pattern of wealth prominence, however, was dictated by contacts with coastal Indians. The formerly patrilineal Alkatcho Carrier bands exalted the position of their chiefs by reinforcing them with potlatch-sanctioned titles borrowed from the patrilineal Bella Coola. The northern Carrier were seemingly involved in a conflict that was never wholly resolved. Village chieftainship was a separable role from potlatch nobility, although the same man might hold both. There can be little doubt, however, that the power of the village chief enabled him to assume potlatch titles when the effect of the fur trade was felt and the Tsimshian matrilineal pattern began to spread. Since the Stuart Lake pattern was one of individual titles with rights to surplus from tracts of land rather than one of strictly exogamous groups, the feeling was that the titles should be kept in the "phratry" or "company." Inheritance by the sister's son served this end, but in the absence of exogamy it was not the only means to the end. Possibly inheritance by the sister's son was more strictly observed between 1800 and 1850. The present data, which relate mainly to a period beginning shortly after 1850, show such inheritance only when there was marriage between the two principal title groups. But they also show that marriages within the groups were equally frequent and that inheritance by the son or the daughter's husband occurred in these cases.

The fur trade brought about a concentration of the new surplus in the hands of a few men. The half-dozen or so title holders among the Ltsəməshyu group living at Fort St. James helped one another potlatch, and especially they helped the holder of the principal title, *agetas*. Such concentration is fairly common among people who acquire a new source of wealth, even though there may be local mechanisms, such as fear of witchcraft as among the Navajo or ceremonial obligations as among the many corporate peasants of Latin America, for leveling the wealth. In fact, the dissipation of accumulated wealth in the *cargos* or ceremonies of the peasants has a certain resemblance to the potlatch, except that the *cargos* are rotated and do not affirm sharp status differences.

Following the culmination of the nobility-potlatch pattern, there appeared processes which are worldwide in general terms. Access to manufactured goods, desire to use the surplus of one's effort for personal benefit, contact with Europeans, and the impingement of concepts of individual land-use rights which are in conflict with traditional rights undermine the earlier patterns. In more specific terms, wealth afforded by nonmigratory, conservable, wild resources led to the particular pattern of the family-held trapping territory which is precisely like the Mundurucú family-held tapping territory.

The Stuart Lake Carrier in 1939 had lost most native and nobility-potlatch institutions. Their society, like that of the Mundurucú and Montagnais, consisted of individual families held together by common dealing at the trading post and by enforced association with one another owing to isolation on small reservations and strong race prejudice among the whites.

BIBLIOGRAPHY

GOLDMAN, IRVING
  1941. "The Alkatcho Carrier: Historical Background of Crest Prerogatives," *American Anthropologist*, 43:396-418.

JENNESS, DIAMOND
  n.d. *The Indians of Canada*. 2d ed. National Museum of Canada, Bulletin 65, Anthropological series No. 15.

LAUT, AGNES C.
  1918. *The Conquest of the Great Northwest*. 6th ed. 2 vols. New York.

MORICE, A. G.
  1890. "The Western Dénés," in *Proceedings of the Canadian Institute*, 3d ser., 7:109-74.

  1895. "Notes Archaeological, Industrial, and Sociological on the Western Dénés," in *Transactions of the Canadian Institute*, 4:1-222. Toronto.

  1905. *History of the Northern Interior of British Columbia, formerly New Caledonia*. 3d ed. Toronto.

MURIE, OLAUS G.
  1935. Alaska-Yukon Caribou. *North American Fauna*, No. 54, U.S. Department of Agriculture, Bureau of Biological Survey, Washington, D.C.

MURPHY, ROBERT F., and JULIAN H. STEWARD
1956. "Tappers and Trappers: Parallel Processes in Acculturation," *Economic Development and Cultural Change*, 4:No. 4:335-55.

10

The Direct Historical Approach to Archeology

One of Steward's more important contributions to archeological theory, "The Direct Historical Approach to Archeology" was published in *American Antiquity* (vol. 7, pp. 337-343, 1942), which has consented to its reprinting in the present volume. An application of the method outlined by Steward may be found in his classic essay "Ecological Aspects of Southwestern Society," which also appears as Chapter 9 of his *Theory of Culture Change*, published by the University of Illinois Press in 1955.

In recent years considerable attention has been given to theoretical statements and to concrete applications of what is called the "taxonomic method" in archeology. Although this method is not necessarily in conflict with the direct historical approach to archeology, a growing preoccupation with the former has definitely been at the expense of the latter. The direct historical approach, although employed more or less for many years, has not received formulation comparable to that of the taxonomic method, nor have its potentialities for planned research programs and its possible integration with recent types of historical ethnographic research received full recognition. Even, therefore, if it is unnecessary to argue its value, it seems timely to attempt a statement that may help clarify its procedures and research possibilities.

Methodologically, the direct historical approach involves the elementary logic of working from the known to the unknown. First, sites of the historic period are located. These are preferably, but not necessarily, those of identifiable tribes. Second, the cultural complexes of the sites are determined. Third, sequences are carried backward in time to protohistoric and prehistoric periods and cultures. This approach has the crucially important advantage of providing a fixed datum point to which sequences may be tied. But, far more important than this, it provides a point of contact and a series of specific problems which will coordinate archeology and ethnology in relation to the basic problems of cultural studies.

The direct historical approach to archeology was first deliberately used in the Southwest about 1915 by Nelson, Kidder, Spier, and Kroeber[1] and in New York State by Parker and Harrington about the same time.[2] In areas like the Southwest and Middle America, where many of the more conspicuous sites were only recently abandoned and where a connection between historic and prehistoric cultures was obvious, it was almost an inevitable approach. In all these areas it was possible to start with historic sites and, through stratigraphy, or seriation,[3] or both, to carry sequences backward beyond the point where the trails of the known, historic peoples faded out.

Despite this fruitful beginning, the full value of the direct historical approach seems not to have been recognized until much later. It is, in fact, a striking commentary on the divergent interests of archeology and ethnology that in the Southwest the gap represented by the four hundred years of the historic period remained largely unfilled, while archeology devoted itself mainly to prehistoric periods, and ethnology, to the ceremonialism and social organization of the modern Pueblo. And yet it was during this four hundred years that the Pueblo had contacts with one another, with the nomadic and seminomadic tribes, and with the Spaniards, that account for much of their present culture. There are only a few happy exceptions to the general indifference toward this period.[4] Similarly, interest in New York seems recently to have drifted away from problems of history to those of taxonomy.[5]

In most areas, use of the direct historical approach was delayed because historic sites were difficult to find or because other practical considerations interfered or simply because attention had been directed away from problems involving history or ethnology. For the Southeast, however, Swanton had assembled documentary evidence on the location of many sites of historic tribes.[6] Following his leads,

[1]Nelson, 1916: Kidder, 1916. See also Kidder, 1924, pp. 84-95; Spier, 1917; Kroeber, 1916.

[2]Parker, 1916; also Parker and Harrington, 1922.

[3]This method was employed by Kidder in the Rio Grande Valley (1915), and was stated more explicitly by Spier (1917).

[4] For example, A. V. Kidder's long and detailed studies of the historic Pueblo of Pecos, now published in full; F. W. Hodge's partially published studies of Hawikuh, an old Zuñi site; and J. O. Brew's recent excavations of Awatobi, an old Hopi village. E. C. Parsons has called attention to some of the types of study that will help relate archeological and ethnological data in the Southwest (1939, vol. 2, p. 1212; 1940).

[5]W. N. Fenton (1941) showed the possibilities for use of the direct historic approach to archeology in the Iroquois area and assembled abundant materials (1940) that could be used for this approach.

[6]Contained in many of Swanton's works. For his complete bibliography, see Swanton, 1940, pp. 593-600.

Collins identified Choctaw pottery in 1925,[7] and other historic wares were subsequently determined by several workers, especially Ford, Willey, and Walker. Ford has now succeeded in carrying a sequence for the lower Mississippi Valley back from the historic tribes through several prehistoric periods.[8] Meanwhile, sequences have also been established through use of the direct historical approach by Strong and Wedel in the Plains,[9] by Collins in the Arctic,[10] by Parker and Ritchie in New York,[11] and elsewhere. In short, history is being rapidly blocked out and it is now becoming possible to describe archeological materials in terms of time and space, the first elementary step toward understanding culture change.

The northern Mississippi Valley has yielded less readily to the direct historical approach. But it is hoped that the ethnographic survey of historical documents being made by Kinietz and Tucker will provide information on historic sites which will facilitate use of this approach. Meanwhile, the archeological data of this, and, to some extent, other areas, are being arranged according to the taxonomic scheme. Basing classification solely on the association of cultural elements, the result is a set of timeless and spaceless categories. Whatever use may be made of these materials, it is to be hoped that the effort to pigeonhole cultural materials by any nonhistorical scheme will not direct attention too far away from historical problems, which are surely the important consideration of archeology. Furthermore, where history has already been blocked out, it is difficult to see what is gained by scrapping a scheme with historical terms and categories in favor of a nonhistorical one.

The direct historical approach is not only crucially important in ascertaining cultural sequences, but, integrated with recent endeavors in ethnology, it has a tremendous potential value to the more basic problems of anthropology. Too often, these problems have been obscured by immediate tasks; techniques and procedures have loomed as ultimate goals. Ethnology tends to ignore the results of archeology, while archeology, concentrating on its techniques for excavation and its methods for description and classification of the physical properties of artifacts, comes to consider itself a "natural," a "biological," or an "earth science" rather than a cultural science. It is too often forgotten that problems of cultural origins and cultural change require more than ceramic sequences or element lists.

[7]Collins, 1927.

[8]See the summary in Ford and Willey, 1940.

[9]The latest summaries are Strong, 1940, and Wedel, 1940.

[10]Collins, 1940, and earlier works.

[11]Parker, 1916; Ritchie, 1932; this preceded the interest in taxonomy.

If anything characterizes historical anthropology today, it is a recognition that valid theories which generalize data of cultural change, process, or dynamics must be based on gradually accumulating information about the specific circumstances which surround particular events. To the extent, therefore, that archeology can deal with specific problems of specific peoples, tracing cultural changes, migrations, and other events back into the protohistoric and prehistoric periods while ethnology traces them forward to the present day, it will contribute to the general problem of understanding cultural change. Its data can be handled directly for theoretical purposes; there is no need for taxonomy.

A few illustrations will suffice to demonstrate the value of the direct historical approach to these basic problems. Using it in the Plains, Strong put the cultures of the area in a new light. Tracing changes in the culture of known, historic tribes back through the protohistoric into the prehistoric period, he showed that the Plains had not been a basically bison-hunting area with a few anomalous, horticultural tribes, as had been generally assumed, but that it had formerly been in large part horticultural. A pronounced shift to hunting had followed the introduction of the horse. This new picture of the Plains required drastic revision of ecological and other theories previously held concerning it. In Alaska, Collins's direct historical approach to Eskimo archeology revealed a long, local development of Eskimo culture which required new interpretations of Eskimo cultural origins and migrations. In the Southwest, the light thrown on Pueblo cultural origins by this approach is too well known to need comment.

On many other similar problems, work has only started. The Navajo and Apache, for example, are obviously Canadian in language though not in culture. Speculation about their cultural origins, their migrations, and their role, if any, in the retraction of the Pueblo area after about 1000 or 1100 A.D. has been almost futile. It is a job for the direct historical approach to Navajo archeology, which has just begun. Similarly, the question of the relationship of the Iroquois to southeastern ethnic and archeological groups and to Ohio archeological complexes will be definitively solved only when archeology has succeeded in tracing the different Iroquoian peoples deeper into the past. The distribution of Siouan peoples in the Plains and in the east also indicates the need of tracing both groups back to the area where they formed a single group and even suggests where ancient Siouan remains are likely to be found.

There are also problems connected with the introduction of new European culture elements during the protohistoric or early historic period that archeology can help solve. We know much about the effect

of the horse. But what about the gun, the steel trap, new trade relations, tribal dislocations, and other factors coming directly or indirectly
from the white man? It is certain that in many cases these produced
revolutionary changes in economy, village types, village distributions,
migrations, tribal contacts, and other features which would afford
information basic to studies of culture change. The archeology of early
historic sites would also help enormously to correct ethnography's
attempts to reconstruct pre-contact cultures.

Every tribe in the country cannot, of course, be traced through its
archeology. But a great number of problems can be solved by combin-
ing data derived from ethnography and from historical documents
with the results of the direct historical approach in archeology. In fact,
if one takes cultural history as his problem, and peoples of the early
historic period as his point of departure, the difference between strictly
archeological and strictly ethnographical interest disappears. Archeology supplements the cultural picture drawn from historic documents and informant testimony. Ethnography explains archeological
materials in their cultural context. And where archeology traces
changes backward into the past, ethnography may trace them forward.
It seems certain that historical acculturation studies, such as Keesing's
Menomini monograph,[12] which traces cultural changes through the
three centuries of the post-contact period and might be called the
direct historical approach to ethnology, are destined to find an important place in anthropological literature. Studies of this kind will overlap
with and be tremendously facilitated by direct historical studies in
archeology.

Whether the objective of cultural studies is a broad cultural sequence
or detailed information on the history of a specific people, the contributions of archeology will be more or less proportionate to its success
in using the direct historical approach. This approach will serve to
remind both archeologists and ethnologists that they have in common
not only the general problem of how culture has developed but a large
number of very specific problems. If archeology feels that applying
itself to cultural rather than to "natural history" problems seems to
relegate it to the position of the tail on an ethnological kite, it must
remember that it is an extraordinarily long tail. Vaillant has said:
"Unless archaeology is going definitely to shift from a branch of an-

---

[12] Keesing, 1939, Kinietz, 1940, also recognizing the importance of distinguishing Indian cultures at different periods within historic times, has ransacked the early literature
for information on culture immediately following contact with whites. It is of some interest that South Americanists, perhaps because most of them have in the past been
Europeans and traditionally have devoted more effort to library studies, have made far
greater use of old sources than North American ethnologists.

thropology to an obscure type of mathematics, an effort must be made to relate the rhythms of cultural development with the pulsations of an evolving human society."[13] This requires a perception of problems that involve more than the physical features of material objects, bare chronologies, or even classifications.

[13]Vaillant, 1935, p. 304.

BIBLIOGRAPHY

COLLINS, H. B., JR.
1927. "Potsherds from Choctaw Village Sites in Mississippi." *Journal of the Washington Academy of Science*, Vol. 17, pp. 259-263.

1940. "Outline of Eskimo Prehistory." In *Essays in Historical Anthropology of North America*. Smithsonian Miscellaneous Collections 100.

FENTON, W. N.
1940. "Problems Arising from the Historic Northeastern Position of the Iroquois." In *Essays in Historical Anthropology of North America*. Smithsonian Miscellaneous Collections 100.

1941. Review of "Roebuck Prehistoric Village Site, Grenville County, Ontario," W. J. Wintemberg, *American Antiquity*, Vol. 7, pp. 290-294.

FORD, J. A., and GORDON WILLEY
1940. *Crooks Site, a Marksville Period Burial Mound in La Salle Parish, Louisiana*. State of Louisiana, Department of Conservation, Anthropological Study No. 3.

KEESING, F. M.
1939. *The Menomini Indians of Wisconsin*. American Philosophical Society, Memoir 10.

KIDDER, A. V.
1915. *Pottery of the Pajarito Plateau and of Some Adjacent Regions in New Mexico*. American Anthropological Association, Memoir 2, No. 6.

1916. "Archaeological Explorations at Pecos, New Mexico." *Proceedings of the National Academy of Science*, Vol. 12, pp. 119-123.

1924. *Introduction to the Study of Southwestern Archaeology*. New Haven.

KINIETZ, W. V.
1940. *The Indians of the Western Great Lakes, 1615-1760*. University of Michigan, Occasional Contributions, Museum of Anthropology, No. 10.

KROEBER, A. L.
1916. *Zuñi Potsherds*. Anthropological Papers, American Museum of Natural History, Vol. 18.

NELSON, N. C.
1916. "Chronology of the Tano Ruins, New Mexico." *American Anthropologist,* Vol. 18, pp. 159-180.

PARKER, A. C.
1916. *Excavations in an Erie Indian Village and Burial Site at Ripley, Chautauqua County, New York.* New York State Museum, Bulletin 117.

PARKER, A. C., and M. R. HARRINGTON
1922. *Archaeological History of New York.* New York State Museum, Bulletins 235-236.

PARSONS, ELSIE CLEWS
1939. *Pueblo Indian Religion.* Chicago.

1940. "Relations between Ethnology and Archaeology in the Southwest." *American Antiquity,* Vol. 5, pp. 214-220.

RITCHIE, W. A.
1932. "The Algonkin Sequence in New York." *American Anthropologist,* Vol. 34, pp. 406-414.

SPIER, LESLIE
1917. *An Outline for a Chronology of Zuñi Ruins.* Anthropological Papers, American Museum of Natural History, Vol. 18.

STRONG, W. D.
1940. "From History to Prehistory in the Northern Great Plains." In *Essays in Historical Anthropology of North America.* Smithsonian Miscellaneous Collections 100.

SWANTON, JOHN R.
1940. Bibliography of. In *Essays in Historical Anthropology of North America.* Smithsonian Miscellaneous Collections 100.

VAILLANT, G. C.
1935. *Early Cultures of the Valley of Mexico: Results of the Stratigraphical Project of the American Museum of Natural History in the Valley of Mexico,*

1928-1933. Anthropological Papers, American Museum of Natural History, Vol. 35.

WEDEL, W. R.
1940. "Culture Sequence in the Central Great Plains." In *Essays in Historical Anthropology of North America.* Smithsonian Miscellaneous Collections 100.

11

Function and Configuration in Archeology[1]

"Function and Configuration in Archeology" was co-authored with the late Frank M. Setzler and first appeared in the archeological journal *American Antiquity* (vol. 4, pp. 4-10, 1938), which has given permission to reprint. The essay was an important theoretical advance in its time and represents an attempt to unite archeological interpretation with social-anthropological concepts. Frank M. Setzler was a specialist in the prehistory of Ohio and the midwestern United States; he was for many years chairman of the Department of Anthropology of the Smithsonian Institution, where he was associated with Steward.

Cultural anthropology is generally considered to be a distinctive discipline which seeks an understanding of the fundamental nature of culture and of culture change. The nature of its ultimate objectives, however, is rarely made explicit, and a lack of agreement exists concerning even the more immediate objectives. There is reason to believe that within the last few years archeology and ethnology are, in many respects, growing rapidly apart instead of contributing to mutual problems. It seems timely, therefore, to inquire whether there really exists a general, basic problem of culture and to what extent archeological research may be brought to bear upon it.

When materials are susceptible to arrangement in time sequences, archeology and ethnology both aim to make historical reconstructions, the latter often depending upon the former for the depth in its cultural picture. Some ethnologists, however, now expressly deny an interest in historical reconstructions. Both disciplines seek to ascertain spatial distributions, though a reason for doing so, especially in ethnology, has

---

[1] "Configuration" herein has its common meaning of design or form in which elements of a culture are arranged and interrelated. In ethnology, "pattern" has been used in this sense for many years. It is unfortunate for clear terminology that in the system of archeological classification adopted for the Mississippi Valley, "pattern" was chosen to designate a complex of elements of a certain magnitude, thus giving it a totally different meaning in archeology and ethnology.

frequently been to infer history. Both subjects are, to varying degrees, concerned with taxonomy, though the use to be made of taxonomy is not always evident. Some ethnology has recently emphasized functional studies, which, however, usually stress kinship and rarely embrace total cultures. Archeology has generally avoided treating data in functional terms. And, finally, much ethnology is treating culture in psychological terms. One searches with difficulty for the common problems which coordinate the research in these two branches of cultural anthropology.

What can be said of the objectives of archeology? There are several immediate aims which seem beyond question. Though individuals have somewhat different interests and though areas present different kinds of problems, all archeology deals with relatively tangible and concrete objects and their significant associations. Each object is a culture element. It is first treated individually, being named and assigned to a broad class of objects, such as pottery, projectile points, and the like. This kind of taxonomy is similar to that in biology. But culture elements rarely occur in isolation. Instead, certain of them are usually found together again and again in greater than chance association. They are usually part of complexes. Another task common to all archeology, therefore, appears to be the identification and naming of complexes. Such complexes are similar to the biologist's floristic and faunistic assemblages.

Archeology is also concerned with the historical arrangement of culture elements. Without reference to time and space, mere classification of elements and complexes has little meaning. Moreover, it is one of the striking characteristics of culture complexes that their contents usually do not remain unaltered in all places and in all periods. A description of the changes which they undergo is history in the narrow sense or, we may say, the raw materials of history. To many persons history is so much a part of archeology that it may seem absurd to underline its importance. But there are some who believe differently.

When complexes have been identified and history in the narrow sense reconstructed, what task remains for archeology? Some day world culture history will be known as far as archeological materials and human intelligence permit. Every possible element of culture will have been placed in time and space. The invention, diffusion, mutation, and association of elements will have been determined. When taxonomy and history are thus complete, shall we cease our labors and hope that the future Darwin of Anthropology will interpret the great historical scheme that will have been erected? There has been a marked tendency to avoid these questions on the assumption that they are unimportant at present. It is held that the urgent need of the moment is to record data which are rapidly vanishing, provided it is done with proper techniques.

We believe that it is unfortunate for several reasons that attempts to state broad objectives which are basic to all cultural anthropology and to interpret data in terms of them should be relegated to a future time of greater leisure and fullness of data. First, although technological advancement is of the utmost importance, techniques alone neither state nor solve problems. Techniques are tools. It is difficult to believe that any tool can be developed to perfection without a definite conception of the purpose for which it is designed. It is, in fact, very probable that techniques for collecting facts which now seem important actually fail to procure other and equally important facts. Techniques, therefore, may be perfected only with reference to their purpose, which involves the question of research objectives. Second, no one will in the future be able to interpret data one-tenth as well as the persons now immersed in them. The increasing variety and volume of accumulated facts and the minutiae of element variations and associations in an area even moderately well known archeologically are forbidding to the nonspecialist. It is only to the extent that archeological findings are interpreted in terms of broad problems that they are useful to the general student of culture.

One wonders whether the frequent limitation of interest to measurements and tabulation of data and refinements of techniques is an unwillingness to grapple with the problem of objectives. Perhaps the fascination of immediate materials, such as pots, celts, and other choice objects which first drew interest to archeology continues to some extent to obscure the matter of their broadest significance. Candid introspection might suggest that our motivation is more akin to that of the collector than we should like to admit.

The intense interest in specimens *per se* is betrayed in many archeological monographs, including those of the authors. We treat materials primarily as items to be described, listed, and arranged historically, but not as devices employed by human beings in important daily activities. This is implied in the use of such descriptive headings as objects of "bone," "horn," "stone," and others based upon materials, instead of such functional headings as "horticulture," "food preparation," "hunting," "fishing," "dress," "adornments," "household," and others appropriate to the culture.[2]

Do we avoid present efforts to interpret data because they have

[2] A tentative effort to use more meaningful categories was made by Barrett, "Aztalan," 1933; Deuel, "Pictorial Survey," 1935; and by Cole and Deuel in "Rediscovering Illinois," 1937. Linton, "The Study of Man," 1936, pp. 394-396, has suggested classifying data under "biological," "social," and "psychological needs."

intrinsic qualities which forbid it? Is it inherently logical to postpone it; or has chance oriented our interest in other directions? We incline to the last explanation. Candor would seem to compel the admission that archeology could be made much more pertinent to general cultural studies if we paused to take stock of its possibilities. Surely it can shed some light not only on the chronological and spatial arrangements and associations of elements, but on conditions underlying their origin, development, diffusion, acceptance, and interaction with one another. These are problems of cultural process, problems that archeology and ethnology should have in common. And it is by no means improbable that in spite of our refined techniques of excavation, ceramic studies, and classification, we are actually overlooking important data, even when doing fieldwork, that would contribute to their solution.

We would like to suggest, therefore, a few points at which archeology may touch the broader and more basic cultural problems, hoping that if we have ventured into the realm of controversy, it may at least elicit other points that have not occurred to us.

First, considerable enlightenment would be provided the general reader of archeological monographs if more information were provided about the general features of a culture. Often ten pages are devoted to the minutiae of pottery temper, paste, and so on, while one page or less describes subsistence and the relationship of the culture to the geographical environment. Such disproportionate treatment of different subjects is by no means always explainable by lack of information about the latter. Even less space is usually accorded data concerning social groups and population distribution and concentration which are indicated by such elements as house remains and village locations.[3] Even when these data are included in a monograph that seems monumental in its detailed completeness, it is often exceedingly difficult to extract them.

Any culture must, of course, rest upon a basic economy which is adapted to its environment. This adaptation is human ecology. To varying degrees, it produces a configuration that interrelates a large number of elements, e.g. food getting, storing, grinding, and cooking. A description of it would, so far as data permit, make explicit the relative importance and kind of horticulture, fishing, or hunting and gathering and the relation of these traits to soils, altitudes, rainfall, flora, and fauna, that is, to the natural landscape. It would ascertain

---

[3] Steward, in "Ecological Aspects of Southwestern Society," *Anthropos*. Vol. 32, pp. 87-104, 1937, endeavored to synthesize archeological and ethnological data on population and social groups. In spite of the great amount of archeological work that has been done in the Southwest, it was, except from a few reports, extraordinarily difficult to extract data on the types and distribution of prehistoric villages.

whether particular types of economy did or did not correlate with certain environments, and whether unlike economies occurred in the same environment. It would also make explicit the kind of villages, evidence of clustering or lack of clustering of houses, number and distribution of villages in an area, and inferences about population density and stability. Such data would have enormous value to an anthropologist, economist, or geographer seeking historical depth in the conditions of population groupings underlying social and political configurations.

It is true, of course, that many areas yield only cemeteries, ceremonial structures, or other limited types of antiquities. It may be sometimes suspected, however, that if the more conspicuous and exciting remains held less intrinsic interest, a more deliberate search would be made for evidence of villages, subsistence, and other features to complete the cultural picture. Surveys to establish the distribution of recognized complexes are, of course, indispensable. But only complete and detailed excavation which is interpreted in the fullest possible degree will afford data pertinent to problems of culture process.

We believe also that treatment of archeological objects would be more meaningful if they were regarded not simply as museum specimens but as tools employed by human beings in some pattern of behavior. This requires a deliberate effort to understand their functional[4] place in the total configuration of activity. Naturally, it is more difficult in archeology than in ethnology to ascertain the function of each implement. The purpose of some we cannot know at all; others may be known only imperfectly. Nevertheless, each had some function. And it is not enough to ascertain, let us say, that a basket was used for gathering or a mortar for grinding. Gathering of wild seeds may have been the sole subsistence, having a basic importance and entailing not only basketry but a whole series of interrelated traits to which basketry was indispensable. Or gathering may have been a minor supplement to horticulture, so that baskets used in gathering were relegated to an unimportant place. Mortars may have been the most efficient implements for grinding the particular species of seeds used by a group, so that the use of mortars rested upon a degree of functional necessity. Or, they may have been no more serviceable than metates, so that their presence is explainable largely as historical accident.

In some areas, definable configurations and functional relationships between certain elements are so obvious as to have compelled recog-

---

[4] "Functionalism," unfortunately, carries a somewhat formidable connotation to many anthropologists. The word has been publicized in connection with analyses of a very narrow segment of culture, namely, kinship systems. It is nevertheless a very useful concept.

nition. For example, in Middle America and the Southwest there was a more or less closely knit complex of elements clustering around intensive horticulture. It comprised large communities, ambitious and permanent habitations, and an elaboration of society, ritual, and ceramic, textile, and other industries. Descriptions of these cultures, consequently, involve more than mere element lists or enumerations of the elements of complexes; they inevitably make more or less explicit the general cultural patterns and the functional position of the elements in those patterns.

It surely cannot be assumed that the culture elements of other areas were not also interrelated in some definable configurations. Yet many monographs merely list elements found in a site as if their sole connection were chance association. The manner in which elements were connected with one another is, of course, no more evident from a mere list of them than the design or pattern of a tile mosaic is evident from a list of the shapes, colors, and numbers of tiles composing it.

Though we stress the importance of seeking configurations, we do not imply that all elements are equally integrated in any culture. The functional place of arrowpoints, basketry, grinding implements, and pipes, for example, may be very dissimilar. Some may have had basic importance, while others were dispensable or variable. Any element, moreover, may have played a very different role in a horticultural, a hunting and gathering, or a fishing culture. Archeology no less than ethnology can gain some insight concerning the functional place of elements in cultures. This knowledge may not only contribute to an understanding of culture process, but may even modify historic and taxonomic conclusions.

The last point may be illustrated with mortuary customs. It has been asked whether mortuary customs are an index to culture. This is really a question of their functional role in the configuration of each particular culture, that is, of their relative susceptibility to change. It may be answered only empirically. Data of ethnology, supplemented by documented records, show that among certain far western tribes mortuary customs have changed with great rapidity. Some tribes substituted burial for cremation because they moved away from an area of sufficient firewood or because they came into contact with tribes which buried. Some shifted from burial to cremation for similar reasons, while others practised either, depending upon circumstances at the time of a death. Though archeology cannot give so precise a statement as ethnology of the functional place of mortuary customs in any culture, its historical sequences usually enable it to give a better statement of the stability of these customs relative to the total culture. If changes in mortuary customs are concomitant with changes in certain other practices, it may be inferred that their functional connection is great; if not, the connection must have been slight. In either event, the value of mortuary customs as an index of culture change cannot be determined *a priori*.

We criticize not commissions but omissions in modern archeology. Though modern field techniques, intensive ceramic studies, listing of elements, and taxonomic methodologies serve important purposes, it is unfortunate that emphasis on them alone should be at the expense of clarifying the general problems. Though the conception of ultimate objectives will develop as the science of archeology matures, we believe that a deliberate effort should be made at present to ascertain whether or not our daily research is likely to fit into a general scheme of cultural research. Otherwise, the fruits of archeology will continue to have little apparent bearing on other fields of cultural research and to hold little interest for persons other than antiquarians.

PART III

Modernization and Complex Societies

12

Concepts and Methods
of Area Research

This essay appeared as Chapter 3 of Steward's book *Area Research: Theory and Practice* (New York: Social Science Research Council, 1950, pp. 95-125) and is reprinted here with the permission of the Social Science Research Council. This chapter introduced his ideas on "levels of sociocultural integration," a theme which he also developed in an article entitled "Levels of Sociocultural Integration: An Operational Concept" (*Southwestern Journal of Anthropology*, vol. 7, pp. 374-390, 1951). The latter article was reprinted as Chapter 3 of Steward's *Theory of Cultural Change* (1955).

Some of the problems and practices of area research have been surveyed in preceding chapters. The present chapter will attempt to present a unified theory and method of area research. This should be considered a tentative rather than an ultimate formulation; it is hoped that it will be provocative.

INTEGRATING CONCEPTS

Any area program, whether of training or of research, requires the participation of many disciplines. It is certainly true in research and presumably true in training that the data of the different social sciences and of the humanities have to be integrated if an area program is to consist of more than a miscellany of unrelated facts. The present uncertainty about integrating concepts may mean that social science is still in a "natural history" or phenomenological stage.[1] Preoccupation with "facts" or with description in area research is evidence of scientific immaturity.

"Integration" has no fixed definition;[2] its meaning depends upon

[1] F. S. C. Northrop, *The Logic of the Sciences and the Humanities* (New York: Macmillan Company, 1947).

[2] Pitirim A. Sorokin, *Society, Culture and Personality* (New York: Harper & Brothers, 1947), pp. 337-341, reviews some of the meanings of integration (and disapproves of them all).

the problem in hand. For present purposes, we shall take integration to mean a functional interdependence of social science and humanistic phenomena within some kind of organizational whole or system. At the first national conference on the study of world areas sponsored by the Social Science Research Council, Pendleton Herring and Talcott Parsons implied that an area whole is something like a biological organism; it was their suggestion that "study of an area, its culture, and its society" might entail cooperation of many disciplines somewhat like that in medical research.[3] This does not mean that area research need adopt the biological analogy, for there are important differences between biological organisms and social systems. Both, however, are organizational wholes, although areas or territorial units are not necessarily self-contained entities like biological organisms. A community, a region, a nation, or any other area society may be a whole only in a relative sense; its organization, though incomplete, may be sufficiently definite to make it the frame of reference within which a variety of phenomena interact. The questions for area studies are: What kind of interaction is meant? What kinds of integrating concepts are appropriate to area wholes? What kinds of problems require such concepts?

The writer's concept of integration is only one of many that underlie various area research projects, and it is necessary to examine some of the others. The natural area is not an integrative concept, for it sets no criteria for inclusion or exclusion of phenomena. Among the more important and current integrative concepts are the individual, culture, and society. More specialized concepts, such as value system, philosophy, and ideology, are emphasized in particular studies, but these are parts of culture—they are master patterns of society, rather than something separable from both society and culture. The individual, culture, and society are here selected as the principal integrating concepts requiring comment because, where social science method is concerned, area studies tend to focus upon one of these. The three concepts are of very different orders.

THE INDIVIDUAL

Failure to distinguish two different concepts of the individual has caused some methodological confusion in social science. The concept of the individual as the "carrier of culture" and the concept of the "cultural personality" have been used as if they were identical. Because culture has no real existence apart from the behavior of actual people, it is sometimes argued that the personality structure of the typical individual is an indispensable feature of any study of society or culture.

[3] Wagley, *Area Research and Training*, p. 5.

"Personality," "society," and "culture" may be brought into relationship for many purposes, but they are very different kinds of constructs, and the respective integrating processes vary greatly.

In any social science study the individual's behavior and products are the basic observable phenomena from which constructs of particular societies and cultures are derived. These constructs are norms or abstractions rather than directly observable phenomena, but they are based on observations of the varieties of behavior exhibited by different individuals. Study of social and cultural behavior deals with individuals as the components of society and as the carriers of culture but not necessarily as psychological entities. The structural and functional whole is social, and the integrating processes are sociocultural, not psychological.

Research problems in which the individual is conceived as the integrative whole are of a different order. The purpose of the previously mentioned studies of cultural personality and of national character was to ascertain how socially inherited modes of behavior are integrated within the typical individual. Whether the society and culture are primitive, with fairly stereotyped behavior patterns, or are contemporary civilizations, with considerable variation in possible behavior and therefore need for choice, the various economic, social, and religious modes of behavior are synthesized, reconciled, or patterned within each person. Every individual acquires a personality structure and tends to find a way of life that involves a maximum of direction and integration and a minimum of internal conflict. The concrete terms of personality structure depend upon the culture, but the processes of personality integration are psychological. They presumably are equally applicable to all people. The different personalities result from psychological adaptation to the sociocultural and natural environments.

If the problem is simply how culture and society affect personality, the inquiry is essentially psychological and does not have direct bearing on broader social and cultural interests of area studies. This problem could also be stated, however, as the effect of personality structure on cultural change. Approached from this point of view, the problem would be to ascertain how established personality types eliminate, select, and recondition new modes of behavior. It would be assumed that a society cannot accept new modes of behavior which are too inconsistent with or cannot be integrated into the prevailing personality types. The problem of how personality affects culture, however, cannot be stated as if culture and personality constituted a closed circle. If, as some studies seem to claim, personality and adult behavior result essentially from childhood training which in turn is determined by culture, it would appear that culture merely creates personality and personality merely perpetuates culture. Obviously there are factors in change which have to be analyzed in social and cultural terms, and while personality undoubtedly conditions change, it cannot be assigned the dual role of cause and effect.

CULTURE AND SOCIETY

Culture is generally understood to mean learned modes of behavior which are socially transmitted from one generation to another within particular societies and which may be diffused from one society to another. A society is a particular group of people whose relationships have a special pattern, but there is no such thing as society in the abstract, for the nature of any such group is determined by its cultural heritage. Culture on the other hand does not exist without societies, and societies have no forms or functions that are not determined by culture. Society and culture are different though complementary concepts. There has been a confusion of culture areas and social wholes, and of cultural change and social change.

In dealing with primitive cultures the anthropological unit of study is a "tribe," which is a society—a structural-functional whole. But many cultural problems have extrasocietal dimensions. Much of the cultural-historical approach has dealt atomistically with culture elements, such as firemaking, metallurgy, agriculture, the family, religious practices, or art styles. Each of these elements may be studied in isolation, being traced through time and space. That a great many elements have about the same territorial distribution gave rise to the concept of the culture area. A culture area, however, is not a society; it includes a number of societies which share a similar way of life. Culture area consequently is not an integrating concept but a descriptive device which presents the common denominator of behavior of several societies.

Studies of primitive cultures led to the concept of culture pattern[4] or configuration, which requires the corollary concept of function,[5] for patterns are means of describing the functional interrelationship of all cultural phenomena or the master plan of a society, even though the criteria of patterns vary. Culture areas as wholes are not integrated by patterns, although they are often approached as if this were the case. Any world area is characterized by a culture and a pattern, but the area

[4] Ruth Benedict, *Patterns of Culture* (Boston: Houghton Mifflin Company, 1934).

[5] "Function" has been conceptualized in many different ways by Radcliffe-Brown, Malinowski, and others. In its simplest meaning, function merely signifies that cultural phenomena are interdependent and interact within some kind of social unit.

is not necessarily an integrated whole and the pattern is not the integrative factor of the culture area. A culture area is a territorial division within which a particular pattern, like any specific culture element or complex, recurs in each of the different societies. Because no two societies are exactly alike, the pattern of a culture area represents merely an abstraction or common denominator of the patterns of the societies within the area.

The various nations of the West, such as Germany, England, France, Greece, or the United States, have different individual patterns, each representing the particular way in which economics, social institutions, political attitudes, and ideological systems are organized and integrated. Distinguishing the West from the East involves a high degree of abstraction. Western science, logic, industrialization, capitalism, political democracy, and many other features are functionally interdependent in the pattern of Western civilization. This does not mean that the West is an integrated whole and the East another whole. It means merely that Western societies have a number of general features in common which distinguish them from Eastern societies. These general features and patterns are abstractions of the more particular and diversified ones which occur in each independent society or nation.

Culture pattern, therefore, is an integrating concept only when applied to particular societies such as nations. It is not the integrating concept for a culture area unless the societies within the area have such interdependence that they form a larger whole, a supersociety coincident with the area. The nationalistic trends in Southeast Asia would be no more than recurrent political and ideological patterns within a culture area—an area of "political pressures"—unless an organized state emerged. The Indonesian Republic represents a step toward formal area unity. Nationalism in India has meant separatism, but the societies and nations of South Asia have, as W. Norman Brown points out, important economic, political, cultural, and religious ties. These may someday cause the culture area to develop into an organized whole, in which all parts fit a single pattern. China was split into two states during its revolution. The functional interdependence of world areas has become so great that in 1943 a United States presidential candidate could write about "one world," a term that has since been used increasingly often. The intersocietal or international connections that give some functional unity to culture areas and the interarea connections that are leading toward one world have not yet become clearly patterned. In fact, they are so fraught with confusion that the literature on area trends and world trends shows considerable disagreement about what is happening.

The differences between the concepts of society and culture mean that social change and cultural change, though closely connected, must also be distinguished. Societies may experience rather drastic changes of certain kinds without any important alteration of their culture. These are sometimes called "social interaction" as contrasted with "social" or "cultural change." Baseball furnishes a rather simple illustration of the difference between social and cultural change. As a cultural institution baseball has certain fairly fixed characteristics: competitive teams, rules, loyalties, and, in the professional leagues, commercial aspects and pageantry. Each team may be considered a society. Within the rules of the game the teams may win or lose; their ailing athletes, the strategy of their managers, and many other factors make for success or failure. Their changing positions within the league represent rather considerable social change. But the fate of a particular team need not in the least affect the rules. The culture of baseball is in fact such that some teams must necessarily succeed at the expense of others in order to perpetuate the pattern. If a certain team is a consistent winner, the proportions of a ball park may be altered to make competition fairer; or if attendance declines, a livelier ball may be introduced or new rules made. But any changes in the culture of baseball are relatively minor and they are devised to perpetuate its basic pattern of fairly equal competition. In any case, what happens to the teams—the societies— does not greatly affect the rules, or culture. But any change in the rules may greatly affect the teams; and in baseball or any organized sport a change in rules is accepted only after extended discussion by participants, whose welfare may be threatened.

The difference between social and cultural change, illustrated in the case of baseball, is equally applicable to other subgroups of a society. In Euro-American societies, for example, there is a pattern of "free enterprise" and competition between business institutions, and whether these are corner grocery stores or international oil companies, the competition is supposed to be based on generally accepted rules. In the nature of things the success of one institution must be at the expense of others. The culture which prescribes the terms of competition is of course not static; but it is significant that when cultural trends begin to favor certain competitors, for example, when monopolies begin to develop too rapidly so that an undue number of competitors succumb, the total society makes an effort to strengthen the pattern of free competition—that is, to halt cultural change—by adjusting the rules so that all competitors have a more equal chance.

The distinction between social and cultural change is important in historical studies, for cultural history is by no means the same as national history. To illustrate the point again by the theme of competition, a culture area may be characterized by patterns of competition between the nations within the area, as in Western Europe. The successes or failures of individual nations which result from the strength or weakness of their rulers, the intrigues of ministers, the strategy of generals in certain battles, and various political maneuvers may be no more than expectable episodes within the cultural framework. All nations cannot win any more than all baseball teams can lead a league. The fate of the individual nations, like the fate of baseball teams, is rarely the same thing as the fate of civilization, a change in culture. A historical approach which interprets the rise and fall of nations or empires as the growth and decline of civilization fails to make this essential distinction.

The rise and decline of the kingdoms in the ancient centers of civilization in Egypt, Mesopotamia, India, China, Meso-America, and the Andes is often described as the development and fall of civilization. It is true that the particular kinds of societies found in these centers did not survive, but most of the basic cultural achievements, the essential features of civilization, were passed on to other nations. In each of these centers both culture and society changed rather considerably during the early periods, and everywhere the developmental processes were about the same.[6] At first there were small communities of incipient farmers. Later the communities cooperated in the construction of irrigation works and the populations became larger and more settled. Villages amalgamated into states under theocratic rulers. Meanwhile building arts, ceramics, metallurgy, weaving, urban planning, writing, astronomy, mathematics, and other fundamentals of civilization were developed. Finally, culture ceased to develop, and the states of each area entered into competition with one another. In the Near East, Mesopotamia and Egypt were culturally stagnant from the Bronze Age (about 3000 B.C.) until the Iron Age, some 2,000 years later. China changed surprisingly little from about 1000 B.C. until one hundred years ago. In Meso-America and the Andes, culture was comparatively frozen between 1000 A.D. and the Spanish Conquest.

When culture ceased to change greatly in these centers, an era of cyclical conquests followed. The conquests conformed to a fairly stable cultural pattern, which was not unlike that of the competition of baseball teams within a league. Each state began to compete with others for tribute and other advantages. One or another state succeeded in dominating the others, that is, in building an empire, but such empires ran their course and collapsed after some scores or hundreds of years

---

[6] Julian H. Steward, "Cultural Causality and Law; A Trial Formulation of the Development of Early Civilizations," *American Anthropologist*, 51:1-27 (1949).

only to be succeeded by another empire not very different from the first. The peak of each empire brought a kind of richness and splendor; between empires, there were "dark ages" and local independence.

For the historian this era of cyclical conquests is filled with great men, wars and battle strategy, shifting power centers, and other social events. For the culture historian the changes are much less significant than those of the previous eras when the basic civilizations developed, or, in the Near East, those of the subsequent Iron Age when the cultural patterns changed again and the centers of civilization shifted to new areas.

The concept of culture is being used in historical studies, but the distinction between social and cultural change is not always clear. Toynbee, for example, writes about the growth and decline of "civilizations" but whether he is dealing with societies or cultures is often quite obscure.[7] It is not surprising that he finds something mysterious and even metaphysical in the decline of early "civilizations" because, failing to distinguish the fate of societies from that of culture, he often seems to mean the decline of nations, not of culture. In a similar way, Spengler reflected the pessimism of Europe after the first world war in writing about the "Decline of the West" as if culture itself had declined rather than particular states, which had lost out in world relations according to the prevailing competitive culture pattern.

A sharper distinction between society and culture would be of assistance in more precise formulation of some of the basic problems of modern world trends. Much of the competition for economic or political power has occurred within the framework, or rules, of a general culture. The industrial revolution brought profound cultural change to Western Europe and caused competition for colonies and for areas of exploitation. Japan entered the competition as soon as she acquired the general pattern. The realignments of power caused by Germany's losses in the first world war and by Italy's and Japan's in the second are of a social order. What new cultural patterns will result from these changes remains to be seen.

The general assumption today seems to be that we are in danger of basic cultural change caused by the spread of communism. Russia acquired drastically new cultural patterns as a result of her revolution. Whether communism has the same meaning in other nations has still to be determined. The Chinese revolution, for example, could be regarded from two extreme points of view: first, that it is essentially an agrarian revolution, a phase in the cycles of Chinese history which have been repeated again and again within a fairly stable cultural frame-

---

[7] Arnold J. Toynbee, *A Study of History*, abridgement by D. C. Somervell (New York: Oxford University Press, 1947).

work that has persisted since the Ch'in or T'ang dynasty; second, that it is a completely new ideology, an entirely new cultural pattern, imported from Russia. Certainly neither explanation is the whole truth, and the outstanding contribution of Fairbank's study is its examination of the processes of revolution and Chinese nationalism to ascertain to what extent the trends conform to China's traditional past and to what extent new patterns are being introduced.

Studies of smaller societies or segments of societies may also fail to distinguish society and culture. In our review of community studies we have seen how many monographs were concerned with social relations within established patterns rather than with cultural patterns themselves. The contrast between social stability and cultural stability, as illustrated by the Old Order Amish of Pennsylvania, shows the need to distinguish social and cultural change.

The distinction between society and culture does not mean that both concepts are not necessary to area research. Culture determines the characteristics of societies and it can only be observed as it is manifest in particular societies. Cultural change almost inevitably causes social change, although the reverse may not always be true.

The distinction between society and culture has several methodological implications. First, culture can be used as an integrating concept in area research only in the case of particular societies. Culture areas which consist of many societies are integrated wholes only in a loose sense. Second, the concept of society requires the corollary though distinct concept of culture, for social change does not necessarily involve cultural change. Third, the nature of any social change is determined by the basic culture and can be dealt with effectively only in terms of culture. Whether the objective is to stop the ravages of competition, eliminate the evils of business cycles, or correct any other social ills, the solution must deal with the basic pattern and not merely with the limited phenomena which are determined by it.

SOCIOCULTURAL WHOLES AS INTEGRATIVE LEVELS

The various kinds of societies whose structure and function are determined by the cultural heritage of the world areas in which they exist are *sociocultural* systems or wholes.[8] A sociocultural system is a unit, the social segments and institutions of which have a significant degree of interrelationship and functional interdependence. Any given socio-

---

[8] *Sociocultural* has various other shades of meaning. For example, Sorokin makes society, culture, and personality an "inseparable trinity." For reasons previously stated, the writer considers personality an integrative concept of a different kind than the concept of a sociocultural whole, even though personality is produced by and may affect a sociocultural whole.

cultural system, however, is an empirically derived construct which represents a particular kind of society in a particular developmental continuum, that is, within a designated world area. Research problems and methods, therefore, have to be adapted to sociocultural systems which are characterized (rather than classified) with reference to two criteria: (1) the cultural tradition which they carry; (2) the relationship of the parts to the whole within the level of development. The first criterion depends upon the principle of cultural relativity. The second requires a theory of sociocultural levels within a developmental continuum.

Within any world area there is a developmental continuum of sociocultural wholes or systems. More complex and territorially larger systems supersede simple localized systems. In the progression from simple to complex, the earlier units and the earlier cultural practices do not entirely disappear. There are survivals of what Sumner and others call "folkways" and "mores" and "folk societies" and "folk cultures." There has been a strong tendency to treat these survivals as if they were preserved like fossils and functioned in the newer sociocultural wholes more or less as they did in the older. For example, the concepts of community and folk society are treated as though they represented absolute and universal entities, whose study requires identical methodology regardless of whether they are independent sociocultural units or dependent parts of larger wholes, which latter vary according to the cultural tradition of the areas in which they are found.

This tendency to apply a given methodology to any "survival" is a result of the assumption that the higher levels of sociocultural systems differ from lower ones essentially in complexity. Because systems of the higher level do not consist merely of more numerous and more diversified parts, it is methodologically incorrect to treat each part as though it were an independent whole itself. For example, in the early eras of Peruvian culture communities were independent sociocultural wholes, but later these communities became dependent parts of states or empires. Still later they were incorporated into the Spanish state of Peru. Today Peru is strongly aboriginal Indian in many respects and also preserves many practices of sixteenth-century Spain. But modern Peruvian culture is not simply a mechanical mixture of elements and patterns of aboriginal Indian, old Spanish, and contemporary Euro-American culture; and Peruvian society cannot be regarded as a structure made up of strictly native villages, of purely sixteenth-century Spanish communities, of modern cities, and of various economic, religious, and political institutions. The older cultural elements, communities, and institutions have undergone qualitative changes, brought about by their functional dependence upon a new kind of whole. A continuum of development is recognizable in Peru's history, but it consists of successive levels—the lines may be drawn at various points—that are parts of a whole which is qualitatively new as well as quantitatively more complex.

In science generally, there is good precedent for dealing with levels of integration. The distinction between the inorganic, organic, and superorganic is a very old concept and it means that the sciences dealing with each level frame their problems in terms of special aspects of phenomena. Thus biology involves principles and processes in addition to and different from those found in chemistry and physics, for the organization of matter known as life has qualities peculiar to itself. Psychological phenomena, although based on neurological structures and functions, have some aspects which are best investigated in terms of themselves, that is, at a psychological rather than neurological or organic level. The particular forms of human behavior known as culture involve something more than psychological processes, and consequently culture patterns and complexes may properly be studied in terms of themselves, that is, through distributional, historical, and comparative methods which represent operations on the superorganic level. Because behavior patterns are concretely manifest in particular groups of people or societies, whose structure and function they determine, sociocultural units represent levels of organization which are not wholly reducible to biological, psychological, or even cultural phenomena.

If the basic concept of levels is valid—and this would not seem to be very debatable—types of sociocultural organization no less than the phenomena of the inorganic and organic levels must be divided into sublevels. In physics, for instance, it is much more convenient to study the behavior of gases as wholes than in terms of each molecule or atom. Even a field equation, which will someday interrelate all physical phenomena in a single formula, will be a poor tool for dealing with everyday problems of mechanics.

In biology the concept of sublevels is extremely important. Sublevels differ according to the nature of the whole, and in each sublevel the principles of organization and the relationships between the parts and the whole are different.[9] The lowest form of unicellular life has properties that are not reducible to chemistry and physics, for life has the distinctive quality of self-perpetuation, which is not found in inorganic matter. Even if a living cell could be created synthetically, it would nonetheless be more practicable for many purposes to treat its life processes in terms of themselves. Multicellular organisms consist not

[9] Alex B. Novikoff, "Integrative Levels in Biology," *ETC.: A Review of General Semantics*, 2:203-213 (1944-45).

merely of cells, but of specialized kinds of cells, each of which has distinctive functions and relationships to other kinds because they are all dependent parts of new kinds of wholes, of higher levels of organization. The cell is incompletely understood if it is not studied as part of an organ; and an organ is intelligible only as part of a total organism. The heart, for example, has specialized cells, which function according to principles of chemistry and cell metabolism; but the heart serves to pump blood in the body, while being affected by respiration, nerve impulses of various origins, hormone content of the blood, and other factors.

This concept of levels is not an argument against reductionism, for there are many problems in all the major divisions of science where reduction of one kind of process to another is not only valid but desirable. Where levels of organization mark divisions between sciences, such reduction often represents an important interdisciplinary approach. Thus nutrition, originating in biology, has utilized chemistry to the point where many foods, vitamins, and other esentials can be produced synthetically. Similarly it could be argued that ultimate explanations of cultural and social change—at least, explanations deeper than those now offered on the social and cultural levels—must take account of biological, psychological, and physical factors. But problems of this kind are peripheral to present considerations. We are concerned with ascertaining the nature of the sociocultural systems at each different level of organization.

According to the principle of sociocultural sublevels, each higher sublevel is more complex than the lower ones not only in the quantitative sense that it has more parts but, as in biological sublevels, that it has qualitatively novel characteristics or unique properties which are not evident in or foreshadowed by the lower ones. That is, the new whole at each higher sublevel induces changes in the very nature of the parts and creates new relationships between the parts and to the whole.

This point may be illustrated with a simple and basic phenomenon. The human family is found in all societies but, like the cell, its nature and functions vary according to the whole. In a few sociocultural units, such as the Eskimo or the Great Basin Shoshoneans, the family more or less constitutes the social, economic, educational, and political whole. The family has persisted throughout world history, but its nature and role in larger sociocultural wholes have changed tremendously. The contemporary American family, for example, has lost many of the primitive functions, while others have been so modified as to give it unique meaning and relationships that are specific to the context of modern civilization.

In the historical development of sociocultural systems, the individual family units amalgamated into larger groups whose nature and functions were very different from those of the family. There are and have been many kinds of primitive multifamily societies, each representing an integrated whole. One variety of multifamily local group is that found in aboriginal Yucatan. The native Maya states collapsed after the Spanish Conquest, and a high degree of local separatism was established among the Indian groups. Gradually and in varying degrees these people were brought under the influence of Merida, a city of the European pattern. Redfield, speaking of Yucatan, characterizes the folk society[10] as small, isolated, close-knit, homogeneous, simple in technology, patterned around kinship relations, having implicit goals and values, and believing in all-pervading supernaturalism. In Yucatan, under the influence of urban or national culture,[11] the many collectivized folk activities became individualized, the all-pervasive supernaturalism receded, much of life became secularized, and the close-knit folk society was disorganized. But the changes in the folk society and folk culture of Yucatan could also be described in terms of their readaptation to a new and higher level of sociocultural organization. From the point of view of the folk society, the individual's life became secularized, individualized, and disorganized. From the point of view of the larger whole or the newer pattern, scientific or naturalistic explanations replaced supernatural ones in many spheres of life; the organized church partly replaced informal, local religious outlets; affiliations with the kin group and the local group were partly superseded by affiliations with urban (or national) occupational, social class, and other special groups; and when the individual ceased to be one of many similar individuals who cooperated in a local homogeneous whole, he assumed a specialized role in a larger heterogeneous system. Folk societies and cultures do not entirely disappear but they are modified and acquire new characteristics because of their functional dependence upon a new and larger system.

These remarks on the transformations in a folk society when it is absorbed into a larger sociocultural unit are intended merely to illustrate the modifications in functions of the former. It is purely a matter of definition whether the folk society is said to disappear when it becomes a dependent part of a larger organizational whole—and there are many definitions and concepts of "folk society."

The concept of sociocultural levels, of course, implies a developmental continuum, but the question of where to draw the lines between levels—that of a developmental taxonomy—must be answered on a

[10] Robert Redfield, "The Folk Society," *American Journal of Sociology*, 52:293-308 (1947).

[11] Robert Redfield, *The Folk Culture of Yucatan*.

comparative empirical basis if the organizational wholes are to be conceptualized in such a way as to facilitate a problem approach in research. Sociological taxonomy has tended to be so logical and abstract as to have little bearing on reality. For example, Sorokin's classification of social groups into families, clans, tribes ("an organized and solidary agglomeration of two or more clans"!), and nations[12] is not based on empirical cross-cultural studies, for few such studies have been made. There are unquestionably typological similarities between societies of the differing cultural traditions represented in the major world areas, but considerable comparative study will be necessary to isolate recurrent dynamics of developmental process and of structural-functional types.

On primitive levels, "family," "clan," and "tribe" are largely unreal concepts. Many primitive peoples never had clans, and "tribe" has a great many meanings. The social typology of primitive peoples is exceedingly complex and has largely to be worked out. One type that has been established cross-culturally is the "patrilineal band," an extended, exogamous, land-owning patrilineal kin group which is found among Australians, Bushmen, Fuegians, Southern California Shoshoneans, and certain other primitive hunters.[13] This is but one of many types of primitive bands, each with its own ecological adaptations, social structure, and functional relations.

The "folk society" is at present a highly abstract construct—almost a definition—rather than a type based on cross-cultural data. Redfield's particular concept of folk society and his statement of the effects of urbanizing influences on it apply specifically to Yucatan. He offers these as hypotheses for cross-cultural testing and not as validated universals. In the different world areas there are hundreds of societies which might be considered "folk" from one point of view or another. For research, the concept of "folk" needs to be concretized in terms of actual sociocultural groups. If certain types are found in several different areas, the concept has operational utility in developmental and functional studies. Setting up a type as a logical construct rather than as an abstraction of forms which occur in concrete situations is likely to have limited use.

Similarly, "nation" is too broad a concept to have much significance, for dozens of wholly unlike societies in the ancient and modern world might loosely be defined as nations. Wittfogel's "oriental absolute state" is a type established cross-culturally on the basis of empirical

---

[12] Sorokin, *op cit.*, p. 251-255.

[13] Julian H. Steward, "The Economic and Social Basis of Primitive Bands," in *Essays in Anthropology Presented to A. L. Kroeber* (Berkeley: University of California Prss, 1936), pp. 331-350.

data. This concept has operational utility because it relates a particular social, political, and economical structure to particular kinds of natural environment and land use in several centers of ancient civilizations.[14]

More realistic types in sociological taxonomy are modern nations, particularly those of the Western world, for they have been extensively studied. It does not follow, however, that nations in other world areas can be approached by use of the concepts developed with reference to these Western nations, because the structure, functions, and values of the former differ from those of the latter. Above all, it is utterly fallacious to conceive of any developmental continuum of social types as representing a sequence of stages through which all mankind passed. Universal developmental stages, such as those postulated by L. H. Morgan, have long since been rejected. Whatever mankind may have in common has to be ascertained by the long and tedious process of detailed comparisons of society with society and area with area. It cannot be achieved by any deductive process.

If a developmental and structural-functional taxonomy is to be useful in studying such problems as the growth of nationalism, economic development, impact of industrialized nations on backward peoples, spread of political ideologies, and other themes of interest, it is necessary first to understand sociocultural units in their particular relativistic area settings before abstracting out structural features or developmental processes that are common to societies in two or more areas.

The concepts of level of organization and of developmental continuum indicate the need of recognizing that in each world area the sequences of sociocultural units consist of successions of new kinds of wholes qualitatively different from previous ones but genetically related to them. Where to draw the lines between levels should depend more upon the particular problem under investigation than on any a priori logical construct. Each sociocultural system can provide the frame of reference within which interdisciplinary data are integrated, but the nature and method of integration will depend upon the level or kind of organization. The higher, more complex levels will require contributions from many more specialized disciplines.

SOCIOCULTURAL SYSTEMS AS RESEARCH UNITS

In this section some research implications of the concept of levels of sociocultural systems will be suggested, but no attempt will be made to prescribe any universal methodology. The general theme of interest,

[14] K. A. Wittfogel, "The Foundations and Stages of Chinese Economic History," *Zeitschrift für Sozialforschung*, 4:26-60 (1935).

the research problem, and the nature of the unit of study determine the methodology appropriate to each project.

Among most primitive peoples the localized unit is the sociocultural whole; the society is small and self-contained and the culture is fairly simple. The ethnographic method can usually be applied by one person since it is comparatively easy to study the functional interrelationship of all aspects of behavior in small independent societies.

As societies become more complex, special social groups begin to cut across local societies, and formal national institutions begin to appear. The whole consists of three kinds of parts: (1) the local units, such as communities, neighborhoods, households, and other special groups, which may be called vertical divisions of the larger whole; (2) special occupational, class, caste, racial, ethnic, or other subsocieties which, like the local units, may have a somewhat distinctive way of life, but which cut across localities and may be called horizontal sociocultural segments; and (3) the formal institutions, such as money, banking, trade, legal systems, education, militarism, organized churches, philosophical and political ideologies, and the like, which constitute the bones, nerves, and sinews running throughout the total society, binding it together and affecting it at every point. The vertical and horizontal sociocultural subgroups make up the total social structure. The institutions as such usually do not constitute sociocultural segments, although they affect and are affected by all segments.

As societies develop to higher levels of organization, the horizontal sociocultural segments and the formal institutions attain increasing importance. In contemporary civilizations they are so important that the institutions have become the specialties of different disciplines. The means of interrelating these fields of specialization in modern area research, however, are not yet clear.

The local units or communities, as we have seen, are treated by many anthropologists and sociologists as if they were independent, self-sufficient, sociocultural systems. Their place in the larger structure is rarely clarified, and the effect of national institutions upon them receives little attention. The methodology for understanding the community in its larger context must be adapted to the particular case. Tarascan communities retain a great deal of folk culture; they have fewer horizontal sociocultural segments and are less affected by national institutions than Middletown in the United States.

The horizontal segments are generally studied with referrence to a total social structure and are identified by such basic criteria as income, social status, and occupation. There has been virtually no application of the ethnographic method to these segments comparable to its use in community studies. Responses to questionnaires, designed primarily to yield quantitative data, have shown some of the outstanding characteristics of horizontal segments. The ethnographic method should also be used in study of these segments, for it is probable that many of them have subcultures just as communities do. It is even possible that in a nation like the United States, the horizontal segments often represent the more important subcultural divisions, which in many cases have a degree of organization. Whereas a Tarascan individual is primarily attached to his family, neighborhood, or community in which even the church, school, and political organizations have more local than national significance, many Americans have few ties with their localities. They may hardly know their immediate neighbors; they may or may not participate in the local Parent-Teachers Association, American Legion, or other organizations; and their principal interests and connections may lie entirely outside the community. They may belong to labor unions, the National Association of Manufacturers, scientific or professional societies, churches, lodges, or other organizations and institutions which ally them more closely functionally with people scattered throughout the nation than with the person next door.

It is probable that there are many interlocality horizontal segments which have true subcultures, and these would be well worth studying. There are indications of such subcultures in certain community studies. For example, the laboring class and the middle-class businessmen of Middletown are culturally different, but does each resemble its own class in other communities? Novelists like Sinclair Lewis are still the principal authority for the hypothesis that middle-class businessmen have about the same culture everywhere. Social science might well set itself the task of investigating this hypothesis.

The formal institutions of the more complex societies are the concern of many special disciplines—economics, government, law, history, literature, philosophy, and others. As most of these developed in the study of Euro-American societies, the concepts of culture, cultural relativity, and sociocultural systems are only now beginning to be used in them. Until recently they were becoming more and more specialized and compartmentalized. Theoretically it should be possible to make as completely integrated an interdisciplinary study of the United States as of a primitive tribe. Practically this will be impossible as long as specialized studies, which will always be necessary, are not more closely coordinated. Just how this will be brought about is not clear, but some of the major themes of interest previously mentioned probably will lead to interdisciplinary studies. Whether the themes are conceived as relating to practical problems or to scientific interests does not matter. Research will be so planned that it will cut across disciplinary lines. Adequate conceptualization of the nature of the sociocultural whole and its parts in each case will indicate the relevance of different fields of specialization to any interdisciplinary approach to the basic themes of interest.

CROSS-CULTURAL PROBLEMS AND METHODS

Previous sections have stressed the importance of problems in area research, of which the scientific goal is to develop a method which will make social and cultural prediction possible. Prediction, however, may be understood differently. By the principle of cultural relativity, which in its extreme sense implies that no two world areas are alike, prediction would mean that the people of any area can be expected to behave "in character" and the task would be to ascertain the cultural particulars which determine their behavior. This principle, however, seems to preclude the possibility of making predictive formulations which are valid for two or more areas. Such formulations would have to be made in terms of recurrent cause and effect, but the extreme relativists see any culture as a unique entity in which all the phenomena are so interdependent that each is both cause and effect.

The problem approach to area research, however, generally implies that certain general trends may be found in the area particulars. For example, the impact of industrial nations upon backward areas has some common characteristics. Emergent nationalism has similar aspects in different parts of the world. The search for general laws is an ideal of many area research workers.

A. V. Kidder, in a mimeographed account of the Carnegie Institution's May program, states that:

> The question . . . is: does culture, although not biologically transmitted, develop and function in response to tendencies—it is perhaps too connotative to call them law—that are comparable to those controlling biological evolution? There seems to be evidence that, in some degree at least, it does. All over the world and among populations that could apparently not possibly have come into contact with each other, similar inventions have been made and have been made in a seemingly predetermined order. Extraordinary similarities are to be observed in the nature and order of appearance among widely separated peoples of certain social practices and religious observances.
>
> These are likenesses, not identities; history, to reverse the proverb, never repeats itself; different environments and differing opportunities have seen to that. But they do seem to indicate that there are definite tendencies and orderlinesses, both in the growth of this compelling force and in man's responses thereto. It is therefore the task of the disciplines concerned with man and his culture—genetics, history, archaeology, sociology, the humanities—to gather and to correlate information which

may enable us more fully to understand these now dimly perceived trends and relationships.

The search for laws or universals has been notably lacking in a comparative cross-cultural approach.[15] Too often the formulations concerning function or process that result from the analysis of a single society are postulated as universal laws. As long as these are not tested in other societies, they are no more than hypotheses and may be no more than descriptions of particular characteristics of our own Western European cuture. Such "laws" as those concerning the behavior of money, the profit motive, or business cycles may not at all be valid for other societies, except as the latter have been drawn into the orbit of Western capitalism, and even in these cases the "laws" may require drastic modification. Characteristics of the family which are correlated with income or social status may apply only to Western civilization. Assumptions about political behavior, such as those which presumably underlie public opinion polling methods, would certainly not be applicable elsewhere—and apparently require some modificaiton to be reliable in our own rapidly changing society.

Fei and Chang[16] have given an interesting illustration of how assumptions about American land use and land tenure cannot be directly transferred to China. They criticize Buck's[17] questionnaire approach to land use in China on the grounds that, "following the American convention, villagers are classified into landowner, part owner, tenant, landless laborers, and nonfarming villagers." They point out that a better understanding of the local variations of Chinese society would show that tenants in Yunnan may work the land of collective clan owners and thus be in a very different social and economic position than are tenants in Kiangsu, who rent from absentee landlords and again that hired labor in some areas may be migratory, not resident.

A serious obstacle to an approach to cross-cultural laws or regularities is the evident belief that a law, whether of developmental processes or stages or of functional dynamics, must apply to all mankind. The objective is usually phrased as the search for "universals." In the article cited,[18] the writer endeavored to show that the immediate aim should be to formulate cause and effect relationships, whether of a

---

[15]This point has been discussed by the writer and its application illustrated in "Cultural Causality and Law: A Trial Formulation of the Development of Early Civilization," *op. cit.*

[16]*Earthbound China*, pp. 2-4.

[17]John L. Buck, *Land Utilization in China* (Chicago: University of Chicago Press, 1937).

[18]"Cultural Causality and Law."

synchronic or diachronic nature, that pertain to delimitable and specifiable conditions and situations rather than to seek universals. Many
formulations may be valid for two or more areas, but the varieties of
world cultures, past and present, differ so greatly because of both area
tradition and sociocultural level that it can hardly be expected that
formulations will hold for all mankind. And there is not the slightest
need that they should.

The study of patrilineal bands[19] is a simple illustration of the procedure in a cross-cultural formulation of cause and effect. The problem
was to ascertain what cultural-ecological factors contributed to the
formation of certain kinds of exogamous hunting and gathering
bands. Relevant phenomena included natural landscape, the nature
and distribution of wild game, hunting technology, population density,
patterns of kinship and exogamy, and relative status of men and
women in the culture. It was found that the adjustment of man to
nature—cultural ecology—under particular conditions brought about
bands that were patrilineal, exogamous, patrilocal, and land-owning.
These features represent an independently recurrent type which is an
abstraction of similarities, although the total culture of each band
consists of innumerable particulars which in their totality are unique.

The method of abstracting recurrent functional interrelationships
in higher sociocultural levels is essentially the same, although its application is far more difficult because the phenomena are not only more
complex and qualitatively different than in simpler societies but their
study has been divided among different disciplines.

Formulations that pertain to a complex society may be illustrated by
hypotheses which were developed by the staff of the Puerto Rico
project. Had the purpose of this project been to describe the culture
according to the concept of the culture area, the task would have been
simply to list those cultural features which comprise the common
denominator of the island, those which it shares with the larger
Ibero-American culture area, and those which it shares with the United
States. But there are many patterns and processes of land use, land
tenure, colonialism, economic and political dependency, natic.1alism,
and other matters which are not limited to Puerto Rico. Each can be
stated as a hypothesis of the causal relationships that may be expected
under stipulated circumstances. Applied to Puerto Rico, it was necessary to specify the particular characteristics of the island that were
related to the hypothesis and to look to different disciplines for relevant data.

Initially the hypotheses were derived from discussions in a seminar

---

[19]Julian H. Steward, "The Economic and Social Basis of Primitive Bands," *op. cit.*

at Columbia University and from readings of the staff. At first one could not be certain whether each formulation was merely descriptive of Puerto Rico's Ibero-American heritage or whether it represented function and process that occur anywhere under designated conditions. The problems or hypotheses therefore had to be stated as pertaining to specifiable conditions. The island's Spanish heritage originally included an agrarian two-class (landlord and peasant) society, concentration of power in the land owners, and a strong church sanction of the system, the church and state being almost inseparable; and it still includes such features as the Spanish language, towns which are built around plazas, patrilineal families, close familial ties, and a dual standard. Puerto Rico, like every other Latin American nation, also developed special charcteristics of its own and it acquired various features from the United States. Consequently any hypothesis about Puerto Rico which might be valid cross-culturally would have to abstract general features from Puerto Rico's particular cultural heritage. If a hypothesis pertained to Puerto Rico's unique characteristics, it would by definition obtain nowhere else. On the other hand, any hypothesis that might be true for all mankind would probably be so broad as to lack real significance. Between these extremes are hypotheses pertaining to conditions that are generalized in varying degrees. For example, hypotheses might pertain to any agrarian society, to any colonial dependency, or to any colonial dependency of a capitalist society.

A very broad, though not universal, hypothesis might be: "In any agricultural society, children are a nonsalaried essential of the labor force." A more limited hypothesis would be: "In any capitalist society, if high male unemployment and seasonal work reduce the relative importance of the male's contribution, woman's authority in the family and society increases; the concentration of productive resources in the hands of one class continues progressively; consumption on credit varies from class to class; power is exercised by higher leaders and delegated to local leaders, rather than the reverse; the lines of political power correspond to the lines of economic power; the production of subsistence commodities progressively diminishes while production for the world market increases; and there is an observable concentration of land ownership in fewer and fewer hands."

For the purpose of cross-cultural comparison and formulation of hypotheses of a more specific nature, some of the basic characteristics of Puerto Rico are: agrarian; dependent upon cash, credit, and industrially manufactured goods; capitalistic, with private ownership of lands and other means of production; and a system of power and social status. To limit the conditions further, Puerto Rico is insular, tropical, and a dependency of the United States after having been a colony of Spain. Conditions could obviously be narrowed to the point where they pertained to Puerto Rico alone and had no cross-cultural validity. It is incumbent upon anyone seeking cultural regularities to designate the point that separates the particulars of a cultural heritage from those features which are more general.

The requirement that a formulation of regularities interrelate as many phenomena as seem to have casual connection may be illustrated by another hypothesis which may have wide cross-cultural applicability: "An agrarian society which is part of a capitalist economy of which class structure is a characteristic, which has access to manufactured goods, and which produces predominantly cash crops, will have individual land-ownership, bilateral inheritance, and competition for markets; the small owner will be at a disadvantage because of lack of credit and relatively greater overhead expenses; and because lands are split among heirs, the ever-decreasing size of the holdings of small owners will reach the point where the owners cannot compete with the large owners and therefore will lose their lands to them." A corollary hypothesis is: "Two basic types of economy, such as capitalist and cooperative, cannot coexist in any society. Therefore, government intervention or other means of reversing the trend just stated can be applied only to a very limited extent; for power resides in the landowners, who could stop the contrary trend if it began to threaten them."

Another hypothetical formulation of regularities, which interrelates a considerable number of cultural features while pertaining to delimitable conditions, concerns the correlates of large and small farms. It is drawn from previous research, especially from Arensberg and Kimball's Irish study: "In a capitalist industrial society, large and small farmers will differ in a number of ways that are causally interrelated and self-consistent. The larger farmer will have specialized cash crops; purchase many essential foods and material goods; have greater credit, smaller overhead, and greater mechanization; make more extensive use of fertilizers and other scientific methods, these deriving in part from his capital available to employ such aids and in part from his greater education and wider contacts. The large owner will belong to the middle or upper class, and thereby participate to a greater degree in the national culture. His laborers will work for wages, purchase more of their needs, have small bilateral family units, and lack cooperation because there are no activities for cooperation. (Here could be included trends toward unionization, etc., although these would have to be postulated with reference to more specific circumstances.)

"The small farmer will grow more general produce, including subsistence crops, and correspondingly he will have less cash income for the purchase of manufactured goods. For this reason homecrafts will supply a portion of his material needs that varies in direct ratio to the portion of his production that brings a cash income. His farming will be less mechanized. It will entail more mutual help, between both relatives and neighbors. Family ties will be more extended. Village cohesion will be greater, being based not only on economic cooperation but on common religious, political, and social interests. Whereas the hired laborer of the large farm is of the lower class, that is, the national proletariat, the small farmer is more independent of the national structure and more locally distinctive in culture, not falling so readily into a class system and not participating in the national system of credit, trade, education, and intellectual and esthetic values."

These hypotheses may apply to total sociocultural wholes or to special parts or aspects of wholes. They illustrate the kinds of formulations which may be made in any study and tested in other studies. They will be applicable only to stipulated conditions. Both the hypotheses and the conditions will doubtless need to be reformulated as they are tested cross-culturally.

Virtually all important area problems can be converted into hypotheses for cross-cultural testing, and these hypotheses can orient research. Historical-cultural particularism is essentially factualism, and it provides no criteria or frame of reference by which to judge the relevance of data. If, however, the more general purpose of social science is to ascertain the regularities, the laws, or the causes and effects in human behavior, specific formulations of postulated regularities must necessarily guide the selection of research problems and of relevant data.

The conditions of the problem approach are that the postulated regularities be so phrased as to: (1) distinguish general and recurrent factors involved in cause-and-effect relationships from locally distinctive particulars of the cultural heritage; (2) be subject to cross-cultural validation; (3) specify the conditions to which they pertain; and (4) interrelate all pertinent phenomena.

Social science literature is filled with suggestions of regularities that may be cross-culturally valid. The present need is to make the implied hypotheses explicit and to subject them to empirical test.

13

The People of Puerto Rico

This selection formed the introductory chapter to *The People of Puerto Rico* (Julian H. Steward *et al.*, Urbana: University of Illinois Press, 1955), and is herein presented with the permission of the publisher. The volume was of singular importance as the first anthropological attempt to describe and analyze a modern, complex society as a totality, using the field techniques of anthropology. Steward's introductory chapter lays out the concepts and methods of the research and discusses the unique problems inherent in its scope. The original illustrations have been omitted in this edition.

RESEARCH OBJECTIVES

The present volume reports a cultural-historical study of the behavior patterns or lifeways of certain of the Puerto Rican people. The study undertook to analyze the contemporary culture and to explain it in terms of the historical changes which have occurred on the island, especially those which followed the transition from Spanish sovereignty to United States sovereignty a half-century ago, and in terms of ecological adaptations of the historically derived patterns to the local geographical environment. Interest centers not only upon the concrete details of cultural form, function, and pattern of modern Puerto Rico and upon their modification from one historical period to another but upon the general processes of historical development. The substantive results of the study are seen as exemplifications of processes which are now occurring also in other world areas, and this volume concludes with some hypothetical regularities of change which appear to operate in different cultures elsewhere.

In order to carry out this broad objective it was necessary to clarify certain concepts and methods and to delimit the scope of investigation. Instead of attempting to ascertain what the culture of the average or typical Puerto Rican was like or of trying to study all of the many special varieties of behavior, we chose to analyze the lifeways of certain special segments and classes which are numerically important. We were concerned especially with the features which characterize and distinguish the people engaged in the major forms of agricultural production—with the small farmers who grow tobacco and mixed crops, with the hacienda owners, and peasants, and the farm laborers of the coffee area, and with the workers on both the corporate-owned and the government-owned, profit-sharing sugar plantations. These products—tobacco, coffee, and sugar—are Puerto Rico's principal cash crops, and the greater part of the rural population is engaged in their production. We were also concerned with the prominent and wealthy families of business and professional men.

We selected municipalities exemplifying these principal types of farm production and sought to determine whether significant differences in the more important aspects of cultural behavior were associated with the type of production and with the individual's status and role within the community. In the field research, we sought to ascertain subcultural differences between certain classes or categories of rural people by analyzing their methods of making a living, family types, social relations, political and religious forms, practices and attitudes, varieties of recreation, and life values. We paid particular attention to differences associated with the individual's position in the community, whether as townsman or rural dweller, farm owner, sharecropper, or laborer, merchant, government employee, wage worker, and the like. The lifeways which distinguish the members of these different segments of rural society are presented as subcultures, as self-consistent patterns which prescribe the behavior of the local group of which the individual is a member.

These local patterns of behavior are conceived as subcultures because they have developed and function within the larger context of the community and insular culture. For this reason they provide insights into the local manifestations of national political, religious, economic, educational, and other institutions. They also illuminate the varied local structuring and cultural characteristics of social classes. They exemplify certain similarities and differences between the local varieties of rural classes and between the rural groups and the new middle classes which have developed largely in response to new insular economic patterns and governmental services.

A special study was made of the prominent families of the island because of their traditional superordinate position respecting all classes, their important role in the power structure, and their unusually close contacts today with North American culture.

In addition to firsthand field studies of the rural subcultures and of the island's prominent families, the project sought to determine the developmental factors and processes that produced these varied subcultures. Puerto Rico's gradual change from an area in which small, subsistence farms predominated to one characterized by several rather distinctive forms of commercial agriculture had to be understood in terms of trends resulting from influences originating largely from outside the island. The appraisal of these trends involved us in matters that are usually not taken into account in "community studies." We had to understand the nature of the national and international framework within which the subcultures developed and to determine the role of the local environment in the differentiation of land use and in the adaptation of social features to the productive processes.

A final objective was to present our conclusions not only as substantive findings concerning particular subcultures but also as a set of theoretical propositions which might illuminate other cultures. We assume that the comparative or cross-culture method of anthroplogy has value in revealing recurrent features of cultural structure, function, and history as well as in pointing up contrasts between cultures of diverse origins and traditions. Because the former ordinarily remain implicit in the data of any particular analysis, providing the reader only ill-defined impressions concerning their cross-cultural significance, we conclude this report with a set of explicit although tentative hypotheses or formulations of regularities that Puerto Rico seems to share with typologically similar cultures in other parts of the world.

In addition to the purpose set forth, other objectives which are prominent in anthropological studies of contemporary populations were given serious thought. For example, we considered how our research might contribute to the understanding of the national characteristics of Puerto Rico as a whole and of the national character, or "personality in culture," which the typical Puerto Rican presumably acquires as the result of nationally shared cultural traits. We concluded, however, that in the analysis of Puerto Rico or any other heterogeneous society it would be methodologically indefensible as well as impracticable to make such research the first order of business. All members of a nation undeniably have much in common. But before the shared traits can be appraised, it is necessary not only to distinguish and trace the sources of the varied components of the national common denominator—for example, features resulting from the imposition of a single system of national laws, participation in a basic national and international economy, use of a common language, observance of similar dietary practices, responses to media of mass communications, similarities of community and family organization, and other characteristics of diverse and heterogeneous origin—but to weigh these traits against the many features which distinguish the members of different communities and sociocultural classes. We therefore employed the traditional method of anthropology of studying all aspects of the behavior of the individual within the context of his specialized community, class, or other subcultural group.

We also considered the possibility of approaching Puerto Rico in the manner of area study programs, that is, of endeavoring to synthesize the data of all social science disciplines in terms of the total, integrated insular whole. If the whole were defined in cultural terms, this would have required study of the political, economic, religious, and other patterns and institutions that function on a national scale and level as well as of features that constitute the distinctive patterns of community and individual behavior. Since Puerto Rico is a fairly small and well-defined area, it appeared that it might lend itself to an attempt to develop the theory and practice of area research.

While we believe that the present research has contributed to the methodology of area studies, there are two very cogent reasons why it was impossible to make a complete area research project. First, adequate analysis of the many special aspects of national culture requires very thorough interdisciplinary coverage, a task completely beyond our financial and scientific resources. Second, the problem of how to interrelate and synthesize the data of the different disciplines so as to achieve a comprehensive interpretation of any national culture as an integrated whole has not yet been solved satisfactorily by the various area study programs.[1] The purposes of area studies range from extremely practical to highly theoretical objectives, and there may be as many frames of reference as there are disciplines. The anthropological frame of reference is culture. Our efforts to understand the local and class subcultures in relation to the total insular culture compelled us to conceptualize the latter in its heterogeneous and complex aspects and to draw heavily upon the disciplines which have devoted themselves to these aspects. While we make no pretense that the present project is an area study, we believe that it indicates some of the lines along which area research might be pursued.

Before explaining the methodology of the present research, however, it is well to acquaint the reader with some of the principal characteristics of the culture and society of Puerto Rico.

GENERAL CHARACTERISTICS OF PUERTO RICO

Puerto Rico is an island some thirty-five miles wide and one hundred miles long lying at the eastern end of the Greater Antilles between Hispaniola and the Virgin Islands. Subtropical and endowed with a

[1]The question of the objectives, methods, underlying concepts, and frames of reference in the interdisciplinary approach of area study programs to contemporary states, nations, and world areas has been analyzed in some detail in Julian H. Steward, 1950.

varied and extremely fertile natural environment, it has been able to produce not only subsistence crops but a considerable variety of cash crops for export to a world market. For the greater part of its four centuries as a Spanish colony, however, Puerto Rico was predominantly a land of small farmers who were permitted to produce little for world trade, except as contraband export evaded Spanish restrictions and stimulated some commercial farming. Knowledge of the subcultures—especially the blends of Hispanic, African, and native Indian features—of these early centuries and of the factors that shaped them is at present very imperfect.

In the nineteenth century, when Spain relaxed her trade restrictions, sugar, coffee, and tobacco became very important as export crops. Regional subcultures began to emerge in response to the distinctive technological, financial, and social arrangements under which these crops were produced. At the turn of the century, Puerto Rico passed to United States sovereignty, whereupon corporate capital from the continent flowed rapidly into the sugar industry, bringing further technological changes and altering the socioeconomic patterns under which the sugar workers lived. United States sovereignty also permitted accelerated change in legal, educational, religious, and other insular institutions, and it facilitated the flow of continental influences of all kinds.

Puerto Rico, however, is by no means a carbon copy of the United States. It has reacted within the terms of its own cultural background, geographical setting, and local traditions to the new institutional framework. The island is still predominantly agrarian, and some 40 percent of the population earns its living by cultivating the land. Sugar continues to be the principal crop, but by no means all of the agricultural population works in sugar. There are many small farmers who grow mixed crops but obtain most of their income from tobacco. There are also coffee producers, cattlemen, dairy farmers, and growers of pineapples, citrus fruits, and other products.

In addition to the rural population, there are town and urban people—governmental, business, servicing, constructional, transportational, and manufacturing personnel—whose numbers are increasing and who are becoming more varied and specialized as a result of developing technology and commerce and of expanding governmental services. Urbanization, though recent, is progressing rapidly, but the great majority of Puerto Rico's 2,285,000 persons counted in the 1952 census—over 668 per square mile, one of the most densely settled areas in the world—are fairly evenly distributed over the land as rural people.

Puerto Rico's population has quadrupled in the last one hundred years and more than doubled in the last fifty years. Despite the constant drain of emigration within the past decade, there is now a considerable population surplus relative to sources of income.[2] Investment capital from the United States greatly expanded sugar production, but it did not leave enough new wealth in the island to take care of the increased population. Local industries offer a partial solution to unemployment, but as yet they have not been extensively developed. Urbanization has been accompanied by the appearance of slums, such as El Fanguito in San Juan and lesser slums in the smaller cities and towns. A low standard of living, seasonal unemployment, malnutrition, endemic disease, and general insecurity are widespread and chronic. Birth control, which is widely advocated as a solution to the economic and social problems, has made little headway and in any event could not remedy the overpopulation which already exists. Land reform and social legislation resulting in government-owned sugar cooperatives, the assignment of subsistence plots to individuals, easier credit for farmers, creation of farm extension services, wage and hour legislation, health and educational facilities, and many other benefits have helped different classes in various degrees without constituting a final or lasting solution.

METHODOLOGY

Anthropology is a comparative newcomer to studies of contemporary complex societies and nations, having traditionally devoted itself to aboriginal, tribal societies. Although the concept of culture and the cultural method which it has brought to these new studies are perhaps its most valuable contribution to social science, it is now very evident that these methodological tools must be revised to have maximum usefulness in dealing with the new subject matter. During the last two decades, the "community study method" has been applied to the examination of complex contemporary societies, but, with few exceptions, these communities have been treated as if they were tribal societies, and little attention has been paid to the larger state or nation of which they are integral parts. When the cultural method has been used in the study of entire nations, it has treated them as if they were tribal societies and emphasized the common denominator of shared behavior traits while largely overlooking or minimizing the many com-

[2]There are perhaps 200,000 Puerto Ricans in New York City alone. C. Wright Mills, Clarence Senior, and Rose Kohn Goldsen, 1950:23. Senior (1953:132) estimated that nearly 300,000 persons were drained off the island between 1942 and 1951. An estimate in 1952 places the number of Puerto Ricans in New York as 321,000. See also Kingsley Davis, 1953.

plex and more institutionalized features as well as the varying sub-cultures.

The need to revise certain anthropological concepts and methods in studies of contemporary societies became very clear in the course of the present research. It was evident that a summation of portraits of the different communities would not constitute a complete picture of the total island. Puerto Rican culture, like that of any contemporary state or nation, is more than a mosaic of its subcultures. There are features above and beyond the subcultures of the communities and socio-cultural classes which must be grasped if community function and acculturation are to be understood. In short, the traditional concepts and methods of cultural studies proved to be a poor tool for dealing with the heterogeneous aspects of the culture of a contemporary society.

THE CONCEPT OF CULTURE

A concept of culture that is applicable to all sociocultural systems, primitive and civilized, is necessarily very broad and general. Culture in the abstract consists of socially transmitted or learned ideas, at-titudes, traits of overt behavior, and suprapersonal institutions. In most anthropological studies it is generally conceived that the totality of these features has an overall unity which is generally expressed in cultural terms as functional integration within a basic pattern or con-figuration, but which may also be expressed in psychological terms as integration within a basic personality type. In either case stress is placed upon the functional interdependence of the different modes of be-havior. The cultural method, therefore, is broadly holistic in that it analyzes all modes of individual behavior and all supra-individual institutions in relationship to one another. It contrasts with a method which undertakes separate studies of each aspect of behavior, such as economics, government, or religion, in isolation.

An operational concept of culture and a workable cultural method, however, must be adapted to the nature of the particular sociocultural system under analysis. Concepts and methods revised for the study of tribal societies are inadequate for dealing with contemporary societies. We shall distinguish "subculture" from "culture," assign new and qual-ified meaning to "national culture," "national characteristics," and "national character," and devise a taxonomy and terminology for designating qualitatively different types of cultures. Until these distinc-tions are made, anthropologists who are experimenting with new applications of their cultural method will be unable to communicate with each other, let alone with fellow social scientists who are dealing with the same subject matter.

Part of the difficulty in readapting methodology stems from anthropology's concept of cultural relativity. As a comparative science, anthropology has traditionally been concerned with contrasts to the extent of placing primary emphasis upon the uniqueness of each cultural tradition. This emphasis logically negates the possibility of a taxonomy which would put different sociocultural systems or parts of different systems in the same category. Terms that are used cross-culturally, therefore, have only very loose meaning if fundamental distinctions in the stages or levels of any developmental continuum from tribal to civilized societies are not made. The lack of clarity between "tribal," "community," "state," "national," and the like has meant in practice that all developmental levels are handled with the methodology which was developed in tribal studies.

Primitive societies are typically small, self-contained, and culturally homogeneous. "Tribal culture" is a construct based essentially on behavioral traits that characterize virtually all members of the society. Although there are some differences associated with sex, age, role, and status, there are no major occupational, regional, or social groups or segments that differ significantly from one another and can be said to have subcultures, and there are no larger, suprapersonal institutions that cannot be understood fairly well by studying the behavior of individuals. The cultural method, which in tribal studies is commonly called the ethnographic method, is to observe a sufficient number of individuals to ascertain the typical or expectable behavior of tribal members which is then described as the culture.

More complex sociocultural systems such as modern nations are not dealt with so easily. The subcultural groups of the latter, such as communities, occupational classes, ethnic minorities, and the like, may be studied by the ethnographic method, but this alone is not enough. Modern nations have certain features, such as governmental structures, legal systems, religious organizations, and economic patterns which differ qualitatively from anything known in tribal culture and which cannot possibly be grasped by ascertaining the behavior of the typical individual associated with them. The concept that culture consists of shared behavior will not at all serve to describe the functions of a government or a system of international commerce.

LEVELS OF SOCIOCULTURAL ORGANIZATION

The several distinctions made here between tribal and contemporary national sociocultural systems are based largely upon the concept of levels of sociocultural integration or organization. The concept of levels of organization underlies the distinctions between the physical, biological, and social sciences, which deal respectively with those phenomena which are organized according to physical principles, with those which are organized according to a life principle, that is, which have the property of self-perpetuation, and with those which are organized on a cultural or superorganic level. Each level has qualities that are unknown in the lower levels and that require distinctive research methods. I have suggested elsewhere (Steward, 1951) that the concept of the superorganic, though useful in distinguishing cultural phenomena from biological and physical phenomena and in clarifying the nature of the subject matter of anthropology, is an imperfect tool for the study of particular cultures. There is need in the cultural sciences as in the biological sciences to distinguish sublevels of organization and to recognize that each sublevel differs from the others not only quantitatively in having greater complexity but qualitatively in having new forms and distinctive principles of organization. Just as a mammal has a respiratory, circulatory, nervous system, and other features not found in unicellular life, so national societies have institutionalized, supracommunity features not found in tribal society. The intricately and delicately structured interrelationship between these features has a distinctive quality.

The concept of levels of sociocultural integration does not of itself carry conclusions as to what levels are significant. As an operational concept it merely points up the need of recognizing qualitatively distinctive characteristics which emerge in the development of any culture and which are found in the internal structure of any "complex" or "civilized" society. The precise nature of the cultural sublevels or organizational patterns will differ in particulars in each historical tradition, but certain general features are fairly universal.

There are a few cultures in the world, like the Western Shoshoni Indians of Nevada or the Eskimo, in which the biological or nuclear family represents the highest level of organization. In such societies virtually all cultural activities are carried on by the family in comparative independence of other families. There are few aspects of culture which may not be wholly understood through analysis of the individual family.

Most primitive peoples, however, are organized in various multi-family societies, such as lineages, bands, villages, and tribes, which have patterns of interfamilial cooperation and interaction. These patterns include collective forms of hunting, fishing, and farming, group worship and ritual, extended kinship relations, tribal warfare, and many other activities which entail suprafamilial organization. These characteristics more or less correspond to those of Redfield's folk society and folk culture (Redfield, 1941, 1947). They are qualitatively different from anything found on a purely family level, and they could not function among families that were largely independent of one another. A still higher level of organization is represented by multicommunity states, federations, and other sociocultural systems, which are integrated through patterns or institutions not found at a community level. The state[3] generally has more or less formal national patterns of government and militarism, a state church, economic patterns which entail some degree of centralized regulation of production and consumption and which usually have an officialdom or bureaucracy and national social classes.

In a developmental sequence through successively higher levels of sociocultural organization, the structural forms and distinctive functions of the lower levels tend to persist after the new patterns and institutions are superimposed upon them. The family continues to be the sexual and procreational unit, and it may retain certain economic, educational, and social functions, although, as part of a larger whole, it is modified in certain ways. The band, tribe, or village does not relinquish all of its functions after becoming part of a state. Its members continue to cooperate in local enterprises, it has its own leaders, and it may retain its traditional religion, even though national forms of production, government, and religion are superimposed upon the local ones. In due time, of course, influence from the national patterns may penetrate to the very lowest levels of organization. In modern industrial societies, for example, extreme specialization in occupations together with the development of transportation, of means of mass communication, and other factors have increasingly leveled local differences and weakened local social integration. The family has surrendered a large portion of its older functions, and those which it retains have become specialized. Local sociocultural segmentation begins to give way to horizontal segmentation, and the individual lives more and more in the context of a socioeconomic class, which has certain uniformities of behavior or culture, rather than as a member of a distinctive community. This is true of the working classes, which have become highly specialized, as well as of the middle classes and the professional and upper classes.

This concept of levels of organization suggests the hypothesis that the higher levels of culture may be changed more rapidly and more readily than the lower ones. When any region or state passes from the sovereignty of one nation to that of another, it has to conform to a new set of national laws, it is integrated in a new economic system, and it may be subject to new religious, military, and social patterns. But it

---

[3]This use of "state" is in no way an attempt to define it. Significant levels will have to be distinguished through empirical research, and an adequate terminology will have to be developed. States differ from one another when they have developed within different local cultural traditions.

retains a great deal of its original local or community organization and custom, and an even larger proportion of familial behavior. A modern sociocultural system, therefore, contains within itself qualitatively distinctive levels of organization, even though the nature and function of each level has been modified by the larger configuration. It follows, therefore, that each of these levels or structural parts must be analyzed in terms of themselves as well as in relationship to the total system.

These concepts have served as a tool in the analysis of Puerto Rico. Contemporary Puerto Rican society is highly diversified and heterogeneous. Our research has shown that there are many subcultures within the larger framework of the national culture and the national institutions. The contemporary diversity is largely the result of differential local effects of the island's participation in world commerce—of agricultural wage labor which has produced a proletariat in one region, of cultivation and sale of a cash crop annual which has made for individual independence and initiative of the small farmer in another region, etc.—but everywhere the cultural lag has been greatest at the community and family level. The encomienda and *repartimiento* under sixteenth-century Spain did not at once eradicate all aboriginal Indian features, and the slave plantation did not at first eliminate those aspects of African culture which functioned on an individual and family level. In fact, a great many features of family and community culture of diverse origin—thatched houses, mortars made of logs, grinding stones, calabash containers, wooden dishes and stools, hammocks, baskets, manioc or yucca presses, and even magic and folk forms of Catholicism—survived until fairly recently among the small, independent subsistence farmers of the interior despite rather fundamental changes in the national institutions. Today, a semblance of uniformity in insular culture as a whole is given by a number of traits of the Hispanic heritage which function largely at the community and family levels—use of the Spanish language, a large family, the double standard in sexual behavior, ritual kinship, and others. These have become differently patterned in each local subculture, but they are not necessarily eliminated by changes at the national level.

NATIONAL SOCIOCULTURAL SYSTEMS

The concept of levels of integration permits certain distinctions between the different aspects or components of the culture of a modern nation that are useful in a study like the present one. The most important distinction is that between *national* (and international) *patterns* on the one hand and *subcultures* or sociocultural segments on the other. Once this distinction is clarified, other aspects of national culture, such as *national characteristics, national character, national cultural achievements,* and *institutional behavior*, may be related to the different levels.

NATIONAL PATTERNS AND SUBCULTURES

National patterns are here considered to be those portions or aspects of culture that function on a national level, for example, the legislative system and legal code, the governmental structure, the educational system, the military, organized religion, money, banking, commerce, public services, and many others. These different national patterns have traditionally been the subject matter of various special disciplines, each of which uses its own distinctive method. Although all of them are part of culture in a broad sense, the ethnographic method is not adapted to the analysis of their principal characteristics.

An ethnographic approach to national institutions or patterns could deal only with what we may call culturally prescribed *institutional behavior,* that is, with the formalized and stereotyped behavior expected of an individual in his capacity as a participant in the institution. This behavior, however, would represent a very incomplete portion of the subculture of the individual or of the larger functions of the institution itself. The laborers, clerks, agents, managers, owners, and the like who meet in the context of a factory conform to certain behavioral expectations of the job situation. While their varied roles and statuses give some clues to their off-the-job status, their total subcultures—their religion, family life, and other features—are not directly manifest in the factory. Similarly, the meaning of the factory in relation to a larger system of technology, credit, distribution, and the like cannot well be grasped by merely observing the behavior of factory personnel. There are many other institutionalized situations, such as the church, school, moving picture theater, baseball park, and the like, which draw persons from various subcultures but which have their own standards of behavior. Even where these situations permit class distinctions, for example, through segregation on an economic or racial basis, which might be manifest through deference shown by lower-class individuals to their superiors, they do not reveal the nature of the subcultural differences associated with the classes.

It is only in a country with well-developed mass communications, a high standard of living, and a relatively high degree of socioeconomic mobility, such as the United States, that the number of institutional situations in which individuals of different subcultures can intermingle increases to the point where shared behavior seems to predominate and subcultural differences are correspondingly reduced. Even in the United States subcultures are by no means completely leveled, but the leveling process has gone so far, especially in the urban centers, which provide a large number of situations for interclass contact, that it would be easy to underestimate the importance of subcultural differences and to overestimate the nationally shared behavior.

The national institutions have functional and structural aspects which are distinguishable from the cultural behavior of the people connected with them. The processes of manufacturing, marketing, and trade, like the principles of money and banking, are studied by the specialized methods of economics, which need not be concerned with how people connected with a factory or bank live. Analysis of governmental structure and a system of legislation does not necessarily pay attention to the subculture of lawmakers. For certain purposes, it may be very important to know the culture of people involved in economic or legislative activities, but there are some aspects of these activities which can best be understood by the specialized methods of economics and political science.

The individual lives within the framework of a set of national institutions, but his daily activities are normally carried out within the context of a fairly small segment of society that consists of people substantially like himself and who therefore may be said to have a subculture. There are two principal types of sociocultural segments. First, there are locally distinctive segments, such as communities, rural neighborhoods, and ethnic minorities, which represent vertical or essentially localized cleavages within the larger society. Second, there are horizontal segments, which follow occupational or class lines and, in some cultures, caste lines. These may crosscut local cleavages. Society at a tribal level has only local or vertical segments, each tribe or segment constituting a comparatively independent functional unit which is not internally class-structured. (There are, of course, many so-called "tribes," such as those of West Africa and elsewhere, which are internally differentiated into segments that extend across local groups.) More developed sociocultural systems, however, have both kinds of segments. The European feudal estate, for instance, was a fairly well integrated society which functioned in comparative independence of the larger society and consisted of two distinct but interdependent sociocultural classes. Modern industrialization and its concomitants have brought new kinds of national patterns or institutions which, though producing nationwide institutions, have caused extreme sociocultural differentiation on a horizontal basis. Occupational specialization has not only divided the laboring class into many special groups but it has created a large number of new middle classes. It has also tended to establish bonds between equivalent segments of different communities. In some cases there may be greater cultural similarities and stronger loyalties between the widely scattered members of the same segments than between members of different segments within the local community.

Virtually all modern communities consist of several distinctive sociocultural segments which are related to one another in a system of social statuses. From this fact we may derive a cultural definition of classes: classes are sociocultural groups or segments arranged in an hierarchical order. But the hierarchy functions principally in the locality. It does not always follow that segments having the same relative status in different localities will be cultural equivalents if the local or regional subcultures are unlike.

During the sixteenth and seventeenth centuries Puerto Rico had a few towns and plantations which were internally divided into a number of sociocultural segments, but the predominant type of rural society was the simple, undifferentiated subsistence farm. In the eighteenth century plantations which grew cash crops and rural communities began to develop on an important scale. Since that time the community, or municipio, which includes the town center and the dependent farm area, has constituted the structural and functional context within which the majority of the people live. Communities are not culturally homogeneous units, like tribal societies, for there are important subcultural differences between town and country and among merchants, artisans, laborers, and the like within the town as well as among landlords and laborers, large and small farmers, and owners and sharecroppers in the country. But the community has a high degree of sociocultural integration. It is the center of primary marketing of produce and ultimate distribution of commodities; it is the locale in which churches, schools, public health, law enforcement, and other services directly reach the people; and it is the place where the people are reared and educated, marry, work, visit, and amuse themselves. It is in the community that the different rural subcultural groups interact with one another in a set of reciprocal, face-to-face relationships.

Although the national patterns or institutions and the subcultural segments are distinguishable and must be treated separately, the two are so interdependent functionally that neither can be understood properly unless it is related to the other. To this end, it was found convenient in the present research to distinguish two aspects of the national patterns: first, the more formal, insular-wide, and institutionalized aspects, such as the governmental and legal system, political parties, labor unions, educational system, export and import trade, money, banking, and credit organizations, churches and official church doctrines, the military, certain organized sports; and, second, the community manifestations of the national patterns.

Governmental agencies, for example, are organized and controlled on an insular or federal basis, but the government agent in a local community has to adapt his work to the "realities" of the situation. Health, education, farm extension work and other services have meaning particular to the community and to the classes within it. One kind of community stresses the value of education while another is indifferent; people utilize the health clinic in some areas but rely on folk medicine in others; and so forth. Similarly, there are great local differences in the manifestations of Catholicism, in political attitudes, and in obedience to the law. Despite the Catholic church's international organization and standardized procedures and doctrines, orthodoxy prevails largely among the upper class, while certain communities have made Catholicism into a cult of the saints and others have mixed witchcraft, spiritualism, and even Protestantism with it. The local manifestation of any national pattern can be comprehended only with reference to the distinctive context of the subcultural segment and the community.

Not all community culture, however, consists of local aspects of formal national institutions. The family, for example, is an entirely local matter. It is true that a type of family may prevail over much or even most of an area and that marriage laws may be established on a national level, but the family is not part of any kind of national structure. It is, therefore, a very different kind of institution than a chain of banks or a political party. The same is true of certain other features of local culture, such as settlement pattern. Both the family and settlement pattern, however, are profoundly influenced by national institutions.

These two aspects of insular institutions, the formal and the local, reflect the traditional division of labor among the social science disciplines and suggest the terms of collaboration. The former are the subject matter of various specialists; the latter, in their community or class manifestations—that is, as characteristics of the different sociocultural segments—lend themselves to a cultural or social anthropological approach. The two lists given here, though very incomplete, illustrate how these two aspects are distinct yet complementary.

A fairly static society which had developed slowly would presumably achieve a comparatively well integrated total culture in which the national institutions and the sociocultural segments would acquire a fairly stable and fixed interrelationship to one another. In the European feudal pattern, communities based on the ownership of large tracts by landlords were functional parts of a state whose governmental, religious, and social system sanctioned and supported the rural land-use and tenure system. But where any parts of the total configura-

Local aspects	*Formal insular or extrainsular aspects*
Subsistence farming	Government regulations and aid
Cash crop production and trade	Insular economy, world markets,
Land tenure	sources of credit, etc.
Settlement pattern	Basic economy, land laws, inheritance
Marriage and family	system
Social classes	None
Occupational groups	Marriage laws
Labor unions	Insular social structure
Local government	Economic system and insular speciali-
Political affiliations and ideologies	zation
Local associations	Labor unions
Church and supernaturalism	National government
Schools and learning	National parties and ideologies
Recreation	National clubs and societies
Hospitals, doctors, curers	Organized churches
	Educational system and media of
	mass communication
	Organized sports, e.g., baseball
	Government health measures

tion are radically altered, the whole is thrown out of adjustment. An understanding of the processes of readjustment requires interdisciplinary collaboration, that is, analysis on both the community and national levels. The Puerto Rican communities, as the chapters on history and on the different communities show, have changed very radically during the four and a half centuries since the conquest. An understanding of these changes requires analysis at the community level of cultural adaptations to land-use potentials and at the national level of insular changes which occurred during the Spanish colonial period and during the American period. Detailed analysis of the national institutions for their own sake was beyond the possible scope of the present project. Nonetheless, we had to consider them at some length in order to understand the national or insular institutional framework within which the communities developed. To this end, we consulted published sources and held a series of extended conferences with specialists in the various subjects.

NATIONAL PATTERNS AND NATIONAL CULTURAL ACHIEVEMENTS

There are certain aspects of any culture, such as art, literature, music, philosophy, science, and ideologies, which are often subsumed under the humanities rather than under the social sciences. Because these commonly represent the highest intellectual and aesthetic attainments of a nation, they are sometimes designated *national cultural achievements*.

In any sociocultural system above the tribal level, however, it is necessary to distinguish the national achievements from the folk achievements. Throughout much of human history, the finest art, music, and literature have been produced for the state or government, or for the classes representing them; and intellectual and scientific discoveries have been made by members of the priestly or ruling classes. Although national achievements tend to filter outward and downward to the general population, they are consumed by all segments of the society only in proportion as there is general education and other means of mass communication and consumption. Otherwise, locally distinctive folk music, literature, art, dance, religious thought, and ideologies may survive.

It is necessary to bear this distinction in mind, for national culture is too often conceived solely in terms of those aesthetic and intellectual achievements which are understood only by the upper classes and which may be litttle known to the illiterate, isolated folk societies. The latter may participate in only limited manifestations of these achievements, as when they take part in religious ceremonialism.

NATIONAL PATTERNS AND THE UPPER CLASS

The subculture of the prominent and wealthy families of Puerto Rico has differed historically from that of the other sociocultural segments in several important respects. It is distinguished not only by its considerably greater wealth and its superordinate social position with respect to the other classes but by its special relationship to the national patterns or institutions and by its role in the power structure.

During most of history, when sociocultural systems have developed to a state level, the national or state institutions have given rise to special ruling classes, whose subcultures might consist in large measure of functions pertaining to the national institutions. This may be illustrated in a somewhat simplified manner by the ancient irrigation civilizations, such as those of the Maya of Yucatán or the Bronze Age Egyptians. The political, religious, and military institutions of these societies produced an upper class of rulers who not only controlled such matters as state irrigation works and distribution of goods, military affairs, government, and religion, but whose subcultural behavior was in large measure determined by their participation in national or state affairs. Management of public affairs was part of their daily life. They were the creators of complex calendars, mathematics, writing, literature, and sytematized ideologies pertaining to the national institutions, and they alone fully understood these matters. Thus they were also consumers as well as producers of the national aesthetic and intellectual achievements to a degree and in ways that were foreign to the lower classes.

In contemporary societies the national institutions have created a much greater range of occupational specializations and statuses than were found in the basically two-class societies of antiquity. Nevertheless, it is normally those persons who are finally considered as upper class far more than any other social segment who understand and control the national institutions, make use of higher education, technological inventions, advanced medicine, and the like, and incorporate the best achievements of national literature, art, music, and the theater into their daily living. The upper class is least integrated in terms of locality, and it is the most cosmopolitan. In many respects its way of life represents an *international upper-class culture*. As technology develops, as the standard of living is raised, and as mass communication is advanced, these national achievements become available to the middle classes and finally to the lower classes. Meanwhile, new national and international features develop, and these too become available first to the upper classes.

This is not to say that all culture change originates in the upper class. Changes in national institutions, as we have seen, may penetrate to the community and family. Moreover, an imbalance may be created in the total pattern by overpopulation, concentration of wealth, realignment of social and economic structure, and the creation of unsatisfied desires in lower and middle classes. These lead to movements of varying magnitudes ranging from individual bargaining, through collective bargaining and political action, to revolution, all producing a change in the power structure and an overhauling of the total socioeconomic system. In Puerto Rico the mass of the people have definitely achieved greater power than they had under the Spanish regime, and many national changes which were initiated because power shifted to the lower and middle classes have reacted upon the total culture.

Meanwhile, the upper class of Puerto Rico retains a prominent, although very unclear, place in the power structure, and its individual members participate to a greater degree than those of any other class in the national institutions. Moreover, they are in a better position than persons of other classes to borrow foreign cultural traits. The chapter describing the prominent families of Puerto Rico will show that they are culturally distinctive largely because of their participation in the national features and their adoption of behavior patterns from outside the island. The upper class may still play an important role in the power structure, but it was beyond the scope of the present project to appraise this role. We have shown, however, that wealth, opportunity, mobility, and contacts have permitted this group to become cosmopolitan. It is upper class in terms of the United States social structure as well as the Puerto Rican, and many of its members reside for extended periods on the continent. It has acquired many of the political attitudes, economic practices, forms of social behavior, intellectual interests, recreational outlets, and other cultural characteristics of wealthy continentals. As Puerto Rican standards of living, education, and other opportunities permit, much culture characteristic of the upper class begins to appear among other classes. To understand the process of acculturation of the masses of the population, however, it is important to recognize that they do not mechanically imitate American behavior or Puerto Rican upper-class behavior. Any borrowing presupposes a basis of opportunity and needs, and, as these factors show marked local variation in the different major regions, borrowed culture becomes readapted to fit the community patterns, as we show in subsequent chapters.

NATIONAL CHARACTERISTICS

We have stressed the importance of viewing the culture of a modern nation as a composite of various subcultures as well as of nationally shared traits which distinguish all members of a nation from the members of any other nation. We now consider the nature of the shared traits or national characteristics.

In tribal society the common denominator of shared traits is more or less coextensive or synonymous with the total culture. It represents family and tribal levels of function and integration, there being no larger patterns. The individual acquires these traits by learning from members of his subcultural group. The national characteristics of a contemporary society, on the other hand, consist of features of various kinds and origins.

There are three kinds of features or traits which may constitute the national cultural common denominator: first, those which arise from more or less compulsory conformity with the basic national institutions which affect all individuals; second, traits of the common cultural heritage, which in Puerto Rico is Hispanic; and third, uniformities produced by means of mass communications. None of these, however, necessarily produces behavioral uniformities.

All members of a nation participate in the same general economy, are subject to a uniform set of laws, may receive somewhat similar public education and other benefits, and be subject to taxation, military service, and the like. But the national institutions themselves actually may produce internal heterogeneity rather than uniformity. An economy of free enterprise and industrialization introduces cash-orientation and competitive striving in all segments of the society it affects, but it also sharpens differences between factory owner and worker, landlord and peasant, merchant and consumer, and other groups. Economic development also entails local specialization, which itself creates sharp differences in patterns of farm production, as this volume shows, as well as in economic status. Participation in education, government, and other national institutions is in turn partly a function of economic status. In general, it can be said that the far-reaching effects of Puerto Rican national institutions under American sovereignty as compared with Spanish sovereignty have increased rather than lessened the island's internal heterogeneity. Moreover, many of the subcultural groups that have developed in response to new national trends are not distinctive of Puerto Rico but are very similar to groups in other parts of the world where comparable economic and political factors have been introduced. Basic national institutions, therefore, cannot at all be considered synonymous with cultural uniformities of individual behavior nor as necesary causes of uniformities.

The second category of national uniformities consists of features derived from the basic cultural heritage. Puerto Rico shares a substantial Hispanic heritage with all other Latin American nations. Certain features of this heritage are commonly adduced as evidence of its vitality and importance: the Spanish language, a double standard and male dominance in the family, ritual kinship, the *paseo*, the town plaza, Catholicism, the lottery, cockfighting, Spanish styles in music, literature, art, and architecture, emphasis upon spiritual and human rather than commercial values, interest in poetry, literature, and philosophy rather than in science and industry, and emphasis upon hospitality and interpersonal relations rather than upon competitive individualism. These components of the Hispanic heritage, however, are of different orders, and not all of them are equally represented among the different sociocultural classes.

The older Hispanic sociocultural system was internally differentiated into two sociocultural classes: the upper class of wealthy landlords and public and church officials, and the lower class of farm workers and artisans. Many of the characteristics commonly considered typical of Latin America are essentially upper-class characteristics which depend upon wealth, leisure, and status and which could not function among the lower classes. The cultivation of philosophical values, the importance attached to rich and warm human relations, and the enjoyment of art, literature, and music presuppose considerable education and financial security. The lower classes, especially those in the tradition of the feudal estate, are too poor and illiterate to support these features. Catholic orthodoxy is largely an upper-class religion, various forms of folk Catholicism being found among the lower classes. Since the double standard implies status and regulated forms of marriage, it is largely characteristic of the upper class. Among the lower class of the corporate sugar plantation, male dominance is greatly weakened and the woman may be the most permanent and potent member of the family. A "double standard" signifying extra-marital relations means little under common-law marriage.

Under the Hispanic culture the two sociocultural classes shared, first, common submission to national laws and other national patterns, which, however, supported and sanctioned the superordinate position and special privileges of the upper class; second, a set of implicit understandings and habitual behavior and attitudes which regulated the superordinate-subordinate relationship which controlled the interaction of the two classes; and third, some forms of customary institutional behavior of a secondary nature, such as cockfighting, the lottery, the *paseo,* and others, which are not strongly connected func-tionally with the national institutions. Class discriminations, however, carried over even into the standardized behavior of situations where the two sociocultural groups mingled. Lower-class members were sub-ordinated to the upper classes in such matters as segregation, even when walking on the streets, while there was and is often actual physical segregation in public conveyances, churches, theaters, cockfight pits, and the *paseo.*

The Spanish heritage, therefore, consists more of features charac-terizing subcultures than of a national common denominator. Where the older social arrangements survive, as in the Puerto Rican coffee area, the upper class continues to some extent to exhibit the so-called "typical" Spanish patterns while the lower class preserves folk patterns. Where the older classes are being weakened and middle classes have arisen under the influence of industrialization, the principal survival of the Hispanic heritage is in language, art, music, and recreational ac-tivities which were not strongly integrated with the older national patterns or the subcultures. The older attitudes which regulated inter-class relations are being weakened.

The situation in Puerto Rico is comparable to that in Japan. Benedict's analysis of Japan (1946) stressed the importance of univer-sally accepted attitudes and behavior traits which governed an individual's behavior toward persons above and below himself in the hierarchy of statuses. In both countries, however, modern influences are breaking down these authoritarian and personalized relationships and substituting more impersonal and commercial standards (Embree, 1939).

In large measure, then, a list of national characteristics of the Spanish heritage consists of secondary features carried at a folk, community, or class level. The national patterns produced differences rather than similarities between the subcultures. Under United States influence many new features have been introduced, such as paved roads, transportation by motor vehicles, sanitation systems, general education, and others. But, as previously mentioned, these have become a common denominator only to the extent that wealth, opportunity, a new cash-orientation, and all that these imply have penetrated to all classes. Actually, there is great variation in the use made of these features. Under United States influence, too, secondary features that are not dependent upon either national patterns or subcultures have been introduced and become uniformities. Baseball, for example, has become the major sport of all classes and regions.

The third major source of the national common denominator is media of mass communications. In contrast to national patterns or institutions, which have a differential effect on subcultures, education, radio, newspapers, moving pictures, and other media tend strongly to level subcultural differences to the extent that economic status will permit change toward uniform national patterns. Constant propaganda and indoctrination affects attitudes toward practices of child rearing, recreation, national political and economic institutions, and even international relations. Mass communications also make national cultural achievements in art, literature, music, and science available to all segments of the population.

Finally, we must mention practices of child rearing and family types, which, according to certain contemporary anthropologists, constitute national uniformities and are the primary factors in the formation of national character. The concept of *national character* is discussed subsequently. We wish only to point out here that whether all members of any nation are really substantially similar in their practices of child feeding, weaning, care, toilet training, swaddling, and the like is purely an empirical question. These practices function on a family level, and they are only indirectly influenced by national institutions. In fact, it is expectable that subcultural groups should differ in child rearing just as they differ in family structure. There are strong class differences in the time the mother can spend with the child, in use of relatives or hired nurses to care for the child, in diet, in number and relationship of siblings and other relatives to the child, in the familial role of the father, and in other crucial factors. In addition, any nation that consists of several ethnic minority groups—for example, Russia, Poland, China, or Mexico, whose political expansion incorporated diverse cultures within a large area, or the United States, which has acquired many ethnic minorities through immigration—will certainly not be uniform in familial patterns. It is only where developed communications begin to penetrate even to the family level that uniformities emerge.

This analysis indicates that the problem of national characteristics is a very complicated one. In Puerto Rico the regional and class subcultures are so distinctive that no single community can be considered to represent the entire island in microcosm. To ascertain the common core of shared behavior would require a carefully devised sampling of the whole island. This common core, however, would not be very illuminating, for most shared traits have a special meaning in each subculture. The lottery is principally a form of recreation to some groups, while to others, where socioeconomic mobility is impossible, it presents the only opportunity to win a stake with which to start an independent business. The *paseo* is a form of courtship in some towns, while in others it is no more than an evening stroll. Ritual kinship, though common to all Puerto Ricans, has several very different functions which reflect local social and economic patterns. All people in the island are striving to better themselves, but specific methods of achieving socioeconomic mobility depend upon the availability of jobs, education, and other factors.

Most features of the common denominator have different local meanings because they are functional parts of the total patterns of the different subcultures. These local differences could not be adequately revealed through a field method of sampling the entire island population by means of a questionnaire covering all aspects of culture. Such a procedure would encounter almost insurmountable difficulties. It would be impossible to frame appropriate questions before the subcultures were known; it would be a forbidding task to sample all aspects of culture in an entire nation; and it would be very difficult to obtain accurate answers during brief interviews. More important, questionnaire results could not reveal the functional relationships between phenomena within the different subcultural patterns. A statistical correlation of variables would show that certain distinctive features were associated with one another, but it would not show why. Results of this type are no substitute for prolonged, intensive, firsthand observation and analysis of each subculture as a whole. At best, a questionnaire approach could provide only a preliminary indication of variables that might warrant more intensive investigation.

NATIONAL CHARACTER

The problem of national character is closely related to that of national characteristics. During the last two decades, interdisciplinary collaboration between psychology, psychiatry, and anthropology has led to the theory that each culture produces a distinctive basic personality type, which is called the "cultural personality."[4] Interest in the cultural personality of nations—"national character" or "personality in relation to nationality"—received a tremendous stimulus during and after World War II, when it was recognized that an understanding of the mainsprings of the behavior of people of foreign nations was essential to successful international relations. The many recent studies of national character have had wide public appeals,[5] and it even seems that anthropology, which was once popularly believed to be a science that dealt with old bones and prehistoric men, is now commonly regarded as a new kind of national psychiatry which is prepared to offer facile generalizations and explanations of the behavior of whole nations.

The concept of cultural personality in unquestionably valid, but there has been much skepticism among anthropologists as well as other persons concerning some of the basic assumptions and methods employed, especially in the analysis of contemporary nations. In the present research, the question of studying the cultural personality was inevitably raised. There is obvious value in understanding the motivations of the Puerto Rican people and in correcting prevalent and erroneous sterotypes. We concluded, however, that the very concept of national character has questionably validity—that national character is a phenomenon of undetermined content, dimensions, and validity —and that in any event the difficulties of approaching cultural personality on a national scale are insurmountable.

The concept of national character implies that all members of a nation share attitudes, motivations, and responses that result from a common core of shared cultural characteristics and experiences. We have already seen, however, that the national cultural common denominator is a complex of diverse components of different origins and functional significance. The family type is generally attributed a major role in personality formation, and some writers go so far as to assume that all national institutions are projections of the family pattern. Actually, however, regional, class, and ethnic differences in family type may greatly outweigh national uniformities. National institutions produce behavior similarities only in a limited sense. They may, in fact,

---

[4] See, for example, Kluckhohn and Murray, 1949; and Hallowell, 1953.

[5] For example, Benedict, 1946; Gorer, 1943 and 1948. Since this was written, Margaret Mead (1953) has definitively and importantly modified the generally accepted approach to national character in stating that the determination of personality in national terms is but an expediency dictated by international crises and that the proper level of investigation of cultural personality is the subcultural group.

lead to strong internal cultural differentiation, and a great variety of subcultural manifestations. Mass communications, which may augment the common denominator of practices and attitudes, are quite undeveloped in many parts of the world and among certain social segments in most parts of the world. We concluded, therefore, that the concept of cultural personality can be applied far better to a subcultural group, where the processes of the individual's socialization as a member of the family and community can be studied in detail and concreteness, than to the more complex and heterogeneous national society.

Another difficulty in determining national character is that the techniques have by no means been perfected. Klineberg's very illuminating review discusses the different techniques (1950:8-92): descriptive accounts by informed observers; description and interpretation by anthropologists (Mead, Gorer, Benedict, LaBarre, Haring, and others); collection of vital and social statistics on insanity, crime, suicide, and other features; psychiatric interpretation; psychoanalytic approaches; interpretation of psychosomatic manifestations, such as hypertension and gastric ulcers; content analysis of cultural products, such as novels and motion pictures; public opinion surveys; attitude studies; intensive interviews; tests and measurements, such as the Rorschach Test and Thematic Apperception Test; the semantic approach, or analysis of word meanings; and review of child training and education, both formal and informal. Klineberg concludes (1950:89-90):

> The fact that such a large variety of techniques have been distinguished in this field of study in itself indicates that no one technique has as yet been judged completely satisfactory. The problem of "national character" or of personality in relation to nationality is exceedingly complex. As a matter of fact, there have been frequent denials of the existence of national differences in personality; many writers have held that such differences would disappear if groups were equated for factors such as economic level, degree of industrial development, concentration in urban or rural areas respectively, age distribution, etc. It seems more probable . . . that, although all these factors must be taken into consideration at every step in the analysis, certain differences will still emerge in the behavior and attitudes of people of different nations. The problem of adequate methodology remains, however. The various techniques that have been distinguished all have something to be said in their favor; they all suffer from the same defect, that their validity has never been fully established.

Finally, even if it were possible to determine with precision the national core of shared cultural traits and of personality characteristics, there would still remain the problem of ascertaining which of the cultural traits produced the personality type. If, for example, it were found that a high incidence of particular kinds of insanity, psychosomatic manifestations, reactions to psychological tests, and other responses diagnostic of personality type were characteristic of all subcultural groups, it would be very difficult to devise an empirical method to determine whether these characteristics were caused by child rearing, family type, similar responses to national institutions, or something else. There is at present no basis for assuming that any single cause has primary importance. Despite the crucial role ascribed practices of child rearing, there is little doubt that children within a single nation are reared in many ways, while particular kinds of child training may be practiced in several nations which have unlike national ideologies.

As the means of identifying national characteristics and of diagnosing national character are so fraught with difficulties, the safest and surest procedure is to work first on a local scale and then to widen the scope of inquiry. If the methods discussed above are applied on a national scale, there arise enormously difficult problems both of sampling and of correlating significant variables. Even if it could be shown that one nation differs substantially from another in general attitudes and behavior, the reasons for the differences could not readily be determined. A further reason for beginning analysis on a smaller scale—on a lower level and in subcultural terms—is that the processes of learning can be more readily understood. An individual's socialization begins in the household and is gradually broadened to include neighbors and members of the community. In this sense, he is not primarily a member of the nation. The influences of national institutions are mediated to him through the locally distinctive patterns of the community and its subcultural groups, and his responses, even to mass communications, are conditioned by the attitudes he acquires as a member of a subcultural group. A scientific analysis of the significance both of national uniformities and of distinctive subcultural features, therefore, must start with the particulars of how the individual is socialized in the context of his family, class, and community.

CULTURAL PERSONALITY AND CULTURE

There is still another problem in the socialization of the individual. Adult personality, attitudes, and values are the result of infant, childhood, and adolescent experiences—his education or "enculturation." Yet in contemporary society the life-demands and required behavior may not at all correspond with learned attitudes and expectations.

In this respect, there may be a sharp difference between contemporary civilization and tribal society. The entire course of education in a tribal society realistically prepares the individual for adult life. In modern society, the individual may be socialized in the context of a particular subcultural group but, because of socioeconomic mobility, come to live in a very different subcultural group. In such cases, the sociocultural demands upon him are very different from those he has learned. In a sense, we are confronted here with the very definition of culture. Culture is usually considered to be learned modes of behavior which are socially transmitted from one generation to another. And yet an individual may find himself in a situation where the culturally prescribed modes of behavior differ sharply from those he has learned.

To illustrate this point, the coastal sugar plantations in Puerto Rico have many workers who migrated from the highlands. As our research shows, the highland patterns are very different from those of the plantations. Yet the highland workers are forced to conform to the basic economic arrangements and to other important patterns of the coast. To a certain extent, the highland attitudes and customs may be retained in the plantation situation, but they do not survive in strength because they are incompatible with the demands of a corporate, mechanized productive system. The individuals from the highlands may suffer from conflict arising from the transition, perhaps to a traumatic degree, but by and large they conform overtly to the expected behavior.

In other words, a cultural study of rapidly changing modern societies might pay primary attention either to the socialized individual or to the cultural demands of the situation, which might or might not correspond to what the individual has learned. If the situation rather than the individual is the research objective, it would be proper to regard the effects of socialization merely as factors which may further or retard cultural change rather than as culture itself.

In the present study, primary attention has been directed to the cultural demands of local situations. Despite a certain amount of socioeconomic mobility, most persons have grown up and worked within the context of a particular subcultural group. These groups and the attitudes and values of their members, however, have been changing fairly rapidly. We recognize that psychological studies of the effects of child training and of other socializing factors would constitute an extremely valuable contribution to our analysis.[6] Such studies should first ascertain the personality type of each subculture, second, deter-

[6] Such studies are being made (in 1953) by the Family Project under the auspices of the Social Science Research Center. The project is under Reuben Hill, director, and David Landy, assistant director.

mine its causes, and third, relate it to the changing cultural demands. Such studies were not made because circumstances prevented us from including in the project a psychologist with appropriate skills. Our analyses of cultural behavior, therefore, must be regarded as the interpretations of anthropologists who were equipped to approach these problems in terms of cultural values and demands rather than of psychological analysis.

DYNAMICS OF CULTURAL CHANGE

The problem of the present research was to ascertain the factors and processes which brought about the development of distinctive rural subcultures in Puerto Rico during recent centuries. The field research was directed toward analysis of the contemporary subcultures, but historical understanding was needed to explain how these subcultures emerged during Puerto Rican history. An obvious line of approach would be to trace the patterns and behavioral traits to their historic sources, to the basic Hispanic heritage, which was originally modified in some degree by African and native Indian features and later by strong influence from the United States. But to consider Puerto Rican culture merely an admixture of features borrowed from different sources would be quite inadequate. Puerto Rico's distinctive colonial position, geographical environment, and location not only caused a selection of features from the Spanish culture but entailed special adaptation of many of these features. Puerto Rican subcultures, especially those of the rural communities, were by no means exact duplicates of those of Spain, and they could not have been duplicates unless the kinds of production had been the same and unless whole farm populations had migrated to the island, bringing their patterns with them. The Puerto Rican rural subcultures were based largely on the production of special crops in distinctive environments, while the rural population was itself a mixture of Indians, Africans, Spaniards, and other Europeans. Similarly, the changes brought about by United States sovereignty entailed further differentiation of land use and productive processes and consequently of related social features.

These processes by which culture is selectively borrowed and adapted to a particular environment, that is, the processes of cultural ecology,[7] are among the most important creative processes in cultural change. No cultural history is simply a chronicle of the diffusion of rigid patterns and groups of culture elements from one part of the world to another. Diffusion is always selective, and the features which

---

[7]The concept and method of cultural ecology have been illustrated by the author in several studies (Steward, 1936, 1937, 1938, and 1945).

are and are not diffused depend not only upon the nature of the receiving culture but upon the environmental potentialities of the receiving area. Moreover, once cultural features are accepted in a new area, they will be adapted to local conditions through a series of creative processes that produce a new or modified culture.

As the adaptations primarily involve land use, the method of cultural ecology requires first an examination of the relationship of technology, or productive processes, to the environment. The initial problem is to determine which types of productive processes are historically available in the lending culture. Next, it is necessary to ascertain the cultural and environmental factors which cause certain of these to be selected by the new area. Finally, the modifications in the productive processes in a new environment must be analyzed and their effects upon other aspects of culture determined. When a particular exploitative technology such as farming is introduced to a new region, the local soils, topography, rainfall, climate, and other environmental factors will usually require modifications in methods of production and in the related patterns of marketing, land tenure, cooperation, and settlement pattern. These latter may in turn have a profound effect upon the structure and function of the entire society. It must be emphasized, however, that the method of cultural ecology does not anticipate particular conclusions as to the precise nature of the adaptive processes or their results. It is merely a methodological tool for approaching the general problem of how new features arise from the interaction of culture and environment. Data from different parts of the world, however, strongly indicate that rather similar changes often ensue when a particular technology is employed in a particular kind of environment. These changes lend themselves to the formulation of regularities of cultural change, a consideration which we discuss in Part IV. The following chapters on the development of Puerto Rican culture, Part II, and the succeeding chapters describing the principal subcultures, Part III, will show clearly that the distinctive features both of the total insular culture and of the regional community subcultures must be explained by cultural ecological processes as well as by culture history.

The point of view from which these chapters are written may be illustrated briefly by the contrasts between Puerto Rico and the American Southwest. Both areas were first parts of the Spanish Empire and later came under American sovereignty, but, despite having the same sources from which to draw their cultures, they developed along distinctive lines because of their different geographical positions and environments. Puerto Rico is subtropical, humid, and insular. It is suited to the production of such export crops as ginger, sugar, livestock, coffee, and tobacco, which were historically available and which have been in demand in the world market at different periods, but it has little mineral wealth. It has ready access via the sea lanes to continental America, Europe, and Africa. The Southwest is arid, and, though part of continental North America, it was fairly isolated from markets duing most of its history. It has, however, a comparative abundance of mineral wealth.

During the early periods of the Spanish Empire, the Southwest, like Mexico and the Andes, supported a class of Spanish overlords who used Indians in encomiendas as virtual slaves to exploit the mineral wealth. Puerto Rico, lacking substantial mineral wealth and at first not in a position to farm extensively for an outside market, became a colony of small farmers. For two centuries, it had a mixture of Iberian, native Indian, and African cultures. How the various culture elements and patterns of these diverse origins merged into a new culture is not known. The only semblance to the Spanish type of hacienda was the livestock ranch, which supplied expeditions to the mainland with cattle, and a few sugar plantations. The Southwest became a largely self-sufficient area when mineral wealth had decreased and Indian labor became scarce, and it produced such crops as beans and wheat for its own use. The environment and location prevented production of anything but cattle and hides for an outside market. Puerto Rico, however, was in an excellent position for export, and, as trade restrictions were lifted, its plantation economy developed rapidly.

Under the American regime, the Southwest became an area of migration from the United States, and Anglo-American culture was introduced alongside the haciendas, the small farms of the Spanish Americans, and the Indians. Puerto Rico drew capital rather than people from the United States, for its sugar lands promised rich returns which corporations could exploit *in absentia*. The only comparable investments in the Southwest are represented by certain large mining interests. Highly mechanized, corporate-owned Puerto Rican sugar plantations and the government-owned profit-sharing plantations, which followed as a corrective to the overly large corporate enterprises, have created new types of rural life.

Contemporary Puerto Rico exhibits an internal diversity of regional subcultural types which are no less explainable by cultural-ecological processes than the differences between Puerto Rico and the Southwest. The Spanish culture, which originally included both national institutions and large rural estates, was available to the entire island. The national institutions—the government, legal system, church, and military organization—were imposed on the island as a whole, but the only subcultures of a predominantly Spanish type were those of the upper classes, while rural subcultures largely reflected distinctive local factors. Mineral wealth was unimportant everywhere, and export crops could not be produced in most of the mountainous interior. The highlands, therefore, became a region of small, independent farmers who grew subsistence crops. Today, the highland pattern has been modified by the introduction of a supplementary cash crop of tobacco and by the establishment of coffee haciendas. The Spanish hacienda pattern developed chiefly on the coastal plains, however, in connection with cattle raising and the production of sugar and ginger. It was based partly upon slave labor in its early phases, but later on free labor. During the nineteenth century, the hacienda penetrated the highlands, where it became the pattern of coffee production. American investment capital was attracted by the possibilities of mechanized sugar production and transformed the Spanish plantations or haciendas into what are virtually company towns—land-and-factory corporate combines. Today, the coffee haciendas represent the principal survival of the older Spanish patterns.

In each of these different regions, environment not only determined the type of land use which was selected from those available in the Spanish and American cultures, but local factors strongly conditioned the subcultures which grew up. South coast irrigation accelerated the inflow of American capital, which produced a subculture that is neither Spanish nor American nor a mechanical mixture of the two but a local adaptation. Similarly, the highlands, which have been least affected by modern productive processes, continue to exhibit a large number of adaptations which have long been distinctive of Puerto Rico.

PROCEDURES AND METHODS

THE COMMUNITY STUDY METHOD

The present research exemplifies what may be broadly classed as the community study method. It represents the application of the cultural method to subcultural groups rather than to the heterogeneous entity that constitutes a total modern national culture. The method is holistic in that it analyzes individual behavior in terms of the total fabric of life—the many-faceted and functionally interrelated modes of behavior, the values, and the attitudes. It contrasts with a procedure that deals with culture on a national scale and treats individuals in their separate capacities as farmers, merchants, laborers, consumers, voters, church members, and the like. The latter yields statistical data from which averages may be deduced and relationships between phenomena may be demonstrated by correlation of variables. The community study method yields explanations of the correlations between variables through direct analysis of their functional nexus within the localized subcultural group.

In Puerto Rico nearly 40 per cent of the people make their living by means of farming, and many more than half live in the context of a rural community. Earning a living, visiting friends and neighbors, going to church, attending school, marrying, rearing children, finding entertainment, belonging to clubs, business associations, and labor unions, obtaining medical care, finding help in time of trouble, and many other activities make up the community subcultures. An individual learns the characteristic responses, aspirations, and attitudes of his class within the community. He shares some but not all of these things with persons throughout the island.[8]

Preliminary surveys of Puerto Rico indicated and field research ultimately proved that the communities represented several strikingly different types of regional subcultures. The more important of these subcultures became the subject of field research, and they are reported in the chapters on Tabara, the community of small farmers of mixed crops and tobacco; on Cañamelar, the community of a corporate-owned sugar plantation; on San José, the community of coffee growers; on Nocorá, the government-owned, profit-sharing sugar plantation, and on the insular upper class which lives in San Juan. These subcultures differ from one another not only in their culture content, that is, in the particulars of behavior, but in their total organization or configuration. Selection of these for field study made it possible to describe Puerto Rican behavior, attitudes, and character with a specificity, concreteness, and detail which would be wanting in a national survey of selected characteristics and in an abstraction of a national type.

As a modern community cannot be adequately understood if, like a tribal society, it is studied solely in terms of itself, it was necessary to devise procedures for taking the total national culture into account. Ideally, the research staff should have included persons from the other social sciences and humanities but as this was beyond budgetary possibilities we had to draw upon published information and upon individual scholars as the need arose.[9] Another methodological need not

[8]In Puerto Rico the municipality is a convenient community unit of study because it is the insular administrative unit. The island is divided into seventy-seven municipios, or communities, each of which has an elected mayor and assembly, whose chief function is to administer schools, health centers, poor relief, and other services of the national government. The communities have 10,000 to 30,000 persons, of whom 10 to 25 per cent live in the pueblo, or town, and the remainder in the dependent farm area.

[9]These procedures and methods have also been described in Steward, 1950.

ordinarly considered in community studies was to ascertain the regional types of rural culture before selecting a community representative of each. Finally, we had to adapt the methods of field research to the larger methodology which has been explained in previous pages.

THE NATIONAL OR INSULAR CULTURE

Modern area-training institutes have the inestimable advantage of providing the student a general and basic knowledge of the various aspects of the total culture of the area in which he will work. As Columbia University has no Latin American Institute, it was necessary to obtain background information about Latin American culture in general and Puerto Rico in particular by other means. Two steps were taken in this direction prior to the fieldwork in Puerto Rico.

First, about eight months before the fieldwork began, Raymond Scheele made a survey of historical sources in order to provide a picture of the changing national institutions and subcultures. He abstracted data on cultural origins and on the cultural effects of Puerto Rico's changing colonial status with particular attention to the economic basis of the social and cultural patterns. The sources contain general information on the economic, political, religious, and social trends that originated largely outside the island and constituted the principal factors causing change in the subcultures. The cultural history presented in Part II deals largely with national institutions. The varieties of subcultures of the period from 1500 to 1815 are being investigated by Eugenio Fernández Méndez, who will publish his material in the future, while the subcultures which emerged after 1815 are described in Part III. Part II accords much greater detail to the period from 1815 to 1948 because national changes during this time are most relevant to our primary interest in the contemporary varieties of regional cultures.

It should be stressed that the very incomplete knowledge of sixteenth- and seventeenth-century Spanish culture constitutes a serious obstacle to an adequate understanding of the culture of any Spanish colony. The national institutions—the crown policies, the church, the patterns of exploitation and trade, and the military—are known in considerable detail and the upper-class subculture may be reconstructed quite readily, but the subcultures of the workers, small farmers, artisans, and other special groups are known only incompletely. It is very difficult, therefore, to determine the extent to which the culture of the early small farmer of Puerto Rico is an importation from Spain and to what extent it is a native product.

A second means of relating the community studies to the national culture was a seminar held at Columbia University prior to the field-work. This seminar included all fieldworkers, except those from the University of Chicago and the University of Puerto Rico, who joined the staff later. It covered primarily the national institutions or patterns—sugar production, other economic activities, United States policies, demography and general statistics, social structure, race relations, and national ideologies. The seminar members reported on published sources, and they heard several guest speakers who had special knowledge of Puerto Rico.

During and after the fieldwork, further information was obtained on national aspects of the culture through consultation with Puerto Rican scholars and specialists and through study of various published sources and documents.

FIELD STUDIES

The project staff spent nineteen months in Puerto Rico, where the research was divided into three phases.

The first phase was devoted to a survey of the island to obtain data on which to base the selection of the communities and subcultures for intensive study. The theory of community selection is discussed below. During the survey, the staff met together frequently to discuss problems and to consult with local scholars and specialists.

The second phase consisted of intensive analysis of the selected communities. A team, consisting in most cases of a continental American and a Puerto Rican, spent a total of about twelve months in the community making firsthand observations. During this time, however, the entire staff met occasionally at the Social Science Research Center at the University of Puerto Rico to compare results, rephrase problems, and discuss methods.

The third phase was devoted to an interpretation of field data, time being allowed for occasional return visits to the communities to check information. As the interrelation of the community subcultures and the national institutions was the principal interest during this time, the series of conferences mentioned above was held with authorities on various special subjects. Before each conference, a list of questions was prepared covering the national features and their local manifestations and functions. The wholehearted and generous cooperation of the Puerto Rican scholars, scientists, government personnel, and political and religious leaders, whose kindness has been acknowledged individually in the Preface, contributed greatly to an understanding of how our communities functioned in their insular setting.

274   *Evolution and Ecology*

COMMUNITY SELECTION: THEORY AND PRACTICE

The basic problems and theoretical assumptions which underlay community selection in Puerto Rico have already been explained. We wished to study representative samples of the ways of life found among a major portion of the island's population. It was clear at the outset that a study of rural communities would account for a large part of the population. In 1947, 39 per cent of the people were farmers and, of the 24 per cent engaged in manufacturing, handicraft, and construction and the 37 per cent engaged in trade, government services, and domestic and other occupations, a considerable proportion lived in the rural communities, and their work was directly related to farm production (Perloff, 1950). Background literature, census data, and other information, however, indicated that the island is very heterogeneous in types of land use and landownership, and we surmised that each of these types would entail a somewhat distinctive subculture. If so, we could not choose a community at random with the assurance that it represented all communities.[10] Nor could we attempt to sample the total rural population with the certainty that a substantial common denominator would be found.

It was first necessary to determine the types of land use and landownership which involved the greatest number of people, and to ascertain their regional extent. Next, we had to find out whether a distinctive subculture was associated with each type of land use. Finally, we had to choose a sample of each regional subculture. The sample should be a unit which included all possible local manifestations of culture—town and farm, owner and worker, school, church, business, trade, and government controls and services—and which had a maximum degree of local organization, that is, which constituted a fairly well integrated sociocultural segment of the island.

To choose among the different types of land use presented certain difficulties. Puerto Rico produces not only sugar, livestock, coffee, tobacco, and other crops which are marketed, but a great variety of garden vegetables and fruits which are consumed on the farm or sold locally. It was obvious that a study should be made of the culture of the sugar region, for more than half the persons employed in farm work are employed in sugar production, and more than one-third of the acreage of cultivated land is devoted to sugar. Sugar also constitutes more than half the value of Puerto Rico's total exports and more than one-third of the value of farm produce. There are, however, several types

[10] The pioneering work of studying a community that is fairly "typical" of the island had been done by Morris Siegel, who studied a town in the southwestern part of the island. This study is unpublished.

of sugar production: corporate-owned mills and fields; government-owned profit-sharing cooperatives; privately owned fields, or *colonos*, which usually send their cane to large mills; and a few individually owned farms and mills. Although there are small sugar growers in certain regions, for example, where a shift from coffee to sugar production is occurring, the general trend has been to concentrate land in large holdings. Corporate holdings, which represent the extreme in this trend, are largest and richest in the south coast, where irrigation is practiced. We therefore selected a south coast sugar community, Cañamelar, which represents a type of production that prevailed on the south coast until legislation attempted to dissolve the large holdings.

To older legislation, which had limited land holdings to five hundred acres, was added the creation of government-owned profit-sharing plantations and small individual holdings. By December, 1947, the Land Authority had purchased about 36 per cent of the corporate holdings, and in 1947-48 it produced over 11 per cent of all sugar produced in the island. This type of production represents a future potential for a great deal of farming in field crops other than sugar. A north coast cooperative, Nocorá, was therefore selected for study. It was hoped that a study might also be made of a north coast community where private owners are shifting from coffee to sugar production and of another community of *colonos*, or private producers, whose sugar is ground at a central mill, or *central*. Such a study, however, would probably have revealed a transitional type, which is in the process of change from the family hacienda to the large plantation, rather than a fairly fixed type, which now and presumably for some time in the future will be found among a substantial portion of the population.

Livestock ranches are of great importance in that the amount of land in pasture is about double that devoted to sugar, while the income from livestock products is second only to sugar. The ranch and dairy farms, however, did not seem to warrant study in the present project, primarily because only a small portion of the farming population works with livestock, and secondarily because the ranches and farms are scattered and do not form communities.

The small farm owners and sharecroppers of the highlands, who grow a great variety of garden crops for their own use and for local sale, constitute about one-third of the total farm population. These people are in the direct tradition of the early subsistence farmers, although about 10 per cent of their land is now devoted to tobacco, their chief cash crop. Tobacco is perhaps a declining crop, at least so far as export is concerned, but it has enabled the small farmers to participate in a world which increasingly requires some ready cash. Moreover, the recent establishment of a cigar factory in Caguas may augment exports. The selection of Tabara as representative of the tobacco and mixed crops region is explained in Part III. Tabara is a type that has long been characteristic of Puerto Rico and is likely to endure for some time; for even a further decline in tobacco may be offset by increased sales of truck garden crops for insular consumption.

It was believed that a community in the coffee area should be studied, even though coffee production involves only 14 per cent of the farm population (310,000 persons in 1939), because coffee was the principal export crop in the nineteenth century and the subculture of the coffee region is most nearly in the Spanish pattern and a majority of the large owners are first- or second-generation Spaniards. The choice of a coffee community, however, presented certain difficulties. We sought a place where there were resident owners and workers, the latter living upon land allotted them for their own subsistence and depending upon favors extended by the owners. In the heart of the area, where such conditions might be expected, it was found that there were many sugar plantations and that a considerable number of workers used needlework to supplement their income. Here, also, seasonal and part-time work and out-migration had disrupted the traditionally face-to-face dependency relationship between owner and worker. San José, on the fringe of the coffee area, however, had just enough production of tobacco and minor crops—it had some sugar, too—to enable the workers to produce their own food and a small cash crop in the off-season on the plots allotted them by the owners. This partial dependency upon cash production represents a trend away from the older type of Spanish hacienda, but San José is less cash-minded than the other communities where wage labor prevails.

The selection of the above-mentioned communities was based not only upon data from the U.S. Census, the Agricultural Adjustment Administration, and other federal, insular, and local agencies but upon information obtained by visits to the communities. Consultations with mayors, school directors, labor union leaders, political committeemen, farm foremen and overseers, farm owners, tenant farmers, merchants, and wage earners provided a general picture of life in the communities as well as a supplement and corrective to some of the published statistics. Where several communities were fairly typical of a region, the final selection was based on additional considerations: the community should not be too large for a team of two fieldworkers to ascertain its general nature within a year, and the people should be amenable to the research. One or two communities were avoided because antagonism had prevented studies in the past. The chapters in Part III explain the choice of communities in greater detail.

The decision to study Puerto Rico's economically, socially, and politically prominent families was based upon theoretical considerations which differed in certain important respects from those underlying the choice of the rural communities and subcultures. And the study involved the fieldworker, Raymond Scheele, in certain problems and methods rather foreign to those traditionally used in cultural analysis. Whereas the rural subcultures were seen essentially as divergent end-products of the processes of cultural change, which were largely although not entirely beyond their control, the prominent families were initially assumed to be not only a subcultural group which itself had experienced change but also an instrument in the change of other groups. It was suspected, although it had not been proven, that in any area which is subjected to strong alien influence the upper or superordinate classes might first adopt new patterns and then transmit them in some form to the other classes.

This rather general and untested hypothesis, however, could obviously not mean that the lifeways of the upper class diffuse outward and downward through a simple process of imitation. The behavior patterns, the ideals, and the attitudes found to be distinctive of the upper class presupposed a basis of wealth and prestige which could not possibly be imitated. The role of the upper class in the acculturation of the Puerto Rican people had to be phrased in terms of two general problems.

The first problem was to ascertain the nature of the subculture of the prominent business families and to determine whether it constituted an ideal toward which other subcultural groups sought to move or were compelled to move. In the research it was soon found that these families had been Americanized—that is, had adopted patterns typical of the United States and especially of the upper classes of the United States—far more than any other group and that their acculturation was patterned largely around commercial enterprises, which were closely tied to United States businesses and which imposed standards not only of economic behavior but of social, political, and other kinds of cultural behavior. It was also found that the United States patterns constituted an ideal for subordinate groups, partly because the lower echelons of employees within any particular business organization are compelled by the nature of the commercial structures to follow many precepts of behavior not only on the job but in their private lives. It thus appeared that many patterns associated with commerce spread downward not only because the members of the lower echelons sought upward mobility but because their very employment depended upon it. This filtering downward of cultural traits did not destroy the differences between classes. It initiated trends, such as those described in the hypotheses in

Part IV, which are making all of Puerto Rico more commercialized and more cash-oriented even while the subcultural differences are becoming more pronounced. The acculturating effect of the prominent families is certainly greatest upon members of their own business organizations, where a face-to-face relationship prevails and where standards of behavior can be enforced. It seems likely that the members of the lower echelons of business adopt these standards as much because their personal security depends upon doing so as because of any desire to alter their way of life in favor of alien patterns. The impact of upper-class standards upon individuals over whom they have no direct control cannot be judged at present, but it seems probable that a kind of chain reaction runs along the axis of a business affecting large numbers of persons in some degree.

The second problem was to ascertain how the prominent families indirectly affected the subcultures of other groups through their influence upon national institutions. Apart from the rather profound Americanization of the personnel in their own business organizations, these families played a significant role in insular commerce and finance, which undoubtedly had some effect upon large numbers of persons with whom they had no direct contact. They also appear to have influenced the economic policy of modern legislation to some extent. No doubt their influence has touched many other aspects of Puerto Rican national life, but precise analysis of its nature and extent would involve complicated problems of national institutions and power structure and of the relationship of these to the upper class on the one hand and to the other subcultural groups on the other. From the point of view of the present study, which is concerned primarily with subcultural groups, Scheele's analysis has served to show various ways in which an upper class might be related to other frames of reference in cultural analysis.

The subcultures and communities selected do not exhaust all of the Puerto Rican rural types. There are Title V communities, which are made up of independent farmers living on small plots provided them by the government. These represent a future potential for many Puerto Ricans, but at present they do not involve any significant portion of the population. There are predominantly Negro communities, which, though small and not very numerous, are alleged to have some surviving African customs. They might have thrown some light on past conditions, though they can hardly be regarded as "fossil communities" which have survived unchanged into the context of modern Puerto Rican life. There are a few communities where a living is made largely or entirely by fishing. And there are needlework communities, where women supplement other sources of income, often to a very important extent, through lowly paid piecework.

In addition to the subcultural types found in these communities, there are other sociocultural segments which should be studied by the cultural method. There are the growing middle classes which are represented to some extent in the communities described here but which extend more or less throughout the island and very likely have similar subcultures. An extremely interesting example is the new inter-community class of war veteran taxi owners and operators. There are also dislocated and perhaps culturally disorganized slum dwellers in San Juan and elsewhere. And there are types of sociocultural segments peculiar to the cities.

Having chosen communities typical of the four most important kinds of agricultural production, we faced the further problem of selecting units of study within the community. The smallest community is Cañamelar with a population of 11,468 in 1950, and the largest is San José with a population of 22,906. Questionnaires could not be used as the principal instrument in community research for reasons previously discussed, yet the communities were much too large for two fieldworkers to obtain firsthand knowledge of all or even of most persons in the time allowed. Before explaining how this problem was solved, we must discuss the field techniques.

METHODS AND TECHNIQUES OF RESEARCH ON SUBCULTURES

The anthropologist sometimes perplexes his fellow social scientists by his seeming failure to follow a rigidly standardized field procedure. It is evidently felt that unless cultural studies, like the laboratory and mathematical sciences, specify in detail and step by step how results are obtained so that anyone can follow the procedures and obtain identical results, the selection of data and the conclusions based on them are somehow haphazard and unreliable. Admittedly, there is danger in cultural studies that many unconsidered factors may invalidate results, and it is certainly the scientist's obligation to show how he has endeavored to be objective and precise. Questionable data, however, are more likely to result from lack of clarity in basic methodology—from obscure problems and use of obsolete or inappropriate methods—than from failure to devise procedures that are comparable in their specificity to those of the "more exact" sciences. There are, as a matter of fact, several reasons why detailed blueprints of field techniques have not been offered in the past and cannot and need not now be drawn up.

In the first place, one of the primary purposes of cultural studies is to identify and record the characteristic features of different cultural groups throughout the world. There is, of course, need for accuracy, but it is unnecessary and impossible to stipulate how the data of an unknown culture are to be gathered when their specific nature cannot be known in advance. The field techniques must follow the dictum that "science is organized and applied common sense"—common sense in that, since no two field situations are alike, procedures may have to be improvised. It should be stressed that the first task is to identify and describe the cultural phenomena, which must precede measurement, comparison, and correlation. Descriptive analysis and statistical handling cannot be performed in a single operation, for qualitative characteristics must be known prior to quantification. A questionnaire could not possibly be used to treat an unknown culture, unless it had a space for every conceivable type of human activity. It is a common ethnocentric fallacy for scholars unaware of this methodological problem to treat the data of foreign cultures in terms of those of the United States. Fei and Chang, for example, have very cogently criticized Buck's use of American categories of land tenure and methods for correlating them in analysis of Chinese data in complete unawareness of the wholly different nature of the latter (Fei and Chang, 1945).

If there appears to be no highly standardized ethnographic procedure, it is because no two field situations are alike. The anthropologist has felt that it is more important to work among the great number of still unknown cultures of the world than to restudy known cultures. Perhaps more restudy would be valuable, and it might well reveal inadequacies of technique. Since research in new fields, however, is the greatest present need, the fieldworker unavoidably faces the need for a certain amount of improvisation. Nonetheless, basic techniques have been developed and discussed during more than half a century of ethnographic field research. If the anthropologist fails to restate them in each monograph, it is because it no longer seems necessary to say that he lived with his people, observed their economic, religious, and social activities day by day, talked at length with informants to obtain explanations of his observations, and read any published sources available—in short, that he used methods of participant observation, interviews, and archival research.

More specialized techniques depend upon the nature of both the problem and the culture. If, for instance, problems of social structure were the paramount interest, and if the society proved to have a complex kinship system, it would probably be necessary to make extensive use of kinship charts, to ask very special questions of innumerable persons, and to devise any number of procedures which were not foreseeable before the study began. The fieldworker might or might not find it profitable to hold frequent directed interviews, to take notes openly, and to ask about certain aspects of culture. Upon occasion he might not consider it advisable to remain in a community. In other words, no two cultures are quite the same, and the competent fieldworker must approach his data not only with a sense of problem, which provides a criterion of relevancy of data, but with an ingenuity for improvising as complications unfold. In the final analysis, orginal and sound research in any science consists of the ability to sense out new relationships between phenomena and to contrive new methods of analyzing them rather than to impose well-tried methods. In comparative cultural studies, the constant discovery of new and frequently unexpected phenomena makes the ability to devise appropriate techniques absolutely essential. What is more, the sensibilities of the people studied must always be taken into account.

Another reason why cultural studies cannot now be carried out by means of rigidly standardized techniques is that problems and interests are changing very rapidly. At the turn of the twentieth century, anthropology was essentially a descriptive and historical discipline, dedicated to recording the salient features of the many different world cultures before they disappeared or were radically altered under the impact of Western civilization. More recently, new aims and interests have developed, each demanding new procedures. The study of culture and personality, for example, has stimulated the recording of case histories and of considerable detail on child rearing and the individual's life cycle,[11] both of which may be interpreted by psychoanalytic or other techniques. Other new and specialized field procedures are exemplified in studies of race relations, social stability, class structure, and other particular subjects. The lack of comparability of results arises not from failure to standardize procedures but from an exceedingly wide range of research interests.

In the present research, we first selected the communities for reasons previously discussed. In order to ascertain the economic groupings within each community, we obtained data on the number and size of land holdings, the total quantity and value of different crops grown, patterns of marketing, credit facilities, farm extension aid, and other factors in land use. These data were readily available from published statistics and from various government and local authorities. In the same way we obtained information on many important aspects of the community as a whole, such as the amount of participation in schools and labor unions, use made of health facilities, and the general nature of political activities.

Many things could be observed directly by the fieldworkers, for example, phases of farm production, the homes, clothing, and other possessions of the people, and the stores, churches, clinics, and other

---

[11]See Gottschalk, Kluckhohn, and Angell, 1945. The emphasis on life cycle in community studies is shown in Martin Yang's *Chinese Village* (1945) and James West's *Plainville, U.S.A.* (1945).

features in the town. Impressions were obtained by walking the streets, riding the public buses, and miscellaneous conversations with a variety of people.

By these techniques it is possible to obtain a general picture of the community, but an understanding of how the various phases of culture constitute a total system of living for the individual required intimate knowledge of people of the different classes. Practices of child training, the nature of family life, the role of ritual kinship, the kinds of social relations, the meaning of education, religious and political attitudes, and life goals can only be grasped by intimate and prolonged association with the people, during which everything is carefully observed and innumerable questions are asked.

The procedures obviously cannot be standardized. There are even certain similarities between the general purpose and methods of the cultural scientist and the journalist or novelist. But there are important differences which consist of more than a common lack of standardized technique. Both seek an understanding of the mode of life and the motivations of the typical individuals of different subcultures. But whereas the novelist creates a composite or synthetic picture, the scientist endeavors to show the range of variation. Whereas the novelist ordinarily employs evaluative terms against a background of his own ethical judgment and thus may indulge in words that evoke emotion in the reader, the scientist reports as objectively—and as dispassionately—as he is able, omitting purple passages. Most important of all, whereas the novelist endeavors to present a description which is good or bad, according to his perception and literary skill, the social scientist seeks not only to describe but to explain. The social scientist, unlike the novelist, works within a conceptual framework which requires that he make his problem explicit, categorize his data, select and reject data according to their relevance to the central problem, and present his conclusions systematically and explicitly in terms of relationships between selected phenomena. One has only to compare highly perceptive but unsystematic works, such as Sinclair Lewis's *Babbitt* and *Main Street* and Granville Hicks's *Small Town* with social science studies such as the Lynds' *Middletown* to recognize the difference.

Fieldwork on the more intimate aspects of community life is an art only in the sense that it requires constant awareness of the sensibilities of the people and constant alertness to take advantage of opportunities to gain deep insights. One cannot enter a home as a stranger and straight off inquire into sex life, family relations, or attitudes toward local authorities. Six months to a year is usually needed to establish rapport. Once rapport is established, the fieldworker participates in the more private aspects of culture and discusses freely the matters he wishes to know about. He can visit and dine in the homes, attend dances, meetings, and fiestas, and learn about attitudes, ambitions, and frustrations. It is very debatable whether an outsider can immerse himself so thoroughly in a culture that he can experience its emotional overtones as well as observe its forms. And it is doubtful whether this is desirable, for it might lead to a degree of subjectivity and empathy that could easily warp his perspective.

Although these techniques require that the fieldworker approach his people with the sympathy of a friend, the intuition of an artist, and the objectivity of a scientist, the data gathered may be as reliable and as directly related to the central problem of inquiry as in the laboratory sciences. If child training is over-emphasized, if social relations are imperfectly understood, if economic activities are attributed too large or too small a role in shaping the culture, if, in fact, the factual reporting is inadequate in any way, the deficiency lies in theoretical orientation or in individual incompetence of the fieldworker, not in techniques of research. Use of too small a sample results from preconceptions about the cultural common denominator and the homogeneity of the culture, not from inadequate field techniques. If a problem is clearly stated, the kinds of information needed will be clear. The techniques of obtaining the information must then be judged with reference to the problem and not in terms of any immutable set of procedures that can be applied to all cultures regardless of the problem or the nature of the culture.

DELIMITATION OF THE UNIT OF STUDY

In the cultural analysis of contemporary societies there are several problems concerning the unit of study which do not ordinarily arise in ethnographic analysis of primitive peoples. First, since the total populations of modern nations are so large, it is necessary to select representative examples of subcultural groups which can be adequately understood by means of the methods of anthropology in the time available. The fieldworker must become intimately acquainted with a local group which is fairly small and whose patterns of behavior he can grasp during his research period. Second, since all members of the group studied may not share a homogeneous way of life, it is essential to determine the nature and extent of any cultural deviation. Third, it may be important in a practical if not a theoretical sense to determine whether the kinds of cultural behavior found within the group analyzed may be reasonably supposed to exemplify substantial portions of the total population.

The need to select a manageably small group for cultural analysis follows from anthropology's holistic approach to all aspects of the behavior of any society. If intimate relations are to be established, especially within a limited period of research, the number of persons studied cannot be too large. The optimum group size and optimum field period both depend upon the situation and the nature of the culture. Many cultural features may be ascertained from published data and statistics, from fairly brief interviews with little-known individuals, and from rapid observations. Other features such as sex attitudes, the nature of the family, interpersonal relations, and basic values are not readily revealed until close personal relations are established. A cultural study of any contemporary group therefore is multidimensional in that a large variety of informants and sources of information are used for different purposes—some for gross statistics and general features, some for various specialized knowledge about particular features of their community or class, and some for those more intimate aspects of culture which are not readily disclosed to strangers.

When the biographical or case history approach is used, six months to a year may be spent studying a single individual or family. On the other hand, a culture which is wholly unknown well merits a report based only on a single day of observation. Generalization is impossible because too many factors are involved, but it seems to be the general experience of anthropologists that the more intimate behavior patterns cannot be understood in less than six months. A year of fieldwork is preferable, and several years are still better. Malinowski's deep insights into Trobriand Island culture were possible because he lived among these people for three years.

It is almost impossible to stipulate optimum group size in relation to time available for research. As a very rough statement, however, it might be said that a fieldworker can grasp the behavior patterns of perhaps twenty to fifty families within a year of research, and that he can learn enough about some fifty additional families to state with reasonable certainty whether they conform to the families he knows intimately, and that he can obtain a pretty good impression of whether another hundred families are generally like those he knows well.

In the present research the number of families studied was extended somewhat by the use of questionnaires (see Appendix). The numbers and kinds of families interviewed by this technique is explained subsequently. It must be stressed that the use of questionnaires was an experiment in technique rather than a basic source of information for the analyses reported in these volumes. The result of principal interest is that the questionnaires verified what had been expected, namely, that people with the same place in the economic arrangements were similar in the other major features of their lives.

The question of whether all the families studied in field research actually share the same subculture has been a fairly minor consideration in anthropological research. Members of tribal societies, which have not been affected by alien influence, generally share the same ideals of expectable behavior, even though individuals may deviate from the norm in different ways. In modern societies, however, the individual's conception of desirable behavior and his conformity with it may be affected by two important factors. First, his own subculture is constantly changing. The normal or ideal behavior shifts, while alternatives and conflicts are multiplied. Individuals, therefore, exhibit a considerable range of variation in their adaptation to the attractions, pressures, and requirements of new goals. Second, because modern commercial society offers incentives and opportunities for upward mobility, many individuals attempt to simulate the patterns of subcultural groups above them in the class hierarchy. For these reasons, the range of individual variation in contemporary societies may appear to be so great that the reality of subcultures is questionable.

Subcultures undoubtedly intergrade with one another to a certain extent, and there are many individuals who cannot readily be classed in one or another subculture. Nonetheless, there are comparatively few aspects of behavior which exhibit continuous variation along any scale of measurement. When total behavior is recorded, there are definite clusters of interrelated features, especially of features which are not readily susceptible to quantification. Such features distinguish subcultural groups rather clearly. Thus, while income, family size, school attendance, and other traits might show fairly continuous gradation within the total population, certain rather basic qualitative features, such as occupation and status in the productive arrangement, kinship patterns, religion, language, and others are fairly invariant among large groups of people. In Puerto Rico the differences between town and farm populations are quite marked, and the farm population, moreover, is classifiable into subgroups based on the nature of the crops, one's role as owner, laborer, or sharecropper, and his relationship to credit and marketing arrangements. Pronounced differences in the family, in social relationships, in political and religious attitudes, in use made of schooling and of other public facilities, in value systems, and in many other features were associated quite consistently with the different subcultural groups of town and rural persons.

In the present project, rural neighborhoods exemplifying principal types of productive arrangements constituted the subject matter of field study. The research workers could expect to understand the behavioral patterns of about one hundred families. In Cañamelar the farmers of the corporate sugar community consisted almost entirely of landless laborers, whose culture was remarkably homogeneous. In each of the other communities the group selected for investigation included several different rural subcultures which were rather clearly differentiated. For example, in San José owners of coffee haciendas and the landless laborers were almost poles apart in a cultural as well as an economic sense although interrelated in the productive system. In contrast there was considerable variation in basic economic features in Tabara, where landownership was widespread. Farm size ranged from small to medium and the income varied correspondingly. Tabara farmers as a whole, however, shared a subculture related to the production of subsistence crops and a tobacco cash crop which set them off as a group from persons in the coffee or sugar areas who might fall into the same categories of landownership and income but who otherwise differed in behavior and outlook.

The third question of whether the varieties of cultural behavior studied exemplify substantial portions of the population beyond the local group is as much a practical as a scientific problem. It is "practical" in the sense that insights gained through cultural analysis are valuable in action programs if they shed light on large numbers of people. It is, however, scientifically defensible to limit analysis to a very small and atypical group, since any understanding of cultural patterns and processes have theoretical value no matter how few individuals are involved. Intensive studies of single individuals or families—as in the case history and biographical methods—or of a half-dozen individuals or families in a population of thousands are quite legitimate. But, once these intensive and limited analyses have been made, there remains the question of what light this throws on the remainder of the population.

This problem is tentatively answered in the present study by the assumption that the major characteristics of subcultures tend to be associated with the principal features of the productive patterns. In each rural subculture and in the insular upper-class subculture, the research strongly indicates that the constellation of basic economic features—the land potentials, the particular cash crops, the mechanization, credit, and marketing facilities, and position in the economic power structure—and familial social arrangements and many other cultural features are so closely correlated in a causal nexus that where the former occur the latter will also be found. As our research was limited in time and therefore in scope, we could not verify whether a second, third, or fourth corporate sugar community would correspond precisely with Cañamelar, whether the patterns of the older type of coffee hacienda would be found elsewhere than in San José, whether all subsistence crop and tobacco growers would be like those of Tabara, whether the workers on all government-owned sugar plantations are similar to those of Nocorá, and whether the prominent business executives in Ponce and elsewhere have followed the acculturational trends of those in San Juan. But we strongly believe that, despite slight modifications resulting from unique local factors, this will prove to be the case.

FINAL SELECTION OF THE UNIT OF STUDY

In the Puerto Rico study, the problem of finding local groups for analysis and of determining their internal range of variation and their wider external significance was expedited by the nature of the local community, or municipio. The municipio is not only the principal political and administrative unit, but it is the unit generally treated in historical and other documents and in statistical material. Each municipio is subdivided into barrios, which are districts of minor administrative importance, and the barrios tend to be subdivided into neighborhoods, or small areas of primary groups with face-to-face relations.

In order to understand the municipio as a whole, it was necessary to analyze its administrative, economic, social, and religious functions and to ascertain what sociocultural groupings were found within the town center. It was impossible to know all the townspeople well because the "urban" population, as counted in the 1950 census, ranges from 1,032 people in Nocorá to 4,105 in Tabara, but it was possible to grasp the principal functions of the town in the total municipio and to gain general knowledge of the sociocultural classes. In the case of the rural population, it was necessary to find individual barrios and to select neighborhoods within the barrios that exhibited the kinds of agricultural life typical of the region. The studies became intensive analyses of representative neighborhoods.

In each community the choice of the neighborhood of concentration was made in about the same way. The fieldworkers first spent several months living in the pueblo or town, becoming acquainted with local life, studying data provided by local agencies, and visiting the rural barrios. The selection of the neighborhoods for intensive study was facilitated by readily available statistical data on land use, landownership, and the nature of employment. On the hypothesis that subcultural differences would be associated with the size of farms, crops grown, and occupation, we chose neighborhoods which exhibited economic patterns typical of many thousands of persons in the region.

As explained subsequently, each of the groups of intensive study numbered from one to three hundred families. Intimate acquaintance with a limited number of these families revealed certain patterns of behavior, which, to judge by general knowledge of the other families, seemed to characterize the entire group. In order to substantiate our assumption that the recorded norms were valid for the larger group, we gave questionnaires to a considerable number of persons beyond the principal informants. These questionnaires (see Appendix) were given at the end of the field research, when we were able to formulate culturally significant questions. There are, of course, many aspects of culture which cannot be treated by this method—e.g., authority structure within the family, the nature of the *compadrazgo,* and so forth—but the questionnaires at least give a clue to the nature of the culture. In general, the results verified our assumption that certain modes of behavior characterize all families within each rural class. Nothing would be added to the analysis contained in this volume by tabulating the questionnaire results.

We now consider the problem of selecting a unit of study in each of the communities.

San José.—San José, a municipio in the western mountains, was chosen because it was believed to represent the "traditional" subculture associated with the production of coffee, despite the invasion of sugar, mixed crops, and needlework in the region. The farms devoted entirely to coffee are generally large, unmechanized, except in processing, and owned by persons of Spanish birth or descent. They represent the family-type hacienda which is characterized by face-to-face, paternalistic relations between owners and workers. In addition to the haciendas, there are small farms producing mixed crops and tobacco as well as coffee.

The municipio of San José, including the town and rural area, has a population of about 19,500 persons, or 3,800 households, which fall into several distinctive subcultural groups. The large coffee lands are still held as family haciendas, but much coffee is produced by small-scale farmers, some classifiable as medium owners and others as peasants. As the field research progressed, it became clear that four socioeconomic groups could be distinguished: (1) landless agricultural workers; (2) peasants holding 10 *cuerdas*[12] or less and small farmers owning 10 to 30 *cuerdas* who supplement their income with wage labor; (3) medium farmers having 30 to 100 *cuerdas* who also do some wage labor; and (4) hacienda owners of 100 and more *cuerdas.*

The rural population numbers about 16,000 persons, or some 3,200 households, and it is divided between eight rural barrios. Some of these barrios have abandoned coffee in favor of cane production and others have adopted needlework to the extent that the older patterns are destroyed. We finally selected the barrio of Manicaboa, which has two neighborhoods of some 100 households each and which includes representations of the four socioeconomic types mentioned. During

[12] A *cuerda* is 0.9712 of an acre.

the year of research the fieldworkers came to know the lifeways of individuals of the different types fairly well. In addition, a questionnaire was finally given to 86, or 43 per cent, of the 200 households. These included 46, or 17.5 per cent, of the farm owners of different sizes and 40, or 15 per cent, of the landless workers.

The town of San José numbers about 3,500, or 600 households. This is too large and diversified a unit to have been studied thoroughly in terms of subcultures. It was possible, however, to grasp the functions of the town in its relationship to the rural area, that is, to determine its role as administrative, religious, political, marketing, and distributional center. It was also possible to determine in broad outline the general nature of its subcultural groups. In addition to a wide variety of contacts with townspeople, the field workers gave questionnaires to 27, or about 5 per cent, of its 600 households.

It cannot be claimed, of course, that every aspect of the municipio culture was fully investigated in the research. Many problems were peripheral to our interests. We are confident, however, that this volume accurately reports the subcultures of workers, peasants, middle farmers, and hacienda owners of Manicaboa. We also believe that it is highly probable that these subcultures typify comparable socio-economic groups associated with coffee production elsewhere in the highlands.

Tabara.—Tabara was selected because its economic patterns are typical of twelve municipios which primarily produce tobacco and mixed crops. (See Chapter 6 for further explanation.) According to the 1950 census, Tabara had a total of some 17,500 persons of whom about 4,200 lived in the town and 13,000 in seven rural barrios. One of these barrios, Quito, is representative of the twelve municipios in the proportion of tobacco it produces, while another, Salvador, is unusual though not unique in producing a somewhat larger proportion of tobacco. The fieldworkers took up residence in a rural house where these barrios adjoin and they had access to neighborhoods in each barrio.

The neighborhoods studied have some 150 families, which includes all sizes of farms and types of land tenure in the area. The great majority of farms are small, being less than 35 *cuerdas*, while the average is 17 *cuerdas*. Three farmers own 35 to 100 *cuerdas*, and four, who are classed as large farmers, own more than 100 *cuerdas*. There is much sharecropping, there are landless laborers, and there are roadside shopkeepers. Of these 150 families, more than 50 became known quite intimately to the fieldworkers. Forty-two questionnaires were given in these neighborhoods, although their primary purpose was not so much to broaden the basis of information as to test the questionnaire method against ethnographic results.

Some subcultural differences were found within the rural barrios, the principal differences being between the medium farmers, small farmers, and landless workers, and it is presumed that similar differences will be found in the other municipios growing tobacco and mixed crops. It is significant that the largest farms produced coffee and were very different from all the tobacco producers.

The general functions of the town were studied by the field staff, and the subcultures were given considerable attention by Sra. de Roca. In addition, thirty-six questionnaires were given to the professional people, large merchants, middle classes, and poor people of the town.

Cañamelar.—Cañamelar had 13,464 persons in the 1950 census of whom 4,105 lived in the town and 9,359 in the rural area. The selection of groups for intensive study, however, was much easier than in San José or Tabara because the entire culture of the municipio is closely tied to the corporation sugar mill and fields. There is only one rural subcultural group, which consists of plantation and mill laborers, there being no private owners or *colonos*. Moreover, the distinction between urban and rural is less sharp than in the other communities because many of the workers live in the town and because many functions of the town are controlled by the mill.

The fieldworkers were generally familiar with the town people but they concentrated on one of the barrios which has three nuclei of population—a *poblado* or settlement along the road where the investigators lived, a *colonia* or cluster of houses on company land, and the *playa* or beach where squatters live. Each of these neighborhoods has about 80 families. Not all families, of course, were known equally well, but all are laborers and all clearly share a very similar subculture. In the *poblado* the questionnaire (see Appendix) was given to 43 families. In addition special data on the family and the standard of living were tabulated for 66 households.

Town life presented a comparatively simple problem because Cañamelar lacks the middle and upper classes found in the other small urban centers. Many of the urban functions of merchandising and of providing health and other services are closely tied to the sugar corporation, while town government is, in a sense, a function of the workers' union.

Nocorá.—In the 1950 census the municipio of Nocorá had nearly 20,000 persons of whom 1,032 were classed as urban and 18,867 as rural. The socioeconomic structure of Nocorá resembles that of Cañamelar in that a large sugar mill—in this case, government-owned—is the focal point of municipio activities and a considerable number of the town people are sugar workers. It differs from Cañamelar, however, in that all sugar producers do not fall into a homogeneous class of wage laborers. In addition to government sugar lands which feed the *central*, or central mill, and which employ as many as 3,000 men, there are some 500 *colonos*, or owners of private sugar plantations, who send their sugar to the *central* to be ground. Although most of the *colonos*, especially on the coastal plain where the principal study was made, own so little land that they must work part time as laborers, a few have comparatively large holdings, which places them in a higher economic and sociocultural class. Nocorá also differs from Cañamelar in that town functions are not so subordinate to the sugar interests. Nocorá has a small middle and upper class of professional people and merchants, some of the latter also owning sugar lands.

The fieldworkers lived first in the "urban" center of Nocorá for three months, where they became acquainted with government officials of the sugar mill, labor leaders, businessmen, and mill workers. Individuals of these different categories were consulted in order to determine the general nature of the community and its functions in municipio life rather than to establish subcultural differences between persons of various statuses and roles. That is, each individual was an informant concerning the nature of the municipio rather than as a representative of a special subculture.

After three months in the town center the fieldworkers moved to Tipan, a community of more than 100 families who worked on the government profit-sharing sugar farm. During seven months' residence there they came to know the general cultural patterns of some 50 families fairly well. After this they lived for eight months in Mango, a settlement of some 30 families of government sugar workers of whom they came to know perhaps 15 quite well. "Very well known" or "fairly well known" are of course relative statements. They mean that in the opinion of the fieldworkers reliable data essential to the present analyses were obtained. The cultural pattern of the government plantation workers is constructed not only from studies of the families just cited but also from fairly extensive knowledge of laborers living in other districts.

The subculture of the *colonos* is based largely upon fairly intimate knowledge of some 25 coastal families which send their sugar to the government mill. Most of these *colonos* own so little land that they have to work as laborers to supplement their income and their standard of living is not very different from the landless workers. A few *colonos*, however, have fairly substantial holdings and high socioeconomic status.

Questionnaires were used in Nocorá largely to ascertain differences between people within the town. Sixty questionnaires were given to individuals not previously known to the fieldworkers. These subjects included the different social and economic classes: professional people, war veterans, workers, and others.

The prominent families of Puerto Rico.—These families were a unit of study in a somewhat different sense than the subcultural groups of the rural municipios. They are characterized by a high income and a high degree of acculturation from outside the island. They are localized only in that most of them happen to reside in the island's capital, San Juan. This group was delimited as a unit of study principally on the basis of income, social status, and economic and political role. Limited in number by the two basic criteria of income and socioeconomic status (see Chapter 10), it represented a highly specialized subcultural group.

With the group so delimited, the research problem was to establish close relations with enough of its members to be sure that the analyses of the behavior patterns were truly representative. The procedure was about the same as in the case of the rural subcultural groups. A considerable number of informants were used because of their specialized knowledge. A limited number of families became known so intimately that the fieldworker was given access to information on the familial and social features of this class. An additional number of families was studied through a questionnaire drawn up especially for this subculture.

IMPLICATIONS FOR AREA RESEARCH

Considerable thought was given to the significance of the present project for an area research program. "Area research," it should be understood, is a very general concept which may merely mean that more or less collaborative research of the different social sciences and humanities is carried on under the auspices of area institutes on various problems pertaining to the major nations or areas of the world.[13] As area research includes almost as many interests, problems, and procedures as there are disciplines, it would be impossible to provide a blueprint for area studies that would satisfy everyone. Since, however, Puerto Rico is very small as areas go and since we dealt in one way or another with virtually all aspects of Puerto Rican culture, the project could be considered an interdisciplinary one in certain respects. While we did not undertake to deal with the island as a whole, our methodology has three features of special interest to area research: first, a clarification of one role of anthropology in an area program; second, a means of conceptualizing the totality of the cultural phenomena in an area unit; third, a method for stating cross-cultural regularities.

---

[13]See Steward, 1950, for a discussion of the theory and practice of area research.

Previous pages have undertaken to show that one of the most useful roles anthropology may play in the analysis of contemporary societies is to study subcultural groups. Nationally shared behavior traits and even large communities, which have diversified aspects, do not lend themselves readily to the holistic ethnographic method. Subcultural groups, however, may be adequately understood only in the context of the total area. It is necessary, therefore, to conceptualize the total area and to devise methods for relating the subcultural group to it.

Areas are defined in many different ways for different purposes. From a cultural or holistic point of view, however, an area must be viewed as a relatively well integrated sociocultural system. It may be a state, a nation, or a dependency, whose people are bound together by common laws and economic institutions and frequently by other features. Puerto Rico is an integrated sociocultural system in that it has a single government and economy—although both are tied to the United States which is a larger system—and its people have a cultural heritage which combines features from Spain and from North America.

The place of the Puerto Rican subcultural groups in the insular setting is essentially an interdisciplinary problem. In order to understand cultural function and change among these groups, it is necessary to relate them to various national features, such as commerce, banking, legislation, governmental services, religious organizations, education, and the like, each of which is the subject of study by some special discipline. A full understanding of the national setting of the subcultural groups would require analysis of how the national institutions interact with one another. At present, however, there is no super-social science, no area science per se, which can integrate all national features in terms of a total configuration. Historians come nearer than anyone to a holistic approach to nations, but most of them tend to accord primary attention to special features, such as political institutions.

In the absence of what might be called a basic "area study science," scholars will draw upon the specialized knowledge of national features as their problem demands it. In the present study, we have had to consult the works of our colleagues in other fields at great length. There are many problems which will counteract the previous tendency to compartmentalize knowledge and to isolate special phenomena from their sociocultural setting. Such diversified subjects as demographic trends, health, environmental adaptations, technological development, money and banking, social structure, political systems, foreign relations, military power, religious organizations and beliefs, ideological systems, and values may be chosen for investigation, but it is becoming clear to everyone that these are interdependent, that they are different aspects of the total national culture, and that an understanding of any one will be incomplete if it is wholly isolated from the others. Moreover, when any of these subjects is studied in its national terms, the nature of the sociocultural system must be adequately conceptualized. The concept of levels of sociocultural organization which distinguishes family, community, and national levels is applicable to all contemporary societies and is useful in any problem of area research.

The present project has one other implication for area research which we consider extremely important. It has endeavored to present its analyses in the form of hypotheses which are applicable to other world areas. Scholars working in other world areas have been prone to view their phenomena in terms of cultural relativity—to stress the uniqueness of the cultural elements and of the total configuration. Current world trends, however, call attention rather forcibly to kinds of social and economic change that take place again and again in different areas. Puerto Rico could be viewed either as a country that is unique in its Hispanic and American cultural heritage and in its particular relationship of dependency upon the United States or as an area which is experiencing many changes similar to those in other parts of the world. Certainly, a description of certain of the problems of Puerto Rico would strike very familiar notes to students of recent trends in Africa, India, China, Southeast Asia, or almost any other part of the world which has been an economic or political dependency. All of these areas are experiencing a sharp increase in population while becoming geared to a worldwide economic system through capital investment, production of export crops or other raw materials, and the importation of manufactured goods. Overpopulation without industrial development has lowered standards of living to the crisis point. Economic and demographic changes have combined with the growth of middle classes created by new trades, businesses, and professions to disrupt traditional social systems and to create new political ideologies and new economic and political power structures. The profound rearrangements within the colonies have affected their external relations; for the individual farmer, artisan, laborer, businessman, and professional finds his place in the social and economic scheme, his personal life, and his political outlook profoundly altered. He may demand greater autonomy in how his problems shall be solved and what course the future shall take. Most colonies have become culturally if not politically nationalistic, and many have already won independence.

The present project was undertaken with an awareness of the similarities as well as of the differences between Puerto Rico and other agrarian areas which have a similar relationship to a powerful nation. These other areas are the subject of analysis in many current research programs, the results of which served to sharpen the sense of problem in the present project. The hypothetical formulations of culture change which are presented in our concluding chapter are based solely on the Puerto Rican data, but they are made against a background of general knowledge of trends in many colonial, agrarian areas. And they are phrased so that they may be tested in areas which have a cultural tradition very different from that of Puerto Rico.

BIBLIOGRAPHY

BENEDICT, RUTH
    1946. *The Chrysanthemum and the Sword*. Boston: Houghton Mifflin.

DAVIS, KINGSLEY
    1953. "Puerto Rico: A Crowded Island," *Annals of the American Academy of Political and Social Science*, vol. 285, pp. 116-22.

FEI HSIAO-TUNG and CHANG CHIH-I
    1945. *Earthbound China: A Study of Rural Economy in Yunnan*. Chicago: University of Chicago Press.

GORER, GEOFFREY
    1943. *Themes in Japanese Culture. Transactions of the New York Academy of Sciences*, series 2, vol. 5, New York.

    1948. *The American People*. New York: Norton.

GOTTSCHALK, LOUIS, CLYDE KLUCKHOHN, and ROBERT ANGELL
    1945. "The Use of Personal Documents in History, Anthropology and Sociology," *Social Science Research Council Bulletin* 53, New York.

HALLOWELL, A. IRVING
    1953. "Culture, Personality, and Society," in *Anthropology Today* (A. L. Kroeber, editor), pp. 597-620. Chicago: University of Chicago Press.

HARING, DOUGLAS C.
    1949. *Personal Character and Cultural Milieu*. Syracuse: University of Syracuse Press.

KLINEBERG, OTTO
    1950. "Tensions Affecting International Understanding," *Social Science Research Council Bulletin* 62, New York.

KLUCKHOHN, CLYDE, and HENRY A. MURRAY
    1949. *Personality in Nature, Society and Culture*. New York: Knopf.

MEAD, MARGARET
    1953. "National Character," in *Anthropology Today* (A. L. Kroeber, editor), pp. 642-67. Chicago: University of Chicago Press.

MILLS, C. WRIGHT, CLARENCE SENIOR, and ROSE KOHN GOLDSEN
    1950. *The Puerto Rican Journey*. New York: Harper.

PERLOFF, HARVEY S.
1950. *Puerto Rico's Economic Future*. Chicago: University of Chicago Press.

REDFIELD, ROBERT
1941. *The Folk Culture of Yucatan*. Chicago: University of Chicago Press.

1947. "The Folk Society." *American Journal of Sociology*, vol. 52, no. 4, pp. 293-308.

SENIOR, CLARENCE
1953. "Migration and Puerto Rico's Population Problem," *Annals of the American Academy of Political and Social Science*, vol. 285, pp. 130-36.

STEWARD, JULIAN H.
1936. "The Economic and Social Basis of Primitive Bands," in *Essays in Anthropology in Honor of Alfred Louis Kroeber* (Robert H. Lowie, editor), pp. 331-50. Berkeley: University of California Press.

1937. "Ecological Aspects of Southwestern Society," *Anthropos*, vol. 32, pp. 87-104.

1938. "Basin-Plateau Aboriginal Sociopolitical Groups," *Bureau of American Ethnology Bulletin* 120. Washington: Government Printing Office.

1945. "Foreword" to *Cultural and Historical Geography of Southwest Guatemala* by Felix W. McBryde. Washington: Institute of Social Anthropology, Publication no. 4, Smithsonian Institution.

1950. "Area Research: Theory and Practice," *Social Science Research Council Bulletin* 63, New York.

1951. "Levels of Sociocultural Integration: An Operational Concept," *Southwestern Journal of Anthropology*, vol. 7, pp. 374-90.

WEST, JAMES
1945. *Plainville, U.S.A.* New York: Columbia University Press.

YANG, MOU-CHIN
1945. *A Chinese Village: Shantung Province*. New York: Columbia University Press.

14

Modernization in Traditional Societies

This paper is the better part of a chapter that Steward had originally written as an introduction to *Contemporary Change in Traditional Societies* (1967) but which was never published. The present essay is actually more general and far-ranging than the introduction that finally appeared, and is therefore more appropriate to this volume. Steward makes several references to the work of his colleagues in the Study of Cultural Regularities project. In order of appearance of their essays in the three-volume work, they are: Edward H. Winter and Thomas O. Beidelman on the Kaguru of Tanzania; Robert A. Manners, who studied the Kipsigis of Kenya; Stanley Diamond, who wrote on the Anaguta of Nigeria; Frederic K. Lehman on the Kayah of Burma; Richard Downs, writing on a Kelantanese village in Malaya; Toshinao Yoneyama, who carried out a comparative analysis of two Japanese farming villages; Charles Erasmus on northwest Mexico; Solomon Miller, who did fieldwork in Peru on a highland hacienda and a coastal plantation; and Louis C. Faron, who studied the history of the Chancay Valley in Peru. The reader interested in pursuing their work is directed to the appropriate chapters of *Contemporary Change in Traditional Societies*.

1. THE INITIAL CULTURE

Any study of change requires a time factor—some knowledge, however sketchy, of the past. The trajectory of a ball in flight could not be judged by a single snapshot. In cultural studies it is obviously not necessary to start with the paleolithic or neolithic periods. Because the major concern is change in the modern world, a perception of direction is possible even though the starting point or initial culture does not extend much beyond the time when the processes of modernization began.

The nature of these processes will be discussed subsequently. Because the term "process" has so many meanings, it should be said here that it refers to a large number of developmental trends, such as increased production, expanding population, individualization of effort, changing goals, and others. This meaning contrasts with repetitive processes, such as those which are employed in making a shoe, purifying water, or cultivating the soil.

Some fundamental transformations of tribal societies occurred after their first contact with the larger world. The acquisition of horses and steel tools by the Plains Indians began before the Indians became integral parts of a larger sociopolitical system. Steel cutting tools and traps initiated important transformations through development of the rubber trade in the Amazon and the fur trade in Canada. There are many other cases in which a single factor brought marked social change. Our concern here, however, is with societies which are at least nominally parts of modern states and which are being exposed to an increasing number of factors that induce change. Influences from the modern world are reaching out with greater impact each year, and, owing especially to improved transportation, they may even leapfrog over great areas.

The date at which modernization becomes recognizable obviously varies in each case, but in anthropological studies it is often within the memory of older informants or their grandparents. This does not mean that one can or needs to reconstruct a complete ethnography as the baseline or initial culture. Knowledge of the past, however, is usually adequate to provide clues about the incipiency of modern processes. That is, projection of trends backward in time helps to judge their trajectory.

Another factor bearing on the choice of the initial culture or datum point is the existence of written records. The tribal societies of Africa had no writing, but outside sources disclose slaving activities in some areas before the colonies were established. This gives some insight into the nature of the early societies and their attitudes toward other tribes and outsiders. There is more historical material on the Yaqui and Mayo of Mexico owing to the Spanish chronicles, which explain how missionaries introduced various features during the seventeenth century. The historical records are fairly continuous for the colonial and republican periods of Peru and for the long history of Japan.

There are no fixed criteria by which to judge how far back into known history it is profitable to go. One can only say that if the factors that shaped the culture and society prior to the impact of modern industrial influences are known, the effects of more recent events may be placed in better perspective. That is, a kind of running start at the problem of recent change is always helpful. Our basic interest, however, is the processes created by the contemporary industrialized world. This is not to say that industrialization in its extreme form, let alone automation, has a direct and full impact upon native societies.

But their influence is spreading so widely that native societies are often caught up in certain aspects of the modern world so that they may skip some of the more gradual transformations of a half-century or more ago.

2. THE CONTEXTS OF CHANGE AND MODERNIZATION

Modernization is stimulated or initiated by factors of outside or alien origin as well as by local circumstances, but these external factors become effective through contexts of different kinds. Borrowing, which is one of many processes to be considered subsequently, may account for change in certain particulars, such as dress or foods, but it does not necessarily create internal evolutionary processes. We are concerned here principally with the supracommunity institutions of the state, or nation, or world to which the native society is exposed, and with the total structure of the national society.

In an earlier study of the subcultures of Puerto Rico (Steward *et al.*, 1956) my colleagues and I endeavored to enumerate those features of the island-wide and even U.S. culture that had brought about modernization of various segments or subcultures of the population. The production of sugar on increasingly mechanized plantations, which in turn were linked with a continental market, quotas, and other advantages, had created a proletariat of wage laborers. Workers on the coffee haciendas, however, had maintained a more personal relationship with their patrons, wherein various benefits partly supplanted wages. Cultivators of tobacco and truck garden crops were independent land owners, and they took advantage of government assistance in farming, health, and education. Among the principal factors of Puerto Rico's context were markets for crops which could be grown, government aid and benefits of various kinds, education (which had been rather unsuccessfully conducted in English until that time), medical help, outmigration to the United States of surplus population, underemployment owing to increasing mechanization of the sugar plantations and mills, and a system of labor unions which was as much politically as economically oriented. Many elements of the hispanic heritage, such as speaking Spanish, cockfights, lotteries, and certain food preferences, persisted, while baseball and other features were adopted from the continent.

Spicer's *Cycles of Conquest* (1962) views the culture history of the Indians of northwestern Mexico and the southwestern United States in the contexts of the early Spanish and later Mexican and U.S. policies and influences. Spicer's approach is a notable advance over the many "acculturation" studies made among Indians of the United States, wherein the reservation system has been more or less taken for granted. Reservations really consist of a very special kind of context.

A distinction must be drawn between factors of potential and actual effectiveness. Any context of modernization contains a considerable number of factors, which become effective according to local circumstances. There is usually a market system, which may rapidly involve the native society in a cash rationale if lands favor production and there is access to markets. There are government laws which may prevent local wars, forbid certain traditional practices, settle land disputes, and set up other requirements in a national code which is enforced by policemen and courts. There is education to which people have access in different degrees. There are missions whose activities in health and education may sometimes be more effective than their spiritual proselytizing. There are usually some government services in health, farming, reclamation, and other fields, which the people utilize under certain conditions. In many areas pacification has permitted drastic change in settlement pattern and land use. As these factors in the national context become effective, evolutionary processes begin to modify local societies, often with great speed.

An important feature imposed from the national level is alienation of native lands to foreign-owned plantations, which creates land shortage and population surplus and in turn provides plantation wage labor. Taxation may also drive people to seek wage labor which they might otherwise avoid. Access to manufactured goods also seems to become an increasing inducement to acquire cash through work on plantations, mines, or other commercial enterprises if not by producing salable commodities. Persons who affiliate themselves with outside enterprises enter special contexts of modernization.

Another important aspect of the larger context may be the existence of multiple societies or structures, which in some cases amounts to a near caste-like hierarchy of closed societies. Such a system effectively retards the impact of modernizing factors upon the native peoples owing to the many restrictions and prohibitions imposed upon them. Societies which are preliterate and unskilled at the time of outside contact are often exposed to racial prejudice, denied skilled jobs, and given little training needed for such jobs. Segregation effectively keeps them in the lower echelons of employment and social status. Probably the most extreme case of discrimination and segregation is the apartheid policy of South Africa, but barriers to upward social and economic mobility are found in some degree in most areas.

Our field studies included two general areas of caste-like multiple societies. In East Africa the distinctions between the Africans, who were the basic, native population, the Asians (largely Indians), who were the skilled workers and entrepreneurs, and the Europeans, who had been the rich land owners and colonial rulers, were very striking. These three groups differed unmistakably in race, language, culture, religion, occupation, and status. In Malaysia very similar distinctions existed between the basic, rural Malay population, the Chinese merchants and businessmen, and the British plantation and mine owners who had formerly been the colonial rulers and civil servants.

Some factors, however, have tended to create a context that is the obverse of these rigidly stratified states. Japan's distinctive history has resulted in great racial and cultural homogeneity. Japan has no important segment of alien population, its lands have not been expropriated for plantations by foreigners, it has no important conflicts of religions, and its rapid and massive industrialization is penetrating all segments of the society. Opportunity for advancement is open to all who can take advantage of it. The only segment of Japan's population which suffers restrictions is the Eta, an outcaste group not unlike the outcastes of India, who are identified by ancestry and habitat rather than by any observable difference in race or manner of living, except their traditional association with butchering and leather work. There is strong evidence, however, that the force of modern industrial development in both India and Japan is lessening the social and economic disabilities of the outcastes.

Rapid industrialization is also minimizing and often obliterating distinctions between ethnic groups in such countries as those of Western Europe and the United States. Although racial discrimination has by no means disappeared in the United States, ethnic and religious backgrounds are diminishing as barriers to opportunities. Ethnicity survives usually as a somewhat vague symbol of group identification.

The Latin American nations, although still short of having realized their full industrial potentials, lacked many of the racial and ethnic prejudices of the Anglo-American countries. Considerable intermarriage and miscegenation produced a large mestizo population in Latin America. Access to the factors of modernization has been determined far more by wealth, which is the principal basis of class, than by culture or race. For this reason, the peoples of Mexico and Peru may become modernized without facing the disadvantages found in so many other parts of the world.

Another important feature of the context of highly industrialized nations is that cultural distinctions between rural and urban societies have so diminished that this dichotomy is losing significance. Such nations consist of sociocultural segments of subsocieties—for example, laborers, brokers, teachers, and dozens of others—who may be drawn from many ethnic groups. Rural populations are tied so closely and in so many ways to the cities and the nation that, but for a contradiction in terms, it would be proper to speak of urbanization of these people. Despite the considerable variety of immigrant cultures brought to the United States, the immigrants have so changed that any distinctive "ethnicity" is becoming little more than identification with their group of origin. Whether urban or rural, third- and fourth-generation immigrants are becoming parts of subcultural groups which comprise peoples of other ancestry.

A crucial factor in any context is environmental potential for production of cash commodities that are in demand and the possibility of getting the products to market. The demand may have different effects if the product is for a world market or a local market. A few years ago in Japan, tomatoes became a popular item of diet and overproduction followed. The following year, however, the farmers were able to change their crops, thanks to land potentials and in part to government experts in marketing analysis. By contrast, the Tanzanian Kaguru have depended largely upon castor beans grown for a world market. Decreased demand for castor oil brought near disaster, and Indian middlemen suffered as much as the Kaguru. In any case demand, whether national or local, is ineffective if the produce cannot reach a market.

The many factors involved in a national or state context may seem so complex as to defy reduction to cross-cultural formulations. And yet the number of critical factors is not very great. Each context of modernization seems complex because a small number of basic factors may be present in different combinations. A simple formula illustrates this point. If the number of factors of external origin that may enter any context is N and the possible number of combinations of these factors ranges from any one to several or all, the possible context consists of X factors. X then is $2^N - 1$. In early stages of modernization, N may be a single factor, such as steel axes. If a second factor is introduced, such as horses, the context may consist of the first, the second, or both—a total of three possible combinations. If the situation may include one, two, three, four, or any combinations of five factors, the total number of possibilities is 31, and if there may be ten possible factors, X is increased to 1,023.

This formula is cited solely to illustrate that the task of determining essential factors may not be nearly as difficult as the variety of contexts suggests. It cannot, however, be used to quantify studies of change or applied directly in any way to problems discussed herein for several cogent reasons. First, the factors are not comparable and therefore not amenable to equations. For example, colonial laws, steel axes, production of cash crops, missions, and improved health are very unlike phenomena. Second, single factors cannot be assumed to be identical simply because they bear a common label. Education, for example, is very different among the Malay, whose formal training is largely religious, the Kipsigis, whose schooling is essentially practical, and the Japanese, who have very advanced education. Third, some seemingly distinguishable factors may actually be different facets of a single factor. Thus, plantation labor where native land has been expropriated and where the native population had already reached its subsistence limits may be inseparable facets of a particular pattern of production, land use, and recruitment of a labor force. Fourth, the effect of any factor may differ in total contexts. Cash production for an outside market has had a far deeper effect in Japan, where there is a highly developed economy and transportation system, than among the Kaguru of Tanzania, who have poor land resources, a limited, external market, and an inadequate network of roads. The effect of cash production will also differ in situations where market crops may be varied according to local demands from those where world markets for such crops as castor beans, coffee, or rubber are beyond local control. Moreover, since the former crops are usually foods whereas many of the latter are not edible, the local community may be unable to consume its export crop. A few crops, such as rice, are notable exceptions. Fifth, a certain factor may be a precondition of particular subsidiary factors and processes, although not all of these may accompany it. Thus missionization may seek to introduce religion, education, health measures, new land use, and technologies, but which of these takes effect depends upon the local situations.

An important but imponderable factor or aspect of the context is the goal of directed change. This is difficult to assess because, although all colonies and states are guided by policies, the specific goals change with the years and they are usually modified in some degree by necessity, so that ad hoc solutions replace avowed plans. The goals of indirect and direct rule have often been contrasted, but their differences are often fictitious and their outcomes may not be very different. The early Spanish encomienda was in theory a system of indirect rule and exploitation, but it was quickly replaced by a system of privately owned haciendas. In order to maintain an alleged system of indirect rule, the British had to appoint chiefs where they did not exist. The result today in East Africa is independence and increasing nationalization of formerly foreign-owned plantations under the rule of a few individuals who had exceptional education. In Indonesia the Dutch system of direct rule had about the same outcome. The state achieved independence and confiscated foreign-owned wealth.

These observations are not intended to compare all kinds of colonialism, let alone trace the historical development of the different policies. The contrasts, however, place the present exposition in better perspective. While all of our areas except Japan had been colonial within the past century or two, specific local factors in part determined the nature of colonialism. Spain's elimination of the Inca emperor in Peru at first entailed minimal changes in local villages, owing partly to the dense population which could not retreat, as the Indians of the Amazon did, partly to the goal of extracting mineral wealth, and partly to the permissive nature of Catholic proselytization. So long as wealth was forthcoming, the practices of community life, including minor religious beliefs, were tolerated. In other colonies, and later in the Spanish colonies, various means of binding labor to produce wealth were adapted to the local situation. These means included discriminatory practices, inducements, and, in land-poor areas, lack of alternative.

3. MECHANISMS AND AGENCIES THAT MEDIATE CHANGE

The mechanisms of change in the contemporary world differ qualitatively in many ways from those which operated in the primitive or tribal world. Aboriginal societies influenced one another through intermarriage, visiting, trade, joint ceremonialism, warfare, and other kinds of social interaction. Today traditional societies are modified by factors in the context of modern states, which requires mediating agencies, in addition to the give and take of social interaction of different ethnic groups.

It is entirely inadequate to think of a contact community in the contemporary world as one in which the native and alien segments of the population freely intermingle and exchange cultural traits. Such exchange occurs only to a very limited degree and is a minor factor in the transformation of native societies. The community of alien rulers and owners of land and other wealth is normally segregated socially and territorially. It rules with the support of courts and police; it introduces new technologies, occupations, laws, and religions; and it holds a superordinate position. The native peoples may imitate (borrow or adopt) dress and other particulars of the foreign culture for prestige reasons, although most borrowed traits require some cash income, and they may be forced to change some of their behavior. More important, however, the native populations are potentially exposed to a set of state-level institutions, which are mediated to them in a number of ways.

The agencies and mechanisms of modernization include both individual persons, who represent outside institutions, and impersonal situations which result from these institutions. Among the former are government officials, including a hierarchy of administrators, civil servants, policemen and courts who enforce laws, traders who give the people access to a market economy, specialists in such fields as health, farming, engineering, and education, missionaries who are variously effective in transmitting religious ideologies, schooling, and health practices, and others. Impersonal agencies which afford potentials for change include the presence of markets, a system of internal transportation that may include highways and vehicles ranging from bicycles to trucks and railroads, and external contacts through steamships and airplanes. Another important agency may be a national language or lingua franca and mass media of communications, which encourage a better informed population and a national outlook. These agencies usually become effective, however, owing to the efforts of individuals, such as economists, merchants, planners and operators of transportation, publishers, and teachers.

The effectiveness of these agencies in introducing change is partly a function of the local potentials for supporting new practices, such as cultivation of cash crops. It also depends somewhat upon the level of sociocultural integration of the native society. A society whose largest permanent unit was the individual family, as among the Nevada Shoshoni, could adopt new practices that entailed interfamily cooperation and adjustments to outside institutions because there were no band, community, or tribal structures that might require modification. Among other North American Indians, such as the Pueblo, strong community institutions together with isolation on reservations retarded change and assimilation into local segments of American rural life.

A corollary of the differences in levels of sociocultural integration between societies is the differences within societies. Within complex states the national-level institutions generally change most readily, the community with more resistance, and the family most slowly. In Peru, for example, factors have transformed the national context through several major culminations while the community and family have retained more traditional culture. Similarly, Japan's national culture has acquired the institutions of an industrial democracy although the farm communities retain many traditional features and the rural families are even more conservative. As both nations become industrialized or modernized in their state-level institutions, however, an increasing number of agencies become effective in mediating factors of change down to the family level. Changes resulting from the exposure of the basic biological or nuclear family to the many outside agencies are becoming very evident in the United States and in Europe.

There are several rough categories or types of situations which facilitate the effectiveness of somewhat different kinds of mediating agencies and mechanisms. First, there are traditional societies which have remained on their own lands and are influenced mainly by personal representatives of the government and other outside institutions. Second, there are missions which usually serve as transitional points between the traditional and the new. Third, there are alien-owned and controlled commercial enterprises, such as plantations, cattle ranches, mines, and others, which constitute subcontexts of modernization and have their own tightly controlled mechanisms of change. Fourth, there are urban centers which afford a great variety of opportunities and mediating agencies, according to the nature and functions of the city, which have neighborhoods or subcommunities that may perpetuate some ethnic distinctiveness, and which create various networks of interpersonal relationships.

Most of our field studies dealt with the first type or category of societies which are rural, agrarian, locally oriented, traditional, and reside on their own lands. Although some of these societies have lost a portion of their lands to representatives of colonial powers and some of their members have moved out into new contexts, our studies describe mainly the changes that have occurred among the remaining or residual peoples. The various modernizing factors that are present as potential influences in the state context are mediated, according to local circumstances, principally by individuals who work among and often live close to the native society but are not genuine members of it.

The number and effectiveness of these agents range from near zero among the Kayah of Burma to a vast complex of governmental representatives in Japan. In some instances, such as the Anaguta of Nigeria and the Malay of Pasir Puteh, many agents are available to the people, but the societies have not reached the breakthrough point where they actively seek their help. The Kipsigis in East Africa have, owing to local conditions of environment and proximity of Europeans, made far greater use of outside agencies than the isolated Kaguru. The Kipsigis' potential for producing food crops for local European towns and plantations ensured them a much better income. While there was little personal interaction between the Europeans and Kipsigis, except during official contacts, the latter could observe and covet some of the amenities of European life. Complete emulation of the Europeans, however, was severely curtailed—even had the Kipsigis desired it—by their restricted incomes. To some extent, moreover, the Kipsigis' productive activities were also limited by government decree, as in the prohibition against owning European breeds of milk cows and the limitation of tea production to two acres per farmer.

Missions are generally agencies which afford training for life outside the traditional society, although permanent residents may tend to collect around mission stations. The effects of missions should not be underestimated. In Latin America many of the fifteenth- and sixteenth-century missions, which were subsequently abandoned, introduced not only a large number of religious beliefs but also new crops, livestock, crafts, and social practices. Notable practices which survive today, two centuries after missionization, are cults of saints, a socio-religious calendar which is based partly upon Catholic holy days and gives prominence to cofradias or brotherhoods, and a system of compadrazgo or co-godparents. Today, Catholic missions in many areas give initial training in the elements of education as well as religious instruction. Seventh Day Adventists are outstanding throughout the world for their medical aid and training in crafts. Individuals who have lived at any mission station for a number of years usually do not wish to return to their native societies and in many cases would not be welcomed by them.

Between the land-owning native society and the various kinds of people who have been resettled or who have gone voluntarily to plantations there are many intergradations. Extreme cases of forced dislocation were the Spanish repartimientos of colonial Latin America, whose communities were moved and settled elsewhere. Slavery was even more extreme. Somewhat less drastic dislocation occurred where the need for money to pay taxes forced individuals to work for fairly short periods on plantations or other European-owned enterprises. Expropriation of lands by foreigners also required that many people enter a wage economy. In all these cases the labor was bound in some degree.

In addition, a desire for the amenities of modern culture led persons to spend months away from home. The result of the increasing importance of cash has been that an ever larger number of individuals, and later whole families, left their home communities to live permanently on plantations.

An important common denominator of most plantations is that people who moved from their traditional lands and societies usually live and work with peoples derived from other societies in single communities where they are subject to many regulations and restrictions but also receive certain benefits. The historic tendency in such contexts seems generally to have been that they began with self-contained estates, such as early haciendas, where the owner supplied subsistence plots, manufactured clothing, and other necessities, gave medical care, and often constructed a church. In more recent years the owner— frequently a corporation—has provided schools, recreation, housing, and other facilities. Many extremely modernized enterprises today are devoted to a monocrop, employ the latest technology, give wages in lieu of subsistence plots and other benefits, and operate on a strict cost-accounting basis with maximum efficiency. The laborers now become a proletariat who meet their own needs with what they can earn, and the owner-worker relationship is depersonalized.

In the subcontext of the various kinds of plantations and haciendas, such as those reported for Peru (see Miller, 1967) and Puerto Rico (Steward *et al.*, 1956), the agencies and mechanisms of change are fairly fixed and compulsory. Whether the workers are transient migrants or permanent residents, they have little choice but to conform to housing, diet, wages and hours, managerial decisions, and even such peripheral matters as recreation, schooling, and health care. Whether ties with the home village and a sense of ethnic distinctiveness linger among permanent residents is probably a function of time—a minimum of three generations.

But additional national factors may be mediated to the workers on modern plantations. Organizers may introduce labor unions. Education and contact with other wage earners together with a weakened sense of allegiance to their traditional tribal or village culture may implant a national outlook and new aspirations. The plantation, then, may constitute an even greater step than the mission toward fuller participation in national life.

The initial drift of rural people to these modern estates or plantations has various motivations, but wages are the main inducement. Cash is needed to pay taxes, purchase food, and acquire such items as cloth, sewing machines, bicycles, steel tools, and various prestige goods. As in the case of migrants even from foreign countries to the United States—for example, Chinese, Italians, and others—the initial goal may be to earn money and return home. In the end, however, an increasing number of migrants become permanently separated from their native communities and land, and they are intensively exposed to a set of agencies and processes that assimilate them to a new kind of subculture. The mechanisms that mediate change on the plantation are far more compelling than those that mediate change on the native lands.

Both kinds of land use—native holdings and plantations—may exist side by side, facilitating the transition of surplus population from one to the other. The White Highlands of Kenya consisted of large European plantations that produced mainly coffee, tea, and wheat. On their private land the Kipsigis grow truck garden crops for local consumption. Although they adjoin some 30,000 acres expropriated by tea plantations, colonial law had limited their tea lands to two acres. But in

Tanzania workers traveled hundreds of miles to spend a few months on the plantations of sisal and other monocrops. Malayan rice paddies are interspersed among rubber plantations, where the people can earn extra cash. The Malays produced some rubber on their own lands, but it was very limited in quantity and inferior in quality.

The Yaqui and Mayo have retained ethnic identity, but they were resettled by the government on ejidos, or farm cooperatives. Economically, these Indians were caught up in a situation that was as compulsory as the plantations. Once a member of an ejido, the individual could not escape the government's managerial controls or the debts for farm machinery and other costs. At the same time, the comparative isolation of ejidos has prevented extensive association with other farm populations of the area, especially with those now involved in great irrigation projects, and with urban peoples. The Yaqui and Mayo have retained much of their traditional social and religious culture, which is a blend of aboriginal features and seventeenth-century mission influence.

In Peru the situations range from fairly isolated, independent, traditional highland communities, which are only now being influenced by outside agencies, through hacienda workers, who are traditional in their use of subsistence plots but modified through wage employment on the hacienda, to landless, migrant, coastal plantation workers, who are subjected to a strong complex of modernizing influences.

The notable exception to these great contrasts in the native land-owning and plantation components of the rural societies is Japan. Owing to her incredibly efficient farm productivity together with great industrial development, Japan's farms average about two acres. There has never been loss of land to foreigners through conquest since the empire was founded, nor development of plantations. The largest holding in 1958 was a corporate-owned estate in the Tohoku district of the north. The agencies of modernization in Japan are so numerous and effective that the nation as a whole must be considered increasingly more urban than rural.

Our project did not include studies of urbanization, although many individual families from the societies investigated had drifted to urban situations. Various published studies (e.g., Southall and Gutkind, 1956; Lewis, 1961) suggest that urban contexts differ from rural and plantation situations in two principal respects. First, the unskilled, illiterate individuals who migrate to the city (educated migrants are an exception) more often than not initially enter slums and acquire a "culture of poverty," as Lewis calls it. Like migrants to the plantations, some retain ties with their native communities and perpetuate those aspects of native culture that can be supported in the city. But the vastly greater number of new occupations, roles, and statuses in the city eventually complete the process of detribalization or loss of functional linkage with the society of origin, and immigrants lose more and more of their ancestral ethnicity as they merge into the many kinds of subcultural groups. Second, because the city, unlike the traditional rural community or even the plantation, consists of many partially unlike subsocieties, a structured system of interactions is created.

In addition to the unskilled workers who enter slums in cities, there are, as I have suggested before (Steward *et al.*, 1956), many who may follow avenues of skills into urban environments. A general skill is literacy, and as Winter and Beidelman (1967) point out in Tanzania, secondary education, difficult as it is to obtain, enables native people to find positions as teachers, clerks, and other lower- and middle-class occupations in the towns. The same is true in Malaya. In most areas technicians, such as mechanics, may find a place in a city or in some part of the larger society outside their own community. In Peru, as discussed subsequently, skills gained on haciendas may help toward employment on plantations or other occupations including those of cities. Japan's large-scale education and opportunities for social and occupational mobility have entailed a massive movement of rural populations into urban and industrial centers. Most American Indians of the United States who have left their reservations are educated, owing to the federal school systems on their reservations, but their eventual adjustment remains to be seen. During recent years they have gone to cities in increasing numbers. Finally, highly trained persons from foreign countries have everywhere added to urban populations.

But there are slums of impoverished, disorganized, and unskilled people throughout the world. One has only to visit such slums as those which are growing in San Juan, Puerto Rico, in Hong Kong, in Singapore, in Harlem and Chicago, in Kampala, Uganda, in Nairobi, Kenya, in Beirut, and even in Kyoto to recognize the lot of the untrained in overpopulated areas. It may require many generations for such persons to become assimilated into any clearly structured segment of the larger society, for their population increase seems to offset and often to outdistance the processes that have brought about adjustments. In many areas, moreover, the acquisition and employment of skills by persons leaving their own communities are severely retarded by the attitudes which prevail in a multiple society. The greater potential mobility in Peru is partly enhanced by comparative weakness of racial prejudice. In Puerto Rico segregation is virtually absent, but the excess population is either crowded into slums on the island or it entered the United States to face difficulties similar to those confronted by American Negroes. Those who, like the Batak of Sumatra which Bruner has described, have adjusted to an urban environment while retaining ties with their rural communities of origin are fortunate.

How rapidly the urban context affects the immigrants depends upon many factors, including the levels of native culture brought into this context. Where community institutions are carried by immigrants, as in the case of the several Chinatowns or the Greeks of Tarpon Springs of the United States, loss of traditional culture is retarded. Perpetuation of the native language, a system of writing, schools, religion, and other community-level features, racial distinctiveness, and segregation by neighborhood buffer the effects of their new environment. When individual families migrate to towns where they cannot speak the language, a phase of disorganization tends to precede reorganization and integration into the urban structure. The rate of reintegration depends upon additional factors, including proximity to the community of origin.

It would be futile to attempt to assess the extent to which change anywhere is directed by creating factors and agencies in the contexts or is permissive. The state usually encourages change but does not always require it. Even those attempts to enforce change may have consequences far beyond their narrow intent. In the British colonies the central authority largely eliminated tribal wars, which in turn encouraged certain innovations. The Kaguru of Tanzania were able to shift their settlements to more fertile areas and to increase their production without fear of raids. Owing mainly to the Indians, who were the middlemen and entrepreneurs, they could market their castor beans and purchase hardware, cloth, ornaments, sewing machines, bicycles, and a limited number of other items. Their involvement in a market economy, however, was largely permissive, and it was limited by their poor lands and their isolation. Even a moral factor seems to have affected their productive activities, for after the disastrous failure of the government's "Operation Ground Nut" (peanuts) in this area, the possible production of tobacco was reported to have been discouraged by the missionaries. On the other hand, missions afforded one of the main opportunities for education. Remoteness from towns and poor roads, however, discouraged many agencies which were effective in other areas.

4. PROCESSES AND CULMINATIONS

Processes have been defined for present purposes as the ways in which factors in the social context, especially factors of alien origin within the colonial or national context, operate to bring about transformations in the traditional society. There is no one-to-one correlation between a factor, the mediating agency, and a process. Single factors may initiate several processes, while different factors may set off similar processes. The important point is that as any process brings about change, its evolutionary effects extend far beyond anything contained in the originating factor. Thus involvement of a society in a market economy through various agencies may eventuate in individualization of productive effort and of ownership of the means of production, which a market economy alone does not require or anticipate. Even when culture change is strongly directed toward particular goals, very unexpected processes and effects are usually encountered.

A necessary complement of process is culmination, for any process is recognizable in part by its consequences. When change is incipient, its nature is somewhat conjectural. It must have become sufficiently effective that its future course may be projected with some degree of certainty. To illustrate the point again with trade, the early exchange of a small amount of local produce for manufactured goods may give little indication of the ultimate effect of complete dependency upon an outside market. One may venture a forecast by examining in retrospect what has occurred among other societies where the same process has run its course or culminated. But any projection of trends based on other cases must be speculative because any process ordinarily operates in conjunction with other processes and is conditioned by special factors. Trade of such natural products as rubber or furs, as in the Amazon and Canada respectively, may have different consequences than trade of agricultural products, and commercial farming itself may take many forms. In each case the particular process is recognizable only when it approaches culmination.

The importance of recognizing culmination as an inherent attribute of process is further underlined by the fact that over long periods of time qualitatively new processes may be introduced before older ones have culminated. Thus early state formation in much if not all of nuclear America seemingly resulted from the interaction of augmented food production, increase and stabilization of population aggregates, and development of theocratic controls. The process of state expansion through military conquests probably began before the theocratic states had culminated, but conquest eventually superseded earlier wars fought to capture sacrificial victims, and became a major determinant of the enlargement and consolidation of states into empires. Most of the various processes of state formation differed qualitatively from those which operated among egalitarian tribal societies in other ways. Internal differentiation created separate classes of rulers, food producers, artisans, and specialists. Such processes were initiated independently in many areas by the agricultural revolution; they were later supplemented and partly supplanted by processes arising from

the industrial revolution, and today they are augmented by automation.

These processes are designated "evolutionary" because they induce
changes or transformations in the native society which are not adopted
from external sources. In those cases where the change is abrupt,
drastic, and disruptive, perhaps they may best be designated "revolutionary," although there are many intergradations between
gradual or orderly transformations and violent disorganization, which
precedes reorganization. Which term is employed in any case is largely
a matter of semantics, but forcibly directed change, loss of lands, or
shift of populations to new settlements, to plantations, or to urban
centers seems frequently to entail a break in a people's continuity with
its past. Accommodation and adjustment to radically new situations too
often follow a period of social and cultural disruption.

Designation of processes as evolutionary also implies that they are
independently generated in each case by similar factors. It cannot be
stressed too strongly, however, that my use of "evolution" does not
imply that any change, including modernization, must follow identical
stages everywhere. To the contrary, similarity of evolutionary change
will result only when the factors, processes, and effects are identical.
The nature of the society subject to certain processes will partly affect
the course of change. Our data strongly indicate, however, that very
dissimilar societies may be affected in strikingly similar ways, provided
one can judge whether the process has culminated rather than remaining incipient. There are, nonetheless, many lines of early and modern
evolution, and a high degree of similarity is recognizable among societies within each line. That is to say, the greatly varied changes among
native societies are probably reducible to a fairly limited number of
evolutionary categories provided they are viewed in the cause-and-
effect terms of processes and their consequences.

Since the many recent writings on cultural evolution ascribe it many
meanings, I would willingly substitute some other term in order to
avoid possible misunderstanding. I apply it to modernization, as I have
applied it in the past to earlier culture change, as a concept of multilinear evolution principally because there is a recent tendency in social
science to recognize the limitations of the earlier view of modernization
among native peoples as diffusion and borrowing from the West and
acculturation and assimilation to Western culture. The following section will examine the inadequacy of the early concepts more closely.

EVOLUTIONARY VERSUS HISTORICAL PROCESSES

The earlier American view of any cultural change, including modifications of native societies in contact with Western or industrial nations,

postulated that the basic process was diffusion or borrowing. It is of course true that innumerable traits of culture have extremely wide distributions, which indicates that they have been transmitted from one society to another. To designate the underlying processes as diffusion and borrowing (adoption would be a better term for the latter since no trait can be considered borrowed if it is not to be returned) implies a rather mechanical operation which lacks preconditions or consequences. It fails to distinguish the various mechanisms of so-called diffusion, it does not identify the kinds of features which may be transmitted by these different mechanisms, and above all it pays no attention to the possible internal processes that may be generated by the adoption of an alien trait.

The traditional concept of diffusion is most applicable to minor items or small bits of culture—to culture elements or traits, which anthropologists used to list and map. The effect of diffusion upon any society was, according to this concept, merely cumulative. Through intertribal contacts, the cultural inventory of a society was augmented by the adoption of elements or element complexes.

Culture history became based upon the concept of the culture area, which is a territory of similar distributions of elements, and age-area interpretations, which postulated centers of creativeness of elements and marginal areas to which few elements diffused.

Diffusion and borrowing lacked several crucial concepts for understanding cultural change. First, an element even so simple as a domesticated plant, pottery, or a religious belief is not borrowed simply because it is available in a neighboring society. Adoption has many preconditions. Acquisition of domesticated plants presupposes an environment suitable for their cultivation and perhaps other factors, such as absence of equally productive natural resources. Pottery of simple kinds has been made by seminomadic peoples, but ceramics cannot play an important role without the preconditions of a reasonably settled life, availability of clays, and need for various forms of pots. Religious beliefs of fundamental importance are not adopted unless they are reasonably congruent with the general world view or are reinterpreted by the local society.

Many items may be adopted without important preconditions—e.g., minor art motifs, games, ceremonial details—but these are trivia in that they are dispensable. The society may take or leave them.

Second, alien features of culture are not simply diffused and adopted in an abstract sense. They are passed along through various mechanisms. Some features, such as useful technologies, may be acquired through observation and imitation. In the case of plant and animal domesticates, the people must come into actual possession of specimens and know what to do with them. A clan system may be introduced through intermarriage, provided the preconditions are suitable. Basketry and pottery techniques, art designs, and other elements may also be transmitted through intermarriage or by other means. Trading facilitates the adoption of many kinds of material objects, provided the techniques for making them are not too difficult. Patterns of warfare may be spread by a kind of chain reaction, each society forcing hostilities of particular kinds upon its neighbors. A typology of the kinds of diffusion might have some value, especially if it were to pay attention to the individual agents and mechanisms by which various aspects of culture are transmitted, but inadequacies would still remain.

A third inadequacy of conceiving diffusion in the traditional way is that the processes generated by diffused or adopted traits are not taken into account. Increase of the cultural inventory by adopted traits does not necessarily disclose internal transformation of the society. Important transformations or evolutionary changes are produced by processes which follow the incorporation of certain crucial traits. The adoption of efficient fishing gear may lead to the utilization of previously neglected rich sea or riverine resources and so increase the size and stability of populations that great social modifications ensue. Adoption of plant and animal domesticates may initiate an incipient phase of increased productive efficiency and eventually lead to the development of great civilizations and states. These social transformations resulted largely from internal evolutionary processes. They did not spread except by conquest or migration. Diffusion will continue to operate, but it adds only superficial accoutrements to the basic structures, such as placing temples on mounds or use of the plumed serpent motif.

There are two broad categories of processes which follow the adoption of alien traits and features: cultural-ecological adaptations and social adaptations. The first includes the kinds of social interaction and cooperation that are appropriate to the exploitation of any given natural environment by means of a special inventory of tools and techniques. The second relates to such modification of a particular society as may be required by its adaptive interactions with neighboring societies. As man's control over nature increases and modern civilizations develop, technology increasingly shapes the natural environment while the processes of adaptation to the complex social environment become more important determinants of change. Vogt (1960) believes that in cultural development values play an increasing role. This, however, need not obviate the possibility of ascertaining determinants, although it complicates the problem.

The fourth inadequacy of the concept of diffusion is that it fails to take into account the significant levels of sociocultural integration, which have special importance in the present context. In tribal society community-level institutions may be affected by processes created by social interaction or diffusion of various kinds from neighboring societies. Family-level institutions are not necessarily greatly changed, although the family members participate in community affairs. In modern societies, state-level institutions constitute a supracommunity complex of factors which affect the community and individual family only as they are intermediated to them in ways previously discussed.

Most of the basic factors of a modernizing context are introduced from the outside, but few of them constitute an inventory of traits which a native society might borrow. Such state- or colonial-level institutions as political and legal systems, law enforcement, markets, religious organizations, transportation and communications, and education are not simple, discrete culture elements. The influences of these features penetrate local societies in ways which depend upon how they are mediated and upon many local factors.

These points will be clearer in the light of the substantive field analyses reported here. At present, a few examples will elucidate my point. Even the diffusion of a simple culture element such as European dress to a native society requires access to cloth, which the society may not manufacture, and thus it has the additional precondition of the means of buying cloth. But it may also entail imitation of Europeans, which in turn rests upon incentives to change. The motivation may be prestige value, if a general European way of life including clothing has acquired appeal, or such clothing may simply be more efficient for some purposes. In industrial plants of Japan, European clothing is simple and safe. In business and office situations the Japanese wear European clothing as part of a Western way of life, but they change to kimonos in their homes. Clothing may also be adopted even though the people do not want it, as in the tropics, where missionary or governmental authorities insist upon "decency." In the case of clothing, then, at least three kinds of diffusion may be involved: prestige, efficiency, and compulsion. And each depends upon preconditions.

Change in style of clothing, however, is more the effect than the cause of the adoption of other features of culture. It probably initiates no processes of internal change. In other cases, very different mechanisms and processes are involved, and "diffused" features may have far-reaching consequences. Most primitive societies adopt—that is, trade for—steel tools, containers, and other hardware which they cannot manufacture because these industrial products are more efficient than their own equivalents. This borrowing, too, has preconditions, such as commodities which can be produced locally or cash from wages or from sales of commodities. The sale of local products is commonly accomplished in the early phases of contact through an individual trader. Once the people become dependent upon the larger society, certain processes of internal economic change may be initiated, although these are in no sense part of the trade situation. That is, these consequences clearly do not result from diffusion as conventionally understood. Societies which may sell natural products through a trader or a market may become so dependent upon their commerce that they cease to produce their own foods and must purchase what they eat. The productive and consuming corporate unit is reduced to the nuclear family. Many Amazon tribes have fragmented into family units which trade wild rubber for manioc, which they formerly grew, and for other outside goods. Most of the Tsimshian and Tlingit Indians of the Northwest Coast have given up preserving salmon and now sell their catch to the canneries, where they live in slum-like shacks. When the fishing season is over, they buy canned salmon from their employers. These transformations and dependencies upon the larger society were in no way planned or intended when the rubber traders or salmon canners set up their businesses. Among the Moenkopi Hopi Indians, Shuichi Nagata (ms.) reports that recent emphasis upon cattle raising, private ownership of recently irrigated lands, and access to wage labor has created a strong trend toward substitution of the nuclear family for the matrilineage as the corporate unit—a trend that was not at all planned by the Bureau of Indian Affairs.

These remarks bring us to a consideration of the inadequacy of the concepts of "acculturation" and "assimilation" as means of understanding the impact of the Western or industrial world upon native societies. The earliest formulation of "acculturation" by Redfield, Linton, and Herskovits in 1936 was based upon the concept of borrowing or diffusion of culture elements. Western society was the giver, native societies the receivers. As elements of the native cultural inventory were replaced by Western traits and as the cumulative effect of borrowed features became overwhelming, the native culture collapsed or succumbed to westernization. The people were then said to have been assimilated. The limitations of this original concept of acculturation were pointed out from time to time, and in 1954 a Social Science Research Council Seminar defined acculturation as change initiated by the conjunction of two or more cultural systems as contrasted with change within only one of these systems. Murphy (1964) argues that there have been few wholly autonomous systems and that there is no essential difference in the kinds of change initiated by the interaction of simple societies with one another or of such societies with complex states.

My previous contention that all so-called borrowing, regardless of the nature of the social contacts, involves internal processes of change supports Murphy's argument. If "acculturation" were to distinguish change in modern times from that in antiquity, it would also have to specify the qualitatively new factors in the modern contexts and processes. It cannot be doubted that new qualities are emerging in modern world culture. The difficulty in applying the criterion of newness is largely in knowing where to draw the line. The history of culture is marked by the constant appearance of new factors and processes of change and of culminations of their effects. A baseline might be the industrial revolution, which created so many new factors, but there is no more reason to consider that acculturation started at this point than at the beginning of the agricultural revolution, or the urban revolution, or at any time during the paleolithic period.

At all times in cultural history, change has been brought about through certain internal transformations that follow the consequences of contact with other societies and include the adoption of traits and practices which initiate evolutionary processes. The processes imply much more than has been contained in the concept of acculturation. If acculturation is to embrace these processes, it is applicable at all times and places, and cannot be restricted to contemporary situations.

The concept of assimiltation is no less inadequate than diffusion, and it must be carefully qualified. A society is gradually, sometimes rapidly, transformed by a number of processes. Its acquisition of alien features has many preconditions and often profound consequences. But no society is assimilated to Western or industrial culture merely through cumulative adoption of Western culture elements. It is assimilated in a very different sense. First, it becomes linked with and affected by state-level institutions in many ways, and it accommodates to other segments of the larger society through various networks of inter-relationships. Second, it may completely lose its ethnic identity and become more literally assimilated to a particular subsociety or sub-cultural segment of the larger society, such as farmers of different kinds, types of laborers, members of various middle classes, and so on.

SOME PROCESSES OF MODERNIZATION

The literature abounds in implicit statements of processes of change. In fact, nearly all analyses of contemporary societies, even when presented without any historic depth, disclose pressures and influences which are now modifying the society. Analyses which are avowedly diachronic and pay major attention to change through time, however, rarely attempt to isolate processes which may have operated cross-culturally. There are a few notable exceptions, but most analyses deal with very general processes.

The classic statement of postulated cross-cultural processes is Redfield's threefold effect of an urban society upon a folk society: individualization, disorganization, and secularization (Redfield, 1941). Redfield's thesis has been highly stimulating and provocative, but it infers the processes of urbanization from a comparison of four communities of Yucatán which range from the Indian, or ideal folk community, to Mérida, the city. More recently, studies by sociologists and anthropologists have paid attention to segments of urban populations. Anthropologists have been especially interested in peoples from primitive, tribal, and traditional rural societies who are comparatively new migrants to the cities. Since the urban center has been regarded throughout history as the locus or "container of civilization," it clearly exposes its residents to a very large number of modernizing factors and processes.

Urban contexts, however, are not identical. The strongly class-structured cities of antiquity permitted the lower classes little upward mobility. There were classes of artisans, but scientific and technological knowledge changed so slowly that it was passed on through families or guilds. Such knowledge today necessitates more and more education, which in turn has made upward mobility inevitable and society very fluid. Moreover, there are more kinds of towns and cities today. A manufacturing town, a university community, and a religious center, for example, may have different agencies and processes of modernization. Urbanization, therefore, is a modernizing process of a very general nature. It may include processes peculiar to different types of cities, and it may share processes with rural areas.

Another characteristic of modern society is the increasing number of situations in which behavior is prescribed but does not constitute a profound or distinctive part of an individual's culture. The conceptualization of the various segments of contemporary cities and states as subsocieties means that their ethnic differences are blurred. All subsocieties are subject to national laws and influences generally, and they usually have a common national language. In addition, they intermingle in the church, the baseball park, the theater, on the street and highway, and so forth, where they conform to implicit rules or to legal requirements. This too is part of culture, but I have called it "situational culture" (Steward, 1956). As social and territorial mobility increases, exposure to the many kinds of situational culture tends to create uniformity.

Within nations, such as the United States, the amount of shared behavior, goals, and ambitions has so increased that an almost depressing uniformity is permeating all segments of society. There are still racial barriers to opportunity, some differences between economic roles and statuses, and vestiges of ethnic background which are becoming more symbolic than real. It would be impossible to place all the social segments in some classificatory system according to clear criteria. There are differences between the segments, but assignment of any segment to some definite taxonomic niche generally raises the virtually unanswerable question of how different is different.

Among native societies, modernizing processes have not run their courses or culminated. Inescapably linked as most of them are with the larger society, sufficient ethnic distinctiveness usually remains to give them a sense of identification. This distinctiveness is usually perpetuated in part by territorial and social isolation and in part by the fact that modernizing processes have rarely culminated.

In order to identify processes which result from different kinds of contexts and are found cross-culturally, though not necessarily universally, we must inquire further into the nature of a process. In general, a process denotes the manner in which change is brought about. It may be recognized in ongoing change, as when the study of a tribe through a period of years shows transformations of land use, land tenure, or social organization. It may be deduced in part from Redfield's kind of age-area approach, wherein differences in a series of communities are assumed to represent stages in the effectiveness of the process, the most remote from the urban center exemplifying the least affected. Or it may be inferred from a purely synchronic analysis of any society which is strongly involved with a larger context and shows characteristics, and often imbalances, which clearly are not traditional.

It happens that terms designating processes commonly terminate with "-ization" or "-ation," but some do not, and it would be awkward to create neologisms in order to make designations of process recognizable in this way. Among a considerable list of general processes, however, there are many terms with such endings: commercialization, proletarianization, missionization, reorganization, education, secularization, factionalization, individualization, disorganization, and urbanization. Since processes are more revealing as they designate smaller and more specific links in a causal chain, it would be helpful to devise terms for the particulars by which the various agencies of change operate. This task, however, leads us to substantive conclusions. The present discussion will be restricted to exemplifications of processes which clarify the theoretical approach and suggest some of the kinds of processes that may be recognized.

It is convenient to begin with Redfield's three principal processes, which, though postulated as the effects of a city upon a simple folk community, have broader implications. In most traditional, primitive, rural communities the individual is normally an integral part of a tightly structured society wherein his relationships to members of his community are dictated by custom. In the city these rural structures and relationships are weakened and may disappear with time. What Redfield did not say about this aspect of urbanization is that the processes of individualization and disorganization, which so frequently mark the first stages of life in the city, are accompanied by the obverse processes of reorganization. The individual may become a member of a neighborhood, an occupational group, a labor union, a club, a status segment of society, and perhaps a church and other special organizations. His life may not be as tightly integrated with people like himself as it was in the native community, but processes of reorganization and reorientation operate in the city. Similarly, secularization means that many aspects of the world of nature, of individual affairs and group destiny, including health, are viewed increasingly in terms of science and medicine rather than of the supernatural. The area ascribed to supernatural influence shrinks, and religious practices and beliefs connected therewith weaken or change in function.

Comparable processes are beginning to operate within rural communities, although their effects differ in some respects from those on the plantation or in the city. As the rural society becomes inextricably and irreversibly involved in a cash or market economy through a general process which may be designated commercialization, individualization of certain features of society may begin. In a society which previously held land in common and granted individual rights on a usufruct basis only as long as the particular plots were cultivated, individuals may begin to claim permanent and transferable rights to the plots. This also involves individualization of productive efforts, and the nuclear family becomes the producing and consuming unit. In time, legal title may be given to individual owners. That such title may conform to European or other alien legal codes does not mean that the practice is simply borrowed from outside sources. Individual ownership would be pointless if the family had not already become the corporate unit owing to the process of commercialization.

Commercialization and individualization have many other manifestations. Erasmus (1956) has shown that cooperative work groups tend to disappear after commercialization has reached the point where the desire for cash makes them an unprofitable luxury. Traditional work groups typically go in succession to the farm lands of each of their members, where the host entertains them in return for their help. Much time is spent in festivities. As the profit motive is strengthened, especially among larger producers of cash crops, workers are hired and paid on an hourly basis. This trend has been noted in all parts of the world, and quite clearly the same processes are involved.

Individualization of economic holdings and productive efforts may have far-reaching effects upon the whole society. Settlements may become dispersed owing to the new kind of land tenure, and clans, lineages, or communities which had been the land-owning units lose an important basis for their cohesion when they no longer control the lands. In addition, community agricultural ceremonialism may weaken as a more scientific understanding of farming is introduced. Secularization, too, tends to introduce a more rational view of meteorology, health, production of wealth, and other matters which had provided the basis for ceremonialism of all kinds and for the world view. Paradoxically, even missionization may remove a large realm of activity, such as health practices, from the supernatural while it attempts to introduce new views about religion. The ceremonialism that survives may become increasingly recreational and social rather than religious in function.

Another process of modernization of native communities is education—a new form of socialization—which provides the people with tools for better commercial transactions, for more effective means of dealing with foreigners, and with the opportunity of acquiring such a wide range of knowledge that their whole outlook is broadened. If the process of education is understood also to include such mass media as newspapers, magazines, and radio, the effect is further to decrease the community's insularity and to implant a national view. Most leaders of the newly emerged nations are persons who acquired advanced education, which itself usually implies extensive travel and a comprehension of matters far outside those of their traditional society.

Variations in the actual effectiveness of particular factors in the social context bring different processes and combinations of processes into operation in different local societies. Frequently, fairly isolated societies become commercialized merely through the presence of trade, and the members of these societies become individualized in productive efforts. Such societies may lack access to education, have no opportunity to travel, produce wealth only by primitive techniques, and retain traditional beliefs about the supernatural, health, and the world around them. Others may be missionized with varying effects upon productive activities, education, and social life and moral attitudes. Permanent residence on a plantation exposes the people very strongly to several processes of change included in the more general process of proletarianization. The initial phases of urbanization may, if the migrants to the city are unskilled and remote from the community of origin, consist of disorganization, which is later followed by special processes of reorganization and reorientation according to many circumstances.

Another general process that usually marks different stages of modernization is factionalization. Divisive trends begin to split the society along lines determined by the effective processes of change. Among the most common factions are the progressives and conservatives, the missionized converts and the so-called "pagans," occupants of different territorial divisions, and nearly always older and younger generations. Factionalism is generated by exposure of segments of the society to such factors and processes as commercial opportunities, education, mission influence, experiences on plantations or in cities, and political ideologies which permeate all societies in the emergence of new nations.

5. SUBSTANTIVE EFFECTS OF MODERNIZATION

The thesis of previous sections has been that modernization is brought about by internal evolutionary processes which are initiated by factors in the larger context, mediated to local societies by various means, and manifested in a variety of sociocultural transformations. The cause-and-effect relationship implied differs from more historical assumptions of diffusion, acculturation, and assimilation. The causality begins with factors in the context which are accepted without inquiry about their ultimate origins. Processes provide the causal links between the contextual factors and the substantive results which are observed in the field research.

Analyses which can isolate out the factors, internal processes, and substantive effects are fraught with many difficulties. Varying degrees of complexity and development of the contexts, distinctions between potential and active processes, recognition of the extent to which processes have culminated, and assessment of the effects of processes upon unlike native or traditional societies make the different cases seem incomparable to one another. Since no case can be tested repeatedly under controlled laboratory conditions, methodology must be adapted to the phenomena. Certain striking similarities, however, are evident within the great variety of cases, and it would be as fallacious to assume that an understanding of causality is completely elusive as to reduce the varied data to a few facile formulations. Some of the methodological precautions deserve special attention.

First, the processes previously discussed are of a highly generalized nature. Individualization, for example, may be applied to many processes such as the effects of urban life upon the family or of commercialization of productive effort upon native land tenure. Individualization is a crude statement of a causal link between several different kinds of factors in the context and their effects. A formulation of causality is more meaningful as it deals with the smaller links and with the particulars of each case. An example previously mentioned is the individualization—i.e. family ownership—of rubber tracts in the Amazon and fur areas in Canada. These fairly simple situations disclose the essential steps, or small links, in the chain of causality. Desire for hardware because of its obvious utility to stone-age people led to exchange of local natural products through a trader. Increasing dependency upon the outside world created an irreversible trend and members of the community became unwilling to share the results of their labor with one another or to allow their headmen to take an unearned share as entrepreneurs. In addition, conservation practices encouraged each family to claim and care for the resources of bounded territories. The culmination of this process was decentralization of community-village or band—and loss of most community endeavors. The single factor of trade gradually transformed self-contained societies into congeries of family units which related to one another and to the larger world mainly through the trader.

A second methodological problem is whether the effects of processes which operate together can be isolated and whether their total effect is merely the sum of each operating alone. This is an empirical question in each case. Many processes, such as the increasing involvement of a society in a cash rationale, seem inexorable in their irreversible trends. But some processes may enhance others, as where education supplements and facilitates the quest for greater cash income. People who lack the means of producing wealth and have no education or skills may turn to wage labor in foreign-owned commercial enterprises. A complex of factors creates the need for cash and determines how a society obtains it. Most processes, it would seem, act somewhat as catalysts upon others.

Third, many processes, especially those which constitute the smaller links, presuppose others. The breakdown of cooperative work groups and the substitution of wage labor presuppose that control of lands has already been individualized and that the profit motive has become an important goal. Out-migration from native communities and lands entails several effects, and it seems usually to have two preconditions: first, desire to earn cash for what it will buy, which may range from bare necessities such as food to satisfaction of acquired tastes, and, second, a shortage of native lands owing to their expropriation by aliens and/or a growing population. Not all people, however, migrate or resettle their communities willingly. There are various government policies of re-settlement which entail particular processes and effects. The massive expropriation of lands and dislocation of the people in the Kikuyu area of Kenya were preconditions of the Mau Mau uprising. In Mexico placement of the Yaqui and Mayo on ejidos has created rather unbreakable financial ties with creditors, much as the company store which has operated on many haciendas and plantations as well as in factory towns has kept the workers perpetually in debt.

Among preconditions of involvement in a money economy, certain steps logically presuppose others. These steps are not universal stages, but they commonly occur. Early contacts of a primitive society with the Western world generally involve direct barter with a trader, unless a system of taxation is immediately imposed upon a conquered society. Exchange through transactions in money, which has symbolic value, is initially viewed with suspicion, and paper money may replace metal coins with difficulty. Many people who are suddenly drawn into a money economy are at first so badly confused that they are readily victimized. A credit economy, which does not necessarily involve cash transactions, is still more difficult to comprehend. Our study of Puerto Rico (Steward *et al.*, 1956) showed that many interior mountain communities had made little use of credit available to them because they did not understand the implications of using their lands as security for loans, of co-signing notes, and other requirements.

So far as these different understandings of the use of money are concerned, any preliterate, subsistence society must undertake difficult steps to make full use of its resources. Manual production of commodities which can be directly traded is not difficult. Deferred rewards wherein a middleman keeps records of credits on his books—and easily cheats the producers—is another matter. Investment in basic capital of production, such as machinery, fertilizer, and other aids, requires more complicated dealings in credit.

A fourth factor which may obscure the effects of processes is perpetuation of form but change in function. A striking case is the Sonjo of the Rift Valley of Tanzania. In the system of men's age-grade societies, a certain age group of Sonjo traditionally went to war. Today, since the area has been pacified and wage labor is available, the age grades are perpetuated but the former warrior group now leaves the community to work. A change of function common to societies of many levels of complexity is the acquisition of recreational functions by religious practices which have been secularized. A religious dance, ceremony, shrine, temple, or rite may lose much of its supernatural significance but be perpetuated because it has recreational and social value. Among the Pueblo Indians much complex ritual today is carried out because it is crucial in supporting social solidarity even while its rain-making, fertility, and curative functions are doubted. In Japan hundreds of thousands of tourists visit the famous shrines and temples as sightseers, whereas only a handful make the trips as truly religious pilgrims. Commercialization of these religious sites has accompanied the recreational functions, for dozens of vendors of foods and souvenirs place stalls outside their gates. The Easter worship at the principal church in San Juan, Puerto Rico, has become an occasion for ostentatious display by the wealthy and for carnival-like celebrations outside the church by lower classes.

Instances in which function rather than structure are modified are so common that they should be designated by a single term, "form-function." Often, too, very unlike traditional forms may acquire the same function. There are, however, limits to the adaptability of traditional forms. A stimulating discussion with the members of the East African Research Institute at Kampala of the possibility that the forty or more clans of the Baganda of Uganda might assume corporate economic functions as commercialization affects this tribe entailed some differences of opinion. It was my own conclusion that while clans might assume new political functions in the modern state, production for profit would make the more skilled, knowledgeable, and enterprising individuals unwilling to share their profits with their innumerable clansmen. Individualization of effort is occurring and is the probable prognosis for the Baganda as well as most societies.

Despite these obvious precautions and qualifications, the modernization of very dissimilar native societies has so many basic resemblances that some order may be found in the confusion. If one views the basic trends of modernization, the number of parallels and convergencies are so great as to suggest that the number of fundamental processes is not large. The formula previously stated for demonstrating how a small number of factors may be combined in a large number of ways in the context $X = 2^N - 1$ is equally illustrative of how a few processes may combine in many ways.

Within the great range of variation of our cases, two important differences must be taken into account. First, a far larger number of factors have entered the context of Japan, as in other industrialized nations, than some of the newly emerging nations. Japan has been able to incorporate more features of the larger, industrial world culture. Second, the effectiveness of potential factors in any given context may range from near zero through varying degrees of culmination.

If Japan still falls somewhat short of other industrial nations in its number of automobiles and roads, television sets and other household appliances, and other material goods, it is rapidly closing the gap. Japan ranks extremely high in the education of all its people, in the development of the sciences and humanities, in rural electrification, in railroad transportation, and in the efficiency of agricultural production. It leads in such fields as ship building, plant genetics, miniaturization, optical equipment, and others. It is highly urbanized. Its farm population constitutes an ever smaller portion of the population while its ties to the cities are making it more suburban. Japan, in short, has a far greater number of factors in its context and active modernizing processes than the newly emerging nations.

The less industrialized and less affluent nations have more restricted contexts, although all are changing with great speed. At the present time, however, the effectiveness of the factors in some cases may remain near zero, as among the Kayah of Burma, whose institutions have scarcely begun to penetrate its isolated societies. In other cases the effectiveness of the potential factors is inhibited not only by isolation of many of the societies but by lack of national wealth. The former colony of Tanganyika had, as Winter points out, an annual budget for all administrative and service purposes smaller than that of the University of Illinois. It is understandable that Tanganyika had few schools, that most of these were primary schools, and that few persons had the means to travel to the limited number of secondary schools which would provide the education necessary for positions outside the native societies. Poor lands, dependency upon an uncertain export crop, and poor roads have retarded complete involvement of these societies in a market economy. The number of individual Kaguru who make their way into the larger society and find a permanent niche in towns is also limited because there are few towns, especially of any size. Tanzania's context at present lacks the wealth to support the great complex of factors which could create a wholly literate society and produce persons accomplished in the sciences, humanities, government and law, and other sophisticated fields. Its societies are entering in varying degrees the early stages of literacy, commercialization, and national awareness.

The situation in Peru contrasts with Tanzania's in important ways. Many native Peruvian communities, especially of the highlands, are traditional mainly in the sense that they have owned or have retained rights to cultivate land on haciendas, but they may make transitional steps toward modernization through several avenues owing to Peru's greater industrial development. The hacienda itself contains many modernizing factors, such as a cash economy, some education, and contacts with national institutions. From the highland hacienda the people may go to the coastal plantations, initially as contract laborers, much as some of the people of Tanzania work for delimited periods on plantations. In Peru, however, a permanent proletarianized population is developing, and this new orientation constitutes a step toward the city.

The processes of modernization, however, would be badly oversimplified if they were thought to become active merely because people had access to them. The Anaguta of Nigeria, whom Diamond (1967) de-

328   *Evolution and Ecology*

scribes as suburban to the European town of Jos, have not responded to the factors of potential change despite their seeming accessibility. The rather static condition and apparent apathy of this tribe raise a number of problems about the hundreds or thousands of other societies which have lost identity and disappeared from history as viable ethnic entities. Loss of traditional culture through proletarianization, as in the case of plantationization, permanent wage labor on other commercial enterprises, or urbanization are common phenomena, but these processes have had little effect upon the Anaguta. Apathy apparently besets many societies which have felt the traumatic effects of sudden and violent impact from the outside world and from disease. The Anaguta experienced both of these, and they had been the victims of slavers before British colonization. Many other societies have suffered similar fates which brought sharp population decline and great social disruption, but they subsequently recovered. Perhaps recovery depends partly upon the size of the society. The large native populations of the aboriginal states and empires of Mexico and Peru initially declined and then reconstituted themselves, whereas many small tribes, such as those which became the "mission Indians" of southern California, were virtually extinct within two generations. The Anaguta are a small society, but they have not yet demised or lost their native culture.

A problem partly related to the last is what factors or features determine the point of breakthrough or the threshold when modernizing processes begin to take effect. Isolation from factors of potential change is an obvious obstacle to modernization. The Kaguru have been described as such a society. Isolation may also be social as well as territorial. The U.S. system of Indian reservations together with racial segregation have greatly retarded change among the Indians. For a number of years during the New Deal of the 1930s, the earlier policy directed toward rapid westernization of the Indians—the period of boarding schools and disposable individual title to lands—was reversed and every effort was made to preserve native culture, or "Indianhood" as John Collier phrased it. These alternating governmental goals, however, seem to have had much less effect than the basic processes. National industrialization entailed greater accessibility of the Indians to outside influences, more education, greater territorial mobility, more job opportunities, and accelerated modernization. In fairly recent years the Indians have begun to find employment off the reservations, aided in some cases by special skills, such as the Iroquois workers on bridges and other high steel construction, and in other cases by sufficient literacy to make their way in towns and cities. There is now a marked drift to the cities, stimulated in part by increasing populations which have put pressures on their lands, but, as in the case of the mass of urban Negroes, complete assimilation of Indians to subcultures or special segments of the city is only rarely accomplished.

A strongly developed multiple society, as in Africa—especially expressed in the apartheid policy of South Africa—and somewhat in Malaya also created social isolation from opportunities. Unlike the Indians of the United States, who constitute less than one percent of the population, the Africans are the overwhelming majority. The multiple society created by colonialism imposed a large number of restrictions upon the native societies, which have dampened their zeal for change and even excluded them from certain pursuits.

In addition to the various obstacles to modernization just examined, there remain inexplicable cases. The great drive of the Kipsigis of Kenya for change contrasts sharply with the comparative indifference of the Malay of Kelantan Province. Both societies have access to roads, plantation employment, markets, and various government services. The present amorphous society and comparative indifference of the Malay to potential factors of change may represent lingering effects of their precolonial status as basic food producers for small sultanates and their Islamic education and traditions, which still place little value upon earning cash. Acquisition of a few metal tools, a rice-husking mill, and very unsuccessful small shops along the highway seem not to have influenced the society very profoundly. Among the Kipsigis, the individualization of all lands, the striving for better education, improved farming, new health measures, and other potential changes are very great. These changes have factionalized the Kipsigis into progressives and conservatives, followers of different leaders, and, above all, into generations. Such divisive trends are much less evident among the Malay, who seem content with the traditional status quo.

Despite all these factors which inhibit the effectiveness of potential processes of change, our comparisons make it obvious that a fairly small number of economic influences have great effect. Different kinds of involvement in a market economy and local potentials for production of wealth repeatedly generate similar processes. These are enhanced or retarded by the traditional culture, by government policies, by a multiple society, by education, by mission training, and by other factors not wholly understood. The very existence of colonies and the factors in their national contexts, however, were initially designed to extract wealth. The native societies have responded to their access to new sources of wealth from the outside, although their responses take several forms and today represent varying stages of culmination.

In the course of modernization, native societies within delimited areas also influence one another through different kinds of social interaction. The basic transformations, however, are caused by internal evolutionary processes which are induced by factors of outside origin.

BIBLIOGRAPHY

DIAMOND, STANLEY
1967. The Anaguta of Nigeria: Suburban Primitives. In *Contemporary Change in Traditional Societies*, vol. 1, ed. J. H. Steward. Urbana: University of Illinois Press. Pp. 361-500.

ERASMUS, CHARLES J.
1956. Culture Structure and Process: The Recurrence and Disappearance of Reciprocal Farm Labor. *Southwestern Journal of Anthropology* 12: 444-469.

KATZ, ELIHU, HERBERT HAMILTON, and MARTIN LEWINE
1963. Traditions of Research of the Diffusion of Innovation. *American Sociological Review* 28: 237-252.

LEWIS, OSCAR
1961. *The Children of Sanchez*. New York: Random House.

MILLER, SOL
1967. Hacienda to Plantation in Northern Peru. In *Contemporary Change in Traditional Societies*, vol. 3, ed. J. H. Steward. Urbana: University of Illinois Press. Pp. 135-225.

MURPHY, ROBERT F.
1964. Social Change and Acculturation. *Transactions of the New York Academy of Sciences*, ser. 2, 6: 845-854.

REDFIELD, ROBERT
1941. *The Folk Culture of Yucatan*. Chicago: University of Chicago Press.

REDFIELD, ROBERT, RALPH LINTON, and MELVILLE J. HERSKOVITS
1936. Memorandum on the Study of Acculturation. *American Anthropologist* 38: 149-152.

SOCIAL SCIENCE RESEARCH COUNCIL SEMINAR
1954. Acculturation: An Exploratory Formulation. *American Anthropologist* 56: 973-1002.

SOUTHALL, A. W., and P. C. W. GUTKIND
1956. *Townsmen in the Making*. East African Studies, no. 9. Kampala, Uganda: East African Institute of Social Research.

SPICER, EDWARD W.
1962. *Cycles of Conquest: The Impact of Spain, Mexico and the United States on the Indians of the Southwest, 1533-1960*. Tucson: University of Arizona Press.

STEWARD, JULIAN H., *et al.*
1956. *The People of Puerto Rico* (with R. A. Manners, E. Padilla, E. R.Wolf, S. W. Mintz, and R. L. Scheele). Urbana: University of Illinois Press.

VOGT, EVON Z.
1960. On the Concepts of Structure and Process in Cultural Anthropology. *American Anthropologist* 62: 18-33.

WINTER, EDWARD, and T. O. BEIDELMAN
1967. Tanganyika: A Study of an African Society at National and Local Levels. In *Contemporary Change in Traditional Societies*, vol. 1, ed. J. H. Steward. Urbana: University of Illinois Press. Pp. 57-203.

PART IV

The American Indian

15

Limitations of Applied Anthropology: The Case of the Indian New Deal

"Limitations of Applied Anthropology" appeared in the first issue of the *Journal of the Steward Anthropological Society* (vol. 1, no. 1, pp. 1-17, Urbana, Ill., 1969) and is reprinted with permission of that publication. The essay appeared during the height of the academic protest against the Vietnam War. Despite a profound moral and political revulsion to that conflict and participation in letters of protest and "teach-ins," Steward was ambivalent about the proper role of the social scientist in such matters. On the one hand he was a citizen, and on the other he had been educated in the tradition of "value-free" and "objective" anthropology taught by Kroeber and Lowie. The struggle between the two, between personal ideals and scientific understanding, is a *leitmotif* of the article, which attempts to present the dilemma as it emerged during the early years of the "Indian New Deal." Steward's views on the relative powerlessness of the social planner may seem unduly pessimistic to many, but they were cast against a perspective that the ways of history are both subtle and powerful, difficult to understand and even more resistant to alteration. This is sound social theory. The originally published article has been edited in the interests of style and continuity.

INTRODUCTION

The contemporary acceleration of the number of social problems and intensification of their seriousness constitute challenges to anthropologists, and to social scientists generally. They raise the question of what, if anything, one may do. There is clearly an increasing number of "concerned" anthropologists, for it is difficult to remain aloof from injustices and crises in the modern world. Yet there is sharp disagreement concerning the proper role of the anthropologist.

One point of view advocates action on the basis of values that one learns from his society and holds as a human being, which in effect calls for abdication of attempts at scientific understanding (Berreman, Gjessing, and Gough, all in *Current Anthropology*, December, 1968). I do not know whether this represents the majority conviction, but its advocates make up in vehemence what they may lack in numbers. Perhaps such admonitions represent "action programs" as distinguished from applied anthropology, since they do not primarily seek to use understanding of culture change and conflict based on social science analysis. Berreman seeks to prove his case by innumerable citations of sociologists who say the same things as he. Gough advocates "revolutionary socialism," apparently on the assumption that since the many activities involved with the CIA and U.S. counterinsurgency efforts are clearly designed to preserve a faulty status quo, anything that causes change will necessarily promote human well-being.

I completely agree with the position stated by Ralph Beals in the same issue of *Current Anthropology* that no matter how imperfect our understanding of cultural transformations may be, the effort to achieve value-free scientific analyses must not be abandoned; abdication of any attempt to approach modern problems through scientific understanding inevitably leads to uncritical support of particular ideologies. A lifetime of research devoted to understanding social evolution or transformations convinces me that, while much remains to be done, mere humanitarianism is a poor guide to action anthropology.

The history of human affairs is marked by repeated catastrophes induced by those who acted on what was generally considered the humanitarian thing to do. As recently as 1887 (Beals, 1968, quoting Helm, 1966) Alice Fletcher in the interest of Indian betterment persuaded the U.S. Congress to pass the Dawes Severalty Act, which led to the rapid sale of reservation lands to whites by the already impoverished Indians. This was not repealed until the New Deal for the Indians in the 1930s, when many Indians were in a far better position to control their own affairs.

There must, however, be a reason why so many anthropologists protest such matters as the Vietnam War, the Dominican affair, U.S. interference in other areas, racial prejudice, and many other contemporary matters. There is, I believe, a set of basic values that are valid cross-culturally and scientifically and that are not merely humanitarian because the sociologists say so. We must remember that before the agricultural revolution nearly all societies had the basic goal of survival. This broad goal contained subsidiary goals such as absence of hunger, pain, and sickness. The crisis areas today are largely those which have not eliminated sickness and hunger despite a world of plenty.

The extent of such dissatisfactions remains to be determined. Added to these are the culturally induced values and the unequal sharing of the surplus goods of the modern technological world. These involve the question of frustration in inability to achieve new kinds of expectations with respect to values that are subjective yet perhaps no less potent than survival values had been. Since the control of surpluses has taken many forms throughout history, the question is whether there are any absolute standards by which to evaluate different societies and to determine whether revolutions are caused by deprivation of survival means or by dissatisfaction in meeting cultural expectations. This has not been answered.

There are limitations to the scientific understanding that anthropology can provide. First, of course, it is limited by lack of adequate attention to human welfare problems, as I attempt to show in this paper. In addition, any manipulation of social change must be done within the context of inevitable trends. When social transformations involve the emergence of qualitatively new phenomena, these cannot be foreseen. To explain them in retrospect has practical value only where they are likely to happen again. Social science becomes a factor in change only when the total complex of forces is understood.

Insight into transformations, however, discloses mounting popular discontent, as today. Therefore, since all cultures are changing, some drastically and by revolutionary means, it is a fair presumption that some intellectuals and anthropologists will recognize and articulate the nature of discontent sooner than others. Indeed, some will become more radical than the masses.

The present paper describes changes in federal policy and the role of anthropologists in the Indian Reorganization Act, or the New Deal for the Indian, of 1934. But the implications of these experiences are not restricted to any single time or social group. They are offered because they demonstrate many of the basic problems encountered in any kind of social betterment program.

The Indian New Deal was extraordinarily humanitarian in motivation and more revolutionary than anything in prior U.S. policy, but it was largely unsuccessful because good intentions were insufficient. It gave anthropologists their first major opportunity to participate in the formation and implementation of policy, but it also found them unequipped with relevant knowledge. It induced frustration, and the major problems are still unsolved today. Above all, it raises the question of whether events could have turned out differently.

I offer no final answer, hoping merely to provoke thought on the basic issues.

THE NEW DEAL FOR THE INDIANS

In 1934 Congress passed the Wheeler-Howard Bill, or Indian Reorganization Act, which not only sought to eliminate the errors and injustices of the former policy of assimilation to American society but to recreate native cultures. The principal guidelines of the New Deal for the Indians were drawn by the late John Collier (1884-1968), who had fought for justice to the Indian as Secretary of the American Indian Defense Association after 1923 and had been appointed Commissioner of Indian Affairs under Interior Secretary Harold Ickes in 1933.

The Collier regime instituted a complete reversal of federal policy. It also drastically altered the position of anthropologists vis-à-vis the Bureau of Indian Affairs (BIA). Before this time the government had impeded ethnographic research, which had been directed toward recording the very aboriginal cultures which federal policy was attempting to eliminate. Now such research was encouraged, for it would show that cultures that the BIA sought to restore were still remembered. During the next several decades, however, it became apparent that the Indian could not be isolated from the tide of modernizing influences stemming from the external society, and today the Indians have entered a new phase of culture change in which these influences are unchecked.

In 1934 anthropologists were ill-equipped with basic understandings of culture change in the modern world. American ethnography at this time had been almost entirely devoted to the reconstruction of aboriginal cultures, even to gleaning bits of language and customs from survivors of tribes that had all but vanished. Under Boasian cultural particularism and relativism, these cultures were conceived in static, culture-area terms rather than as evolving entities. Although by 1934 virtually all Indian societies had been qualitatively transformed in some manner and degree by influences from the larger American society, they were considered thereby to be ethnographically contaminated. Ethnologists were not interested in the factors, processes, and dynamics of change that had occurred during the many years following European contact. In 1936 the late John Provinse, who subsequently became Commissioner of Indian Affairs, asked whether anthropology would cease to exist when native cultures had finally disappeared. Recognition that modified Indian cultures were a proper subject of investigation was first formally stated by Robert Redfield, Ralph Linton, and Melville Herskovits in the memorandum on "acculturation" in the *American Anthropologist,* in 1935. This statement was made to justify a new subject matter, but it did not offer a methodology for investigating modern change, which is still under discussion. The Society for Applied Anthropology was founded in 1941, but it was concerned more with the role of anthropology in problems of the larger American society than with the particulars of Indian modernization.

When the assistance of anthropologists was finally sought by the BIA in 1934, we were unprepared to offer much of value. Despite our knowledge of the particulars of native cultures, the BIA's goal of rolling back time was obviously unrealistic. The effects of modernization could not be halted, but continued assimilation was definitely ✓ opposed by the BIA. The possibility of conceding that modernizing trends would inevitably continue was stoutly denied, and endeavors to minimize their traumatic effects were not considered. Anthropological theory as yet had paid little attention to the effects of modernizing factors so that it lacked ability to make even the most tentative predictions. The Indian New Deal purported to combine the best from the contemporary world with that of traditional culture, and anthropologists could only guess what could and could not be done. The new goals led to such absurdities and frustrations that few anthropologists were able to endure the sense of futility.

PRELUDE TO THE NEW DEAL

The traditional, pre-New Deal policy of assimilation grew out of British colonial goals which few persons had questioned. In the absence of dense native populations, like those of Meso-America and the Andes, which could readily be converted into bound labor, the sparse North American populations were driven off their lands, which were settled by Europeans. Bound labor for plantations was supplied by slaves from Africa. During the first few centuries only a few large, powerful tribes in the east, such as the Iroquois, retained their identity and culture.

By the middle of the last century the frontier had shifted west, and the federal policy of dispossession, pacification, confinement to reservations, and assimilation was formalized by creation of the Bureau of Indian Affairs in 1849. The Bureau of American Ethnology (BAE) was created in 1879 by Major J. W. Powell to furnish information about the Indians on the western frontier, but Powell's main contribution was to identify and classify Indian languages and to take censuses. Otherwise, BAE contributions were little concerned with the processes of assimilation.

By the beginning of the twentieth century the plight of most tribes had become critical. Many were losing their identity, and all suffered from insufficient lands. The condition had been growing worse owing to the possibility of selling individually owned tracts. The boarding schools were brutally run, like military institutions. They deprived the Indian children of contacts with their people, they prohibited use of Indian languages, and they taught little of value for later life after return to the reservation. Reservation agents tried to eliminate native religions and all aboriginal practices, while the government farmers and stockmen had only limited success in improving land use. The national ideal of the melting pot was not succeeding.

Protest against the federal policy was led by various private organizations. The question of federal policy presented a dilemma to anthropologists, for the choice was limited to two extremes. Should native culture be preserved or should assimilation be furthered? Most native cultures had already been transformed, some traumatically, and reversal of these processes seemed impossible. On the other hand, the obvious abuses of enforced assimilation might be mitigated. Although anthropologists were brought into the picture after the Reorganization Act was passed, their role was purely advisory and they had little effect on the federal policies which had already been decided.

THE INDIAN REORGANIZATION ACT AND ITS SEQUEL

The radical reversal of federal Indian policy was made possible by the national climate that supported President Franklin Roosevelt's New Deal, but the new policy for the Indians went much further than that for the nation. It not only sought to halt assimilation and to preserve "Indianhood," but it permitted John Collier to attempt to introduce his own utopian assumptions about native societies.

John Collier, who served as Commissioner of Indian Affairs from 1933 to 1945, was the principal architect of the New Deal for the Indians. He had first become active in various kinds of welfare work involving European immigrants about 1910. In 1923, after several visits to the Indians of the Southwest, he became executive secretary of the American Indian Defense Association. At this time modern life was beginning to threaten the cultures of the Southwest. The new policies which were written into the Reorganization Act of 1934 expressed both Collier's compassionate humanitarianism and his uncompromising crusade to perpetuate native culture. Former Secretary of the Interior Stewart Udall recently wrote that he "worked to establish in law the right of the Indians to determine their own future through self-government; to reverse the devastating erosion of the Indian estate; and to reawaken the Indian to his own heritage." The mystic quality in Collier's beliefs is disclosed in quotations from an editorial in *Smoke Signs-Fire Flames,* May, 1969: "Mr. Collier hacked away at government policy that called for 'civilizing' the Indian. He tried instead to reawaken interest in Indian art and music, folklore and custom. Mr. Collier often referred to the Indian tribes of the Southwest as 'mountain peaks of a submerged social continent.' He maintained that the Indian culture, or 'cosmic soul,' was spiritually superior to that of

White, western civilization." This was truly a messianic or revitalization movement, and Collier was its prophet.

In eliminating the abuses of the former policy, the pendulum swung to the other extreme. Self-governing tribal councils were adopted by democratic vote, and land sales to outsiders halted. Most boarding schools were abolished in favor of local day schools. Medical care was improved. But in attempting to recreate native cultures, a futile effort was made to isolate the Indians from modernizing influences, except as the BIA decided which influences were admissible.

Collier held strong convictions about the nature of aboriginal culture and the possibility of restoring it. "Indianhood" was to Collier a mystique, a way of life, of static quality that did not refer to 1900, 1850, or any particular period. He believed strongly in some form of utopia and frequently referred to the efforts of the Spanish colonists of Paraguay to introduce such a society. He was firmly convinced that native Indian societies had been truly communal, and that acceptance of the Reorganization Act would restore the native condition. Formerly forbidden religious practices were encouraged, and native arts and crafts were supported through the Indian Arts and Crafts Board, created in 1934.

In 1934 W. D Strong was loaned as advisor to the BIA by the Bureau of American Ethnology, and several anthropologists were sent to the field. The following year I took Strong's place, and, together with the late H. Scudder Mekeel, spent a full year working with the BIA. Meanwhile the Soil Conservation Service employed a large number of experts, including a dozen or more anthropologists.

Although the nature of native cultures had been anthropology's former interest and Collier's goal was to recreate these cultures, it was apparent to most of us that the course of modernization could not be halted, let alone reversed to some earlier but unspecified condition of "Indianhood." But as we paid attention to the acculturated Indian, we became aware of our ignorance of the particular processes and factors of modern change. Administration policy, however, left us no alternative but to accept its new goals or disassociate ourselves from the entire program. Today it is clear that modernization had already transformed Indian societies in various ways and degrees, and that the most useful role anthropology might have played would have been to deal with each tribe individually so as to help cushion the shock of inevitable changes. The utopian fiction regarding the communal nature of native societies and the possibility of instituting a uniform policy for recreating the "superior" Indian cultures left no place for dissent.

Different tribes, however, had been modernized in various ways and degrees. Some of the Rio Grande Pueblos had already become hispanicized towns, and the "mission" Indians of southern California were culturally extinct. A comparatively few, mostly in Arizona and New Mexico, retained basically Indian patterns, but acceptance of the reorganization plan with all its implications by no means always fitted their notions of proper action. The Hopi, owing to isolation, had remained among the most traditional societies, but, as Richard Clemmer (1969) shows, the various villages such as Hotavilla were unwilling to surrender their independence to an all-Hopi tribal council. On the other hand, as Shuichi Nagata has shown (1969), the Hopi from Hotavilla and Oraibi who established themselves at Moenkopi near the joint Pueblo-Navajo reservation headquarters had split into conflicting factions of traditionalists and progressives, the latter accepting a modern, cash-oriented life. The Navajo, who were intended as the showpiece of the New Deal, resisted for various reasons. For one thing, the program of stock reduction, although badly needed for soil conservation, did not appeal to an already starving people. The Indians of Alaska had abandoned their native villages and economy to live in shacks near the fish canneries. They sold all their catch to the canneries, only to buy canned fish between salmon runs. In the Great Basin arbitrary territorial units became the alleged native basis for self-government, and my own findings based on years of research in the areas were regarded as an attempt to sabotage the program.

Many tribes were already assimilated beyond the point of no return, and they were unwilling to give up their lands for community purposes. Other Indians retained reservation affiliation in order to benefit by any government subsidies. Moreover, the generation gap had become very serious in many tribes. When I informed Collier that the young men who collected admission fees to the Sun Dance at Fort Hall, Idaho, boasted of keeping the money, he declared in shocked disbelief that no Indian would betray the communal trust, and took this as further evidence that I was trying to undermine his program.

One strong motivation for the Indians' acceptance of the new tribal councils was their hope of profiting from a federal loan fund. Long accustomed to handouts in partial fulfillment of treaty obligations, the chance to borrow was seen as another gratuity. The true significance of the loans, however, was almost completely obfuscated by hundreds of pages of legal jargon stipulating conditions upon which the lawyers could not even agree among themselves. Among the extraordinary requirements to obtain a loan was the guarantee that the Indians would keep their yards swept clean.

There were many examples of inherent conflict in the efforts to revive native culture. The decline of Navajo sandpaintings distressed the BIA, but when I pointed out that success in introducing modern medicine would undermine the shaman who made sandpaintings, I was told that it would be understood that the Indians would go to the modern physicians for organic illness but to the shaman for functional and psychosomatic ailments. The Indians were to have the best of their own culture and of Western civilization.

The Board of Arts and Crafts succeeded in reviving some excellent Pueblo pottery and Navajo blankets, though these, like any handicraft, began to price themselves out of the market. At one point, it was proposed that Navajo weavers and Pueblo potters teach their arts to the impoverished Great Basin Indians, who had no crafts. The extraordinarily fine basketry woven in western Nevada had already been abandoned because the women could earn more taking in laundry.

With the carryover of the pre-New Deal federal personnel, the revival of native crafts sometimes reached the point of absurdity. The Alaska Indians, who had established a fair market for miniature totem poles made with carpenter shop facilities, were ordered to make them only with aboriginal tools. On the Southern Ute reservation the head of the carpenter shop was distressed because the boys were now making native love flutes, which they played under the girls' windows at night. Locking all the outbuildings, he said, could not stop the deterioration of morals.

SUBSEQUENT CHANGES

Modernizing trends continued despite the government's effort to halt them. Tribal councils served as business organizations to some extent, but they were handicapped by the principle of collective endeavor that the BIA had insisted on. In addition to furthering local business enterprises with considerable financial and technical help from the government, the tribal councils were permitted by the Indian Claims Act to sue for all the lost lands and resources for which they had not been compensated. These lengthy suits grind on, and it is estimated that they will not be completed for decades.

Meanwhile, the reservations were being exposed to an increasing number of linkages with and influences by the larger society. Military service during World War II had made enduring impressions. As the Indians became more fully aware of what money could buy, they sought additional cash incomes. The "Hopi Hotshot Fire Fighters" were sent to the West Coast forests. Busloads of Navajo traveled to Utah and Idaho for the harvests. The Iroquois became famous high steel workers in construction around New York City. Colonies of Indians began to develop near the railroad yards at the West Coast terminals.

During the last two decades there has been a mass exodus from the reservations to cities. The number of Indians involved is difficult to estimate, because the BIA had ruled that any person with one-eighth Indian ancestry was entitled to benefits as a member of his tribe. Estimates that between one-quarter and one-third of the Indians have left their reservations, though only approximations, indicate a substantial urban trend. One estimate gives 100,000 Indians in Los Angeles, where not over half a dozen were born, and other cities also have large Indian populations. Little trained for skills needed for urban employment, many of these urban Indians live in pockets of poverty, like other minority groups.

It is too early to know what adjustment will be made to the city, for few Indians have had more than twenty years urban experience. About two decades ago it was estimated that 20,000 Tarascan Indians from Mexico had worked for several years in the steel mills of Gary and Muncie, Indiana, and then returned to their tribe. It is doubtful whether North American Indians will find the means of satisfying their new wants on the reservations. Meanwhile, however, the local association of members of different tribes in a pan-Indian alliance will undoubtedly represent the first stages of adaptation.

While the specific steps toward assimilation depend upon many factors, at least a generation will be required. Indians, no less than second- or third-generation Puerto Ricans and the innumerable blacks who have "passed" into the larger society, will become detribalized in time.

EFFECTIVENESS OF APPLIED ANTHROPOLOGY

Successful applied anthropology presupposes that goals are attainable by rational means. This means generally that the social scientist attempts to achieve goals approved by society rather than to alter them, and in so doing he has sufficient knowledge of cause and effect to know the outcome of particular courses of action. In the case of the American Indian, we were unable to affect the goals either before the New Deal or afterward.

In a recent paper (Steward, 1971) I ventured the hypothesis that the basic goal during all but the last few thousand years of hominid evolution had been survival, which required hundreds of rational decisions but allowed little latitude for variation, except in certain stylistic features. After the so-called "agricultural revolution," however, the production of subsistence surpluses permitted the evolution of socially derived goals that were not supportable by any absolute standard such as survival. New types of social structure placed control of production in the hands of limited segments of society, the nature of which was determined by cultural evolution rather than by biological necessity. Because these evolved without foresight or planning, and indeed emerged so gradually that the processes of change were not recognized, they were accepted with little question as divinely given parts of the eternal nature of things. No logic could have altered such goals.

Until recent centuries the role of reason was restricted to effecting adjustments within the larger system. The industrial revolution, however, initiated internal social changes. The emergence of new classes of manufacturers, merchants, and bankers weakened the essentially two-class system of landlords and peasants, broadening the basis of competition. The diffusion of knowledge and ideologies, expedited by printing, enabled social philosophers to articulate and thereby to intensify the discontent of the have-nots. Few social philosophies, however, went far beyond popular feelings. The wars of independence of the Western hemisphere sought freedom from European imperialism but not complete internal economic egalitarianism. The ideal of free enterprise and private property was extended rather than eliminated by the American and French Revolutions. The Russian Revolution of 1918 was the first attempt to transform the basic goals and revise the internal structure of a major nation. But the nature of the Russian state and of the others that have followed the same general model continues to experience transformations.

American colonialism followed the British policy of displacement of the aboriginal inhabitants with minor regard to their welfare or even survival. Any compensation for their treatment was thought to consist of their assimilation to the superior Western European civilization, except for the few who believed that the Indians represented idyllic natural man. It was not until the end of the last century that the failure of the means of assimilation became evident.

The New Deal for the Indians was remarkable in that its policies were as radical as those of the Russian Revolution. It undertook to redirect culture change toward communal, utopian societies that were presumed to have existed earlier and to establish them within the larger framework of free enterprise. In so doing, it also attempted to reverse modernizing trends.

The new Indian policy was messianic, compassionate, intolerant, and unrealistic, and it presented anthropologists a dilemma. The pre-New Deal efforts at assimilation had been disastrous, but the new goals were unattainable for several fundamental reasons. First, the egalitarian goal of the new policy could not be realized within the context of a larger society based on competition and social stratification. This policy represented a partial revolution—an attempt to revolutionize the Indian subcultures without affecting the total national culture. Although many persons thought that a national revolution might occur during the Great Depression, the Roosevelt measures served to perpetuate the American system.

Second, the factors and processes of modernization continued to affect Indian societies to the point that many had lost their identity and others were in various stages of transformation. These changes entailed unavoidable and often traumatic conflict between generations and factions, which at best could only be mitigated but not averted. All Indians were undergoing fundamental readaptations from a variety of institutions based on a subsistence economy to a dependency linkage with national institutions. Even if anthropology had a body of theory about modernization, it would not have been permitted to use it, for the utopian dream of preserving "Indianhood" was unassailable. The impotence of applied anthropology in dealing with government policies represented an impasse.

Since no modern nation occupies a permanent evolutionary niche with static goals, the larger question is whether social science can be effective in modifying national goals. The goals conceived by social science are not established on the basis of pure reason. They respond to the same evolutionary processes that create popular dissatisfaction with the status quo. The present widespread discontent with the establishment has taken many forms, which in fact appear to be articulated more often as estrangement than as positive goals. There is little doubt, however, that these are symptomatic of evolutionary transformations that will create new, and probably now unforeseeable, kinds of society, with or without violent revolutions. If social science were able to forecast the inevitable trends, it could have great effectiveness. Meanwhile, its role is necessarily limited to furthering goals that are generally acceptable to existing society.

BROADER IMPLICATIONS

The New Deal for the Indians was significant in demonstrating the extremely circumscribed role of anthropology in altering government policy even though this policy was based on objectives that were contrary to modern trends. It raises the problem everywhere of whether applied anthropology should and could stem or ameliorate the effects of modernization.

The possibility of halting modernization seems small. Even if this could be accomplished, members of traditional tribal societies, including Indians, are not in agreement on modernization. There have always been segments of society which come into conflict with other segments on this issue. Are the present Indian movements, like the

Afro-American movements, attempts to bring solidarity by creating a synthetic culture which can underlie a revitalization movement? Would it have been better to continue the earlier policies of assimilation, despite the disorganization and trauma they caused, and would modern Indians be in a better position to participate in modern society? Has anthropology sufficient insights into the causes and effects of modernization to make statements about its inevitability?

Other questions involve the humanitarian component of anthropologists' actions. Can we support humanitarian goals with reasonable scientific proof of their value and workability?

This question was posed by opposition to the Vietnam War. I joined my colleagues in signing a full-page statement of protest in the *New York Times* and subsequently participated in local teach-ins. Opposition to the war has gathered momentum, though I suspect that it is because of the government's deceit concerning the course of the war and a slowly growing national conviction that the expenditure of American lives and dollars is accomplishing nothing. Pondering the total situation later, it seemed to me that the social and economic purposes of the United States had barely been mentioned and that anthropologists could have marshaled their knowledge of the causes of revolutions and appeal of communist ideologies in underdeveloped nations. There was opposition to the horrors of bombing, use of napalm, and killing of innocent villagers, which represent humanitarian factors, but not to the extent of pacifist opposition to any warfare. I still hold with those who oppose the war, though I believe that a stronger case could have been made if we had spoken as social scientists.

BIBLIOGRAPHY

BEALS, RALPH
> 1968. "Comments on Social Responsibilities Symposium," *Current Anthropology*, vol. 9, pp. 407-408.

BERREMAN, GERALD
> 1968. "Is Anthropology Alive?" *Current Anthropology*, vol. 9, pp. 391-396.

CLEMMER, RICHARD
> 1969. "The Fed-Up Hopi: Resistance of the American Indian and the Silence of the Good Anthropologists," *Journal of the Steward Anthropological Society*, vol. 1, no. 1, pp. 18-40.

GJESSING, GUTORM
> 1968. "The Social Responsibility of the Social Anthropologist," *Current Anthropology*, vol. 9, pp. 397-402.

GOUGH, KATHLEEN
> 1968. "New Proposals for Anthropologists," *Current Anthropology*, vol. 9, pp. 403-407.

HELM, JUNE
    1966. *Pioneers of American Anthropology.* American Ethnological Society, Monograph 43. Seattle: University of Washington Press.
NAGATA, SHUICHI
    1969. *Moenkopi Pueblo,* University of Illinois Studies in Anthropology, No. 6. Urbana: University of Illinois Press.
STEWARD, JULIAN H.
    1971. "Underdeveloped Nations: Predictability and Manipulability of Modernizing Trends." In *Essays on Modernization of Underdeveloped Societies,* ed. A. R. Desai. Bombay: University of Bombay, Department of Sociology, Pp. 138-148.

16

The Ceremonial Buffoon of the American Indian

"The Ceremonial Buffoon of the American Indian" is a shortened version of Steward's doctoral dissertation and first appeared in the *Papers of the Michigan Academy of Science, Arts and Letters* (vol. 14, pp. 187-207, 1931). The article has never been republished before, despite its considerable interest for students of the history of anthropology as a unique and little-known facet of Steward's work.

Those who are accustomed to thinking of the American Indian as sober and stone-faced will be surprised to learn that he not only laughed as frequently as his white-skinned cousin, but actually introduced into his most sacred ceremonies a comedian whose primary business was to delight the spectators.

The subject of laughter has long been an open field for all manner of students of human nature. Rarely have two bagged the same game. All have made the serious mistake of attempting to formulate a type stimulus to laughter from the humor of a single culture, namely, our Euro-American civilization, although a few rash theorists have fancied a "racial" difference in what things are funny.

It cannot be supposed that an anthropological approach to laughter can solve all the subtleties of this manifestly difficult problem. A review of humor in distinctly different cultures, however, may provide a least common denominator to the humor of the world and thus clear the ground for sounder psychological theorizing. The problem then may be restated in anthropological terms, "To what extent does culture predetermine what is laughable?"

The American Indian furnishes abundant material for a tentative answer to this problem, but it must be remembered that our attention is to be centered upon the institutionalized humor exhibited by the ceremonial buffoon. Humor of everyday occurrence, to be sure, was much in evidence in native life, but this is not available for our purpose because observers have paid little attention to it and made less record of it. The antics of the buffoon, on the other hand, have been well described.

The ceremonial buffoon, however, did not have universal occurrence in North America. The idea of setting aside one person or a group of persons to act as both sergeant-at-arms and comedian seems to have originated, as an historical complex, but once, either in Mexico or among the ancestors of the Pueblo tribes of New Mexico and Arizona, and from its early source to have diffused to several culture areas of North America. The clown was especially prominent in the Southwest, the Plains Area, California, and on the Northwest Coast.[1] What diffused, however, was the idea of setting aside a special person as buffoon, not a particular set of notions about the comic. In other words, a "pattern" diffused whose content was to be filled in somewhat differently in each culture area.

A classification of the themes of humor employed by the ceremonial buffoon permits a twofold division: (1) traits of comedy common to all peoples regardless of culture, and (2) traits of comedy peculiar to each culture area.

COMIC THEMES OF UNIVERSAL OCCURRENCE

The greater number of the comic devices employed by the clowns of native America are based upon situations which are regarded as humorous in every culture. Although as employed by the Indians these devices are rude and smack strongly of the soil and are not comparable to the fine-spun themes of the highly intellectualized European comedies, they are nevertheless basic in all cultures. They center about matters which possess the greatest emotional appeal in any cultural group; they are "human interest" themes.

These may be grouped in four main categories: (1) themes of humor in which sacred and vitally important ceremonies and sometimes persons are ridiculed and burlesqued, or, at times, themes of the nature of practical jokes, which riotously disregard those folkways and mores which are so essential to the smooth functioning of society; (2) themes of humor based upon sex and obscenity; (3) themes based upon sickness, sorrow, misfortune, etc., and important activities in daily life; (4) caricature and burlesque of foreigners.

1. BURLESQUE OF THE SACRED

This class of comic situations comprises one of the most common

---

[1] See Map 2 for the distribution of the clown. [The map has been omitted in this edition—Ed.]

themes of buffoonery. The clown is the person par excellence who is privileged to ridicule, burlesque, and defile the most sacred and important ceremonies, persons, and customs. He is licensed to behave as no ordinary mortal would dream of behaving. He is held accountable for nothing. In his transgression of custom lies much of his comedy. Those mores which are ordinarily observed most rigorously and which are held in great esteem are the subjects of the most pleasurable comedy. As Bandelier says of the Koshare, the "delight makers" of the Pueblo Indians, "nothing is sacred; all things are permitted so long as they contribute delight to the tribe."[2]

A few illustrations from the wealth of material at our disposal will exhibit the clown in this role in different cultures.

Among the Pueblo Indians of the Southwest, clowns are present at the god-impersonating dances to perform comic side-plays on the central theme of the ceremony. They burlesque the *kachina* dancers, dancing out of time, stumbling, grimacing, and doing things ordinarily taboo. At a Jemez Pueblo dance a clown is reported to have irreverently sprinkled his fellows with sand and ashes in imitation of the ceremonial sprinkling with corn-meal and pollen;[3] at Zuñi the Newekwe clown society speaks in Spanish or English before the gods, a thing strictly taboo to ordinary people. The latter once rigged up an imitation telephone and pretended to converse with the gods, although gods are not supposed to speak.[4] The Hopi Koyemsi or "Mudheads" perform separate dances of their own in ludicrous imitation of the *kachina* dancers. The clown of the Navajo Night Chant dance joins the masked dancers in a wholly erratic and unorthodox manner. He gets in their way, dances out of time and awkwardly, sits on the ground, rocking to and fro peering foolishly at people. When the other dancers have departed, he continues dancing until he discovers his mistake and then runs after them. Sometimes he imitates the leader, trying to anticipate him in giving signals for the dance.[5] Even sacred sleight-of-hand performances are burlesqued so as to reveal the secrets.[6]

The buffoon of the religious dances of California performs in a similar manner. Among the Northwestern Maidu his chief stock-in-trade is to parody the ceremonial leader and burlesque the dancers. He enters the dance house after the dancers have come in, munching food. The leader reprimands him and asks him to take part in the dance. A bantering dialogue ensues. Whenever the shaman tries to make a

[2] 1890a, p. 137.

[3] Reagan, 1915, pp. 423-427.

[4] Parsons, 1917, pp. 229-233.

[5] Matthews, 1902, pp. 150-151.

[6] Matthews, 1887, pp. 443-444.

speech, the clown parodies his remarks. He steals tobacco and is again reprimanded. When he finally joins in the dance, he does so languidly, frequently stopping to eat.[7] In the Wintun Hesi ceremony, the acme of Wintun ceremonialism, the clown directs his comic assaults at the leader. "When the captain of the host village was singing as he marched slowly about the inside of the dance house, one of the clowns stationed himself before the captain and marched slowly backwards in step with him, while delivering joking remarks concerning the latter's ability to sing and the particular song he was voicing. This did not seem in the least to disconcert the singer who continued to sing in his gravest manner; but his song was not received with the usual seriousness."[8]

In general, the Northwest Coast religious concepts imposed a pattern of behavior on the buffoon which was too rigid to permit this type of clowning, but instances of this kind have been reported from the Quinault[9] and the tribes of eastern Puget Sound.[10]

The same thing was true in large measure of the clown of the Plains, as among the Cree,[11] Ojibway,[12] Arapaho,[13] and others, especially in the northern Plains, where the pattern was less clear-cut.

Even in Central America, where drama tended to be divorced from religious ceremonies, the Maya are said to have had at their feasts and entertainments jesters who were clever in mimicry and caricature and did not spare even the chief men,[14] while the priests of the Aztec sometimes contributed to the fun of religious ceremonies by throwing mud balls at the actors and praising or censuring the performances in a jocular manner.[15]

That this type of humor is not unique in America is apparent at once from brief reflection on comic themes in our own culture. Even among other primitives it was prominent. Thus in Samoa a jester's dance is performed by men and women of rank to provide comic relief to the dance of the very sacred *taupo* (the woman of highest rank and divinity).[16] The African Masai dances had similar frivolity.[17] The primitive Konds of India actually permitted ridicule of the goddess to whom human sacrifice had been made.[18]

[7]Dixon, 1905, pp. 315-317.
[8]Barrett, 1919, p. 457.
[9]Olson, personal communication.
[10]Gunther, personal communication.
[11]Skinner, 1915, pp. 528-529.
[12]Skinner, 1914, pp. 494-504.
[13]Kroeber, 1907, p. 192.
[14]Bancroft, 2:711-712.
[15]*Ibid.*, 2:291-292.
[16]Mead, pp. 114-115.
[17]Barrett, personal communication.
[18]Chambers, 2:266-270, from Elliot, *The Indian Village Feast*.

In the foregoing examples the keynote of the comedy is what is commonly called "comic relief." Indeed, in nearly every instance it is the very thing which is regarded with greatest reverence or respect which is ridiculed.

A great deal of ruffianism is also exhibited by clowns. Things and persons are not at all respected. The Zuñi Newekwe and Koyemshi indulge in all manner of acts of physical violence. The Hopi clowns have tussles, tormenting each other with cactus branches, stripping breech-clouts, and such-like.[19] The Papago clowns visit people's houses, upsetting things,[20] and, like them, the Miwok clowns run about after dances, prying into houses and wrecking what they can lay hands upon.[21] The Cahuilla "funny man" of Southern California annoys people by throwing water on them or dropping live coals down their backs.[22] And in like manner the Huichol clowns of Mexico torment people with "botherations" and prevent their sleeping by shaking rattles near their ears, or by tugging at their clothing.[23]

To a very large extent, rowdyism characterized the clowns of the Northwest Coast. The Haida often greeted their feast guests at the shore, "playing pranks" with their baggage, bursting it open, and doing similar things, all of which the visitors "expected and were prepared for."[24] The Kwakiutl Fool dancers, when excited by their possessing spirits, ran about with lances, knives, or clubs, hitting people, or in serious cases even stabbing and killing them. Disliking clean and beautiful things, they attempted to break, destroy and soil them.[25] The Nootka,[26] Bella Coola,[27] and Haida[28] had clowns who behaved largely in this manner.

2. HUMOR OF SEX

The prominence of sex humor in our own Euro-American civilization need not be pressed. It is equally, sometimes more, prominent in American Indian cultures. The importance of sex humor is the inevitable result of the powerful biological sex drive. Closely associated are matters of obscenity and the excrementitious.

The Koshare and Newekwe societies of the Southwest are pre-

[19]Fewkes, 1898, pp. 293-294.
[20]Mason, 1920, pp. 17-23.
[21]Gifford, manuscript.
[22]Strong, 1929, p. 166.
[23]Lumholtz, 1907, pp. 185-186.
[24]Swanton, 1909, p. 168.
[25]Boas, 1897, pp. 468-471, 664.
[26]Sapir, 1911, pp. 22-27.
[27]Boas, 1892, p. 917; 1897, p. 469.
[28]Swanton, 1905, p. 173.

eminently associated with sex. They are in fact specifically phallic societies. The Jemez clowns make advances toward women[29] and the Zuñi Koyemshi, who wear imitation penes,[30] encourage sex license during the Shalako ceremony.[31] The Hopi clowns, who are said to be very fond of women, caper with female impersonators. The Hehe's *kachina* mask, in fact, is decorated with phallic symbols.[32] Obscenity and handling of filth run riot in certain ceremonial occasions in the Southwest.

Among the non-Pueblo tribes of the Southwest there was also a considerable preoccupation with sex in the activities of the clown.

In California, among the Yokuts, obscene and pretended phallic advances toward young girls formed part of the stock-in-trade of the clown.[33] The Yuki clowns hold each other's privates in their frolics.[34]

Obscenity, although not prominent, was not lacking on the Northwest Coast. Elliot has described scatological practices of various groups of Alaskan Eskimo.[35] During a comic interlude of a Kwakiutl ceremony a man jests with a chief's daughter, making pointed references to sex.[36]

The clown in the Plains was much concerned with the phallic, which constituted a frequent theme of humor. The Arapaho clown was permitted sex license and obscene behavior. His phallic activities were facilitated by the use of a root by means of which he magically paralyzed and thus secured the women of his fancy.[37] The Ponca clowns were said to crawl up and touch a woman's genitalia in full daylight,[38] and the Hidatsa clowns were permitted incest, despite the usual strength of the incest taboo.[39]

Among the Fox, east of the Plains, a mule dance in which a man imitating a stallion performs indecent antics was a great amusement. Other dances and songs of the Sauk and Fox were highly obscene.[40]

By the Eastern Dakota phallicism was intimately associated with the Heyoka complex.[41] The Heyoka clowns were believed to have great supernatural power which, among other things, enabled them to

[29]Reagan, 1915, pp. 423-427.
[30]Parsons, 1917, pp. 321-322.
[31]Stevenson, 1904, pp. 224-227, 235-236, 276-277; Cushing, 1920, pp. 601-607; Parsons, 1917, pp. 187-188.
[32]Fewkes, 1900, pp. 128-129.
[33]Gayton, field notes.
[34]Kroeber, 1925, p. 186.
[35]Bourke, pp. 142, 207-209, 391-392.
[36]Boas, 1897, p. 546.
[37]Kroeber, 1907, pp. 188-189, 191-196.
[38]Skinner, 1915, p. 789.
[39]Lowie, 1913, pp. 284-290.
[40]Michelson, personal communication.
[41]Pond, p. 232.

satisfy their libido. As part of the Winged Head complex, this belief runs eastward all the way to Maine.[42] Among the Iroquois and various tribes of the Southeast, certain dances furnished occasions for sex license.[43]

Themes of sex and obscenity were common in the ceremonies and performances of the tribes of Middle America.[44]

Lewdness was also highly typical of the humor of cultures other than those native to the New World. The Samoa jester's dance, for examples, was in large measure salacious.[45] The Feast of Fools, which survived in Europe until the middle of the sixteenth century, included a licensed desecration of the church and riotous buffoonery which was largely of an obscene nature.[46] In fact D. M. Robinson has derived the earliest Greek comedies from the phallic songs of the Bacchic dancers and revellers.[47]

3. MISFORTUNE

This class of humor is based upon situations and activities which are fundamental to human existence and which are frequently sources of pain, trouble, and unhappiness. The clown often pretends to be crippled, infirm, or destitute. He is clad in rags and goes about as though starving, begging for food. He enacts scenes of household strife and marital difficulties. He burlesques activities of hunting and fishing, food-gathering and horticulture. Gluttony, too, is employed, for it is an exaggeration of an extremely important daily activity.

In the Southwest the Jemez Koshare dress in rags, carry crooked wands, and wear cornhusks in their hair.[48] The clowns of the Jemez Piñon dance perform in rags, begging for food. One of these beggars is impersonated by the governor of the Pueblo.[49] A Navajo stunt on the last day of the Mountain Chant ceremony is the impersonation of a dull-witted, decrepit, and short-sighted old man. He enters in a woefully ragged suit, carrying a crooked bow and misshapen arrows. He totters into the dance space, where he stumbles on a yucca plant and howls with pain. In his effort to find it, he lacerates himself thrice more, complaining in a weak shaky voice. When he has marked the spot and the way back to it, in an exaggerated imitation of the old Indian way of

---

[42]Speck, personal communication.

[43]Speck, 1907, pp. 138-140; 1909, pp. 129-130; 1911, pp. 204-205; Swanton, 1928, p. 534.

[44]Bourke, 1891, pp. 435-436; Brinton, pp. xxii-xxvii, xli-xliv.

[45]Mead, pp. 114-115.

[46]Bourke, pp. 11-23.

[47]In J. Hastings, *Encyclopaedia of Religion and Ethics, s.v.* Greek Drama.

[48]Goldfrank, 1927, pp. 53-55, 90-91, 93.

[49]Thompson, 1889, pp. 353-355.

doing things, he goes off to find "his woman," and brings her back to pick the yucca fruit. Soon he returns with a tall, stalwart man, dressed to represent a hideous, absurd-looking old granny.[50]

The Southwestern clowns are strongly addicted to gluttony; in fact, the Hopi *kachina* Paiakyamu is called the "Hano glutton,"[51] and the Jicarillo Apache clown wears festoons of bread around his neck.[52]

The California Maidu clown is represented as a lazy, stupid person. During the dance two men representing hunters enter. They ask the clown whether he has seen any deer. He answers that they may have gone by when he was asleep. At another time this clown pretends blindness, which leads to absurd episodes. On still another occasion he staggers in with a bundle of splinters which he carries with prodigious effort, grunting and staggering. He spears a fish with so much vigor that the spear is driven entirely through it and then ten men are required to land it.[53]

On the Northwest Coast, the ceremonial perverseness of the Kwakiutl Fool dancer gives him something of a destitute character. He wears a costume of rags, but this is said to be because he dislikes clean and beautiful things, which he always attempts to destroy.[54]

In the Plains and East Woodland, rags were the common garb of the ceremonial buffoon, and begging a favorite amusement. The Cheyenne Contrary Society dressed in tatters.[55] The Winnebago clowns, shabbily clothed, begged for food, pretending to be impoverished and destitute.[56] The clowns of the Plains Cree, Plains Ojibway, and Assiniboine were characteristically represented as poor and in need.[57] Even the Iroquois False Face Society dressed in rags and made begging tours.[58]

It is reported that in Central America the Aztec comedians commonly mimicked and ridiculed the deaf, lame, blind, deformed, and ailing,[59] and during the feast to Tlaloc priests "dressed like merry-andrews" went from house to house begging food.[60] The "Pilatos" of the Totonac festival of Corpus Christi, like the "old man" of the dances

---

[50]Matthews, 1887, pp. 440-443.
[51]Fewkes, 1903, p. 120, Pl. LVIII.
[52]Russell, 1898, p. 371.
[53]Dixon, 1905, pp. 298, 304; Powers, pp. 310-312.
[54]Boas, 1897, pp. 469, 516.
[55]Grinnell, 2:206.
[56]Radin, 1923, p. 384.
[57]Skinner, 1915, pp. 528-529; 1914, pp. 494-504; Lowie, 1909, pp. 62-66.
[58]Skinner, 1914, pp. 494-504; Smith, 1888, pp. 184-193.
[59]Bancroft, 2:291-292.
[60]Bancroft, 3:334-335, 339.

of the northern part of Mexico, represents himself as poverty-stricken. He wears rags, a black derby, and a wooden mask.[61]

4. BURLESQUE OF STRANGERS

The humorous quality of burlesque of foreigners lies in incongruity. It is a pleasurable break from conventional patterns which is not restrained by emotions of sympathy. These are usually directed against white men who are ordinarily the subjects of greatest emotional feelings, whether fear, envy, or contempt.

A characteristic Santo Domingo theme is the "bull and horse" ceremony, which depicts the first arrival of the white men, missionaries and traders, in ludicrously ragged costumes. A mock bullfight is held, followed by songs of "London Bridge Is Falling Down" and "Good Night Ladies." At the end the "traders" produce a suitcase and the Indians buy from them with paper money.[62] A Santa Clara fiesta enacts the arrival of the United States soldiers in a covered wagon, their drunkenness and finally their fight with the Navajo, in which they are worsted until Utes come to the rescue.[63] A Hopi Powamu ceremony of 1928 caricatured American white girls. The "*kachina* girls," impersonated by men, were dressed in an incongruous attire of skirts, riding boots, sombreros, and six-shooters, and they carried vanity-boxes. The Navajo buffoon furnishes great amusement simply by wearing a great false mustache and an exaggerated imitation of spectacles and other belongings of the white neighbors.[64]

The California clown had less leaning toward this type of humor, but we must note that the Yurok burlesque of a Karok fleeing from vengeance after eloping with another man's wife is of this order,[65] and so is the custom of the Southern Maidu of burlesquing the dance of their northern neighbors.[66]

The best illustration from the Northwest Coast comes from the Kwakiutl. An interlude in a potlatch ceremony introduces four men dressed as police officers. They set up an American court, one acting as judge. A woman is arrested for being absent from the preceding part of the ceremony, tried and fined $70 worth of blankets, which is afterward distributed in her name as potlatch gifts. This episode was introduced in 1865 and had been continued up to the time of Professor Boas' visit in 1897.[67]

[61]Nuñez, pp. 191-199.
[62]Gaastra, p. 67.
[63]*El Palacio*, 10: 12, 1921, anonymous.
[64]Matthews, 1902, p. 433.
[65]Kroeber, 1925, pp. 58-60.
[66]Ralph Beals, personal communication.
[67]Boas, 1897, pp. 562-563.

Of similar cast is the Winnebago dance in which buffoons caricature white men,[68] and the Iroquois New Year dance, in which there are imitations of white men skating, locomotives, and the like.[69] The same theme was common in Central America.[70]

CULTURALLY DETERMINED HUMOR

That there should be some cultural differences, even within cultures, in what is laughable, is to be expected. For while the type stimuli to laughter—the pleasurable relief, the incongruous, the caricature, etc. —are forms which are not dependent upon cultures, the concrete situations into which they are set vary a great deal. The incongruous, for example, depends upon local cultural traits and patterns. The native African chief bedecked in a top-hat is ludicrous to the European; to his African subject he is the personification of magnificence. For the European has been so conditioned to top-hats that this constitutes an incongruity, a conflict of meaning. The African is not so conditioned.

In general, however, the points in which laughter varies among groups of men are not so far reaching as those themes which are shared by all. It has been shown empirically that the universal themes of humor concern matters of greatest emotional interest, and these do not differ materially with culture. Humor that differs with culture is more likely to concern folkways and things of material culture.

A further factor, however, making for cultural difference in the humor which is expressed through the clown is that the clown is seldom purely a comedian. His noncomic duties have frequently affected his comic behavior. For he is, in addition to comedian, a member of some society whose duties may entail important curing, fertility or military functions. The influence of such factors will be elucidated in the following discussion.

THE SOUTHWEST PHALLICISM

It has already been demonstrated that phallicism and obscenity constitute universal themes of humor. It must be recognized, however, that these themes, which are particularly emphasized in the Southwest, are more prominent among American Indians than, for example, in our own Euro-American culture.

Obscenity and scatology are carried to the extreme in the Koshare, Newekwe, Wöwöchim, and Manzrau societies of the Southwest, and, to judge from their frequency, are major sources of humor. Funny as

[68]Chandler, personal communication.
[69]Smith, 1888, pp. 184-193.
[70]Bancroft, 2:285-286.

these are to the natives, however, they have elicited only emotions of repugnance and disgust from even the ethnologist. Here clearly is a definite cultural difference in humor, and the reason is not obscure.

The concept of fertility is, as Haeberlin[71] has shown, prominent in Pueblo thought and ceremonialism. Fertility has been essential to the very survival of the villages; the keynote of their ceremonies is taken from this necessity. As humor is likely to strike at those things which are of greatest importance, this has come to be the dominant note of Southwestern humor. Moreover, the foremost and oldest clowning societies, the Koshare and its derivatives, are concerned in their sober moments with fertility and rain-making rites. It is not surprising, then, that as clowns these societies repeat the serious themes in clowning fashion.

CALIFORNIA

In California distinctive comic differences may also be attributed to general cultural differences. These depend upon the conditioning occasioned by the differences in the ceremonial functions of the clown and are shown for instance in the contrast between the clown of the Northwestern Maidu and Patwin and that of the Pomo and Yuki, or, in other words, between those tribes which had the Hesi ceremony and those which lacked the Hesi and stressed the secret or ghost society. In the former the clown served as speaker to the chief and was purely a mundane personage, not even resorting to disguises for his comedy. Among the Pomo and Yuki clowning was not set aside for special personages, but was carried on by men who were primarily ghost impersonators, secondarily comedians, and whose humorous aspect was merged with an unworldly character. The Patwin and Maidu clowns' performances seemed frankly ludicrous, avowedly for sheer entertainment. Among the Pomo and Patwin the clown was primarily an antinatural being, a ghost, and the grotesque dress, strange behavior, and contrary nature were as much an attempt actually to represent such a being as to produce a ludicrous impression. Moreover, within these tribes an atmosphere of sacred unnaturalness, even in regard to the buffoonery of the clowns, is attested by the fact that the audience was prohibited from laughing.

The traits of the Coyote type of clown are mainly to be attributed to Southwestern influence. In large measure, however, this portrayal has been exaggerated by the tricky, obscene characteristic of Coyote, which in western mythology has served to make coyote tales subjects of constant amusement. The Coyote clown represents, then, to a minor degree a cultural difference.

[71] 1916.

THE NORTHWEST COAST

The Northwest Coast has imposed a virile cultural pattern upon the activities of its clowning societies. The Kwakiutl Fool dancers are primarily a hereditary society, the members of which are possessed during the winter dance season by their spirits. This possession causes excitability, madness, unnatural behavior, and it is provoked by the members of the opposing moiety.[72] The behavior of possessed individuals causes general excitement rather than specific laughter. There is, however, some difference in the character of the madness of the various societies. The Fool dancers tend more toward the comic than the others, although it is not their chief aim. They, as well as the Cannibals and Bear dancers are closely associated with war, and they carry weapons of war—a lance, knife and club. Their military character is also evident in their behavior. When supernaturally excited they attack people by throwing stones, hitting them with sticks, and, in serious cases, stabbing and killing them.[73] This of course is beyond the bounds of humor. In a sense it represents the trait of practical joking carried to a serious extreme, and this extreme follows from their character as a "possessed" military society.

There is, however, a certain humorous turn to the characterization of the Fool dancers. They are represented with enormous noses, in which lie their personalities and their power. Neophytes to the society are initiated by being rubbed with mucous.[74] They possess a real Cyrano de Bergerac complex in regard to this organ. Any allusion to noses irritates them and to have their noses struck causes them to go out of their heads. When in a fury they do not dance, but run about like madmen, throwing things about, striking people, and breaking things.[75] People irritate them by pulling or spitting on their noses.[76]

The Haida persons, who are "made *gagixit*," exhibit a madness comparable to that of the Kwakiutl Fool dancers. They rush about town, rolling over, running through people's houses, making fun of their canoes, and crying through the woods. People do not venture out, and if anyone is caught in the woods, his clothes are torn off and his person ridiculed. They may pull canoes out of the water and break them. The *gagixit* may be caught. For example, on one occasion an inflated seal stomach was hung up and he was called. He came crying, "A ha, ha, ha," rolled under the stomach and went away. When he

[72]Boas, 1897, p. 420.
[73]*Ibid.*, pp. 468-471.
[74]*Ibid.*, pp. 468-469.
[75]*Ibid.*
[76]*Ibid.*, pp. 523, 545.

returned he was seized and taken to the dance house, where he later danced accompanied by spirit songs. At least part of the function of such individuals is to destroy property which the potlatching chief afterward pays for.[77]

THE PLAINS: CONTRARY BEHAVIOR

In many respects the ceremonialism of the Plains stands in sharp contrast to that of the other areas considered in this paper. As the Plains tend more toward individual rites and interests, this important ceremonial setting does not permit the type of clown found elsewhere. Societies joined through visions, for example, had their private ceremonies. Public, communal ceremonies were less common. These rituals were in fulfullment of private promises or to gain personal ends. They centered largely around visions in which the individual rather than the community sought benefits.

With such latitude in behavior and regalia as was permitted by the lack of rigid patterns in the Plains, it might seem that a great range of comic devices would have been possible. As a matter of fact, the Plains clown was dominated and characterized by contrary speech and action. This is generally rationalized as the result of a vision, chiefly of thunder or lightning, which causes one to behave in an unnatural manner. The strength of this association with a vision and the peculiar nature of contrary speech and action brought this into great vogue as a comic device. At the same time the individualistic nature of Plains ceremonialism made it possible that it should also develop into aberrant forms in the military societies. For Plains ceremonialism permitted indefinite variations, and vision-given ritual constantly recombined old elements.

Typical features of Plains ceremonialism are exhibited in the Dakota Heyoka society. This society was joined by a vision of thunder or of Wakinyan, and such a vision made one *heyoka,* or antinatural,[78] and largely governed his subsequent behavior.

The peculiar traits of the Heyoka have been explicitly and fully described for the Dakota. The desires and experiences even of the Heyoka deities are all contrary to nature. "In the winter they stand on the open prairie without clothing; in the summer they sit on knolls wrapped in buffalo robes and yet they are freezing." The initiation ceremony to the Heyoka society is somewhat stereotyped, but the outstanding features is an antinatural trick, the boiling-water per-

[77]Swanton, 1909, p. 173.
[78]Wissler, 1912, pp. 82-85.

formance. In drawing meat from boiling water the performer's hand is protected by certain roots, probably the mallow. During the initiation ceremony the Heyoka members are present dressed as clowns and must act in a contrary manner.[79] Besides the boiling-water trick, the Heyoka may splash boiling water on their backs and legs, complaining that it is cold.[80] They exaggerate the unnatural atmosphere by singing individually and discordantly.[81]

The prominence of contrary behavior threw other comic devices into the background, but the essential point is that the members of the Heyoka were in grave danger of thunder and lightning if they did not perform these contrary ceremonies, so that they were clowns by the direst necessity, by the imperative demand of a vision.

Examples from other tribes will illustrate the predominance of the contrary concept in Plains humor. The Ponca Heyoka were quite similar to those of the Dakota, but the Thanigratha, "Those-who-imitate-madmen," also contrary, were more purely clownish. They might, for example, ford a stream by stripping one leg and hopping across on the leg which was clad.[82]

The Cheyenne Contrary society is also controlled by this concept. Like the Heyoka, it is joined by people who fear thunder and lightning. The society lodge is constructed with the skin wrong side out and the poles outside the skin; the pipe used in the ceremony is assembled incorrectly; the members dress in rags, walk backward, reverse the sitting posture by lying on the ground with their feet up, and say the reverse of what they mean; they tumble about and dance clumsily.[83] They carry red bows and arrows which they use in reverse manner, and they dart about in an eccentric way "like lightning in a storm," for it is said that the "thunderstorm has with him people who act this way."[84]

The Plains Ojibway clown-doctors, Windigokan, combined the serious and humorous aspects of contrary behavior. They were contrary in their play, their warfare, and even in their curing. They too were foolhardy in war. On one occasion twelve of these clowns assembled with their leaders who said: "I am not going to war. I shall not kill Sioux. I shall not scalp four and let the rest escape. I shall go in the daytime." They departed that night and soon met a large body of Sioux. Instead of fleeing they danced until the Sioux, thinking them deities, made offerings to them. Suddenly they drew their weapons and killed four of the Sioux, frighten-

[79]*Ibid.*
[80]Dorsey, 1894, p. 469.
[81]Lowie, 1913, pp. 113-116.
[82]Skinner, 1915a, p. 789.
[83]Grinnell, 2:204-310.
[84]*Ibid.*, p. 329.

ing the remainder. After scalping the four enemies, the leader said: "Now my old men [they were all youths] you must not run home as fast as you can." On another occasion they performed as clowns, being terrified at stumps, fleeing from dogs, and being thrown into spasms at drum beats.[85]

SUMMARY

Those differences which exist between the comic practices of the various American Indian clowns follow in part from the differences set up through different cultural values, in part from purely historical accidents. The emphasis in the Southwest on sex, obscenity, and scatology arose from the supreme importance in the area of the concept of fertility. The unusual prominence of the same things among the nomads of the Southwest and tribes of California arose largely from a cultural connection with the Pueblo tribes. The importance of ceremonial madness on the Northwest Coast was the upshot of a peculiar turn of development and determined the basic character of the clown in that area, while the assignment of clowning to a military society further exaggerated the clown's obstreperous and violent behavior. In the Plains the association of clowning with societies born of visions gave the organizations a typical Plains cast, while a historical accident which originated contrary behavior—probably in a single group—lent the societies their characteristic flavor.

CONCLUSIONS

The high degree of "psychic unity" of man in regard to things laughable is explainable in terms of similar conditioning under different cultures of an innate response. There is no evidence to demonstrate any differences between races in the unconditioned stimuli which produce laughter. All indications point to laughter as an innate response to pleasurable stimuli. To the extent, then, that different cultures find similar things comical, there has been a similar conditioning to things painful and pleasurable. This means simply that sickness, misfortune, poverty and the like, and physiological necessities affect all groups of men alike. They are equally charged with emotional interest, and pleasurable or comic relief from them is everywhere sought.

[85]Skinner, 1914, pp. 500-505.

BIBLIOGRAPHY

BANCROFT, H. H.
1876. Native Races of the Pacific States. 5 vols. New York.

BANDELIER, ADOLF F.
1890. The Delight Makers. New York.

BARRETT, S. A.
1919. The Wintun Hesi Ceremony. Univ. Cal., Publ. Am. Archaeol. and Ethnol., 14:437-488.

BOAS, F.
1892. Eighth Rep. on the Indians of British Columbia. Brit. Assn. Adv. Sci., meeting of 1891, pp. 408-474.

1897. The Social Organization and Secret Societies of the Kwakiutl Indians. U.S. Nat. Mus. Rep. for 1895: 311-738. Washington.

BOURKE, JOHN G.
1891. Scatalogic Rites of All Nations. Washington.

BRINTON, DANIEL G.
1883. The Güegüence; a Comedy Ballet in the Nahuatl-Spanish Dialect of Nicaragua. Philadelphia.

CHAMBERS, E. K.
1903. The Mediaeval Stage. 2 vols. Oxford.

CUSHING, FRANK H.
1920. Zuñi Breadstuff. Ind. Notes and Monogr., 7: 1-673.

DIXON, ROLAND B.
1905. The Northern Maidu. Am. Mus. Nat. Hist., Bull. 17.

DORSEY, J. O.
1894. A Study of Siouan Cults. Bur. Am. Ethnol., Rep. 2: 351-544.

FEWKES, J. W.
1898. The Growth of Hopi Ritual. Journ. Am. Folk-Lore, 11: 173-194.

1900. The New Fire Ceremony at Walpi. Am. Anthropol., New Ser. 2: 80-138.

1903. Hopi Katcinas. Bur. Am. Ethnol., Ann. Rep., 21: 13-126.

GAASTRA, MRS. T. CHAS.
1925. Santo Domingo "Bull and Horse" Ceremony. El Palacio, 18 (No. 4): 67-69.

GOLDFRANK, E. S.
1927. The Social and Ceremonial Organization of Cochiti. Mem. Am. Anthropol. Assn., 33.

GRINNELL, GEO. B.

1923. The Cheyenne Indians. Their History and Ways of Life. 2 vols. New Haven.

HAEBERLIN, H. K.

1916. The Idea of Fertilization in the Culture of the Pueblo Indians. Am. Anthropol. Assn., Mem. 3: 1-55.

KROEBER, A. L.

1907. The Arapaho. Am. Mus. Nat. Hist., Bull. 18: 1-230; 279-454.

1925. Handbook of the Indians of California. Bur. Am Ethnol., Bull. 78.

LOWIE, ROBERT H.

1909. The Assiniboine. Am. Mus. Nat. Hist., Anthropol. Papers, 4: 1-270.

1913. Dance Associations of the Eastern Dakota. *Ibid.*, 11: 101-142.

LUMHOLTZ, CARL.

1907. Symbolism of the Huichol Indians. *Ibid.*, Mem. 3 (Whole Series): 1-228.

MASON, J. ALDEN

1920. The Papago Harvest Festival. Am. Anthropol., New Ser., 22: 13-25.

MATTHEWS, WASHINGTON

1887. The Mountain Chant, A Navajo Ceremony. Bur. Am. Ethnol., Ann. Rep., 5: 385-468.

1902. The Night Chant, a Navaho Ceremony. Am. Mus. Nat. Hist., Mem. 6: 1-332.

MEAD, MARGARET.

1928. Coming of Age in Samoa. New York.

NUÑEZ Y DOMÍNGEZ, JOSÉ DE J.

1927. Corpus Christi in My Native Region. Mexican Folkways, 3: 191-202.

PARSONS, ELSIE CLEWS.

1917. Notes on Zuñi. Am. Anthropol. Assn., Mem. 4: 151-327.

POND, G. H.

1889. Dakota Superstitions. Minn. Hist. Soc. Coll., 2: 215-257.

POWERS, STEPHEN.

1877. Tribes of California. Contrib. North Am. Ethnol., III. Washington.

RADIN, PAUL.

1923. The Winnebago Tribe. Bur. Am. Ethnol., Ann. Rep., 37: 35-560.

REAGAN, ALBERT B.
1915. Masked Dancers of the Jemez Indians. The Southern Workman, Aug., 423-427.

ROBINSON, DAVID M.
"Greek Drama" in J. Hastings, Encyclopaedia of Religion and Ethics.

RUSSELL, FRANK.
1898. An Apache Medicine Dance. Am. Anthropol., 11: 367-372.

SAPIR, EDWARD.
1911. Some Aspects of Nootka Language and Culture. Am. Anthropol., 13: 15-28.

SKINNER, ALANSON.
1914. Political and Ceremonial Organization of the Plains-Ojibway. Am. Mus. Nat. Hist., Anthropol. Papers, 11: 475-511.

1915. Societies of the Iowa. *Ibid.*, 11: 679-740.

1915a. Ponca Societies and Dances. *Ibid.*, 11: 777-801.

SMITH, DE COST.
1888. Witchcraft and Demonism of the Modern Iroquois. Journ. Am. Folk-Lore, 1: 184-193.

SPECK, FRANK G.
1907. The Creek Indians of Taskagi Town. Am. Anthropol. Assn., Mem. 2: 99-164.

1909. Ethnology of the Yuchi Indians. Univ. Pa. Museum, Anthropol. Publ., 1: 1-154.

1911. Ceremonial Songs of the Creek and Yuchi Indians. *Ibid.*, 1: 155-245.

STEVENSON, MATILDA C.
1904. The Zuñi Indians; Their Mythology, Esoteric Societies and Ceremonies. Bur. Am. Ethnol., Ann. Rep. 23.

STRONG, WILLIAM D.
1929. Aboriginal Society in Southern Calif. Univ. Cal., Publ. Am. Archaeol. and Ethnol., 26: 1-249.

SWANTON, JOHN R.
1905. The Haida of Queen Charlotte Islands. Jesup North Pac. Exped., vol. 8, pt. 1.

1909. Contribution to the Ethnology of the Haida. Am. Mus. Nat. Hist., Mem. 8, pt. 1.

1928. Religious Beliefs and Medical Practices of the Creek Indians. Bur. Am. Ethnol., Ann. Rep., 42: 473-673.

THOMPSON, GILBERT.
  1889. An Indian Dance at Jemez, New Mexico. Am. Anthropol., 2: 351-355.

WISSLER, CLARK.
  1912. Societies and Ceremonial Associations in the Oglala Division of the Teton-Dakota. Am. Mus. Nat. Hist., Anthropol. Papers, 11: 1-99.

17

The Foundations of Basin-Plateau Shoshonean Society

This article was first published in *Languages and Cultures of Western North America: Essays in Honor of Sven S. Liljeblad* (ed. E. Swanson, Jr., Pocatello: Idaho State University Press, 1970, pp. 113-151) and is printed here with the permission of the publisher. This is a singularly important essay, for it is probably Steward's most lucid summation of Great Basin society, as well as a clarification and updating of his interpretation of Shoshoni culture. As a footnote to this note, Steward's acquaintance with Liljeblad was mainly through careful study of each other's works and through correspondence. The extent of agreement between them on Shoshonean cultures was remarkable, as was their mutual admiration. Some of the original illustrations have been omitted in this edition.

I. INTRODUCTION

I undertake here an analysis of aboriginal Basin-Plateau Shoshonean society, paying special attention to the clusters of intermarried nuclear families which are its basic components, tracing the interrelationships of such clusters in large aggregates that comprise a network of inter-married and cooperating units, examining the nature of alleged territorial groups that have been designated "bands," and assessing the significance of the larger groupings that are considered "tribes."

Particulars necessary to reconstruct the character of the smaller social units can no longer be obtained by fieldwork (for a summary, bibliography, and discussion of the present status of Great Basin research, see d'Azevedo *et al.*,1966), while important new ethnohistorical sources will probably be rare (Malouf, 1966; Cline, 1966; DeQuille, 1963). The Indian Claims cases gave expert witnesses for plaintiffs and defendants an opportunity to unearth all possible ethnohistorical sources. Plaintiff's testimony for the Ute of Utah, Southern Paiute, Northern Paiute, Yahuskin Northern Paiute and Shoshone-Bannock has been summarized by O. C. Stewart (1966). The evidence and arguments prepared by me on the Ute and by Dr. Ermine Wheeler-Voegelin and me on the Northern Paiute remain unpublished. In drawing on this material, I express gratitutde to Dr. Wheeler-

Voegelin, who regrettably could not find time to co-author this paper with me.

While anthropologists necessarily became adversaries in the Claims cases, it has been pointed out that the plaintiffs and defendants tended to enlist expert witnesses whose views supported their positions.[1] In the case of the Shoshonean groups, as I shall show, the disagreements are implicit in the history of anthropology. On the one hand, there is a traditional tendency to begin analysis with the largest social units — the "tribes" and "bands"—and to accept the presuppositions that they own and defend territory, have cohesion based on common interests and identification, and submit to an overall chief. Since bands are assumed to exist among all hunting and gathering peoples, their presence among the aboriginal, foot Shoshoneans has not been questioned. Mounted bison-hunting Ute bands and warring Northern Paiute bands are not distinguished from alleged aboriginal, pre-horse bands. The smaller components of these bands are accorded little attention.

During the last two or three decades, however, anthropological theory has given us new tools for analysis of social structure. The vast amount of material assembled and discussed in the conferences on Man the Hunter in 1966 (Lee and deVore, eds., 1968) and on Bands in 1965 (Damas, ed.,1969) demonstrate the fundamental importance of starting analysis with the smallest cohesive groups—the "family cluster," "task group," "local band," or "primary subsistence bands"—and then tracing the interaction of these groups in expanding spheres. It has been found in many cases that interaction becomes so diffuse within the larger aggregates that the term "band" has little meaning. In the Basin-Plateau area the present need is to interpret what has already been recorded by means of a coherent theory and consistent procedure.

[1]The very serious charge has sometimes been made that the witnesses altered their views at the request of the attorneys—in blunt terms, that we were bought. O. C. Stewart's unfortunate statement (1966, p. 203) concerning "the attempt by the Department of Justice to avoid payments" to the Indians and his implications that anthropologists' views concerning "tribal lands held long before the Indian Claims Commission cases" were altered must be categorically denied. It must be remembered that attorneys for the plaintiffs received a percentage of the settlement as their fee, while attorneys for the defendants worked on a fixed salary. In my own experience, the Department of Justice asked only that I present and interpret the facts according to my own understandings.

Differences between anthropologists were very real in some cases, and I would prefer to view them as matters of scientific fact and theory. There is no question, however, that attempts to discuss scientific propositions which have been forced into terms of American legal principles and to have discourse between scientists mediated through attorneys badly clouded the areas of genuine scientific disagreement. The lack of direct discussion between anthropologists tended to exaggerate and entrench some long-standing anthropological presuppositions, which I shall discuss here.

In proceeding from the small, cohesive units to the larger social aggregates, I shall draw on Kelly's fieldwork among the Kaibab Southern Paiute (1964) and my own studies of Western Shoshoni and certain Northern Paiute (1938), which now may be viewed in new perspectives. There are few comparable data on social groups smaller than the alleged bands of the Northern Paiute. Lowie (1924), Loud (1929), Kelly (1932), Park *et al.* (1938), O. C. Stewart (1939, 1941), and others who studied the Northern Paiute of Nevada and Oregon could probably have obtained very few necessary particulars on the nature of the components of bands for the period before the Indian wars that would disclose the composition and activities of the subsistence groups and their interactions with one another. All of these sources, however, strongly suggest that these small groups were comparatively independent. My own description of bands among Owens Valley Paiute (1933) will be re-examined in the light of later research.

The many element lists taken among Shoshoneans were unfortunately wholly unsuited for presentation of social structures. My analysis of Shoshonean society (1938) had to be published separately from two sets of element lists (1941, 1943). O. C. Stewart's element lists for the Northern Paiute (1941) and the Ute (1942) name alleged bands but do not analyze them on their components.

The repeated allegation that the aboriginal Shoshoneans were organized in bands is understandable partly as a heritage of a generation or so ago, when all hunters and gatherers were ascribed bands, and partly as confusion of the mounted Ute and Northern Shoshoni hunting bands and of the resistance groups of the Indian wars with pre-horse social groups. It was more than a half-century after the Indian wars and more than a century after mounted hunting bands had developed that anthropologists first did fieldwork among the Shoshoneans. They readily accepted the bands and chiefs already known to settlers, army officers, and administrators, for they were interested in roughing out the culture of major groups within an enormous area. It was not until several decades later that there were enough fieldworkers to investigate smaller divisions and that new theories had given relevance to previously ignored facts.

A striking illustration of the shift of interest from the maximum group, or what was formerly called "band," to the smaller divisions is the contrast between Helm's and Father Morice's reports. Morice's data on the Dogrib Athapaskans gave the band average as 287 persons (1906-10) Helm has distinguished these large groups as "regional bands" and shown that they are no more than groups of identification, whereas the "local band" of some 10 to 20 persons constitutes the permanent subsistence unit (Helm, 1969a, 1969b).

Today, "band" can have no precise definition. Although it generally signifies cohesion and interaction between families that constitute a group of permanent membership, it may range in size from a few families that are closely related to many families which include some not related, or it may be structured on unilineal or bilateral principles, and interaction between the families may take many forms. There can, therefore, be no *a priori* list of characteristics by which a band is defined. The attributes of territory ownership, overall chieftainship, unique dialect, and group identification, which are repeatedly postulated for the Shoshoneans, are purely traditional presuppositions. In fact, Shoshonean society, like that of several other hunters and gatherers, consisted of strongly integrated small units, which had increasingly weaker ties in the larger aggregates.

A very fundamental feature of Basin-Plateau Shoshonean society is the remarkable absence of any traditional institutions other than nuclear families. There were no men's initiations or secret societies, no marriage-regulating clans, moieties, segments, or lineages, no age-grade or women's societies, and no ceremonials, recreational activities, or warfare that united all members of what were later called "bands." Shamanistic activities were concerned with individual illness, rarely with matters of group interest. Dances and gambling were basically local activities. The Ute sun dance and Southern Paiute mourning ceremony were post-reservation.

Owing to the absence of traditional features, the structures observed in the Basin-Plateau area can be more readily recognized as the results of cultural-ecological processes. It will be shown that the small family cluster based on bilateral principles was the inevitable response to areas of meager resources, low population density, and an annual cycle of nomadism, whereas increased interaction between family clusters in pre-horse days resulted from more abundant resources within closely spaced microenvironments, greater population density, and permanent villages. There is no evidence, however, that intensified interaction between family clusters or communities created strong suprafamily, or band, institutions. In Part II, such features as property rights within bounded territories, band leadership, and common group activities will be examined in relation to the serveral types of subsistence activities and other responses to the environment, including the crucial factor of sources of water. Because it is commonly claimed that language differences distinguish bands and tribes, the evidence on dialects will be considered.

Mounted bison-hunting bands evolved among the Northern Shoshoni and Ute but it has not been shown that these were a continuation of pre-horse bands. In fact, there is very good reason to believe that these mounted Ute bands never became fixed in membership. O. C. Stewart is certainly correct that horse nomadism tended to blur territoriality. Both Ute and Northern Shoshoni bands unquestionably represented amalgamations of small, earlier groups of foot Indians who had limited range, and they continued to vary in membership during their comparatively brief history. The same is even more true of the Northern Paiute, who became dislocated from much of their territory and amalgamated in units of changing composition and leadership in wars against the whites. In fact, some designation such as "war party" might be more appropriate than "band," since hostilities against whites probably never involved all members of local groups. I shall show later how a dichotomy into peace and war factions tended to develop.

Neither Ute nor Northern Paiute bands survived relocation to reservations, where they rapidly lost their functions. Ute bands had existed little more than a half-century and Northern Paiute bands only 30 years. No longer able to hunt bison or war against either whites or other Indians and stripped of the attending war honors and of tipis and other features of material culture borrowed from the Plains, Ute society was reduced to family units. When I visited them several times in the 1930s, there seemed to be little new suprafamilial reintegration of the people with reference to institutions of the larger state and national societies.

II. FACTORS IN SOCIAL DEVELOPMENT

1. Subsistence Factors

MULTIPLE SUBSISTENCE PATTERNS

Societies are rarely characterized today merely as hunters, fishers, or food collectors. It was shown in the Conference on Hunters (Lee and deVore, eds., 1968) that vegetable foods comprise some eighty percent of subsistence everywhere except in very high latitudes. The proportion may have been even greater in the Basin-Plateau area, but the very scarcity of game may also have required that a greater proportion of time be devoted to hunting than in areas where game was more abundant, for meat, skins, and rabbit furs were extremely important to the Shoshoneans. Moreover, the particular species of plants and animals utilized were less important than their distribution, abundance, means of obtaining and storing them, and the kinds of social groups involved in exploitative activities. For this reason, the concept of an Old Desert Culture or Tradition with its emphasis on seed gathering as a kind of monolithic phenomenon must be viewed cautiously.

In the Basin-Plateau area, like most other areas, there was a multiple subsistence in that different categories of plant and animal foods entailed certain distinctive activities which affected the nature of complementarity between the sexes and cooperation between individuals, families, and groups of families. Each subsistence activity was related to the characteristics of the species, its abundance, seasonality, distribution, and technology for obtaining it. But seed gathering tends to be competitive, and, in most of the Basin-Plateau area there was no game comparable to bison that shaped so much of Plains Indian society.

Rabbits and antelope were most abundant in broad valleys, but, while they were hunted most profitably when driven by large groups of both sexes, such hunts were unpredictable. Corrals made this hunting possible with antelope, nets with rabbits. Mountain sheep were usually stalked and ambushed in the high mountains, and deer driven or ambushed in lower mountains and valleys by small groups of men. Vegetable greens, seeds, roots, and insects were typically collected in the lower hills and valleys by women. Pine nuts, the winter staple of the southern half of the area, were harvested in the fall by both men and women. In certain localities, fish and waterfowl had exceptional importance, and these were usually taken by men who used an extraordinary number of devices.

Some of these foods were seasonal, although their abundance varied annually according to rainfall. Others, especially antelope herds, required a number of years to re-establish themselves. Some foods could be found with fair certainty in particular localities; others, especially pine nuts, were unpredictable.

Another aspect of the multiple subsistence is that the different resources were often extracted from contiguous but dissimilar and fairly small *microenvironments*, a concept that has been developed with great profit by archeologists (Chang, 1967, pp. 57-60). While the northern and southern portions of the Basin-Plateau are somewhat dissimilar in general features, more important differences are associated with biotic zones at different altitudes in mountain ranges and mesas. The principal encampments, whether permanent or not, were preferably made along the bases of mountain ranges and mesas, where springs or streams were concentrated and from which the people could range through the resource areas of the higher altitudes and the valley flats.

The clearest case of the relationship of microenvironments to society is Owens Valley, where general fertility permitted an unusually dense population and accessibility of principal foods enabled social groups to remain in permanent villages. The valley is 20 to 30 miles wide and bounded on each side by ranges that reach 14,000 feet. The Sierra

Nevada on the west had zones favorable to deer and mountain sheep, while its great altitude which was nowhere less than 10,500 feet, captured considerable rainfall which flowed onto the valley floor at 4,000 feet, spreading out to create fertile marshes and seed lands, before flowing into Owens River. The valley was also the source of rabbits and antelope. The Inyo and White Mountains form a continuous range on the east, which, although in the rain shadow and comparatively dry, had vast areas in the piñon-juniper zone about 6,000 and 8,000 feet, which attracted pine nut harvesters from both east and west. These mountains also had sufficient vegetation to support deer, mountain sheep, and antelope.

The Rocky Mountains, Uintah Mountains, and Wasatch Mountains may also have afforded comparable diversity within microenvironments in some localities, but I know of no direct evidence relating to the social effects of this diversity. The runoff of rainfall created many streams and some major rivers, but these alone did not necessarily support fertile vegetation, for those which flow through wide valleys water only an extremely narrow strip along their borders, while others, especially the Colorado River and its tributaries, are deeply entrenched for long stretches in canyons.

Western Nevada, where the Humboldt, Carson, Walker, and Truckee rivers flow into marshlands and lakes, is most comparable to Owens Valley in local fertility, although it lacked great mountains, except the Sierra Nevada to the west, and its fertile areas lay between large unwatered deserts. Its potential for supporting a dense and permanently settled population, therefore, is questionable.

Except for these well-watered regions, the environment presented serious obstacles to human occupation, and Shoshonean population was sparse and social groups nomadic. Steppe and semideserts grade into vast arid regions with little water or vegetation, such as the Black Rock Desert of western Nevada, the Great Salt Desert and Sevier Desert of western Utah, and the Mohave Desert of southern California, while the whole of southern Nevada and adjoining California are low, hot, and desert, except for a few mountain ranges. Regions of high elevation, such as the Kaibab Plateau and other plateaus and mesas along the Colorado River, are well watered and support vegetation and game, but they are too cold for permanent human habitation. Thus the environmental preconditions of permanent settlements and band organization were extremely limited.

Portions of the Basin-Plateau area might have been more effectively utilized by means of what Downs (1966) calls manipulative as contrasted to exploitative activities, such as incipient farming among a few Southern Paiute, irrigation among certain Northern Paiute, and planting wild seeds, which I have fully discussed (1938). The concept of incipiency, which Downs urges, citing Braidwood and Willey (1962), I defined in 1949 as the beginning of a new activity which has not yet culminated in its social effects. Irrigation, especially on the Colorado Plateau, once utilized streams to support an Anasazi-type culture, but among the Southern Paiute its use in farming was no more than a supplement to gathering wild seeds, and its effect was merely to create a stronger tie of the family cluster to its watering place or winter camp.

TRANSPORTATION

Transportation involves the possible range of people over territory in two quite different ways. First, the advantages of horse transportation over walking are obvious, and it has received much attention. I need only mention here that the wide range of certain Northern Paiute bands reported by early sources would obviously have been impossible without horses. Because, however, not all members of these bands possessed horses, the picture that emerges is one of mounted warriors who frequently moved without their families.

The other factor, which had paramount importance among foot Indians, was the ability of groups to transport water in many of the extremely arid areas. This merits special consideration.

WATER SOURCES, WATER TRANSPORTATION, AND GROUP MOVEMENTS

Shoshonean settlements, especially winter camps, had to be located near water. The several large rivers that flow through the Basin-Plateau area had limited value for this purpose because they are in valleys or canyons, too far from basic resources. Winter camps, therefore, were made in mountains or along the foot of mesas from which springs issued. During the annual subsistence trek, however, sources of water were critical in delimiting freedom of movements, and, since children, food, equipment, and water had to be transported if dry camps were to be made, ability to transport water was vital.

Lee's data on the !Kung Bushmen (1965) are highly suggestive concerning the Shoshoneans although not necessarily applicable in all particulars. He reports tests which show that a normally active person requires a daily minimum of 72 ounces (about 2¼ quarts of water, 4½ pounds, or $9/16$ gallons). Two active adults would thus require 9 pounds or 1⅛ gallons. A family of five will have variable needs, depending on the size of the children. Small children will require less water, but in traveling they may have to be carried or they may slow the pace.

The Shoshoneans have somewhat greater body surface and weight than the Bushmen, but Lee's estimates may indicate minimum needs of people while traveling in summer temperatures in the nineties. Two adults with their children would have a daily requirement of 1⅛ gallons or 9 pounds of water for themselves alone, and probably half again as much for their children. Whereas, the Bushmen used ostrich egg shells and animal stomachs, the Shoshoneans used pitch-coated basketry ollas, which I estimate to have held not over 2 gallons each. A two-day trip would therefore have required at least 1½ ollas of water. The burden would include 27 pounds of water, all essential equipment—especially if the family is not to return immediately to a base camp—varying amounts of food, and perhaps an infant or small child. In view of the loads and the slow pace, 15 or 20 miles is probably the maximum daily travel, which would limit a two-day travel between waterholes to 30 or 40 miles.

There are, of course, many variables, such as temperature, humidity, difficulty of terrain, and health and strength of the individuals. While greater distances could probably be covered in emergencies, 30 or 40 miles is probably as far as they would plan to travel away from water. In many of the higher ranges, springs can be found even where there are no streams, but as the country becomes more generally arid it is extremely important that the family groups not undertake a trip unless they know exactly where the next water is located. The Bushmen had a great advantage over the Shoshoneans in that succulent roots supplied considerable water in parts of their territory.

If water limited cross-country travel and the radius from any spring for food gathering, it was partly offset by the great importance of mountain ranges, for the quantity and variety of resources and the number of springs increased with the altitude of the range.

2. THE DESERT CULTURE OR TRADITION

The sequence of prehistoric cultures over many millennia has limited relevance to the present analysis. Owing to the general acceptance of the idea of a Desert Culture or Tradition, a few considerations may be offered.

First, whether the area remained basically arid or experienced important fluctuations, there were always local differences in precipitation that were no less important than in recent times. It is quite unwarranted, therefore, to postulate a homogeneous society, that has variously been characterized as "bands," "nomadic bands," and even "patrilineal bands." As I shall show subsequently, independent family clusters were the maximum social units of some areas, whereas permanent villages which somewhat affected marriage arrangements and created larger, more cohesive societies, existed in other areas.

Second, as Swanson has indicated (1966), we cannot assume that the climate and culture remained the same for some 10,000 years. Greater precipitation increased the extent of grasslands and forests, decreased lake salinity, augmented the size of rivers, and made fish and waterfowl more abundant. There is evidence of major camp sites far from present sources of water. It is quite possible that in the past certain kinds of flora and fauna were relatively more important, which could have given certain subsistence patterns predominance over others. To judge by petroglyphs of identifiable animals, for example, mountain sheep must have been extraordinarily numerous, especially in the south. In western Nevada, aquatic resources of many kinds were perhaps more abundant in periods of larger streams and less saline lakes. If the basic exploitative devices had the same efficiency as in modern times, population may even have been greater.

An assessment of prehistoric sites should take into account their probable locations with reference to water and evidence of water transportation. Since fur clothing has been preserved since 6000 B.C., evidence of skin water bags or of basketry ollas might be discovered. Those who contend that the climate has not really changed should explain how the early Indians transported water between springs and creeks.

3. Social Factors

TERRITORIALITY AND PROPERTY

Social groups in the Basin-Plateau area obviously had to confine themselves to familiar territory, for knowledge of the location of resources, including water, precluded indefinite and random wandering in strange terrain. That a group exploited about the same territory each year, however, did not imply exclusive claims to or defense of its resources. An informant's statement that "this was our territory; we owned it" is almost invariably followed by the further statement that anyone was free to use the resources. In fact, while the small family clusters of Western Shoshoni traveled during the summer, they exchanged information with other clusters concerning the whereabouts of seeds and game and especially about the prospects for the pine nut harvest in different mountains.

The Kaibab Southern Paiute claimed, according to Kelly, that each family cluster owned the watering place to which it customarily returned each winter, but this meant no more than that a cluster of families made the watering place its preferred headquarters or principal encampment. A similar association of family clusters with winter camp sites at springs, provided the local foods were adequate to support all the people, occurred among the Western Shoshoni, Northern Paiute, and Southern Paiute in the general area east of Owens Valley.

Family ownership of individual pine nut trees and groves and band ownership of groves among Northern Paiute has been claimed by O. C. Stewart (1941). It is incomprehensible how individual trees could be singled out from hundreds of thousands for ownership. Band ownership is explained only in one case: the area "was owned by the band, yet it was subdivided among the individuals who claimed certain spots; notwithstanding this, everyone got piñon nuts where he wanted without payment or permission, unless the 'owner' was on the spot" (1941, p. 440). This may mean that habitual gathering of pine nuts within a convenient distance from the camp or village created a sense of priority, but it hardly indicates exclusive rights that were enforced. In fact, there is no clear reason for rights at all, since a locality that produced a harvest had more than enough for everyone. My own data on Owens Valley are open to the same criticism.

The notion that bands owned hunting rights to all game within its boundaries is really quite meaningless. Rabbit drives were held within very small territories when there were enough people and rabbits. Property concepts pertained to the rabbit nets and the distribution of the killed animals. When deer were taken by means of blinds and traps along migration trails, ownership involved the blinds and other paraphernalia, and use of these at a particular spot. Bow hunting was a very different matter, for if a deer were hit it might have to be pursued for hours or even days, during which it did not observe band boundaries. Mountain sheep and antelope also were hunted by special methods which did not take territoriality into account.

There was ownership of fishing localities, especially along rivers with large seasonal fish runs, where traps, weirs, or other devices that required cooperative construction and use were placed. Similarly, local bands of Canadian Indians assembled at particularly rich and convenient fishing sites during the ice-free fishing season, where they used structures and equipment. These sites were not owned by the larger regional band.

Exclusive ownership also pertained to other things on which work had been expended: irrigation ditches, irrigated areas, cultivated crops, hunting blinds, corrals, traps, and houses. None of these could have involved whole bands.

An assessment of northern Owens Valley consistent with the evidence now available is that because the villages were larger, more closely spaced, and more permanent, and because irrigation augmented the naturally flooded areas, seed crops within a very few miles of the habitations were claimed. Although I had doubted that irrigation was aboriginal, Richard Patch has since informed me of a long ditch in Fish Lake Valley that is covered by a huge sand dune and that seems definitely to have been pre-white, and a few years ago the Paiute of Pyramid Lake were engaged in litigation about water rights, stating that they had irrigated with certain streams before the whites came. This is not conclusive proof, but if some of these local groups depended upon nearby concentrations of seeds, whether irrigated or naturally flooded, use rights would be very strong. This is especially true because seed gathering, unlike hunting, is competitive.

Since Shoshonean society was built of clusters of nuclear families, it is highly probable that these continued to be the basic subsistence units, except in cases of cooperation, as in irrigation or collective hunts. Possibly supracommunity institutions had begun to emerge owing to the integrating effects of the permanent villages, community sweat house, and some festivals in Owens Valley. But it does not follow that such incipient band institutions created the notion of ownership of territories.

Subsistence and territoriality involve very different factors in the case of mounted bands, as among the Ute, Northern Shoshoni, and Bannock. One need only note the many localities where these bands were reported by ethnohistorical sources to recognize the absence of territoriality in major hunting expeditions. These bands had preferred headquarters until they were finally moved to reservations, although they did not return to them every year. The groups and localities involved in obtaining vegetable foods and small game, which constituted major resources, are virtually unknown.

BOUNDARIES

O. C. Stewart has placed major emphasis upon boundaries and published 30 maps in an effort to fix limits of so-called Shoshonean bands and tribes (1966). I ascribe very little importance to such boundaries for several reasons. First, the nature of social groups is best demonstrated by maps showing the clustering of habitation sites, the locations of resources, and the movements of people. Such maps would leave enormous areas quite blank. Second, tribal distributions cannot be indicated by firm lines. Along the whole area of Northern Paiute–Western Shoshoni contact there were bilingualism and intermarriage in a zone up to 100 miles wide. Where peoples such as the Western Shoshoni and Ute were separated, the lines on a map would have to go around the deserts, not through their middle. Third, as I shall show, the extent of certain groups, such as so-called Southern Paiute bands, the Southern Paiute as distinguished from the Ute, and the Northern Paiute penetration into the Shoshoni area of Idaho, is a matter to be determined by word lists which are generally lacking.

Whatever persuasiveness the presentation of bounded "tribal" areas had in the Claims cases, we should not be beguiled by our own expediencies. A line on a map is simply a visual aid. If subsistence areas or linguistic groups overlap or interdigitate, or if there are unoccupied areas, a clean line is more tidy if less accurate than a fuzzy zone. And, if languages are to be represented by colors, these are conveniently confined within lines.

CHIEFTAINSHIP

Unless authority patterns are related to activities requiring supervision, the general allegation that a local group or band had a "chief" is meaningless. The most common leader, or so-called "chief," among the Shoshoneans, was the head of the family cluster, who was obeyed by common consent if he had qualities of leadership. Special chiefs for such activities as rabbit or antelope drives or mudhen hunts had very transient authority. Most of the so-called band chiefs were, as I shall show, war leaders, whose authority did not extend to other activities. In these cases, moreover, such bands and chiefs were contingent on possession of some horses. They fluctuated in membership, overlapped territorially, and ranged over areas far vaster than could be covered on foot.

4. LINGUISTIC FEATURES

Certain generally accepted conclusions regarding band and tribal dialectical distinctiveness are open to question owing to the lack of evidence other than informants' statements in the case of bands and to the significance of linguistic samples in the case of tribes. Accuracy of phonetic or phonemic recording is incidental.

Evidence of any lexical distinctiveness can be related to social groupings on the basis of two assumptions. First, a society whose members have intensive interaction with one another but limited contacts with other groups will develop a distinctive dialect, but, second, a population of scattered small groups which interact through a loose-knit but continuous network will develop cumulative lexical differences between widely separated areas but lack internal dialectical boundaries. An informant's statement that people some distance away spoke a little differently is, therefore, entirely inconclusive as to whether there is a dialectical boundary or merely cumulative lexical differences. In the absence of word lists, a determination between these alternatives cannot be made.

The period when the linguistic evidence is recorded is also crucially important. After more or less isolated local groups have been dislocated from their habitats and amalgamated in larger, more nucleated aggregates of increased social interaction, original differences will gradually be leveled. If an alien language is introduced, especially if it is imposed through schools, the native speech becomes modified. A school situation not only enforces bilingualism, but it removes children from parental influence to a degree unknown among native social aggregates and creates greater interaction within age groups. Successive generations on a reservation where children attend school, therefore, not only tend to lose any dialectical distinctiveness of their pre-reservation parents but, as Indians invariably remark, their native speech becomes "corrupted." Miller (1966) has usefully discussed some of these points.

In order to ascertain dialectical differences among the Western Shoshoni, I recorded lists of 100 words from 14 local groups (1938). These lists are strikingly similar. They showed only occasional lexical changes and no dialectical frontiers. I doubt that phonemic transcriptions of sounds heard by the most acute ear would have altered the comparative significance of these lists. Kelly's belief that each Southern Paiute band was characterized by distinctive dialect is apparently based entirely on informants' statements, for we have no word lists from each of her bands.

In 1934 Kelly (p. 548) wrote that within the Ute-Chemehuevi division "the linguistic relationship is quite close, so close in fact that the northern and eastern [Southern] Paiute do not distinguish sharply between themselves and the Ute except on cultural grounds" and that "the Paiute north and east merge with the Ute," the same being true of the Southern Paiute and Chemehuevi to the west, but (1934, pp. 548-49) she states that "there is an unbroken series of closely related dialectic groups" among the Paiute. Since we have no word lists for these supposed dialectic groups, the evidence may also be interpreted as differences without frontiers. My own data on Southern Paiute social groups of the Ash Meadows, Pahrump Valley, Death Valley, and Panamint Valley region (1938) disclose no bands, and my word lists show no dialects. O. C. Stewart's lists of words for several Ute and Southern Paiute groups (1942) also fail to show clear differences even between these so-called tribal groups.

It is expectable that lexical differences should have developed within so widely distributed a people as the Southern Paiute, but if there were any dialectic frontiers it seems probable that they occurred at deserts, canyons, and other natural barriers.

I have not investigated the nature of the linguistic evidence among the Northern Paiute, except for a few word lists I took in eastern

California and portions of Nevada where the Northern Paiute adjoined Shoshoni. These word lists together with the general absence of bands make it hardly credible that any dialectic frontiers occurred except where natural barriers precluded frequent contacts and communications.

In the case of all three divisions of Shoshoneans, or Numic, it should be remembered that nearly all local groups, except those of the Western Shoshoni, have been on reservations for a hundred years, and that the children of several generations have been exposed to schools. Although local, pre-reservation dialects may have been preserved by some of the very old people, the factors causing change, including intermarriage between individuals of former local groups, would have to be carefully controlled. It is certainly entirely impossible today to obtain evidence of the dialects of the innumerable pre-white bands that have been postulated.

Linguistic evidence must also be used cautiously to demonstrate "tribal" distinctiveness within the three major divisions of Shoshonean. The Northern Paiute generally lack social groupings that would create frontiers, except that the Bannock have apparently been separated from other speakers of Northern Paiute for a long time. In the Shoshoni-Comanche division, I can recognize no marked breaks from the Western Shoshoni through Idaho to the Lemhi Shoshoni, although the Fort Hall and Lemhi had somewhat integrated social groups which might expectably have some dialectic distinctiveness. The Wyoming Shoshoni were a distinctive group, and the Comanche separated off from them at least 200 years ago. Although a Death Valley Shoshoni told me that a Comanche he met at school spoke exactly the same language, there were cumulative differences within Shoshoni-Comanche and probably some frontiers. The hypothesis of a separation of several hundred years of Wyoming Shoshoni and Comanche from the other Shoshoni based on glottochronology is reasonable.

The linguistic distinction made between the Ute and the Southern Paiute is difficult to understand. Miller (1966, pp. 74-75), using the data of earlier studies and employing glottochronology, estimates that these languages have been separated for about 600 years. The question is not the linguist's competence within his own methodology but the significance of his samples, which in this case is a matter for the ethnologist and ethnohistorian to determine. Hale (1958, 1959) had used a Ute sample taken by J. P. Harrington and a Southern Paiute sample taken by Sapir, probably from the Kaibab. But neither Harrington nor Sapir was concerned with the nature of Shoshonean society or with ethnohistory.

There were obviously lexical differences between the many small Southern Paiute groups within their wide territory, whether these were represented by homogeneous dialects of bands or cumulative differences. The Ute also had small social units in the pre-horse period, which certainly differed lexically between western Utah and the Rocky Mountains. But these groups were steadily amalgamated into bands and then into reservation populations, which would have reduced dialectical differences, especially within each younger generation. Comparisons, therefore, cannot be based on the assumption that any particular lexical sample represents a homogeneous tribal language. To the contrary, samples obtained from different reservations, from individuals of different ages and local origins, and at different periods would certainly yield dissimilar results.

The most tenable interpretation of Ute-Chemehuevi is that it constituted a basically similar dialect from the Rocky Mountains to the Mohave Desert and Death Valley, but that it varied where geographical and possibly social barriers interrupted communications, but it was in no way divided into Ute and Southern Paiute languages. Ute is, as Kelly observes, a cultural distinction. Local groups became Ute rather than Southern Paiute upon acquiring horses and the cultural features associated with them.

III. THE SHOSHONEAN FAMILY CLUSTER

1. THE NUCLEAR FAMILY AND FAMILY CLUSTER

The present analysis will discuss the nuclear family and its association with other families in small clusters or primary subsistence units, and then sketch the interactions of family clusters in expanding networks. This will lead to a consideration of bands in Part IV. Although particulars requisite for the analysis of family clusters are not available for all Shoshoneans, I believe that there are sufficient data to support the thesis that all Shoshonean groups, with the possible exception of some bison hunters, had formerly been based on such primary family or kin clusters. It is also possible to demonstrate that the family cluster was necessarily bilateral.

Data on group composition are almost exclusively from Kelly's studies of the Soutern Paiute, especially the Kaibab (1964), and my own material on the Northern Paiute, Shoshoni, and Southern Paiute who occupied California and southern Nevada east of Owens Valley (1938). I select these groups from my earlier monograph for reappraisal because I knew them best, having spent many years in the area and obtained fuller genealogical and census data than from elsewhere. New phrasing of problems has given these data a certain relevance not formerly evident.

Although Kelly and I did our fieldwork in the 1930s, our censuses, which represent the period of the 1880s, are so consistently similar that they must provide a generally accurate picture, despite certain omissions and inaccuracies of detail. Our informants were adult by the 1880s, which is only a decade after the Powell and Ingalls censuses (1874a, 1874b, 1876). My Shoshoni and Northern and Southern Paiute groups, moreover, had remained on ranches or attached to towns near their places of origin, whereas most other Shoshoneans had been relocated and intermixed on reservations. Limitations on our data include frequent uncertainty about grandparents, great-grandparents, and other relatives beyond siblings and spouses. I was able to obtain somewhat better data than Kelly on genealogies and on the origins of individuals married into local groups. By 1880, disease had undoubtedly somewhat reduced the populations, but there is no reason to conclude that this had altered basic patterns.

Very little information on the camp sites, composition, and interactions of family groups is available for the pre-horse and pre-white Ute, Northern Shoshoni, and Northern Paiute, for these small groups had been dislocated and amalgamated with one another owing to Indian wars and resettlement on reservations by the mid-nineteenth century. In all of these cases there are references to fragmentation of the larger society into family groups during seasons of food collecting, but we simply do not know the nature of these groups or their duration.

In emphasizing the importance of the nuclear family in 1938, I also stressed the clustering of intermarried families. The nuclear family had a high degree of independence because it did in fact frequently shift its allegiance from one cluster to another, but it rarely lived alone. The cluster characteristically consisted of intermarried families, each family living in a separate "camp" or house but all wintering together and traveling from spring to fall as a cooperating subsistence unit. The cluster was bilateral in nature. Multicluster aggregates constituted temporary alliances for a few cooperative activities, such as hunting, or other associations where local resources could support unusual numbers of people.

The fundamental importance of the nuclear family requires reemphasis because Lévi-Strauss (1963, pp. 31-51) has questioned whether it is structurally an independent social unit in the sense that it retains its essential characteristics despite entering dissimilar contexts and whether its very existence as well as its nature is not subordinate to its larger context. Lévi-Strauss ascribes the nuclear family secondary importance to the relationship between brothers-in-law—and between the wife giver and the wife taker—which is manifest in the parent-child, uncle-nephew, husband-wife, and brother-sister relationship and in types of marriage prescriptions and proscriptions and in authority patterns. It takes two families to produce the marriage partners that comprise the nuclear family. Lévi-Strauss's interpretation implies that the patterned relationship between these two families has primary importance.

The primacy of the nuclear family among the Shoshoneans is validated by two considerations that I believe to be tenable in all other societies. First, the nuclear family rests upon a biological complementarity between husband and wife in procreation and cultural complementarity in care and socialization of children, subsistence activities, and other roles. If the father surrenders certain functions to the mother's brother, it represents a secondary modification of the nuclear family under specific conditions. Second, these conditions consist of patterned marriage rules and postmarital residence that regularize the relationship between brothers-in-law. Where marriage and residence are extremely variable, the relationship between brothers-in-law will be too haphazard to permit any consistent association with, and patterned behavior between, any relatives except man and wife and parents and children.

The Shoshonean groups I consider here lacked any fixed patterns of postmarital residence and contacts between brothers-in-law. Empirical data show that children of either sex might remain with their parents or leave to marry into other groups, so that brothers-in-law might be brought into close association in some cases but remain a great distance apart in others, and children might or might not be members of the same family clusters as their various aunts or uncles. The nuclear family was more conspicuously stable as viewed in these variable contexts.

The interrelationship of phenomena that determine the nature of the Shoshonean family cluster is as follows:

1. The nuclear family was basic everywhere, and it was not part of any larger, marriage-regulating structures such as clans, lineages, moieties, or marriage classes.

2. Relationship extended bilaterally from the nuclear family.

3. Several nuclear families associated with one another in subsistence activities and at winter sites, because, *a,* cooperation between families gave each greater security, and, *b,* the winter camps were strategically located with reference to water, fuel, and local foods and therefore attracted as many families as the subsistence area could support.

4. Children of both sexes remained with their parents' group if possible, but there were no unilineal tendencies or preferences that created exogamous patrilineages or matrilineages.

5. Because local resources usually limited the family cluster to a maximum of four or five families, the nucleus consisted of locally born consanguines: parents, children, and grandchildren and siblings and first

384 Evolution and Ecology

cousins. Spouses usually came from elsewhere. The cases of marriages between local persons would, if we had genealogical data, probably be shown to be with second or third cousins. Empirically, the ratio of endogamous to exogamous marriages is about one to six or seven.

6. The composition of the local group was extremely variable, owing to sex ratios at birth, fertility, and survival. Although the nucleus of consanguines generally included both sexes, women predominated in some cases and men in others.

7. The principle of bilaterality, therefore, was inevitable. Groups were not large enough to maintain themselves if unilineal principles were enforced.

8. Marriage into other groups or family clusters was contracted with a frequency that was more or less proportionate to the distance of these groups, although groups tended to be concentrated in localities with sources of water. Marriage partners were most often found ten to fifteen miles away, but in many cases they were thirty to fifty miles distant.

9. The network of marriages thus weakened with distance from a particular group, while it extended indefinitely from one group to another until blocked by natural barriers. The network extended freely across so-called tribal lines, between Northern Paiute, Shoshoni, and Southern Paiute where they were in contact.

Where basic subsistence resources are augmented so as to increase population density and support closely spaced, permanent villages, the need to find marriage partners from great distances will diminish, more nuclear families will live in continued association, the relationship between brothers-in-law and other kin will become regularized, and population aggregates consisting of many family clusters will participate in various activities. The foundations of a band or proto-band will be laid. The transportational facilities of the horse will have the same effect as increased resources in permitting larger social groupings. These factors will be discussed in Part IV.

2. Northern Paiute and Western Shoshoni Family Clusters

The exemplifications presented here are mainly from Deep Springs Valley and Fish Lake Valley as published in my monograph (1938). These valleys lie east of Owens Valley across the massive White and Inyo Ranges, but they are separated from each other only by a low pass. Deep Springs Valley is roughly 10 by 20 miles and had four or five habitation sites. Fish Lake Valley is nearly fifty miles long but fairly narrow; it had eight sites. Its eastern end, which is close to Death Valley and various sites east of Death Valley, was occupied mainly by Shoshoni, but they freely intermarried with Northern Paiute and with some Southern Paiute with whom they were culturally identical.

The censuses of these two valleys show that each local aggregate or family cluster had one to five "camps" or nuclear families, but averaged only two families, that the clusters ranged from four to twenty-nine persons, but averaged only 12.4 persons, and that the individual nuclear family varied from two persons to a total of 12 but averaged 6.2 persons.

These groups are difficult to analyze in terms of residence rules, especially for the people of Deep Springs Valley, who shifted their winter residence site so often that the entire population might be considered one. "Uxorilocal" adds nothing to "matrilocal," and "virilocal" is no more precise than "patrilocal," for none of these terms implies whether postmarital residence was within a hundred yards or fifty miles of the residence of one or the other spouse. Of 43 married couples, 20 were siblings who remained with their parents and took spouses from elsewhere, 15 were first cousins, and 8 were persons of unknown relationship but possibly second or third cousins. In six cases marriage was with a resident of the local group, which means that consanguinity was not traceable within four or five generations.

Since the family clusters were fairly widely spaced in this generally arid area, most marriages were contracted within five to ten miles, but some up to thirty miles, and a few with Owens Valley and Long Valley fifty miles away. Reassessing Owens Valley, where I did not obtain census data, in the light of the present data, which show that 11 of 43 marriage partners came from Owens Valley to Deep Springs and Fish Lake Valleys, it appears that Owens Valley was not as endogamous as I had supposed. To some extent, this might be explained by greater mobility achieved toward the end of the last century, but it probably also means that the Owens Valley population was dispersed in more village sites than I recorded and that contacts between families and family clusters were made in the pine nut areas of the Inyo and White Mountains which were utilized by people from all three valleys.

Two sample genealogies from Fish Lake Valley and one from Beatty, sixty miles to the southeast, are given in the figure. In all of the censuses the basic core was siblings and sometimes first cousins who remained with their parents and brought spouses from elsewhere. The ratio of one marriage in six to a local person shows the high probability that local residents were consanguinally related except for some marriage partners. The lower part of the figure shows one of the few cases where siblings married siblings, although more complete genealogies of spouses who came from elsewhere would probably show more cases. Such multiple marriages between siblings—brothers to sisters or brother and sister to sister and brother—was viewed as a binding obligation by Owens Valley informants, although I have no census data to support it. The denser population and closer spacing of habitation

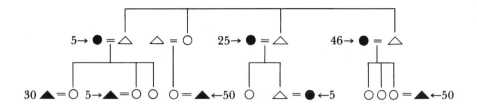

Site 26   Tunava, Fish Lake Valley

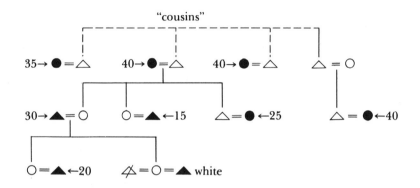

Site 27   Sohodühatü, Fish Lake Valley
(4 camps)

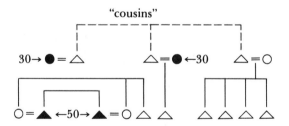

Site 53   Near Beatty, Nevada

Family or "camp" clusters of Western Shoshoni and Northern Paiute east of
Owens Valley in Fish Lake Valley and near Death Valley. These are sample
censuses showing local variations. Site 26 is mixed Northern Paiute and
Shoshoni. Site 27 is predominantly Shoshoni. Site 53 is Shoshoni but includes
a few Southern Paiute. Solid symbols represent spouses for other clusters or
habitation sites. Numbers with arrows indicate distance away in miles of origin
of spouse.

sites in Owens Valley would facilitate this preference, for more potential marriage partners were accessible. Such marriages might also bring brothers-in-law into more frequent contact, and explain the traditionally close relationship between brothers-in-law that I had occasion to observe first-hand. Whether it would create a patterned avuncular relationship is another problem.

3. SOUTHERN PAIUTE

Kelly's Kaibab Southern Paiute census data (1964) are consistent with those for the Western Shoshoni and Northern Paiute just described, although they do not show the place of origin of spouses who married into the local groups and the genealogies are less extensive.

The minimum social unit among the Kaibab was a local cluster of camps or nuclear families, which traveled together hunting and gathering seeds and returned each fall to the same winter camp. These camp sites or headquarters were at water sources which were convenient to firewood and to resources of the mesas and valleys and which were said to have been owned, although other persons were not prevented from drinking the water and families readily moved to other water sources. Such "ownership" may have been connected with domesticated plants, which Kelly's informants thought were acquired a hundred years ago, but Escalante's journal suggests they were known in Southern Paiute territory in 1776 (Bolton, 1950). In either case, people would return each fall to their gardens.

The Kaibab winter resident site or family cluster had one to 7 camps or families, which averaged about 7.5 persons each compared with about 6 for the Western Shoshoni. The total camp cluster ranged from 4 to 39 persons and averaged 12, which was also nearly the same among the Western Shoshoni. Owing to incomplete census data and reduction of the population by disease, the aboriginal figures must have been greater, but this would not have greatly affected the group composition.

Southern Paiute kinship, like that of all other Shoshoneans, was basically bilateral. In a local cluster of 12 persons, probabilities are against its inclusion of potential marriage partners, and in only 9 cases, or about one-fourth of the marriages, both spouses appear to have been members of the same local group. This compares with about one-sixth among the Shoshoni. In one cluster of 7 camps and 35 individuals, relationship between these camps or families is not indicated. They may have been first cousins, but chances that they were second cousins and therefore more marriageable are greater.

Kelly states that informants expressed a preference for matrilocal residence, although its practice is in doubt. Her census data show that the kinship nucleus in 12 cases was brothers, in 2 cases sisters, and in 11 cases siblings of both sexes.

The winter sites, of camp clusters, were somewhat grouped in ten major areas where water sources were concentrated. Kelly's map shows that the sites in some of these were fairly close while others were scattered within 10 to 30 miles. These differing degrees of proximity largely determined intergroup cooperation, and this extended across boundaries of so-called bands to other nearby groups. Aggregates larger than the camp cluster, however, were ephemeral, and there was no cooperation that involved the entire membership of any group that might be considered a "band." In fact, it is hardly credible that all persons in the Kaibab area that extended about 100 miles north-south and 70 miles east-west could maintain meaningful contact with one another. There were no "band" chiefs, ceremonies, or other activities, and no claim to resources within a "band" territory. Informants were unclear about boundaries. The sole criterion of band was thought to be a distinctive dialect, but I have shown that this has no support.

The broad picture of the Kaibab Southern Paiute, therefore, is like that of the Northern Paiute and Western Shoshoni previously discussed, and like that of the Ash Meadows and Pahrump Southern Paiute (Steward, 1938). Local groups intermarried and on occasion cooperated with other groups in a network that extended even across so-called band and tribal divisions to natural barriers.

IV. SHOSHONEAN BANDS

1. THEORY OF BANDS

A considerable literature on the theory of bands has appeared in recent years. Its most important contribution consists of analysis of the kinship structure of the smallest components, as I have undertaken for the Shoshoneans in Part II, and examination of the expanding spheres of interaction within the largest aggregate. This contrasts with the more common approach to Shoshonean bands and "tribes," which assumes that larger aggregates always existed and had such attributes as territoriality, a distinctive dialect, and overall headmen or chiefs.

In examining the nature of Shoshonean bands, it is necessary first to distinguish aboriginal tendencies toward bands from mounted buffalo hunters and from very transient predatory bands of the Indian wars. These distinctions have not been adequately made, with the result that Northern Paiute bands, which are largely those mentioned by mid-nineteenth-century explorers, army officers, and Indian Office administrators, were accepted by anthropologists, who endeavored to relate them to informants' testimony. The extensive disagreement between anthropologists is very understandable. Service's Western Shoshoni "bands" (Service, 1962) are based on evolutionary theory and backed by Powell's conceptions of a hundred years ago. Southern Paiute bands, although postulated by O. C. Stewart, are now regarded by Kelly (1964) as no more than dialectic divisions, and even this characteristic has not been proven.

Where explanatory rather than purely descriptive analysis is offered, O. C. Stewart (1966) and Service (1962) hold entirely different theories. O. C. Stewart's earlier assertions regarding Northern Paiute bands (1933) and apparently his later ones regarding native Ute and Southern Paiute bands (1942) seem merely to follow the traditional anthropological presupposition that all food hunters and gatherers were organized in this manner, for he offers no explanation of why this was so. His later hypothesis (1966) offers a biological explanation in postulating that man shares a tendency with all mammals to occupy and defend territory against trespass. He writes, "I subscribe to the theory that the notion of territoriality is very fundamental among mammals. It has developed strongly among aborigines. The whole notion of tribal and linguistic boundaries being fairly fixed and definite is a good one." Mammals remain in fixed territories and "other members of the same species entering the territory are often challenged, and such trespass is the basis for contest. This has been observed among the primates of Africa" (1966, pp. 168-169). This contention is strikingly similar to Ardrey's (1966) very dangerous attempt to justify war on the grounds that all animals including man are innately territorial and fight other groups to protect their territories.

Although O. C. Stewart has listed what he alleges to have been territorial bands among the Ute and Southern Paiute as well as the Northern Paiute (1942), his contention regarding mammalian territoriality pertains principally to so-called "tribes"—the Ute, Southern Paiute, and Northern Paiute. In the Court of Claims cases, where he was expert witness for the plaintiffs, these tribal units had to prove that they had been identifiable groups, which, from time immemorial, had occupied and utilized resources within delimitable territories to the exclusion of other groups. The theory of innate territoriality was thus suitable to the legal requirements of the claims cases, and it has a certain scientific appeal in its simplicity and universality, which obviates the need of deeper inquiry.

This theory, however, is negated by O. C. Steward's own data, which show that neither band nor tribe members did in fact repel trespassers. The case for territoriality among chimpanzees, baboons, and gorillas is quite misleading since it is postulated on a human model (Steward,

1938). In fact, it is incredible that a broad assumption based on certain observations of mammalian behavior should entirely preclude consideration of cultural factors that are involved in the various forms that rights to natural resources take among human beings.

Service, in contrast to O. C. Stewart, deduces from evolutionary theory that patrilocal bands had existed in the Great Basin but disappeared after white settlement; he derives these from an upper Paleolithic stage, and he offers Powell's reports in support of them among Shoshoneans. I shall show that unilineal groups could not have existed among the Western Shoshoni. The censuses taken by Kelly among the Southern Paiute and by me among the Western Shoshoni, which represent a period within ten years of Powell's field investigations, show no trace of patrilocal or patrilineal bands. As for Service's distress at my lack of faith of a man "so famous for scientific rectitude and perspicacity as was Powell . . . ," I give Powell major kudos as a redoubtable soldier, intrepid explorer, and promotional genius, but an examination of his unpublished manuscripts while I was a member of the Bureau of American Ethnology revealed incredible ethnographic naïveté. Powell simply held the views about bands that were current during his period.

2. THE BASIS OF HUNTING AND GATHERING BANDS

While the irreducible minimum social unit of societies known ethnographically is the nuclear family, such families rarely live in isolation. Among hunters and gatherers, who live under harsh conditions and whose social aggregates must be rather widely spaced, a single nuclear family would survive with difficulty. A cluster of families, therefore, tends to remain in close association, constituting a fairly permanent subsistence unit. This cluster of families is so small—from two to rarely over five, except where there is unusual local abundance of foods—that the preference of children to remain with parents creates a nucleus of siblings with their spouses. As social interaction extends to other family clusters, the number and strength of interrelations generally decreases. My earlier category of "composite bands" (1936) does not take this into account.

Any kind of band, therefore, is built principally of kinship units. In most cases, however, the small family cluster necessarily consists of bilaterally related families, because, owing to the fortuitous ratio of sexes at birth, the nucleus may consist only of female siblings and first cousins, of male siblings and first cousins, or of both. A unilineage could not be perpetuated because probabilities are against sufficient male or female births each generation to establish and maintain a unilinear, exogamous kinship unit. The patrilineal band I discussed some years ago (Steward, 1936) was much larger than the family clusters of the Shoshoneans, and averaged some 40 to 50 persons. A Shoshonean family cluster of 10 or 20 persons would have too many cases with no male births to ensure the continuation of a patrilineage. The same would be true of matrilineages.

It is possible, of course, that the combination of denser population, larger groups, and factors that predispose to unilineal descent may in the past have caused patrilineal bands. Earl Swanson writes me that there is evidence of patrilineages among the contemporary Northern Shoshoni. Elsewhere, however, all Basin-Plateau Shoshoneans were basically bilateral, even where population aggregates exceeded the size of the family cluster.

Among bilaterally organized societies, the northern Athapaskans are perhaps most strikingly similar in basic units to the Shoshoneans. Despite differences in environments and exploitative technologies, the adaptive processes have been much the same. Among the Dogrib, a small cluster of nuclear families related consanguinally through parents and children is what Helm (1969a) has designated the "local band," as contrasted with the maximum group or "regional band" which is no more than a group of identification. Between these extremes were various intermediate groupings of varying composition and duration associated with seasonal activities. Helm (1969b) cites Chang (1962) on the methodological importance of distinguishing settlement pattern, or territorial arrangements of people, from community pattern, or social arrangements, and she calls attention to the need to explain residence in terms of security, useful alliances, and other variable factors as well as residential rules. These points became evident in my 1938 analysis, for both the residence and social affiliation of any nuclear family were determined by resource limitations of particular localities, survival rates which made some clusters too large and others too small, and sex ratios, all of which affected availability of marriage partners.

Among both the Shoshoneans and Athapaskans, interaction of local bands or family clusters with one another became more diffuse with distance. Among the Western Shoshoni and Southern Paiute, it extended to where deserts, large mountain ranges, or major canyons imposed severe limitations on interactions. Among the northern Athapaskans it extended greater distances and "regional bands" are extremely large, for winter travel by means of dog sleds or toboggans and summer travel by canoes permitted extensive contacts within drainage areas, but beyond these interaction was curtailed by large lakes and divides.

The Eskimo had a considerable variety of social groupings, each adapted to various parts of their habitat. Many of these, including those among the Central Eskimo, were bilateral bands much larger than those of the Shoshoneans, for strategic sealing and fishing sites supported a considerable population for long periods. Although a few bands had only 10 to 20 persons, others had as many as 150. The larger bands thus could marry endogamously (Damas, 1968, 1969; Balikci, 1968), although exogamous marriages created a wide network of kinship ties. Only 10 percent or less of the members of the Shoshonean family cluster married endogamously. Many of these Eskimo aggregates, therefore, represent bands that were not primarily kinship units. Lee found that the basic unit of the !Kung Bushmen consisted of 2 to 10 families, or 10 to 30 persons, which was the stable aggregate that cooperated in subsistence, and while marriage relations extended very widely, social interaction decreased outward from these "bands" (1965, pp. 41-53).

Birdsell (1968) proposed, on the basis of certain Australian data, that some half-dozen families, or 20 to 30 persons, is a "model" of the basic and minimum viable social unit. While particular units may drop below this minimum, owing to various factors, a rather similar unit seems to have been basic to the Shoshoneans, Athapaskans, perhaps the Bushmen, some Australians, and the Alacaluf (Steward and Faron, 1959).

A comparative view of food-extracting societies based on bilateral kinship thus shows that the most cohesive unit is the smallest viable group, which tends to be a kin group, whereas the maximum group of social interaction is the least cohesive and to designate it a "band" means very little. Such "bands" had none of the characteristics ascribed by O. C. Stewart to the Northern Paiute, Southern Paiute, and the pre-horse Ute bands. Only those hunters, gatherers, or fishers who have extraordinarily abundant local resources are grouped for substantial periods in large, cohesive bands that have supra-kin features. In some cases settlements and communities are permanent, as among Alaskan Eskimo and on the Northwest Coast, and the term "band" is no longer applied.

In the Great Basin, it is possible that exceptional resources in certain localities, or areas with a number of microenvironments, predisposed society to incipient bands or proto-bands in aboriginal times, but these must be clearly distinguished from mounted bison-hunting bands and from predatory and warring bands that developed during the Indian wars after white settlement. There is absolutely no scientific justification for assuming that bands and chiefs named by army officers, explorers, settlers, or Indian Office officials were aboriginal features that survived drastically changed conditions.

3. ABORIGINAL BAND TENDENCIES

I have previously mentioned that unusual concentration of resources within microenvironments in portions of the western slopes of the Rocky Mountains, the piedmonts of the Uintah and Wasatch Mountains, and the well-watered regions along the eastern side of the Sierra Nevada Mountains might have provided preconditions favorable to incipient band development. We have few hints of aboriginal society in these areas, except that a tendency of small groups to remain fairly independent in subsistence activities connected with food collecting seems evident.

In 1933 I had postulated that bands in Owens Valley had most of the characteristics traditionally ascribed bands, but subsequent research in southern Owens Valley indicated only loose social aggregates. In the perspective of more recent comparative analyses of bands, it now seems more appropriate to designate the northern Owens Valley aggregates only as incipient or proto-bands. They were based on an unusually dense population, permanent villages, access to abundant resources within several microenvironments, and a high degree of interaction between villages within a fairly delimited area. The social interaction involved some cooperative hunting, annual festivals, community irrigation, use of a permanent sweat house, extensive intermarriage, and probably far more visiting than was possible between the widely spaced communities to the east. But there was no warfare, except vaguely remembered friction with people west of the Sierra Nevada Mountains, no dialectic frontiers, no limitation of marriage to other members of the band, and no hunts that involved all band members. There may have been several sweat houses, each conveniently located near house clusters, and it is not certain that dances involved more than a few local groups. The property rights, as previously suggested, were probably based on use-ownership principles, and these seem not to have been defended with much determination. In northern Owens Valley, therefore, these can be considered bands only in the sense that the people utilized resources within certain customary limits, interacted with one another more than with people farther away, and perhaps had a sense of identification with other members of the band.

4. NORTHERN PAIUTE WAR BANDS

The Northern Paiute who extend through western Nevada into Oregon probably had foci of settlement in the comparatively well-watered regions of western Nevada and of the Harney and Malheur Lakes and Owyhee and Snake Rivers of Oregon, but these were separated by vast deserts, such as the Black Rock Desert, and by areas which had few high mountain ranges. Any social interaction between local family clusters of foot Indians would expectably be with other clusters that were accessible and not with those within the band boundaries drawn by O. C. Stewart (1939). Indeed, significant interaction would quite obviously have been impossible within territories as large as O. C. Stewart's Koa'agai band, which has an area 65 by 175 miles, or the Wada band, which is 100 by 150 miles. Any band tendencies among the Northern Paiute, as in other parts of the world, would necessarily be among people in fairly localized regions of high population density. We have no detail on the size or composition of the local family clusters of these Northern Paiute or on the location and degree of permanence of their camps. Various sources, however (Park *et al.*, 1938; Kelly, 1932), mention that small groups were involved in food collecting but fail to indicate any band function whatever.

It was the custom of many of the Northern Paiute as well as many Western Shoshoni to name people after a food or some other characteristic of an area. This was definitely not a band designation among the Shoshoni, and this feature alone does not prove bands among the Paiute. A Jack Rabbit Eater might become a Wada Seed Eater if he moved to the area where the latter was a characteristic food, just as a New Yorker becomes a Chicagoan after transferring his residence. Park (1938, pp. 622-23) specifically denies territoriality or permanent membership of families in any group.

The confusion of attempting to identify and map bands from informants' testimony is very evident in the case of the Southern Paiute, especially in the area between the Kaibab and the Ute. Where Kelly (1934) placed the Kaibab, Panguitch, and Kaiparowits (the last two thought by some informants to have been Ute), O. C. Stewart (1942) locates eight bands. He places three more to the north of these, divides Kelly's San Juan band into two bands, and locates the Shivwits where Kelly's Uinkaret are. One must conclude that obliging informants gave band identification and location a good try but did not know what it was all about.

Northern Paiute bands are those which were recruited by various chiefs during the Indian wars, and which, owing to their fluctuating membership and shifting territories, could not be bounded and were not aboriginal. Hostilities began in western Nevada in the 1840s, when the flow of immigrants and livestock began to destroy native resources. By 1850, some 42,000 persons and 60,000 head of livestock passed through Fort Laramie to continue on along the California and Oregon trails (Kagan, 1966, p. 171). As ranchers fanned out to settle the more attractive areas of Nevada and Oregon, some of the principal sources of native foods were converted into wastes of brush and weeds. Indian hostilities accelerated during the 1850s and lasted into the 1870s, when most of the Paiute were placed on reservations, in some cases along with Shoshoni.

The accompanying map, which is based on research done by Ermine Wheeler-Voegelin and me for the Northern Paiute claims case and cannot be supported here by all the documentation we used, shows where some of the most frequently mentioned chiefs were reported between 1860 and 1877, with the exception of Winnemucca, who was mentioned much earlier. The dashed lines enclose the territories in which Winnemucca, Natchez, Paulina, Ocheo, Wewawewa, and Egan were encountered. These areas cover distances of more than 250 miles, and the territories overlapped one another while bearing no relation to O. C. Stewart's map (1939). It is fairly obvious that leaders attracted followers from men who had acquired horses, which were essential to their great territorial mobility. Their activities consisted of eluding the U.S. Army while committing depredations on ranches and mining communities. Not all the chiefs indicated on my map were in power during the whole period of the Indian wars. Some led bands for brief periods and were followed by more persuasive or successful men. The range of these chiefs tended to converge in eastern Oregon toward the Snake River where the rugged terrain of the Owyhee Mountains afforded refuge.

Among these chiefs Winnemucca commanded most attention, owing partly to the publicity given him by his daughter, Sarah. That he achieved prominence and covered a large territory should not be taken to mean that the Northern Paiute verged on true tribal nationalism (O. C. Stewart, 1939). All of the Paiute shared a similar culture, and, especially after the wars, many of them developed a sense of common destiny with previously isolated local groups. As late as the 1920s, however, the Paiute of Owens Valley and Mono Lake had no idea that people spoke their language in northern Nevada and Oregon.

In cross-cultural perspective these Northern Paiute and other Shoshonean militaristic bands were somewhat similar to the predatory mounted bands which developed in response to white settlement in many other areas. Serious reduction of native resources, dislocation of native population aggregates, acquisition of horses, and the introduction of livestock and ranches which could be raided amalgamated local groups under persuasive leaders. Predatory activities were combined with other band functions, especially hunting, in such widely separated societies as the Tehuelche and Puelche of Patagonia, the Comanche and other tribes of the Plains, some of the Apache, and the Ute. The Northern Paiute predatory bands had brief duration, partly because they had never had a subsistence basis in big game hunting.

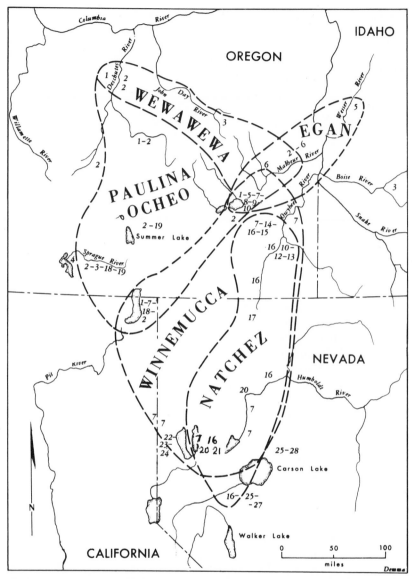

Reported locations of Northern Paiute chiefs between 1860 and 1877. Dashed lines are territories of chiefs named on map. Numbers are locations of following chiefs: 1. Wewawewa. 2. Paulina. 3. Howlock. 4. Mashenkasket. 5 and 6. Egan or E. E. Gant. 7. Winnemucca, first reported much earlier. 8. Oites. 9. Buffalo Horn. 10. Leggins. 11. Tau-wa-dah. 12. Mawuha. 13. Paddy Gaps. 14. Namara. 15. Its-a-da-mah. 16. Natchez. 17. Black Rock Tom. 18. Ocheo. 19. Chocktoot. 20. Sue. 21. Tonoyiet. 22. To Repe. 23. Ge-nega. 24. War-se-que-orders. 25. San Joaquin. 26. Wahi. 27. Had-sa-pokes. 28. Oderie.

5. UTE BANDS

I have attempted to show that the Ute are simply those Ute-Chemehuevi who acquired horses and adopted many Plains features about 150 years ago. They occupied western Colorado to the deserts of western Utah. A similar transformation occurred among the Northern Shoshoni and Comanche somewhat earlier. In both groups the change has correctly been attributed to the mobility permitted by the horse, which made large encampments and joint hunting and war parties possible. My earlier hypothesis that the westward spread of this culture was limited by grasslands that would support horses, however, needs qualification. Other Shoshoneans did, in fact, acquire some horses, and the warring Northern Paiute bands could not possibly have covered their enormous territories on foot. Somewhat greater emphasis, therefore must be placed on the value of horses to the Ute and Northern Shoshoni in bison hunting, which was far greater than in hunting deer, antelope, or mountain sheep. Bison occurred in some numbers west of the Rocky Mountains in Northern Shoshoni and Ute territory until after these Indians acquired horses. Possibly mounted hunting hastened the extinction of the bison west of the Rockies toward the middle of the last century, and led the Ute and Northern Shoshoni to cross the continental divide with greater frequency.

The general trend of change in Ute society since Escalante's journey in 1776 is increased consolidation of the people in fewer and larger groups until, about a century ago, the Ute were restricted to reservations. Escalante is the principal observer of pre-horse Ute (Bolton, 1950). In western Colorado he encountered several Ute groups which had some horses but were not described as wholly mounted, consolidated, mobile bands. In Utah he found unmounted Ute in the region of Utah Lake and the lower Sevier River, but he offers few particulars on the several villages of these people. He named chiefs at Utah Lake, but this tells us little. Miera y Pacheco's map of Escalante's expedition shows a "Cumanche" village on the southwestern shore of Utah Lake, and it notes that these people controlled the country north of the lake. "Cumanche Yamprica" (Shoshoni Yampa Eaters) located in north-western Colorado were said to be a feared group of horsemen who prevented the Ute from crossing eastward to the Uintah Basin, which then was unoccupied, although it later became a major center of Ute habitation and finally the location of the reservation. Escalante's designation of the Sevier River people as "Barbones" ("bearded ones") brings to mind Hiller's photographs taken on the Powell expedition of several remarkably bearded old men apparently of the Las Vegas Southern Paiute group (Steward, 1939).

By the 1820s, a half-century after Escalante, all Ute-Chemehuevi peoples as far south as the lower Sevier River of western Utah had acquired horses and were called Ute. Their mobility is indicated by a report of the Ashley-Smith expedition, 1822-1827 (Dale, 1918), that several thousand Indians believed to be Ute wintered on the Green River above the Yampa River and others at the mouth of the Uintah River. The Timpanogs or Timpanogots at Utah Lake had horses by 1840 (Russell, 1921) and probably earlier, while the Pahvants farther south were also mounted by this time.

By the middle of the last century the Ute had formed highly mobile bands of hunters, warriors, and traders, who ranged northward into Wyoming and across the Rocky Mountains to the east. Whiterock on the present Uintah Ute Reservation became a trading post in 1832, 32 years before the reservation was established. Walker's band of Timpanogots from Utah Lake were reported at various localities eastward to the Green River.

As white settlers entered Colorado and Utah, the Ute bands acquired a predatory character. The Timpanogots and Pahvant west of the Wasatch Mountains, however, were rapidly subjected to the pressure of Mormon settlements after 1847, and they began to drain off toward the east, although some held out for two decades. Similar consolidation began a little later in Colorado.

The identification and localization of different Ute groups at this time are confused by the proliferation of names of groups and chiefs and the reports of groups at different locations, and it would be entirely futile to attempt to relate these groups to alleged territorial bands of pre-white or pre-horse Ute. An example is the so-called "Yampa," which, like food-named groups in Nevada, was probably applied to any Ute who frequented the Yampa River region where they collected yampa roots. The accompanying figure, however, shows that between 1834 and 1872 "Yampa" were reported through most of the Ute territory and even beyond it. These Ute were apparently amalgamated with those of the White and Grand Rivers on the White River Reservation, and at one time were placed on the Uintah Reservation.

The Ute of various local areas began to amalgamate after 1850, a process that was accelerated after 1868, when very few local groups remained separated. Nearly all Ute became placed on the Uintah and Ouray Reservation in Utah and the Southern Ute Reservation in southwestern Colorado.

Final pacification was not achieved with removal to the reservations, and a dual chieftainship developed. The peace chiefs were men who admonished the Indians to remain on the reservations, whereas the war chiefs recruited followers for predatory raids off the reservations. A similar dichotomy was marked among the Apache, and there was

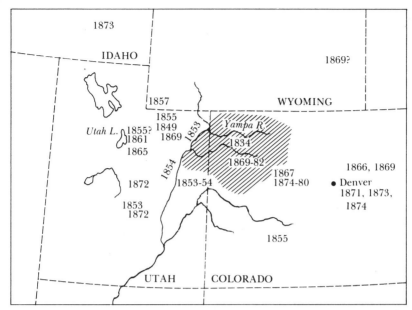

Reported locations of "Yampa" Ute at different dates. Shaded area is probable territory of principal range.

evidence of it also among the Northern Paiute. Such a dichotomy has long been considered basic to North American Indians, and possibly it was aboriginal among some tribes, but most Indian warfare consisted of raids by small groups of recruits to take scalps or captives or carry out reprisals and did not involve tribes as wholes. Among the Iroquois, Algonkians, and their neighbors in the northeast, raiding parties in the aboriginal tradition became confused with post-white national warfare, which allied the Indians with the French or British in the struggle to control the fur trade and required tribal commitments to war or peace. The extent to which the dichotomy between peace and war chiefs elsewhere was connected with wars involving Europeans merits further study.

V. SUMMARY

The Shoshoneans are remarkable for the absence of suprafamilial institutions that structured their society in pre-horse and pre-white times. Cultural-ecological adaptations clearly delimited society among the historic Western Shoshoni and Southern Paiute to basic aggregates of no more than about five nuclear families which comprised a cohesive

400 Evolution and Ecology

subsistence unit. These family clusters were too small to have developed unilineal principles, and they were consequently bilateral. But kinship extended outward from each cluster to other clusters through marriages contracted in both lines of descent.

If the origin of the Numic languages was somewhere in southern California and Nevada, proto-Numic society must have been like that of the Western Shoshoni and Southern Paiute; for the deserts of this region could not have supported much larger populations one or two thousand years ago. During the expansion and differentiation of the three Numic divisions, other populations were displaced, including those of eastern Nevada, Utah, western Colorado, and part of Idaho, who had derived an agricultural base from the Anasazi. But Numic type of land use in these regions probably did not permit much greater population than to the west, for the streams and rivers afforded no great quantity of food unless they were used for irrigation.

In those portions of the Basin-Plateau area where higher population densities developed, society continued to be based on bilateral principles. This meant simply that although marriage was still limited to individuals usually beyond a first-cousin relationship, more marriage partners were locally available, and association and interaction between family clusters were more frequent. As such interaction became more regularized, proto-bands perhaps began to emerge, as in northern Owens Valley and possibly in western Nevada. But proto-bands must be conceptualized as enhanced bonds between local population aggregates, which extended indefinitely from one area of intensive settlement to another, and not as participation of all persons within fixed boundaries in any joint activities.

The Northern Shoshoni and Ute, who had lived within the range of the bison, evolved mounted hunting bands after acquiring horses. It seems unlikely that resources were so concentrated that there were many aboriginal areas of high population density and closely spaced communities. Bison hunting presumably did not create patrilineal bands, for I have postulated (1936) that such bands were a response to hunting small herds of nonmigratory game. The Plains Indians did not develop patrilineal bands, and bands of this type were unknown in the Basin-Plateau area, although I have been erroneously cited several times to the effect that they did occur there.

After 1840, warring predatory bands—or, more accurately, recruited resistance and marauding parties—emerged among many Northern Paiute, for they required a mobility that would have been impossible without horses.

With the reservation period, beginning in the 1860s and 1870s, the Ute rapidly lost their entire superstructure and embellishments of Plains traits acquired a half-century earlier. The so-called bands of the

Northern Paiute, which did not represent any basic change in aboriginal society, endured only 30 years.

The concept of tribes among Shoshoneans is an anthropologist's fiction. Dialectic divergence of the three divisions of Numic, of course, does not mean that each division had an internally homogeneous dialect. Ute is a cultural term, and it signifies neither tribal integration nor a sense of identification. Southern Paiute lacked even band divisions. Shoshoni-Comanche was spoken by a number of quite dissimilar sociocultural groups. Northern Paiute had mounted hunting bands only in the case of the Bannock, who were closely allied to local Shoshoni.

There is no scientific definition by which all of these groups can be classed as tribes. As plaintiffs in the claims cases, however, a sense of identification has been enhanced. This is part of a larger picture that is emerging among American Indians wherein a sense of deprivation and common problems and destiny is utilizing old symbols to further a new concept of Indianhood. Not only isolation on reservations but de facto segregation of the enormous number of recent Indian migrants to cities have furthered these attitudes. While specific potential benefits are at stake in tribal claims, the new trend is increasingly supratribal or pan-Indian.

The general problem for future research is first to identify the new contexts within which the Shoshoneans are being affected by the larger, contemporary industrial society. In some cases, specific linkages and dependencies on external economic, political, educational, and other institutions are being created on the reservation. In other cases, potential exposure to a larger range of modernizing institutions and social contacts exists in urban contexts. But these potential factors of change may remain latent until the Indians have effective access to them. The first problem, therefore, is to ascertain the preconditions that activate latent influences. For many years the reservations seem to have reduced Shoshonean societies to an aboriginal basis of bilaterally related nuclear families, except as schools, some farming, and wage labor penetrated from the larger world. The second problem in analyzing changes in Shoshonean society is to trace the responses, realignments, and adaptations of the family groups to specific modernizing influences, whether on the reservation, in rural contexts, or in urban settings.

BIBLIOGRAPHY

ARDREY, ROBERT
    1966. Man, the Territorial Animal. Life, V. 61, No. 10:50-59.

D'AZEVEDO, WARREN L., WILBUR A. DAVIS, DON D. FOWLER, and WAYNE
SUTTLES, editors
    1966. The Current Status of Anthropological Research in the Great
    Basin: 1964. Desert Research Institute, Technical Report Series, No. 1,
    Reno, Nevada.

BALIKCI, ASEN
    1968. The Netsilik Eskimos: Adaptive Processes. In Man the Hunter,
    Richard Lee and Irven deVore, editors. Aldine Publishing Company,
    Chicago.

BIRDSELL, JOSEPH B.
    1968. Some Predictions for the Pleistocene Based upon Equilibrium Sys-
    tems among Recent Hunters. In Man the Hunter, Richard Lee and Irven
    deVore, editors. Aldine Publishing Company, Chicago.

BOLTON, HERBERT E.
    1950. Pageant in the Wilderness. The Story of the Escalante Expedition
    to the Interior Basin, 1776. Utah Historical Quarterly, 18:1-265.

BRAIDWOOD, ROBERT J., and GORDON R. WILLEY, editors
    1962. Courses toward Urban Life. Viking Fund Publications in An-
    thropology, No. 32.

CHANG, K. C.
    1962. A Typology of Settlement and Community Patterns in Some
    Circumpolar Societies. Arctic Anthropology, 1:28-41.

    1967. Rethinking Archaeology. Random House, New York.

CLINE, GLORIA
    1966. Comments on History. In Current Status of Anthropological Re-
    search in the Great Basin: 1964. pp. 240-52. Desert Research Institute,
    Technical Report Series, No. 1, Reno, Nevada.

DALE, HARRISON C., editor
    1918. The Ashley-Smith Explorations and the Discovery of a Central
    Route to the Pacific, 1822-1829, with the Original Journals. Cleveland.

DAMAS, DAVID
    1968. The Diversity of Eskimo Societies. In Man the Hunter, Richard
    Lee and Irvin deVore, editors. Aldine Publishing Company, Chicago.

    1969. Characteristics of Central Eskimo Band Structure. In Contribu-
    tions to Anthropology: Band Societies, Proceedings of the Conference
    on Band Organization, Ottawa, 1965, David Damas, editor. National
    Museums of Canada, Bulletin No. 228, Anthropological Series No. 84.
    Ottawa.

DANGBERG, GRACE M.
    1963. The Term Political Applied to Family Organization among the
    Great Basin Indians. Nevada State Museum Anthropological Papers,
    No. 9, pp. 35-39, Carson City, Nevada.

DAVIS, WILBUR A.
1966. Theoretical Problems in Western Prehistory. In The Current Status of Anthropological Research in the Great Basin: 1964. pp. 147-166. Desert Research Institute, Technical Report Series, No. 1, Reno, Nevada.

DEQUILLE, DAN (WILLIAM WRIGHT)
1963. Washoe Rambles. Westernlore Press, Los Angeles, 41. (Reprinted from Golden Era, July 28-Dec. 1, 1861).

DOWNS, JAMES F.
1966. The Significance of Environmental Manipulation in Great Basin Cultural Development. In The Current Status of Anthropological Research in the Great Basin: 1964. pp. 39-56. Desert Research Institute, Technical Report Series, No. 1, Reno, Nevada.

FOWLER, DON D.
1966. Great Basin Social Organization. In The Current Status of Anthropological Research in the Great Basin: 1964. pp. 57-74. Desert Research Institute, Technical Report Series, No. 1, Reno, Nevada.

HALE, KENNETH
1958. Internal Diversity in Uto-Aztecan, I. International Journal of American Linguistics, 24:101-07.

1959. Internal Diversity in Uto-Aztecan, II. International Journal of American Linguistics, 25:114-121.

HELM, JUNE
1969a. The Structure of Bands among the Arctic Drainage Déné. In Conference on Bands held in Ottawa, Canada, 1965. David Damas, editor.

1969b. Remarks on the Methodology of Band Composition Analysis. In Contributions to Anthropology: Band Societies, David Damas, editor. National Museums of Canada, Bulletin No. 228, Anthropological Series No. 84. Ottawa.

KAGAN, HILDE HEUN, editor
1966. The American Heritage Pictorial Atlas. American Heritage Publishing Co., Inc., New York.

KELLY, ISABEL
1932. Ethnography of the Surprise Valley Paiute. University of California Publications in American Archaelogy and Ethnology, Vol. 31, No. 3, pp. 67-210, Berkeley.

1934. Southern Paiute Bands. American Anthropologist, Vol. 36, pp. 547-60.

1964. Southern Paiute Ethnography. University of Utah Anthropological Papers No. 69.

LEE, RICHARD BARRY
    1965. Subsistence Ecology of the !Kung Bushman. University Micro-
    films, Ann Arbor.

LEE, RICHARD, and IRVEN DEVORE, editors
    1968. Man the Hunter. Aldine Publishing Company, Chicago, Illinois.

LÉVI-STRAUSS, CLAUDE
    1963. Structural Anthropology. Basic Books, Inc. New York, London.

LOUD, L. L.
    1929. Notes on the Northern Paiute, Appendix 2 of L. L. Loud and M. R.
    Harrington, Lovelock Cave. University of California Publications in
    American Archaeology and Ethnology, 25:152-164. Berkeley.

LOWIE, ROBERT H.
    1924. Notes on Shoshonean Ethnography. Anthropological Papers of
    the American Museum of Natural History, 20:191-314, New York.

MALOUF, CARLING
    1966. Ethnohistory in the Great Basin. In The Current Status of An-
    thropological Research in the Great Basin: 1964. pp. 1-38. Desert Re-
    search Institute, Technical Report Series, No. 1, Reno, Nevada.

MILLER, WICK R.
    1966. Anthropological Linguistics in the Great Basin. In the Current
    Status of Anthropological Research in the Great Basin: 1964. pp. 75-112.
    Desert Research Institute, Technical Report Series, No. 1, Reno,
    Nevada.

MORICE, A. G.
    1906-10. The Great Déné Race. Anthropos, I:229-278, 384-509,
    695-730; II:1-34, 181-96; IV:582-606; V:113-42, 419-43, 643-53.

PARK, WILLARD Z., *et al.*
    1938. Tribal Distribution in the Great Basin. American Anthropologist,
    40: 622-638.

POWELL, J. W., and G. W. INGALLS
    1874a. Statement of Major J. W. Powell made before the Committee on
    Indian Affairs as to the condition of the Indian Tribes West of the Rocky
    Mountains. House of Representatives, Miscellaneous Documents, No.
    86, pp. 1-11, 43rd Congress, 1st Session, 1873, Washington, D.C.

    1874b. Report of J. W. Powell and G. W. Ingalls, Appendix B of the
    Commissioner of Indian Affairs for 1873, pp. 409-414. Washington,
    D.C.

    1876. Communication in Report of the Commissioner of Indian Affairs
    for 1876. Washington, D.C.

RAGIR, SONIA, and JANE LANCASTER
1966. Analysis of a Surface Collection from High Rock Canyon, Nevada. Notes on Western Nevada Archaeology, University of California Archaeological Survey Report No. 66, Berkeley.

RUSSELL, OSBORNE
1921. Journal of a Trapper. Boise, Idaho.

SERVICE, ELMAN R.
1962. Primitive Social Organization: An Evolutionary Perspective. Random House, New York.

STEWARD, JULIAN H.
1933. Ethnography of the Owens Valley Paiute. University of California Publications in American Archaeology and Ethnology, 33:233-350. Berkeley.

1936. The Economic and Social Basis of Primitive Bands. In Essays in Honor of A. L. Kroeber, pp. 331-350, University of California Press. Berkeley.

1938. Basin-Plateau Aboriginal Sociopolitical Groups. Smithsonian Institution, Bureau of American Ethnology, Bulletin 120. Washington, D.C.

1939. Notes on Hillers' Photographs of the Paiute and Ute Indians Taken on the Powell Expedition of 1873. Smithsonian Miscellaneous Collection, Vol. 98, No. 18.

1941. Culture Element Distributions: XIII. Nevada Shoshoni. Anthropological Records, 4 (2):209-59. University of California Press, Berkeley.

1943. Culture Element Distributions: XXIII. Northern and Gosiute Shoshoni. Anthropological Records, 8:263-292. University of California Press, Berkeley.

1949. Cultural Causality and Law: A Trial Formulation of the Development of Early Civilizations. American Anthropologist, 51:1-27.

1955. Theory of Culture Change. University of Illinois Press, Urbana.

1967a. Perspectives on Modernization. In Contemporary Change in Traditional Societies (Julian H. Steward, editor), Vol. I, Introduction and African Tribes, pp. 1-55. University of Illinois Press, Urbana.

1967b. Cultural Evolution Today. Christian Century, Vol. 54, pp. 203-207.

1968a. Cultural Factors and Processes in the Evolution of Pre-farming Societies. In Man the Hunter, Richard Lee and Irven deVore, editors. Aldine Publishing Company, Chicago.

1968b. Hunting as a Factor in the Evolution of Social Structures. In Man the Hunter, Richard Lee and Irven deVore, editors. Aldine Publishing Company, Chicago.

1969a. Observations on Bands: In Contributions to Anthropology: Band Societies, David Damas, editor, pp. 187-190. National Museums of Canada, Bulletin No. 228, Anthropological Series No. 84. Ottawa.

1969b. Postscript to Bands: On Taxonomy, Processes, and Causes. In Contributions to Anthropology: Band Societies, David Damas, editor, pp. 288-295. National Museums of Canada, Bulletin No. 228, Anthropological Series No. 84. Ottawa.

STEWARD, JULIAN H., and LOUIS A. FARON
1959. Native Peoples of South America. McGraw-Hill Book Company, New York.

STEWART, OMER C.
1939. The Northern Paiute Bands. Anthropological Records, 2:127-49. University of California Press, Berkeley.

1941. Culture Elements Distributions. Northern Paiute, XIV. Anthropological Records, 4:361-466. University of California Press, Berkeley.

1942. Culture Element Distribution XVIII, Ute-Southern Paiute. Anthropological Records, 6:231-355. University of California Press, Berkeley.

1966. Tribal Distributions and Boundaries in the Great Basin. In Current Status of Anthropological Research in the Great Basin: 1964. pp. 167-238. Desert Research Institute, Technical Report Series, No. 1, Reno, Nevada.

SWANSON, EARL H., JR.
1966. The Geographic Foundations of the Desert Culture. In The Current Status of Anthropological Research in the Great Basin: 1964, pp. 137-46. Desert Research Institute, Technical Report Series, No. 1, Reno, Nevada.